Maqāṣid al-Sharī'a and Contemporary Reformist Muslim Thought

Maqāṣid al-Sharī'a and Contemporary Reformist Muslim Thought

An Examination

Edited by
Adis Duderija

palgrave
macmillan

First published in 2014 by
PALGRAVE MACMILLAN®
in the United States—a division of St. Martin's Press LLC,
175 Fifth Avenue, New York, NY 10010.

Where this book is distributed in the UK, Europe and the rest of the world, this is by Palgrave Macmillan, a division of Macmillan Publishers Limited, registered in England, company number 785998, of Houndmills, Basingstoke, Hampshire RG21 6XS.

Palgrave Macmillan is the global academic imprint of the above companies and has companies and representatives throughout the world.

ISBN: 978–1–137–32385–9

Library of Congress Cataloging-in-Publication Data

Maqasid al-shari'a and contemporary reformist Muslim thought : an examination / edited by, Adis Duderija.
pages cm
Includes bibliographical references and index.
ISBN 978–1–137–32385–9 (alk. paper)
1. Maqasid (Islamic law) 2. Law reform. 3. Islamic law.
I. Duderija, Adis, 1977–

KBP442.M368 2014
340.5'911—dc23 2014003108

A catalogue record of the book is available from the British Library.

Design by Newgen Knowledge Works (P) Ltd., Chennai, India.

First edition: September 2014

10 9 8 7 6 5 4 3 2 1

I dedicate this volume to my loving wife,
Sri Megawati, whose unselfish willingness to
accommodate my academic career, which has taken
us across continents, is greatly appreciated

Terima kasih, Sayang

Suamiku

Contents

Figures and Tables

Figures

Tables

Acknowledgments

I would like to thank all the contributors to this volume. In particular, I would like to thank and acknowledge the wonderful efforts of David L. Johnston, who took time to review several chapters in this volume. Any mistakes that remain are solely mine.

Notes on Transliteration and Other Conventions

The transliteration system used in this volume is in accordance with the International Journal of Middle East Studies. The editor makes a distinction between technical terms and names. The Qur'ān and the Sunna are not italicized. The names of scholars are not considered technical terms and thus no diacritics are used and they are not italicized. The initial *hamza* and *tā' marbūṭa* are not transliterated. Both *alif* and *alif maqṣūra* are transliterated with ā. In the bibliography, the original spelling and transliteration of the works have been retained. All dates are Common Era unless otherwise indicated with (A.H.) in few references.

Contemporary Muslim Reformist Thought and Maqāṣid cum Maṣlaḥa Approaches to Islamic Law: An Introduction

Adis Duderija

The basic rationale behind bringing out this volume is that although many noteworthy works have been written on issues pertaining to Muslim reformist thought and the concept of maqāṣid al-sharī'a, there still remains a need for a study that examines the role and the usefulness of maqāṣid al-sharī'a as a philosophic-legal cum hermeneutical tool for the purposes of, what I broadly term here, "the contemporary Muslim reformist project" (as is briefly defined later). This book aims to accomplish this by, at times, critically examining how this concept is used in contemporary Muslim reformist thought in relation to a number of specific philosophical, legal, ethical, social, and political issues.

Contemporary Muslim reformist thought is a complex and diverse phenomenon consisting of a number of discourses and actors with different reform agendas and priorities. Perhaps its lowest common denominator is the idea that various aspects of the inherited premodern Islamic tradition, especially aspects of Islamic law, with respect to its underlying worldview assumptions, episteme, and various methodologies underpinning this body of knowledge, are not adequately equipped or need serious reform/rethinking in meeting the many challenges Muslims are facing today, in the context of forming a majority versus Muslim minority society. These reformists differ in the manner in which they conceptualize and employ the concept of maqāṣid al-sharī'a, and they assign to it different hermeneutical positions in their overall approach to Islamic legal theory. This book specifically contributes to expanding our understanding of the role and usefulness of the maqāṣidi-based approach in contemporary Muslim reformist thinking, both Sunni and Shiʿi, by examining the arguments espoused by some of the main contemporary theoreticians behind this approach.

This volume aims to answer two main questions and others related to them:

1. How exactly are the various proponents of contemporary Muslim reformist thought employing the concept of maqāṣid al-sharīʿa for the purposes of their reformist agenda?
2. How useful or effective is the concept of maqāṣid al-sharīʿa, understood as both a classical legal hermeneutical construct developed by premodern Islamic legal theoreticians as well as its contemporary reconceptualization/reinterpretation, in meeting the challenges Muslim reformist thought is responding and seeking to find solutions to?

Hermeneutical Employment of Maqāṣid cum Maṣlaḥa Approaches in Islamic Legal Theories: A Brief Outline of Past and Present Efforts

According to Auda, maqāṣid al-sharīʿa "is a system of values that could contribute to a desired and sound application of the *Shari'ah*."[1] This concept has been employed as a legal hermeneutical tool in premodern Islamic law (or legal theory, *uṣūl ul fiqh*,[2] to be more precise) at least since the third century Hijri.[3] It is based on the idea that Islamic law is purposive in nature, that is, to mean that the law serves particular purposes (e.g., promoting people's benefit and welfare and protecting them from harm) that are either explicitly present in or can be derived from the fountainheads of the sources of Islamic law, namely, the Qurʿān and the Sunna. Maqāṣid al-sharīʿa is also an umbrella term that includes many other concepts that have been closely linked to it in the premodern Islamic tradition, most notably the idea of public interests (*al masaliḥ al-ammah*)[4] and unrestricted interests (*al-masaliḥ al-mursala*),[5] as well as other principles such as istiḥsān (juridicial preference), istiḥsāb (presumption of continuity), and avoidance of mischief (*mafṣada*), all of which are considered to be directives in accordance with God's will.[6]

As ably documented by Auda,[7] past and present works that referred to or employed the maqāṣid (apart from those cited in this section) range from Al Tirmidhi Al-Hakim's (d. 296/908) *Al-Salah wa Maqāṣiduha*,[8] Abu Zayd Al-Balkhi's (d. 322/930) *al-Ibanah 'an 'ilal al-Diyanah/Masaliḥ al-Abdan wa al-Anfus*,[9] Ibn Babawayh al-Qummi's (d. 381/991) *'Ilal al-Shara'i*,[10] and Al-'Amiri al-Faylasuf's *al-I'lam bi-Manaqib al-Islam*[11] to those classical works that deal with the concept of maqāṣid more systematically, such as Abu Al-Ma'ali Al-Juwayni's (d. 478/1085) *Al-Burhan fi uṣūl al-Fiqh*,[12] Al-'Izz Ibn Abd Al-Salam's (d. 660/1209) *Qawa'id al-Ahkam fi masaliḥ al-Anam*,[13] Shihab al-Din Al-Qarafi's (d. 684/1258) *al-Furuq*,[14] Ibn Al-Qayyim's (d. 748/1347) *I'lam al-Muwaqqi'in*,[15] and Al-Shatibi's (d. 790/1388) *Al-Muwafaqat fi uṣūl al-Shari'a*,[16] to those maqāṣid-oriented works among modern Muslim scholars such as R. Rida's (d. 1354/1935) *Al-Wahi al Mohammadi: Thubut al-Nubuwwah bi al-Qur'ān*,[17] Ibn Ashur's (d.1392/1973) *Maqāṣid al-Shari'ah al-Islamiyyah*,[18] Al-Qaradawi's (b. 1926/1344) *Kayf Nata'aamal Ma'a al-Qur'ān al-'Azim*,[19] and T. Al-Alwani's (b. 1935/1353) *Maqāṣid al-Shari'ah*.[20]

The premodern jurists' idea of maṣlaḥa was developed to ensure that the maqāṣid of Islamic law are preserved and protected when adjudicating legal cases.[21] Since both maqāṣid and maṣlaḥa are premised on essentially the same principle (i.e., the purposive nature of Islamic law) and ultimately serve the same purpose (promoting social welfare of the people), they are found to be acting in harmony with each other.[22] As such, interpretational models (manahij) that highlight the importance of these principles in reforming premodern Islamic law will be referred to in this volume as maqāṣid cum maṣlaḥa approaches to Islamic law.

Premodern Muslim scholarship recognized that neither in the Qur'ān nor in the Sunna do we find a definite list of all the maqāṣid or the masaliḥ. Premodern jurists, as a product of their ijtihad, have identified several maqāṣid (e.g., Al Ghazali has identified five such objectives, namely, preservation of life, religion, reason, progeny, and property)[23] and have formed the opinion that the masaliḥ are potentially limitless and change according to time and context.[24]

Importantly, the majority of premodern jurists restricted the scope of the maqāṣid to those falling outside the realm of 'ibādāt (worship rites) and some explicit and unambiguous Qur'ān–Sunna injunctions (muqadarāt) such as the fara'id of inheritance, and the (corporal) punishments hudūd.[25] Additionally, although maṣlaḥa and maqāṣid have been recognized as legitimate and important principles in Islamic law by a vast majority of jurists, they have differed on the question of the scope and the hermeneutical positioning of the maqāṣid cum maṣlaḥa approaches to Islamic law vis-à-vis the clear and decisive legal rulings found in the Qur'ān and the Sunna.[26]

For example, the four main Islamic schools of thought differed somewhat on the issue of the scope of maṣlaḥa. Al-Shafi'i did not consider it as an independent source of law because it did not restrict itself to the basic religious sources such as the Qur'ān and the Sunna and considered that maṣlaḥa was a pure product of reason. He was of the view that the Qur'ān and the Sunna were fully inclusive of all of the concepts and issues pertaining to people's welfare.[27] Malik and Abu Hanifa considered maṣlaḥa as an independent source of law but restricted its scope only to cases in which there was an absence of clear Qur'ān and Sunna evidence and not when maṣlaḥa was going against the clearly (and decontextually) interpreted Qur'ān and Sunna injunctions. As far as Ibn Hanbal is concerned, he considered maṣlaḥa to be an auxiliary source of law and an appendage of the maqāṣid al shari'ah.[28] Thus, when it comes to incorporating the concept of maqāṣid al-shari'a into the theoretical formulations of Islamic law, it is evident that among medieval jurists legal aims (maqāṣid) were not considered by any school of jurisprudence as a distinguished legal source similar to that of qiyās, istiḥsān, or maṣlaḥa mursala.[29]

However, there have been some important dissenting voices among premodern jurists who have gone beyond these limits imposed on the maqāṣid cum maṣlaḥa approaches. One of the first premodern Muslim scholars who endorsed the concept of maṣlaḥa as the essence of and the ultimate purpose in interpretation and the very objective of the Qur'ān and the Sunna was Najmal-Din Al-Tufi (d. 716 AH). For example, in Moosa's examination of Al-Tufi's work, he comes to the conclusion that Tufi considered maṣlaḥa as having a regulatory function over all other established sources[30] and gave it "a universal and humanist status in the [Islamic] law" by giving preference to public interest (maṣlaḥa) over a clear meaning of the text, thereby "subordinating the text to the divination of the universal intentions and purposes of the Shari'ah."[31] Furthermore, Moosa maintains that in Tufi's thought,

> in terms of function and philosophy, the sources of law were actually representations of public interest... and stressed that ethical values and the priority of the sociological purposes of law over epistemology, [were] in line with the meta-purpose of law.[32]

Al-Tufi was not alone in this. According to Moosa, Abu Hamid al-Ghazali (d. 1111 AH), another central premodern Muslim jurist and theologian, although at first not taking the principle of maṣlaḥa as one of the sources of *uṣūl*-ul fiqh, considered that in several instances the maṣlaḥa doctrine "secures the purpose of revelation (maḥafaza 'ala maqṣud al-shar)."[33] Moosa summarizes Ghazali's approach to the question of maṣlaḥa by stating:

> If one examines the primary sources—The Qur'ān and Sunna—carefully, he [Ghazali] said, one will find that maṣlaḥa is indeed implicitly and

> explicitly evident as the purpose of the law. Ghazali thus endorsed maṣlaḥa stealthily, progressing from disparaging it as "fanciful" at first, to viewing it later as the grounds of all legal pronouncements to be found in the canonical sources.[34]

Al-Shatibi (d. 790 AH), a thirteenth-century scholar from Muslim Spain, and one of the most systematic theoreticians behind the maqāṣid cum maṣlaḥa approach to Islamic law, considered al-maqāṣid to be "the fundamentals of religion, basic rules of the law, and the universals of belief (*uṣūl al-din wa qawa'id al-shari'a wa kulliya al-milla*)."[35] For contemporary Muslim thinkers such as H. Hanafi (b. 1935–), M. Al-Jabiri (d. 2010), and N. Madjid (d. 2007), maqāṣid and maṣlaḥa dimensions of Islamic law are seen as the essence of the Qur'ān and that interpretations founded on these interpretational mechanisms can take precedence over clear Qur'ānic text.[36]

However, these minority voices were too few and came too late to significantly shape the Islamic law. Kamali notices this dimension of the premodern *uṣūl-ul-fiqh* by stating:

> Another aspect of the conventional methodology of *usul*, which merits attention, is its emphasis on literalism and certain neglect, in some instances at least, of the basic objective and the rationale of the law. The early formulations of usul have not significantly addressed this issue and it was not until al-Shatibi who developed his major theme on the objectives and the philosophy of Shari'ah (maqāṣid al-shari'ah). Al-Shatibi's contribution came, however, too late to make a visible impact on the basic scheme and methodology of usul.[37]

Echoing this sentiment is Muhammad Fathi al-Darini, a contemporary Syrian legal scholar, who maintains that there has been no inductive or logical study of the *philosophy* and the *purposes* of the premodern Sunni Muslim jurisprudence in the discourse of law and legal theory.[38]

Similarly, contemporary scholar Auda asserts that the premodern theories of maqāṣid were studied as a secondary topic within *uṣūl al fiqh* under the category of unrestricted interests (al-masaliḥ al-mursalah) or as an appropriate attribute for analogy (munāsaba al-qiyās) and not as an independent discipline or as premised on the basis of forming a "fundamental methodology."[39]

Thus, an increasing number of contemporary Muslim scholars have become acutely aware of these lacunae in the premodern theories with regard to the hermeneutical employment of the maqāṣid cum maṣlaḥa approaches to Islamic law that present an important avenue for their various reformist projects.

Modern and contemporary scholars have also broadened the scope of the five traditional maqāṣid. For example, Rashid Rida (d. 1935) included reform and women's rights in his theory of *maqāṣid*[40]; Muhammad Al-Ghazali (d. 1996) added justice and freedom to the premodern five maqāṣid[41];Yusuf al-Qaradawi (1926–) included human dignity and rights in his theory of maqāṣid; Ibn Ashhur included values such as equality, freedom, and orderliness, among others, in his as part of universal maqāṣid of Islamic law;[42] Taha Al Alwani[43] included the concept of developing civilization on earth (ʿimrān); and Attia identified 24 essential maqāṣid (in contrast to the classical five as per Al-Ghazali) falling into four-level realms (individual, family, umma, and all humanity).[44]

The works of these scholars are important contemporary contributions that aim to fill this hermeneutical gap left by the premodern maqāṣid cum maṣlaḥa approaches to Islamic law. This contemporary Islamic scholarship on the maqāṣid cum maṣlaḥa approaches to Islamic law not only builds upon the premodern but also, importantly, both expands the scope of the maqāṣid cum maṣlaḥa and, in fewer cases, elevates hermeneutically these approaches above the clear nuṣūs (texts) found in the Qurʿān and Sunna. More significantly, it also at times evaluates these efforts from a critically constructive perspective. The purpose of this volume is to bring to the forefront some of these contemporary reformist discussions on the maqāṣid cum maṣlaḥa approaches to Islamic law.

Chapter Outlines

This book consists of nine chapters. In chapter 1, I discuss Hashim Kamali's scholarly engagement with the concept of maqāṣid al-sharīʿa as a tool for Islamic law reform. I closely examine his numerous writings on the subject with a particular focus on how he employs it for the purposes of reforming Islamic law. I describe the nature of Islamic reform in Kamali's thought as encapsulated in the two terms he frequently employs: tajdid haḍari (civilizational renewal) and siyāsa al-sharīʿa (*maqāṣid al-sharīʿa*, a compliant method of governance). I also discuss how Kamali's understanding of the nature and delineating features of the Qur'ān, the Sunna, and the relationship between revelation and reason creates a space for reforming Islamic law. In addition to this, I focus on some specific methodological considerations (including maṣlaḥa, istiḥsān, ijtihād, ijmāʿ, qawāʿid [legal maxims], ḥikma, ʿilla, and asbāb al-nuzūl) that Kamali discusses in rethinking existing premodern uṣūl al-fiqh mechanisms for reform purposes by linking them to the concept of maqāṣid. Apart from these I also discuss the main arguments outlined by Kamali regarding the need for and the importance of maqāṣid-oriented Islamic law reform and describe his original contributions to the topic of the nature and the salient features of maqāṣid and their identification. Finally, I outline Kamali's proposal on the new methodology of maqāṣid and his views on the future tasks and challenges for maqāṣid-oriented uṣūl.

In chapter 2, David L. Johnston examines the contribution to and some of the reasons behind Yusuf al-Qaradawi's late career interest in the maqāṣid al-sharīʿa approaches to Islamic law. In particular, Johnston asks a pertinent question whether such approaches to Islamic law are going to, in the long term, demote rather than promote the authority of traditional ulama like Qaradawi himself, something that Al-Qaradawi would find inimical to his own reformist agenda based on his well-known commitment to the principles of Islamic moderation (wasaṭiyya).

In chapter 3, David Warren's contribution provides us with an absorbing exploration of how Tariq Ramadan, in his capacity as the director of the Centre for Islamic Legislation and Ethics (CILE), has attempted to give shape to a new methodology of applied ethics in Islam, in the very particular context of Doha, Qatar. Warren argues that while at first it appears that the chosen location for CILE was based primarily on logistical and financial considerations, it might also be seen as an effort to facilitate CILE's establishment and link with the legal tradition, which in the end effect it aims to dissolve. Warren ultimately opines that this move represents both the marked ambition and the upcoming difficulties for CILE's project, given that its apparent success depends in no small part upon those conservative "*ulamā*" who currently hold very different understandings of what the project entails to those who are heading it.

In chapter 4, Liakat Takim examines the question of the employment of *maqāṣid al-sharīʿa* and *maṣlaḥa* in Shīʿism in general and in contemporary reformist Shīʿism in particular. Takim demonstrates that, historically speaking, in Twelver Shīʿism there are very few discussions on the objectives of *sharīʿa* rulings. He argues that this is probably due to the fact that Shīʿī jurists, not being involved in the political process or decision making of the state, were simply not required to rule on political *maṣlaḥa*. However, he further argues that contemporary reformist-minded Shīʿī scholars emphasize more rational approaches to Islamic hermeneutics that privilege the Qurʾānic core values over the ḥadīth, and he also adds that the employment of *maqasid* cum *maṣlaḥa*–driven hermeneutics is increasingly being resorted to among this circle of scholars.

In the fascinating chapter 5, Aydogan Kars investigates how modern scholars in Turkey perceive and conceptualize the higher objectives of Islamic law. Kars identifies and discusses four distinct approaches with respect to how the concept of maqāṣid al-sharī'a is employed vis-à-vis the idea of "reform" of Islamic law, including: (1) the "traditionalists" or "renewalists," who "define *al-sharī'a* as having a comprehensive ethical-cum-legal flexible worldview that is capable of renewing itself with its authentic tools, one of which is the *maqāṣid al-sharī'a*"; (2) the contemporary academicians, who attempt to stay aloof from "reform versus renewal" discussions and controversial debates on various issues pertaining to religion and are engaged in production of highly specialized academic knowledge concerning various aspects of (maqāṣid) *al-sharī'a*; (3) the "revisionist" academicians, as labeled by Kars, who approach the concept of maqāṣid *al-sharī'a* from their broader "revisionist" Qur'ān-Sunna hermeneutic that integrates scholarship on post-Enlightenment Western hermeneutics into classical Islamic hermeneutical thought; and (4) the "secularists," who regard *al-sharī'a* exclusively in legal or ethical terms and who consider "secularism" to be in harmony with the concept of maqāṣid *al-sharī'a*.

In chapter 6, Sadek critically assesses Rachid al-Ghannushi's employment of *maṣlaḥa* in his sociopolitical reformist project. He argues that Ghannushi's understanding of how to preserve the Islamic character of the state ultimately undermines the gains he achieves through *maṣlaḥa*. namely, that the Islamic state treats all its citizens as free and equal agents. Sadek concludes with an interesting *maṣlaḥa* inspired solution for Ghannushi's political model.

In chapter 7, Moosa provides us with a fascinating discussion on the critical rereadings of Al-Shatibi's work among contemporary Maghrebi scholars, including the critiques of Al-al-Jabiri, 'Abd al-Rahman, and Al-Marzuqi. Moosa asks how contemporary (uncritical) appropriations of Al-Shabiti's work relate to the traditional practice of Islamic law and whether the former will eclipse the other over time.

In chapter 8, I seek to demonstrate that one important component in developing a Qur'ānic hermeneutic, and thereby an Islamic legal one, is to take into account the Qur'ānic presuppositions evident in its text/content as well as in the preclassical nature of the Qur'ān-Sunna discourse, based on their hermeneutically symbiotic, dialogical, ethico-religious, and purposive nature. I use some aspects of male-female gender dynamics and slavery as case studies. In this respect I argue that this nature of the Qur'ān-Sunna discourse with respect to these sociolegal issues would seem to suggest that the deeply embedded contextual patriarchal and slavery practices not only do *not* form the inherent components of their worldview but also that the overall Qur'ān-Sunna principles premised on the alleviation of unjust practices at the time of the Prophet mitigated these practices and paved the way toward their future complete abolition.

In chapter 9, I outline in some detail a new, non-patriarchal, or gender-symmetrical, reinterpretation of Muslim family laws by making a synthesis between, and incorporating, new maqāṣid approaches to Islamic law and non-patriarchal Qur'ānic hermeneutics. I argue that based on contemporary maqāṣid approaches and gender-egalitarian Qur'ānic hermeneutics, new maqāṣid pertaining to Muslim family law can be derived, from which non-patriarchal Qur'ān-Sunna hermeneutics can be developed. This hermeneutical model can account both for the patriarchal nature of the classical *manahij* of the Qur'ān and the Sunna as not being inevitable, as well as provide an important foundation, in addition to other hermeneutical methods, for the fostering of gender-symmetrical Muslim family laws.

Notes

1. Jasser Auda, "A *Maqasidi* Approach to Contemporary Application of the *Shari'ah*," *Intellectual Discourse*, 19 (2011), 193–217, 194.
2. For the purposes of this volume, I will use Islamic law and Islamic legal theory interchangeably although strictly speaking these two are not the same.
3. See, for example, Imran Nyazee, *The Outlines of Islamic Jurisprudence* (Islamabad: Advanced Legal Studies Institute, 2000), 162–175.
4. See Abdul al-Malik Ibn Abdullah, Al-Juwayni, *Al-Burhan fi usul al-fiqh* (annotated by Abdul-Azim al-Deeb) (Qatar: Wazarat al-Shu'un al-Diniyyah, 1400 AH), 183.
5. See Abu Hamid Al-Ghazali, *Al-Mustasfa fi 'ilm ul usul*, Vol. 1 (Beirut: Dar al-Kutub al-Ilmiyyah, 1413), 172.
6. See Hashim Kamali, *The Principles of Islamic Jurisprudence* (Cambridge: Islamic Texts Society, 1991), 235.
7. Auda, Y., *Maqasid al-Shari'ah as Philosophy of Islamic Law* (London: IIT, 2008). I have kept the spelling of the listed works as found in Auda.
8. Ahmed Al-Raysuni, *Nazariyyat al-Maqasid 'ind al-imam al-Shatibi*, 1st ed. (Herndon: IIIT, 1992).
9. See Muhammad K. Imam, *Al-dalil al-irshadi Ila maqasid al-Shari'ah al-islamiyyah* (London: Maqasid Research Centre, 2006).
10. Ed. Mohammad Sadiq Bghar al-ulum (Najaf: Dar al Balaghah, 1966).
11. Ed. Ahmed Ghurab (Cairo: Dar al Kitab al-'Arabi, 1967).
12. Ed. Abdul Al Azim al-deeb (Mansurah: Al-Wafa, 1998).
13. (Beirut: Dar al-nashr, n.d.).
14. Ed. Khalil Mansour (Beirut: Dar al-kutub al-'ilmiyyah,1998).
15. Ed. Taha Abdul rauf Saad (Beirut: Dar al Jil, 1973).
16. (Misr: Matba'at al maktabah al-tujariyah, 1920).

17. (Cairo: Mu'asasah 'izz al-din, n.d.).
18. Ed. El-tahir el-Mesnawi, Kuala Lumpur, Al-fajr, 1999.
19. 1st ed. (Cairo: Dar al-Shoruq, 1999).
20. 1st ed. (Beirut: Dar al-Hadi, 2001).
21. Nyazee, *Outlines of Islamic Jurisprudence*, 134.
22. See Al-Ghazali, *Al-Mustasfa fi 'ilm ul usul* (Cairo: Makba'at dar al-kutub al-misriyya, 1997).
23. Ibid.
24. Kamali, *The Principles of Islamic Jurisprudence*, 235.
25. Ibid.
26. In relation to this question the maṣlaḥa categories developed by the premodern Islamic jurists have been classified into (1) recognized *maṣlaḥa* (*maṣlaḥa mutabara*): the *maṣlaḥa* that has been clearly stated in the Qur'ān and the Sunna, or has gained the consensus (*ijmā'*) of the *fuqahā'*; (2) nullified *maṣlaḥa* (*maṣlaḥa mulgha*): the *maṣlaḥa* that is in clear contradiction to the Qur'ān and the Sunna, and does not have the support of the *fuqahā'*; and (3) conveyed *maṣlaḥa* (*maṣlaḥa mursala*): the *maṣlaḥa* that is not in explicit agreement or disagreement with the Qur'ān or the Sunna or the *ijmā'* of the *fuqahā'*. See Muhammad Shalabi, *Talıl al-ahkam* (Cairo: Matbaat al-Azhar, 1943), 281.
27. Muhammad Al-Buti, *Dawabit al-maṣlaḥa fi al-sharı'a al-islamiyya* (Damascus: al-Maktaba al-Amawiyya, 1966), 377.
28. Ibid., 369.
29. Yasir S. Ibrahim, "Rashīd Rida and Maqāṣid al-Sharī'a," *Studia Islamica*, 102/103 (2006), 160.
30. That is, Qur'ān, Sunna, *ijmā'* and *qiyas*.
31. Ebrahim Moosa, "The Poetics and Politics of Law after Empire: Reading Women's Rights in the Contestations of Law," *UCLA Journal of Islamic and Near Eastern Law*, 1 (2001–2002), 1–28, 11. Al-Tufi uses words that the maṣlaḥa is "qutb maqsud ash-shar"—the aim and the very pillar of religion.
32. Ibid., 11.
33. Ibid., 5
34. Ibid., 10.
35. Jasser Auda, *Maqasid al-Shari'ah as Philosophy of Islamic Law* (London: IIT, 2008), 21.
36. Yudian Wahyudi, *The Slogan "Back to the Qur'an and Sunnah—A Comparative Study of the Responses of Hasan Hanafi, Muhammad Abid Al-Jabiri and Nurcholish Madjid*, PhD dissertation (Canada: McGill University, 2002), 266, 285.
37. Hashim Kamali, "Methodological Issues in Islamic Jurisprudence," *Arab Law Quarterly*, 11 (1996), 5.
38. M. Fathi Al-Darini, *Khasa'is al-Tashri al-Islami fi'l Siyasa wa 'l Hikma*, Damascus, 1987. Cf. Tahir Ibn Al-Ashur, *Alaysa al-Subh bi Qarib? Al-Shakirah al-Tunisiyyah li-funun al-rasm* (Tunis, 1988), 237.
39. Auda, *Maqasid al Shari'ah*, xxv.

40. Rashid Rida, *Al-Wahi al Mohammadi: Thubut al-Nubuwwah bi al-Qur'an* (Cairo: Mu'asasah 'izz al-din, n.d.).
41. Muhammad Al-Ghazali, *Nazart fi al-Qur'an* (Cairo: Nahdat Misr, 2002).
42. Ibn Ashur, Tahir. *Maqāṣid al-Shari'ah al-Islamiyyah*, ed. El-tahir el-Mesnawi (Kuala Lumpur: Al-fajr, 1999).
43. Taha Al-Alwani, *Issues in Contemporary Islamic Thought* (Washington and London: IIIT, 2005).
44. Gamal Eddin Attia, *Toward Realization of the Higher Intent of Islamic Law (Maqasid al Shari'ah): A Functional Approach*, trans. Nancy Roberts (Kuala Lumpur: IIIT, 2010), 116–151.

CHAPTER 1

Islamic Law Reform and Maqāṣid al-Sharīʿa in the Thought of Mohammad Hashim Kamali

Adis Duderija

Introduction

Mohammad Hashim Kamali is one of the leading contemporary scholars writing on the concept of maqāṣid al-sharīʿa as well as Muslim reformist thought. The purpose of this chapter is to closely examine his numerous writings on *maqāṣid al-sharīʿa* with particular focus on how he employs this concept for the purpose of reforming Islamic law. In the first section of this chapter, I describe the nature of Islamic reform in Kamali's thought as encapsulated in the two terms he frequently employs: *tajdīd haḍari* (civilizational renewal) and *siyāsa al-sharīʿa* (*maqāṣid al-sharīʿa*–compliant method of governance). In the second section, I discuss how Kamali's understanding of the nature and the delineating features of the Qurʾān, the Sunna, and the relationship between revelation and reason creates space for the reform of Islamic law. In the third section of this chapter, I focus on some specific methodological considerations Kamali discusses in rethinking existing premodern *uṣūl al-fiqh* mechanisms for reform purposes by linking them to the concept of maqāṣid. These include *maṣlaḥa*, *istiḥsān*, *ijtihād*, *ijmāʿ*, *qawāʿid* (legal maxims), *ḥikma*, *ʿilla*, and *asbāb al-nuzūl*. In the fourth section, I discuss the main arguments outlined by Kamali for the need for and the importance of *maqāṣid*-oriented Islamic law reform. I also describe his original contributions to the topic of the nature and the salient features of *maqāṣid* and their identification. Finally, I outline his proposal on the new methodology of *maqāṣid* and his views on the future tasks and challenges for *maqāṣid*-oriented uṣūl.

Brief Biographical Note

Mohammed Hashim Kamali was born on February 7, 1944, in Lalpur, Nangarhar, Afghanistan. He received his bachelor's degree in law and political science from Kabul University in 1965 and his master's degree in law (comparative law) and his doctorate from the University of London in 1972 and 1976, respectively. Most of his teaching career has been spent at McGill (Montreal, Canada) and the International Islamic University (Kuala Lumpur). He has been very active in a number of committees and has chaired several of organizations. He is the founding chairman and CEO of the International Institute of Advanced Islamic Studies, Malaysia, and editor-in-chief of its journal, *Islam and Civilisational Renewal*, that began with publication in 2008.[1]

Nature of Islamic Law Reform: Tajdīd Haḍari and Siyāsa al-Sharīʿa

Kamali has been advocating for reform in Islamic thought and in Islamic law and legal theory, in particular, for well over two decades. His call for reform is framed under two important concepts, namely, the notions of civilizational renewal (*tajdīd haḍari*) and *siyāsa al-sharīʿa*. What underlies both of these reform-related concepts is Kamali's acute awareness that for Islamic law reform to take place, it must be authentically grounded in Islamic legal theory (*uṣūl al-fiqh*) and in the broader Islamic intellectual and cultural heritage generally.[2]

Kamali's conceptualization of this authentic reform is captured in two concepts that he employs regularly, namely, *tajdīd haḍari* and *siyāsa al-sharīʿa*, on which I shall elaborate next. All of his reform-related efforts must therefore be viewed through this larger prism of the need for authentic reform. The idea of *tajdīd haḍari* is often employed by Kamali in the context of defining and discussing another major concept in his thought, namely, Islam haḍari, or civilizational Islam, which has a strong Malaysian-specific context. Since the purpose of this section of this chapter is to shed light on the employment of the concept of *tajdīd* as a tool for Islamic law reform, I am interested in discussing the Islam *haḍari* concept only insofar as it is useful for us to understand the nature of *tajdīd* as a means of Islamic law reform in Kamali's thought. In his discussion of the definition, nature, and scope of Islam haḍari, Kamali asserts that the idea of *tajdīd*, or renewal, is central to it because it is "germane to every aspect of Islam haḍari and is an entrenched aspect of Islam as we have known it."[3] Importantly, apart from noticing its value of "authenticity" as a concept that is firmly rooted in the history and the normative sources of Islam, Kamali defines *tajdīd* as an inherently open and contextual process that, unlike *taqlīd* and *ijtihād*, cannot be subject to a predetermined methodology and framework.[4] He argues further that *tajdīd* is representative of "the need for renewal, interpretation and ijtihād"[5] especially on issues that do not have a historical precedent in the Islamic tradition. Kamali defends the need for tajdīd not only on the basis of its embeddedness in the Islamic historical experience but also by asserting that Muslim communities have, over time, "lost touch" with the "original impulse and premises of Islam," which have been diluted or even lost due to "taqlīd, colonialisation, and rampant secularism."[6]

Significantly, Kamali, in the context of delineating the scope of tajdīd, links this concept with that of maqāṣid. Here he makes a distinction between two types of tajdīd, both of which he considers to be valid and authentic. The first type of tajdīd can be directly linked to, and is subsumed under, the five essential maqāṣid. The second kind of tajdīd does not need to be traced back to the five essential maqāṣid and is valid as long as it does not alter "the immutable norms and principles of Islam," by which Kamali means the basic beliefs and pillars of Islam. In the case of this second type of tajdīd, Kamali believes that it is not necessary to provide affirmative evidence from the Qur'ān and Sunna in order to prove tajdīd's acceptability.[7] Finally, Kamali considers tajdīd to be a dynamic process/concept that is both specific and responsive to the prevailing societal circumstances to which it is being applied at any given point in time.[8] Such a characterization and definition of tajdīd clearly permits Kamali to widen the scope of reform that is not bound by the legal methodologies inherited from the past.

The tajdīd haḍari approach to reform is closely linked to another important reform-related concept as devised and employed by Kamali, namely, that of siyāsa al-sharīʿa. Kamali uses this phrase to refer to a *method of governance* that is in accordance with the goals and objectives of al-sharīʿa. Siyāsa al-sharīʿa, according to Kamali, is a comprehensive doctrine and in its widest sense applies to all government policies—political, legal, social, civil, military, or administrative—be it in areas where the al-sharīʿa provides explicit guidelines or otherwise.[9] Unlike previous twentieth-century "secular" approaches to reform in the Muslim world, siyāsa al-sharīʿa by its very name is suggestive of a sharīʿa oriented policy that, as an instrument of flexibility and pragmatism in al-sharīʿa, is devised to uphold the cause of justice and good government, especially when the rules of al-sharīʿa are found lacking in guidance or fall short of addressing certain situations or developments. Kamali repeatedly highlights that the policy measures that are taken in the name of siyāsa al-sharī'a must be al-sharī'a compliant, as "the purpose of it is to generally to facilitate rather than circumvent the implementation of sharī'a."[10]

Kamali, in his numerous writings, has unequivocally expressed his view of the need for Islamic law reform for a number of different reasons both internal and external to the religious tradition. In this context he remarks:

> The increased isolation of sharī'a from the realities of law and government in contemporary Muslim societies accentuates the need for fresh efforts to make the al-sharī'a a viable proposition and a living force in society. Our problems over taqlīd are exacerbated by the development of a new dimension to taqlīd as a result of Western colonialism which has led to indiscriminate imitation of the laws and institutions of the West. The prevailing legal practice in many Muslim countries, and indeed many of their constitutions, are modeled on a precedent that does not claim its origin in the legal heritage of Islam.[11]

Elsewhere he states that the recent Islamic revivalist thought has increased Muslim awareness of the need to renew links with their heritage and find their own solutions to the issues that concern them by returning to the al-sharī'a as its most civilizationally distinct and tangible aspect. He emphasizes, however, that these efforts must attempt to relate the al-sharī'a to the living conditions of the people and be relevant to the contemporary needs and realities of Muslim societies. In this context, he has identified areas that require urgent reform. These include issues relating to political leadership and methods of succession; support for constitutional government and democracy; support for fundamental constitutional rights and liberties of the individual; abuse of the doctrine of jihad by militant Muslim extremists; disability of non-Muslims in the matter of giving evidence in the courts of justice; patriarchal nature of Islamic legal (fiqhi) rulings pertaining to polygamy and divorce; death penalty for apostasy; and some of the fiqhi positions relating to women's rights and their participation in the affairs of government.[12] According to Kamali, for reform to take place, this would entail an imaginative reconstruction and ijtihād including revision and modification of the rules of fiqh so as to translate the broad objectives of the al-sharī'a into the laws and institutions of contemporary society.[13]

Importantly, the nature of Kamali's envisaged reform, apart from its emphasis on authenticity, is conceptualized in very pragmatic and realistic terms. It favors a gradual and realistic approach to legislation and social reform that is averse to abrupt revolutionary changes.[14]

Kamali's awareness of the need for such an approach to Islamic law reform is evident, especially in relation to traditionally more sensitive issues such as that of gender relations. For example, with regard to gender equality, Kamali opines that this should be addressed from within the tradition and the prevailing conditions of each society, and that one should "avoid the tendency of putting an Islamic veneer on some foreign ideas which may be altogether unfamiliar to the Muslim law and culture." He adds further that to correct the imbalances of history naturally takes time and reflection over newly emerging issues such as gender equality, the achievement of which is a long-term engagement in Muslim majority contexts. As such, reforms should be aimed in such a manner that they "strike the middle ground between idealism and reality and between traditional and modern social values" and start from less to more sensitive issues.[15] The need for this nature of reform is justified by the still prevalent customs and attitudes among Muslim masses, and there are prospects of a backlash from more conservative sections of the Muslim umma. Kamali adds that the success of reforms will also depend upon factors such as the presence of democratic and consultative methods, the extent of their dissemination through various persuasive media outlets, and the existence of vibrant civil-society engagements.[16]

Consistent with the principles of tajdīd haḍari and siyāsa al-sharīʿa, Kamali's reform is not conceptualized as a clear epistemological and methodological break with the premodern Islamic legal tradition. Instead, he advocates for a reform that aims to the fullest extent possible to utilize the legacy of premodern Muslim thought, including Islamic law and legal theory. This is clearly evident in the following statement:

> The proper approach [to reform] is surely to utilise the best potentials of that [premodern Islamic legal theory] methodology but also to reform it by identifying the problems in regard to each of its particular doctrines and then to find ways of resolving them. We may also need to depart from some of the strictures of the conventional methodology and its unfeasible propositions, but we do not propose to throw, as it were, the baby out with the bath water. The basic approach must surely be one of continuity and imaginative reform which might well entail taking bold steps along the way as well as adding new dimensions to the existing methodology of uṣūl al-fiqh.[17]

If this is so, on what grounds does Kamali frame the possibility of this reform of Islamic law and legal theory in particular?

Avenues and Methods of Reform

In this section I describe Kamali's understanding of the nature of and the delineating features of al-sharīʿa, the Qurʾān, the Sunna, and how the relationship between revelation and reason creates a space for reforming Islamic law.

The first significant element in Kamali's conceptualization of al-sharīʿa for reform purposes is that al-sharīʿa has certain aims and purposes (maqāṣid). At the broadest level, these include the realization of people's welfare (maṣlaḥa) with regard to their worldly life as well as the hereafter and their protection from corruption and evil.[18] Importantly, Kamali asserts that this description of the aims and purposes of al-sharīʿa includes its laws both in the sphere of rituals (*ʿibādāt*) and civil transactions (muʿmalāt). In this context he argues that the overall purpose of the majority of Islamic laws and values, especially those concerning the rituals and morals (*akhlāq*), is to train the individual to be more God conscious (taqwā) and a better human being by becoming a beneficial member of the society in which he/she lives. Significantly, he also emphasizes that the underlying message of Islam is the realization of people's benefits (maṣlaḥa), which are closely linked to the purposes and objectives of al-sharīʿa.[19]

Having stated that in the very concept of al-sharīʿa certain aims and objectives are inherent,[20] Kamali also refers to the *nature* of al-sharīʿa in a particular manner. As a corollary to the argument about the aims or purposes of al-sharīʿa, he refers to it as being primarily an ethico-religious values-based construct, which is essential to the primary message of Islam, its safeguarding, and its continued future relevance. He argues against the dominant view as espoused by both many (pre)modern Muslim jurists and Western scholars of Islam of the legalistic nature of al-sharīʿa as forming its core. In this regard he makes an important distinction between the legal and moral aspects of al-sharīʿa.[21] The former are only peripheral to its original message and purpose.[22] Importantly, he argues that the laws of al-sharīʿa, including the clear texts of the Qurʾān and ḥadīth, must not be isolated from their proper purposes. Significantly, he also makes an assertion that maintaining harmony with the spirit of al-sharīʿa may at times entail a certain departure from its letter.[23]

Making a clear conceptual distinction between al-sharīʿa and fiqh is another very prominent feature of Kamali's thinking in relation to the possibility of reform of Islamic law. He considers al-sharīʿa to be closely related to and mainly grounded in Revelation (wahy), whose only sources are the Qurʾān and the Sunna. Fiqh is a legal science developed by jurists and is therefore a product of ijtihād, of human reason. Kamali considers al-sharīʿa, which comprises in its scope not only law but also theology and moral teaching, to be a wider concept than fiqh, which primarily addresses practical legal rules. For Kamali, the al-sharī'a originates in the Qur'ān and it consists of both specific rulings and broad principles of legal and moral import. Kamali argues further that clear and specific injunctions of the Qur'ān and the Sunna constitute the core of the al-sharī'a and the understanding that they impart is expected to be self-evident and leaves little room for interpretation. While al-sharī'a provides general directives, the detailed solutions to particular and unprecedented issues are explored by fiqh. Fiqh is therefore an understanding of al-sharī'a and not al-sharī'a itself. Whereas al-sharī'a demarcates the path that the believer has to tread in order to obtain guidance, fiqh means human understanding and knowledge. Fiqh is thus positive law that does not include morality and dogma. It is a "mere superstructure and a practical manifestation of commitment to al-sharī'a values."[24]

By making these distinctions Kamali prepares the ground for the argument that Islamic law as contained in fiqh manuals is subject to critical scrutiny and criticism that opens up avenues for its reform.

Closely related to this al-sharī'a-fiqh ontological, epistemological, and conceptual distinction is Kamali's notion of the balance between the changeable and the unchangeable aspects of al-sharī'a. In this context he argues that al-sharī'a always aims at striking a balance between continuity and change. In the category of the unchangeable aspects of al-sharī'a, Kamali identifies the fundamentals of the faith and the pillars on which it stands, the basic moral values of Islam, clear injunctions on halāl and haram, the injunctions of al-sharī'a concerning 'ibadāt, and some of its specific rulings in mua'malāt such as the rules of inheritance and prohibited degrees of relationship for marriage purposes. In the changeable aspects of al-sharī'a, he includes the larger part of mua'malāt, that is, criminal law, government policy and constitution, fiscal policy, taxation, and economic and international affairs.[25]Another important aspect of Islamic law reform is based on his understanding of the nature of the relationship between reason and revelation, which according to him is one of complementarity. The following quote encapsulates well Kamali's thinking on this issue:

> Revelation expounds the purpose of the creation of man, the basic framework of his relationship with the creator, and the nature of his role and mission in this life. Revelation also spells out the broad outline of values that human reason should follow and promote. Without the aid of revelation the attempt to provide a basic framework of values is likely to engage man in perpetual doubt as to the purpose of his own existence and the nature of his relationship with God and His creation. Revelation

> thus complements reason and gives it a sense of assurance and purpose which helps prevent it from indulgence in boundless speculation. Reason is man's principal tool for the advancement of knowledge but the merit and demerit of that knowledge is ascertained with the aid of revelation. Reason is the torch light which illuminates man's path in the material world of observation and investigation whereas revelation is the source of transcendental knowledge of the world beyond perception. One is the realm of investigation and the other of faith and submission to divine providence. Islam's vision of reality, truth, and its moral values of right and wrong are initially determined by revelation and then elaborated and developed by reason.[26]

The nature of ethical value in Islamic law (or in the Qur'ān and the Sunna), which Kamali does not explicitly discuss, is generally conceptualized as being objective, although he is somewhat ambivalent on this issue as can be ascertained from the quote:

> The basic structure of the moral values of Islam, although of divine provenance, is entirely consistent and in harmony with reason. The moral virtues of justice, realisation of benefit and truth, or the evil of dishonesty and transgression, for example, have been articulated in the Qur'ān and Sunna. These are basically unchangeable and rationality is neither expected, nor does it have the authority to reverse them into their opposites. It may thus be concluded that revelation and reason are generally consistent on the basic structure of moral values and legal injunctions of Šarīʿa. The definitive injunctions, namely the wajib and haram, are determined by the revelation and they are on the whole specific and inflexible.[27]

Elsewhere he states that "reason is a credible basis of judgment in the absence of relevant revelatory text, provided that the judgment arrived at is in harmony with the general spirit and the guidance of the revealed scripture."[28]

This reasoning leads Kamali to the conclusion that there exists a convergence of values between the al-sharīʿa and natural law and of Islam as din al-fiṭra (the natural religion) with natural values. He emphasizes that although each moral-legal system has distinct approaches to the question of right and wrong, the values upheld by both are substantially in agreement as both presuppose and are based upon the notion that the moral values are derived from eternally valid standards, "which are ultimately independent of human cognizance and adherence." The only difference between the two lies in the locus and manner of their attribution/justification (moral values determined by God vs those inherent in nature).[29]

The earlier conceptualization and understanding of al-sharīʿa by Kamali is premised on a certain understanding of the nature of the Qurʾān and the Sunna, its fountainheads. He identifies several features of the nature of the Qurʾān and the Sunna that make them considerably interpretationally "flexible," "dynamic," and accommodative of reformist thinking. First, such a feature is with regard to the nature of the Qurʾānic message and its laws, which Kamali maintains is goal-oriented both in the sphere of ʿibādāt and muʿamalāt.[30] Second, the Qurʾān and the Sunna are primarily embodiments of certain ethico-religious values. In his words:

> A cursory perusal of the Qurʾān would be enough to show that the Qurʾān's primary concern is with values and objectives such as justice and benefit, mercy and compassion, uprightness and taqwa, promotion of good and prevention of evil, fostering goodwill and love among the members of the family, helping the poor and the needy, cooperation in good work, and so forth. The Qurʾān may thus be said to be goal-oriented, and that it seeks to foster a structure of values which has a direct bearing on human welfare. It is, for the most part, concerned with the broad principles and objectives of morality and law, rather than with specific details and technical formulas that occupy the bulk of the uṣūl works.[31]

Third, the Qurʾān and its injunctions of sociolegal import[32] as the principal source of al-sharīʿa in particular come in form of primarily general principles. He adds that when the Qurʾān does provide more specific detail it does so for the purpose of gaining a better understanding of the general principles. He also argues that the greater part of the Qurʾān, including its legal verses (*ayāt al-aḥkām*), consists of general (*ʿamm*) and unqualified (*mulṭaq*) expressions and as such they are on the whole open to further interpretation.[33] Kamali also asserts that the Qurʾān is expressive too, at numerous places and in a variety of contexts, of the goals, purposes, rationale, and benefits of its laws such as *raḥma* (mercy), *hudā* (guidance), protection of life, and so on[34] in the spheres of *muʿmalāt* as well as *ʿibādāt*.[35] He considers that this maqāṣid nature of Qurʾān is also signified by the fact that there exists a theme-oriented Qurʾānic commentary genre known as tafsīr *mawḍūʿī*, whose approach, as we shall see later, is conceptualized by Kamali as being goal-oriented.[36] Kamali also considers that the most notable companions of the Prophet, as embodiment and perpetuators of the Sunna of the Prophet, especially Caliph Umar, took a rational approach toward the text and message of the Qurʾān and the Sunna and that their understanding and interpretation of the text was not confined to the meaning of words but also included its underlying rationale, effective cause, and purpose.[37]

The reason for this interpretationally flexible nature of the Qur'ān, argues Kamali, is because the Qur'ān wanted the Muslim community and its leaders, the Ūlū l-amr, to elaborate on them in light of prevailing conditions.[38] This feature of the Qur'ān, asserts Kamali, is best demonstrated by the fact that the Qur'ān is in need of an elaboration of its meaning (*deutungsbedürftig*) and requires a great deal of explanation,[39] which is often but not sufficiently comprehensively provided by the Sunna.[40]

Another feature of the Qur'ān, which is accountable for flexibility and change in the al-sharī'a as identified by Kamali, is the presence of speculative (*zannī*), in contradistinction with definitive (*qaṭ'ī*), rulings throughout the holy Book. Kamali argues that a ruling of the Qur'ān may totally or partially fall under one or the other of these two categories. A qaṭ'i text, which leaves little room for interpretation and ijtihād, is one in which the language of the text and the ruling that it conveys is "clear, self-contained, and decisive," whereas the zanni texts of the Qur'ān, which Kamali identifies as forming its larger part, are "open to interpretation, analysis, and development."[41] The following quotation of Kamali provides an accurate and concise summary of the earlier mentioned aspects of the nature of the Qur'ān and the Sunna that make it conducive to reform:

> The sources of al-sharī'a are of two kinds: revealed and nonrevealed. The revealed sources, namely the Qur'an and Sunna, contain both specific injunctions and general guidelines on law and religion, but it is the broad and general directives which occupy the larger part of the legal content of the Qur'an and Sunna. The general directives that are found in these sources are concerned not so much with methodology as with substantive law and they provide indications which can be used as raw materials in the development of the law.[42]

Another important delineating feature of the Qur'ān and the Sunna, which makes them inherently dynamic, *according to* Kamali, is the notion that, outside of the sphere of the *'ibādāt*, they are rationalist in essence. Kamali refers to the concept of ta'līl (ratiocination) in the Qur'ān as evidence to support this view. In this context he asserts that the Qur'ān "expounds on numerous instances and in a large variety of themes, both legal and nonlegal, the rationale, cause, objective, and purpose of its text, the benefit or reward that accrues from conformity to its guidance or the harm and punishment that may follow from defying it."[43]

Kamali supports the taʿlil nature of the Qurʾān and its laws by making reference to many instances in the Qurʾān where the exercise of sound reasoning and judgment is affirmed, and rational thinking, observations, and conclusions made on their basis are encouraged. Importantly, Kamali links the taʿlil nature of Qurʾān and its laws to the concept of maqāṣid al-sharīʿa (and maṣlaḥa). He argues that ratiocination in the Qurʾān means that the laws of al-sharīʿa are "not imposed for their own sake, nor for want of mere conformity to rules, but that they aim at the realization of certain benefits and objectives," and "when the effective cause, rationale, and objective of an injunction is properly ascertained, they serve as basic indicators of the continued validity of that injunction." This, in turn, implies that when a ruling of al-sharīʿa outside the sphere of rituals "no longer serves its original intention and purpose, then it is the proper role of the mujtahid to substitute it with a suitable alternative because the failure to do so would mean neglecting the objective (maqṣud) of the Lawgiver."[44]

Summarizing this section, the following words of Kamali are instructive and representative of his thinking:

> To summarize, the occurrence of taʿlil in the Qurʾān, Sunna, and the precedent of the companions and the prominence that it takes in the conduct of ijtihād clearly indicates that Islamic jurisprudence, outside the sphere of *ʿibādāt* is rationalist in essence and premised on a set of higher values such as justice and maṣlaḥa, which constitute the basic objective and rationale of all of its legal injunction. Taʿlil and ijtihād must, of course, be guided by the textual injunctions (nuṣūs) of al-sharīʿa but since maṣlaḥa is the overriding goal and objective of al-sharīʿa, the nuṣūs should not be read in isolation from it. A technical and plausible reading of the nuṣūs which is oblivious to the public welfare and inspired only by considerations of conformity and literalism should therefore be avoided.[45]

Another salient characteristic of the Qurʾān and the Sunna that makes al-sharīʿa dynamic and open to change is the idea of their contextualist nature or what Kamali refers to as the unmistakable presence of the time-space factor[46] in them. Although the general import of the Qurʾān and the inspiration and guidance that it provides tend to transcend particularities of time and space, the Qurʾān also contains specific provisions and concrete rulings, which "like most of the Sunna, involves a time-space element." If this element is ignored, argues Kamali further, it results in fragmentation and neglect of the internal values of the Qurʾān and the Sunna.[47] As one argument for the presence of the time-space factor in the Qurʾān and the Sunna (and therefore al-sharīʿa), Kamali cites the practice of the Prophet to accept the majority of social values of seventh-century Arabia.[48] An additional argument in favor of the contextualist nature of the Qur'ān can be found in Kamali's assertion that "God Most High revealed His message to the people in contemplation of their capacity at receiving it and the realities with which they were surrounded in Makkah and Madinah respectively."[49] The concepts of progressive revelation, abrogation, and replacement of some of its own laws are also cited as evidence of the contextualist nature of the Qur'ān and the Sunna.[50]

Methodological Considerations in Rethinking Classical Uṣūl al-fiqh for Reform Purposes and Their Connection with Maqāṣid al-sharī'a

In this section I focus on some specific methodological considerations that Kamali discusses in rethinking existing premodern uṣūl al-fiqh mechanisms for reform purposes by linking them to the concept of maqāṣid. These include maṣlaḥa, istiḥsān, ijtihād, ijmā', qawā'id (legal maxims), ḥikma, 'illa, and asbāb al-nuzūl. Before I do so, I briefly examine why Kamali considers the reform of classical uṣūl al-fiqh to be necessary.

Kamali repeatedly states that there are a number of weaknesses in classical uṣūl al-fiqh methodologies, which make them unsuitable for meeting the manifold contemporary challenges in Muslim societies (and therefore Islamic law). One such problem is that classical uṣūl al-fiqh is burdened with "technicalism and literalism" and that the methodologies on which uṣūl al-fiqh and ijtihād are premised are based on medieval societal values. Another significant factor that impedes the contemporary viability of classical uṣūl al-fiqh, according to Kamali, is the doctrine of taqlīd, which is responsible for the purely textualist approach to Islamic law and a decline of ijtihād. Additionally, Kamali forms the view that there has been insufficient theorizing about the philosophy of maqāṣid in classical uṣūli thought. Finally, he feels that classical uṣūl al-fiqh methodologies have neglected the concept of maqāṣid and have subsumed it under a very literalist legal methodology apparatus.[51] In this context he laments as follows:

> Since the legal theory of uṣūl is meant to translate the value structure of the revelation (wahy) into operative formulas and ensure that ra'y and ijtihād are the carriers of these values, it would follow that the objectives and values, rather than technicality and literalism, should have been the overriding theme and preoccupation of uṣūl al fiqh. But the legal theory of uṣūl actually traversed a different course, and it was not until Abu Ishāq Abu Ishaq al-Shatibi (d. 1388) and his predecessors, 'Izz al-Din ibn 'Abd

> al-Salam (d. 1262) and Abu Hamid Muhammad al-Ghazali (d. 1111) that maqāṣid were added as a new chapter to the legal theory of uṣūl. Yet even these developments proved to have had a limited impact. A certain degree of attention that was paid to the maqāṣid seems to have come somewhat late, that is, at a time when the climate of imitation and taqlīd was too entrenched for this fresh development to bring about any significant change in the generally accepted formulations of uṣūl al fiqh from their conventional mould.[52]

Consistent with his tajdīd haḍari approach described earlier, Kamali employs and adapts the earlier outlined maqāṣid-allied concepts existent in classical uṣūl al-fiqh to argue for a maqāṣid-oriented uṣūl al-fiqh as an authentic and legitimate way of reforming Islamic law. I turn my attention to each of them by primarily highlighting their links with the concept of maqāṣid al-sharīʿa/maqāṣid-based uṣūl.

The first maqāṣid-allied concept is that of maṣlaḥa, which is premised on the idea that laws exist first and foremost for the purpose of serving public welfare and the interests of people. Kamali argues that maṣlaḥa as a legitimate Islamic law doctrine has been underutilized by the traditional scholarship. Having systematically outlined and analyzed the traditional maṣlaḥa doctrines as evident in major Sunni schools of thought, he argues against their restrictive understanding of this legal mechanism, which, as the bottom line, states that the general principles of the Qurʾān, from which maṣlaḥa principles and values can be derived, can only be applied to special cases that are grounded in or supported by explicit dalāl (indicants) found in scriptural texts. He makes this assertion because, in Kamali's view, this doctrine unjustifiably confines the general objectives (maqāṣid) of the lawgiver as illustrated in the Qurʾān itself. Kamali also forms the view that the doctrine of maṣlaḥa, when it is conceptually and methodologically in agreement with the principle of the maqāṣid al-sharīʿa, is indispensible for the contemporary relevance of the Islamic law.[53] Kamali, following Abu Hamid Muḥammad al-Ghazali (d. 1111), understands and employs the doctrine of maṣlaḥa almost interchangeably with maqāṣid "as the benefit or interest behind the introduction of law." He describes maṣlaḥa as primarily a utilitarian concept associated with the notion of securing material benefits but also associates it as a cause that leads to the al-sharīʿa's maqāṣid or indeed at times identifies it as the maqāṣid itself. He considers that the maqāṣid are the "ultimate purpose of maṣlaḥa and [are a] degree higher than it."[54] The only distinction he makes between the two is that maṣlaḥa is circumstantial and changeable whereas maqāṣid have more constancy and permanence. On this basis Kamali views maṣlaḥa as an important legal mechanism that can be employed for Islamic law reform purposes. Maṣlaḥa, furthermore, for Kamali, is in essence a rational concept because most of the benefits of this world are identifiable by human intellect, experience, and custom, even without the guidance of al-sharīʿa. Importantly, he also considers this principle of maṣlaḥa to be valid in relation to making moral judgments about right and wrong.[55] In this context he states that the function of al-sharīʿa in essence is to only provide a "set of criteria and guidelines so as to prevent confusion between personal prejudice and maṣlaḥa." This is, however, not the case regarding benefits pertaining to the hereafter, and those which combine the benefits of this world and the next, for these, argues Kamali, can only be identified by the al-sharīʿa.[56]

Istiḥsān, the doctrine of juristic preference for certain interpretations of Islamic law over others, is another maqāṣid-allied concept through which Kamali sees the potential of Islamic law for reform. Asking the question whether istiḥsān can be used as an instrument of coherence and consolidation between the uṣūl al-fiqh and the maqāṣid, Kamali answers in the affirmative. This is so because, unlike the concept of maqāṣid, he is of the view that istiḥsān forms an integral theme and topic of uṣūl al-fiqh, which is inherently generic and versatile. Furthermore, he asserts that istiḥsān has a strong affinity with the concept of maqāṣid because "the evidential basis, rationale, and purpose of istiḥsān are almost identical with those of the maqāṣid al-sharīʿa." He forms the view that there is "a considerable parity, both of substance and form,"[57] between istiḥsān and the ends and purposes of al-sharīʿa (i.e., maqāṣid al-sharīʿa) because the basic theme and philosophy of the maqāṣid are almost identical with that of istiḥsān. These include securing justice, benefit, and dignity; finding ways to remove and eliminate hardship; as well as responding to the exigencies of necessity and custom. Istiḥsān can thus be seen as an important tool of harmonizing uṣūl al-fiqh with maqāṣid (in addition to fine-tuning maqāṣid-oriented methodology) into a more coherent and organic unity, including in the areas of aḥkām.

In his words:

> Since istiḥsān is endowed with a methodology that looks in two directions: the textual proofs, ijmāʿ, qiyās, maṣlaḥa and custom on the one hand, and the goals and purposes of al-sharīʿa, such as equity and fairness on the other, and since it seeks to realise the ends of al-sharīʿa through the evidential support of its means, it offers a unique methodology for synthesizing the two undigested chapters of Islamic jurisprudential thought. The theory of istiḥsān is focused on finding a better alternative to a ruling or evidence of al-sharīʿa when its application has frustrated one of the

> objectives or maqāṣid of the same. The maqāṣid lacks this focus and does not provide for a modus operandi and istiḥsān can fill in this gap.[58]

Reconceptualization and innovative thinking about ijtihād (independent legal reasoning) is another important mechanism through which Kamali envisages the capacity of Islamic law for reform. His view of ijtihād is closely linked with the idea of maqāṣid. Indeed, maqāṣid are seen as the principal extension of ijtihād. In this context he argues:

> In a real sense, almost the whole of our discussion of the maqāṣid is focused on ijtihād. The maqāṣid only serve the purpose of opening up the avenues of ijtihād and enhance the ideational substance and foundation of ijtihād.[59]

Kamali proposes that the maqāṣid al-sharīʿa should be utilized as a framework for ijtihād in all its forms, especially with respect to issues on which the Qurʾān and ḥadīth texts may be silent but which fall under the umbrella of its broader goals and objectives. Kamali identifies the need to open up the theory of ijtihād by reducing its heavy reliance on the methodology of uṣūl and qiyās (analogical reasoning) and aligning it in the direction of greater flexibility and resourcefulness that the maqāṣid approach offers. This maqāṣid-oriented ijtihād would, according to Kamali, indeed encourage innovative thought and legislation not only in the area of Islamic law but also in economics, sociology, and science.[60] For this to happen, Kamali argues that the classical doctrine of ijmāʿ, as one important source of Islamic law, should be opened up so as to represent the consensus of the community in general (i.e., both political and religious leadership) as a legislative vehicle for the maqāṣid-oriented ijtihād instead of it being confined to the consensus of the religious elite as per traditional doctrine. As such ijmāʿ can play a positive role in the democratization of the legal theory and the entire political system in the Muslim world.[61] Moreover, Kamali proposes that ijtihād and ijmāʿ should be merged to form the "ordinances of the Ūlū l-amr."[62] The Ūlū l-amr constitute the earlier described modified ijmāʿ and are in charge of formulating such ordinances. These Ūlū l-amr, in turn, are to be guided in their decision making, including in the sphere of the aḥkām, both by specific injunctions and by the general objectives, philosophy, and spirit of the al-sharīʿa. He refers to this modified ijtihād-ijmāʿ concept as aḥkām Ūlū l-amr and derives it from the Qurʾānic principle of tawḥīd. Kamali forms the view that this concept of aḥkām Ūlū l-amr is very comprehensive and unifying (hence tawḥīd) as it "seeks to comprise and subsume, in addition to ijmāʿ and ijtihād (and its sub-varieties such as istiḥsān, qiyās, istiṣla), the juristic principle of blocking the means to all that is reprehensible, the fatwa of the Companion as well the goals and purposes, or maqāṣid of the al-sharī'a." He argues further that "all of these are visualized as sources and formulas that may be utilized as basic data, or selected directly for enforcement, through the modality of aḥkām Ūlū l-amr" as a modified form of ijmā'.[63]

Legal maxims (qawā'id) are another maqāṣid-allied concept and a juristic mechanism that can be utilized for the purposes of Islamic law reform according to Kamali. He defines legal maxims as "theoretical abstractions in the form, usually, of short epithetical statements that are expressive, often in a few words, of the goals and objectives of al-sharī'a."[64] They consist mainly of statements of principles that are derived from the detailed reading of the rules of fiqh on various themes. Kamali argues that there is great affinity between legal maxims and the maqāṣid by the virtue of the fact that legal maxims provide useful insights into the goals and purposes of al-sharī'a. This is so for the reason that legal maxims consist mainly of abstract ideas and as such are not particularly affected by the legacy of taqlīd. Kamali goes on to say that *that* is the reason why they can be more readily utilized as aids in the renewal of fiqh and contemporary ijtihād and serve as an effective tool for a better understanding of maqāṣid al-sharī'a.[65] This usefulness of legal maxims in relation to maqāṣid is well evident in the following statement of Kamali:

> It is due to their versatility and comprehensive language that legal maxims tend to encapsulate the broader concepts and characteristics of the al-sharī'a. They tend to provide a bird's-eye-view of their subject matter in imaginative ways without engaging in burdensome details.[66]

Another legal mechanism supportive of a maqāṣid-oriented uṣūl al-fiqh is the concept of ḥikma (wisdom) as explained by Kamali. He defines it as a beneficial consequence of al-sharī'a and as a whole or part of it. Significantly, Kamali asserts that Islamic legal rulings are informed by underlying ḥikma, which are in essence the maqāṣid.[67] Ḥikma, according to Kamali, is goal- and purpose-oriented and as such it can also signify the objective of legislation. He adds that in this sense ḥikma is identical to maqāṣid.[68]

The concept of 'illa gives further credence to a maqāṣid-driven uṣūl al-fiqh that is necessary for meaningful reform of Islamic law because, opines Kamali, in the terminology of legal theory one of its meanings is the effective cause and attribute of a ruling (ḥukm) of al-sharī'a for which it was legislated, as well as its ḥikma. As such 'illa, when not restricted to its purely analogical function as in the case of classical uṣūl al-fiqh, is related to and supportive of the concept of maqāṣid.[69]

Finally, the Qur'ānic science of asbāb al-nuzūl (occasions behind revelation) is another principle that buttresses Kamali's maqāṣid-oriented Islamic law reform project. Its importance for a maqāṣid-oriented uṣūl al-fiqh lies in the fact that, in Kamali's thought, it provides a vista to detach Islamic law from analogy, speculative thought, and literalism and in turn shifts the interpretational focus onto the broader context of revelation for the purpose of identifying the rationale and purpose behind Islamic laws. He also argues that a rationalist approach based on the maqāṣid is supported by asbāb al-nuzūl literature because this literature is an elucidation of the original intent and context of law.[70]

To demonstrate how asbāb al-nuzūl are differently employed in classical uṣūl al-fiqh from that in a maqāṣid-oriented one, Kamali discusses the example of mutilation for punishment for theft and argues that the classical uṣūli approach that relies on semantics and analogy would be unable to identify the ʿilla behind this law or to provide a satisfactory response beyond mere speculation to such questions as to why theft was made punishable with mutilation and not, for example, by imprisonment or whipping. A maqāṣid-oriented approach would employ the asbāb comprehensively. Therefore, argues Kamali when attempting to formulate a rational response that could explain the punishment of mutilation for theft, the jurist would reflect on the time, place, and circumstances in which the law in question originated. As such the jurist would consider factors such as the fact that the punishment of mutilation for theft was practiced by the Arabs before the advent of Islam; that Arab society consisted largely of nomads who traveled with their camels and tents in search of pastures, and it was not feasible under the circumstances to penalize the thief with imprisonment because this would require durable structures and guards, feeding and care of inmates, and so on. He further adds that since there were no protective barriers to safeguard the property of people, society could not afford to tolerate proliferation of theft. Mutilation of the hand of the thief also provided the kind of punishment that disabled the thief from persisting in his wrongdoing,[71] and it served as a "visible mark on the offender to warn people against his menace." Therefore, Kamali concludes that the physical punishment of mutilation was *the only* reasonable option and thus an eminently rational punishment for theft. With this analysis Kamali implies that this form of punishment for theft is no longer the only or the most reasonable manner of punishment in this day and age.[72]

Making the Case for the Viability and Importance of Maqāṣid-Oriented Reform of Islamic Law

In this section I discuss the main arguments outlined by Kamali for the need for and the importance of maqāṣid-oriented Islamic law reform beyond those mentioned earlier. As the next step I describe his contribution to the topic of the nature and the salient features of maqāṣid and their identification. Finally, I outline his proposal on the new methodology of maqāṣid and the future tasks and challenges for maqāṣid-oriented uṣūl.

Kamali presents a number of arguments as to why there is a need for a maqāṣid approach. In no ambiguous terms Kamali is a strong advocate of the great importance of maqāṣid al-sharīʿa in authentic Islamic law reform and for its wider acceptance in the Muslim world. His first argument in favor of a maqāṣid approach-based reform, which is consistent with his siyāsa al-sharīʿa/tajdīd haḍari philosophy outlined earlier, is Kamali's assertion that civilization renewal is more likely to take place if embedded in a suitable al-sharīʿa jurisprudential framework that is provided by the maqāṣid approach and that the rejuvenation of Islamic thought is better served via means of maqāṣid-oriented ijtihād.[73] Second, the significance of the maqāṣid approach, according to Kamali, goes beyond the purely intra-Muslim issues as it can subsume all monotheistic religions and contemporary human rights law (with minor reservations that he does not explain) "because its scope includes material and spiritual benefits to all humanity."[74] Kamali considers that the main aims and purposes of the maqāṣid approach are to provide a methodological tool for safeguarding not only the principal values of Islamic law but also the basic values common to all people.[75]

Another argument Kamali presents for the need for a maqāṣid-based approach to reform is derived from his statement that "maqāṣid al-sharīʿa embody al-sharīʿa itself because the goals of al-sharīʿa are constitutive of al-sharīʿa."[76] In other word al-sharīʿa and maqāṣid al-sharīʿa are coterminous and conceptually inseparable. Another consideration that adds to the importance of maqāṣid approach is that it offers a comprehensive reading of Islam and its al-sharīʿa that is particularly meaningful to harmonizing the al-sharīʿa with the realities of social change and as a means of revitalizing the uṣūl.[77] He also asserts that the maqāṣid approach encourages greater flexibility in ijtihād.[78] Importantly, Kamali forms the view that contemporary conceptualizations of maqāṣid provide scope for innovative approaches to al-sharīʿa that are dynamic in nature and are in close affinity with contemporary human rights discourses. Thus, he argues, these contemporary approaches offer a preferable methodology for coming to terms with and adapting to a number of challenges (he names democracy, human rights, good governance) faced by the Muslim majority world within the framework of al-sharīʿa.[79] The importance of maqāṣid approach as a methodological cum educational tool is also based on the consideration that it is "naturally meaningful to understand the broad outlines of the objectives of al-sharīʿa in the first place before one tries to move on to the specifics." By this he means that "an adequate knowledge of maqāṣid equips the student of the al-sharīʿa with insight and provides him with a theoretical framework in which the attempt to acquire detailed knowledge of its various doctrines can become more interesting and meaningful."[80]

In what follows I describe Kamali's original contributions to the theory of maqāṣid that concern their nature, how they are identified, and the broader methodology underpinning it.

Regarding the question of the nature of the maqāṣid, Kamali forms the view that they are dynamic and subject to change in tandem with social change and that they resonate more strongly with advancement of essential human rights. In other words, he subscribes to the view that the maqāṣid can evolve with the evolution of civilization. As such Kamali argues for an open-ended scale of values for maqāṣid because "as al-sharīʿa has no limit nor do the maqāṣid values."

In this context his words are instructive:

> Our understanding of al-sharīʿa is one of continuing relevance, development, and growth through independent reasoning (ijtihād), renewal, and reform (tajdīd,iṣlāḥ). Hence the goals and purposes of al-sharīʿa must also remain an evolving chapter of the juristic and civilisational edifice of Islam.[81]

In addition to the maqāṣid identified by classical and some modern scholars he identifies social justice, equality, fundamental freedoms and rights,[82] cultivation of human intellect through education and science, and cooperation as additional maqāṣid.[83] Kamali also describes the nature of maqāṣid by maintaining that they must be constant/permanent (ṭabit), zahir (evident), general (ʿamm), and exclusive and that they must operate without any sociotemporal constrains.[84]

Kamali has also developed novel ideas in relation to the issue of the methodology of identification of maqāṣid. In this context he has identified a number of what he terms "principal indicators" or methods of identifying maqāṣid. These include clear and definitive texts (nuṣūs) found in the Qur'ān and ḥadīth: istidlāl (sound reasoning); al-ʿaql (reason); al-tajriba (experience); al-fiṭra (innate nature); and al-istiqrāʿ (corroborative induction). Interestingly, and importantly, Kamali argues that these methods of indication of the maqāṣid can also be employed in combination with one another provided certain conditions are met such as: that a maqāṣid validated by clear and definitive nuṣūs cannot be put into doubt by any other indicator; that as the result of this combination of indicators no maqāṣid of equal standing conflict with each other; that in the case of a conflict arising between the evidential basis of two maqāṣid, recourse to the rules of interpretation pertaining to conflict and preference (al-ta'arud wa-l tarjih) can be taken; and that maqāṣid identified fulfill the conditions of permanence, self-evidence, exclusiveness, and generality.[85] He also adds that the credibility of the maqāṣid is greater if it is identified by a larger number of indicators but that their essential validity can be established on the basis of just one such indicator.

Kamali's important contribution to maqāṣid is also found in the area of identifying a method for their relative appraisal and internal hierarchy. Since not all maqāṣid embody or protect values of equal importance to al-sharī'a, Kamali argues that they are hierarchical and, therefore, their relative importance needs to be appraised. By hierarchical, he means appraising the relative strength or weakness of one maqāṣid in relation to another. With regard to this question, he develops an innovative methodology that identifies systematically the intrinsic merit of various maqāṣid indicators beyond those employed by classical thought (as per al-Shatibi). This methodology helps in the correct placement and order of various al-sharī'a goals. The first such indicator is the presence or otherwise of texts (nuṣūs) in the Qur'ān, ḥadīth, precedent of the Companions and their general consensus (ijmā'). If texts are present, appraisal would involve the relative clarity of text/s, whether it/they is/are speculative (zannī) or definitive (qaṭ'ī), clear and self-explained (muḥkam), or ambiguous and obscure (mujmal), and so on. Another indicator is with reference to how much benefit (maṣlaḥa) they would realize or how much evil (mafṣada) they would prevent. This is a rational evaluation based on contextual considerations and involves decision-making processes regarding the comprehensiveness and generality of the benefit realized or evil prevented. Kamali includes the five scale of moral values (al aḥkām al ḫamsa), the classification of sins into major and minor, and the literature pertaining to the pillars and essentials of Islam (arkān al islam) as existent in classical fiqh thought as further helping with the appraisal of the maqāṣid. Furthermore, Kamali argues that the nature of punishments prescribed by the al-sharī'a for certain conduct is another tool in assisting appraisal of maqāṣid because these punishments are indicative of value and purpose. Those that carry the lesser punishment embody a value of lesser importance to al-sharī'a and vice versa. Kamali also evokes the principle of al-wa'ad wa al-wa'īd or the relative strengths the texts contain in reference to promise of reward or threat/warning as a mechanism for the appraisal of maqāṣid. Finally, the last indicator concerns the relative prominence of a ḥukm, and therefore the value pursued, in the Qur'ān and the Sunna by means of how frequently they have been mentioned in them.[86]

Another major contribution of Kamali is the development of a systematic methodology behind the maqāṣid-oriented uṣūl theory. He repeatedly states that there is a need to develop a more robust and systematic maqāṣid theory that would have a high level of methodological accuracy in order to avoid any arbitrariness or bias in identification of maqāṣid. This he considers to be a crucial factor for any authentic and widely acceptable Islamic law reform. He notes that a lack of a systematic methodology of maqāṣid was an important factor behind the traditional scholars' reticence to give prominence to the maqāṣid-oriented approach because in the absence of such methodology, the speculative element that was involved in the identification of maqāṣid was perceived by them to be too great.[87] In order to achieve this methodological accuracy, Kamali proposes to establish a "learned council" that would be in charge of the process of identification of maqāṣid and their verification.[88] In his words:

> Collective ijtihād and consultation would be the best recourse for ensuring accuracy in the identification of maqāṣid. It would certainly be reassuring to secure the advice and approval of a learned council as to the veracity of a maqāṣid that is identified for the purpose of policymaking and legislation. This could be a standing parliamentary committee that comprises expertise in al-sharīʿa and other disciplines and its task would be to verify, suggest, and identify the more specific range of goals and purposes of al-sharīʿa and law in conjunction with legislation and government policy.[89]

Cognizant of the importance of methodological accuracy in the new maqāṣid theories, Kamali himself has attempted to develop such a theory. One aspect of it concerns novel interpretation of the Qur'ān itself based on what he terms the "newly developed genre of tafsīr," or the "maqāṣid-based tafsīr." Kamali finds antecedents of this new tafsīr genre in the existence of thematic-based tafsīr (tafsīr mawḍūʿī), which aims to uncover the unity of theme and content in the Qur'ān. The complementary nature of mawḍūʿī and maqāṣid tafsīr stems from the fact that the identification of a goal or purpose is only possible once one has interpretationally taken into account all of the evidence pertaining to a particular theme or subject matter, which is the very task of the tafsīr mawḍūʿī. Reflecting this unity of theme and content in the legislative sphere of the Qur'ān would be the task of the maqāṣid-based tafsīr.

Another novel aspect of Kamali's maqāṣid-based tafsīr is that it interpretationally unifies what we could term as "the ethico-religious dimensions" of the Qur'ānic message with those dealing with the aḥkām when interpreting the legal Qur'ānic injunctions. Kamali argues for the validity of this approach by stating that the Qur'ān is not meant to be a law book but a book of moral and spiritual guidance and as such this implies that the aḥkām verses must share a common purpose with the ethico-religious teachings of the Qur'ān. This, in turn, increases the scope of evidence of ayāt upon which aḥkām are to be made. It integrates the ethico-religious verses with those of the ayāt al aḥkām, all of which are used as indicators (dalāl) to help identify maqāṣid. This same methodology would also apply to the Sunna, that is, to aḥkām al ḥadīth. With respect to maqāṣid in the Sunna, Kamali adds further that the detailed rulings of ḥadīth must be interpreted in light of the maqāṣid as done by Companions and that specific requirements of the Sunna can be relaxed, interpreted differently, or reversed if these actions realize a higher maqāṣid of al-sharī'a.[90]

Conclusion

Having spent over three decades in efforts to raising awareness of the importance of a maqāṣid-oriented al-sharī'a and in developing a more systematic methodology of maqāṣid uṣūl, Kamali is aware of the fact that the maqasid-oriented approaches to Islamic law and legal theory will not be a universal panacea for the complex and diverse challenges Muslim societies are facing in the twenty-first century. He, for example, acknowledges that the theory of maqāṣid would need to be further developed, nuanced, and refined before it can play a positive role in the civilizational renewal of the Muslim world and the reform of Islamic law in particular. However, he is optimistic about the potential involved in developing the maqāṣid discourse, which is gaining increased scholarly attention. He interprets this growing interest as evidence that the maqāṣid are seen to have the potential to respond constructively, authentically, and positively to the contemporary needs and realities of Muslims.[91]

Notes

1. http://www.hashimkamali.com/index.php/about. Last accessed December 12, 2013.
2. Hashim Kamali, "Methodological Issues in Islamic Jurisprudence," *Arab Law Quarterly*, 11 (1996): 33.
3. Hasim Kamali, *Civilisational Renewal: Revisiting the Islam Hadhari Approach: Definition, Significance, Criticism, Recognition, Support, Tajdid and Future Directions* (Kuala Lumpur: Arah Publication, 2008), 83.
4. Hashim Kamali, *IAIS Malaysia: Exploring the Intellectual Horizons of Civilisational Islam* (Kuala Lumpur: Arah Publications, 2008), 6.
5. Kamali, *Civilisational Renewal*, 52.
6. Ibid., 57.

7. Ibid., 60.
8. Ibid,. 65.
9. Hashim Kamali, *Shari'ah Law: An Introduction* (Oxford: Oneworld, 2008), 226.
10. Ibid., 225.
11. Kamali, "Methodological Issues," 4.
12. Kamali, *Shari'ah Law*, 173–174.
13. Ibid., 37.
14. Ibid., 59.
15. Ibid., 268.
16. Ibid., 273.
17. Kamali, "Methodological Issues," 33.
18. Kamali, *Shari'ah Law*, 32–33, 232.
19. Hashim Kamali, "Maqāṣid al-šarīʿa: The Objectives of Islamic Law," *Islamic Studies*, 38 (1999):193–208, 194–196. On the link between maṣlaḥa and maqāṣid al-šarīʿa, see the main text later.
20. Kamali, *Shari'ah Law*, 27–28.
21. Ibid., 49.
22. Ibid., 2, 5.
23. Ibid., 135, 229.
24. Kamali, *Shari'a Law*, 16, 39, 41. Cf. Hashim Kamali, "Shari'ah and Civil Law: Towards a Methodology of Harmonization," *Islamic Law and Society*, 14 (2007): 391–420, 395.
25. Kamali, *Shari'ah Law*, 49–50.
26. Kamali, "Methodological Issues," 14.
27. Ibid., 17.
28. Hashim Kamali, "Maqāṣid al-šarīʿa and Ijtihad as Instruments of Civilizational Renewal: A Methodological Pespective," *Islam and Civilisational Renewal*, 2 (2011): 259.
29. Hashim Kamali, "Istiḥsān and the Renewal of Islamic Law," Occasional Paper 58, 2004, Islamic Research Institute, Islamabad. Accessed November 26, 2013. http://www.hashimkamali.com/index.php/publications/item/119-istiḥsān-and-the-renewal-of-islamic-law.
30. Kamali, *Shari'ah Law*, 194.
31. Hashim Kamali, "Issues in the Legal Theory of Usul and Prospects for Reform," *Islamic Studies*, 40 (2001): 13.
32. Here he identifies things such as the textual rulings of the Qur'ān on the fulfillment of contracts, the legality of sale, the prohibition of usury, respect for the property of others, documentation of loans and other forms of deferred payments, the Qur'ānic injunctions on the subject of justice, respect for truth, and giving testimony in its cause principles of government such as consultation, equality, and basic rights. He also identifies Qur'ānic legislation on civil, economic, constitutional, and international relations as falling into this category. Ibid., 51.
33. Kamali, *Shari'ah Law*, 49.

34. See also our discussion on ta'lil earlier.
35. Kamali, "Issues in the Legal Theory," 13.
36. Kamali, "Maqāṣid al-šarī'a and Ijtihad," 250. Cf. Kamali, *Shari'ah Law*, 27. We will have more to say on this in the main text later.
37. Kamali, *Shari'ah Law*, 247.
38. Ibid.
39. Encapsulated by the vast and long tradition of its commentary and exposition in the genre of tafsir.
40. Kamali, *Shari'ah Law*, 21.
41. Kamali, *Shari'ah Law*, 52; Kamali, "Methodological Issues," 3.
42. Kamali, "Methodological Issues," 3.
43. Qur'ānic evidence Kamali provides for ta'lil nature of the Qur'ān and its laws are reference to the proclamation on just retaliation (*qisās*) that "in qisas there is (saving of) life for you, you men of understanding" (2: 179); the prohibition of wine-drinking and gambling being premised on the rationale of preventing "hostility and rancor" among people and interference with the remembrance of God (5: 91). Legal alms and charities are levied in order to prevent the concentration of wealth among the rich (57: 7). With reference even to the prophethood of Muhammad, "We have not sent thee but a mercy to mankind" (21: 10). Mercy *in* this text and communication (5: 92) and warning *in* other places (22: 49), Hashim Kamali, "Fiqh and Adaptation to Social Reality," *The Muslim World*, 86 (1996): 62–76.
44. Ibid. Also Kamali, *Shari'ah Law*, 55.
45. Ibid., 78.
46. Kamali acknowledges Taha Jabir Al Alwani a contemporary scholar who has also written on the concept of maqaṣid as the originator of this phrase that he is borrowing.
47. Kamali, "Methodological Issues," 11–13.
48. Ibid., 22.
49. Ibid., 9.
50. Ibid., 10.
51. Kamali, "Maqāṣid al-šarī'a and Ijtihad," 245. Cf. Kamali, "Issues in the Legal Theory," 11–14.
52. Kamali, "Issues in the Legal Theory," 14.
53. Hashim Kamali, "Have We Neglected the Shari'ah-Law Doctrine of Maṣlaḥa?," *Islamic Studies*, 27 (1988): 287–303.
54. Kamali, "Maqāṣid al-šarī'a and Ijtihad," 248.
55. Which reinforces my statement in the main text earlier that Kamali subscribes to ethical objectivism. See page 20 of this chapter.
56. Kamali, *Shari'ah Law*, 35.
57. Kamali, "Istiḥsān and the Renewal of Islamic Law," 13.
58. Kamali, "Istiḥsān and the Renewal of Islamic Law," 13.
59. Kamali, "Issues in the Legal Theory," 14.
60. Kamali, *Shari'ah Law*, 303–304.

61. Kamali, "Issues in the Legal Theory," 19–20.
62. A Qur'ānic designation of those who are in charge of public affairs of the people.
63. Kamali, "Issues in the Legal Theory," 22.
64. Hashim Kamali, "Legal Maxims and Other Genres of Literature in Islamic Jurisprudence," *Arab Law Quarterly*, 20 (2006): 80.
65. Ibid.,78–80; Cf. Kamali, *Shari'ah Law*, 304.
66. Kamali, "Legal Maxims," 82.
67. Hashim Kamali, "Law and Ethics in Islam: The Role of the Maqāṣid al-šarīʿa," in *New Directions in Islamic Thought*, ed. K. Vogt, L. Larsen, and Ch. Moe (New York: I. B. Tauris, 2009), 24–25.
68. Kamali, "Maqāṣid al-šarīʿa and Ijtihad," 247.
69. Ibid.
70. Kamali, "Issues in the Legal Theory," 30.
71. In this context he notices inconsistency between the Qur'ānic punishment for illegal intercourse with that of theft since the former did not require mutilation of the relevant organ while the latter did. Hence, the argument about the speculative nature of classical uṣūli qiyās.
72. Kamali, *Shari'ah Law*, 130–131.
73. Kamali, "Maqāṣid al-šarīʿa and Ijtihad," 267.
74. Kamali, "Maqāṣid al-šarīʿa and Ijtihad," 249.
75. Kamali, "Law and Ethics in Islam," 23; Kamali, "Maqāṣid al-šarīʿa and Ijtihad," 245.
76. Ibid., 245.
77. Kamali, "Shari'ah and Civil Law," 416.
78. Ibid., 417.
79. Kamali, "Maqāṣid al-šarīʿa and Ijtihad," 245.
80. Kamali, *Shari'ah Law*, 139.
81. Kamali, "Maqāṣid al-šarīʿa and Ijtihad," 266.
82. Kamali, "Law and Ethics in Islam," 31.
83. Kamali, "Maqāṣid al-šarīʿa and Ijtihad," 255–256.
84. Kamali, "Law and Ethics in Islam," 24.
85. Kamali, "Maqāṣid al-šarīʿa and Ijtihad," 257.
86. Kamali, "Law and Ethics in Islam," 39–42.
87. Kamali, "Issues in the Legal Theory," 15.
88. Kamali, "Shari'ah and Civil Law," 418.
89. Kamali, *Shari'ah Law*, 136.
90. Kamali, "Maqāṣid al-šarīʿa and Ijtihad," 251–255.
91. Kamali, "Methodological Issues."

CHAPTER 2

Yusuf al-Qaradawi's Purposive *Fiqh*: Promoting or Demoting the Future Role of the *'ulamā'*?

David L. Johnston

This chapter is about a high-profile Muslim scholar who rather late in his career turned to the now-popular legal methodology of the maqāṣid al-sharī'a. Although I delve into some of the details of his legal theory, I am also interested in probing what is behind this strategy. A media figure of global proportions, Shaykh Yusuf al-Qaradawi has consistently seen himself as a leader of mainstream Sunni Islam with the God-given mission of leading it on the "middle" path (read "moderate," or wasaṭi), away from the ultraconservatives, whether they be the literalists or Salafis on one side, or the liberal Muslims enamored of Western values on the other. Yet Muslims cannot find this middle path and stay on it, Qaradawi holds, without strengthening the authority of Islam's legal experts, the 'ulamā'.

This chapter argues that, besides his gradual intellectual attraction to this "purposive" methodology, Qaradawi's use of it in the 1990s and 2000s dovetailed nicely with his political posturing as an *'ālim* of international standing both within the Muslim community and beyond it. Further, I contend that his adoption of this approach to legal theory did not in the least affect his long-held views as expressed in his fatwas and other writings. So in light of the evident stirrings of change and even turmoil within Islamic legal circles today, I ask one important question in my last section: Isn't this focus on the higher purposes of God's law more likely to undermine the authority of the traditional *'ulamā'* class in the long run, and especially in a twenty-first century marked by a radically democratized public sphere?

Perhaps the most popular Muslim scholar and preacher of the early twenty-first century, Yusuf al-Qaradawi's scholarly output in the domain of *fiqh* (applied Islamic jurisprudence) over the last 50 years is astounding. Yet beyond the sheer volume of his writings (over 130 books to date),[1] his popularity stems from his ability to write accessible texts on current challenges facing the Muslim *umma*, from his preaching in various high-profile venues, his sponsorship of the influential web portal IslamOnline.net, and his interactive teaching style on the ever-admired *Sharia and Life* program on Al-Jazeera TV.

Having written his doctoral dissertation at the Al-Azhar University in Cairo in 1973 on the applicability of Islam's charitable giving (*zakāt*), Qaradawi became an actively sought after consultant in the booming Islamic financial sector. More importantly, ever since he founded the first student chapter of the Muslim Brotherhood at Al-Azhar University in 1946 (at age 20), he has been associated with the organization in one way or another all his life.[2] The most telling sign of this connection was his appearance in Cairo's Tahrir Square to lead the Friday prayers days after the revolution had swept away President Hosni Mubarak (February 18, 2011). The throng of well over a million worshippers come to hear him bears eloquent witness to his Brotherhood credentials, his Egyptian roots, and his enduring popularity there, despite 50 years of self-imposed exile in Qatar.[3]

It was Qaradawi's Brotherhood connection too that created invitations for his lectures and seminars over the years in Europe, Asia, Africa, and America, in addition to his growing reputation as a prolific scholar. Soon after his arrival in Qatar, he was asked to establish the Sharia faculty for the University of Qatar, which opened in 1977, making him a traditional *'ālim* mandated by the state to set up training for a new generation of 'ulamā', at home and abroad. From the 1980s onward, he began to think more strategically about what could be done to leverage the presence of a highly educated Muslim population in the West.[4] This preoccupation bore fruit in the 2000s when he was named president of two influential Islamic organizations: the European Council for Fatwa and Research[5] and the International Union of Muslim Scholars (founded in 2004).[6]

Still, Qaradawi's global influence truly began with his satellite TV presence on Al-Jazeera starting in 1996. Ehab Galal argues that "Qaradawi *and* al-Jazeera have succeeded in combining new transnational media with Islamic thinking in a modern framework." In fact, he continues, "not only has *Sharia and Life* for many years been the only religious programme at al-Jazeera, the programme has also become a model to imitate for other new

Arab satellite channels." Since his constant goal has been to unite the world *umma*, reasons Galal, "Qaradawi takes part in a redefinition of a Muslim public sphere."[7]

Several scholars have noticed Qaradawi's intentional use of the new media.[8] First, there was his fatwa program on Qatar TV, *Hadi'l-Islam*, where he appears alone sitting at a desk and answers questions sent to him by mail. Then he forged a partnership with the initially state-funded but now mostly independent satellite network, Al-Jazeera, to launch *Sharia and Life*, which broke the timeless Islamic atmosphere of *Hadi'l-Islam* by having Qaradawi interact with a host, providing background pictures of global hot spots where Muslims are victims and having people call in by phone. Whereas *Hadi'l-Islam* aims to inform and educate a regional audience, through *Sharia and Life* Qaradawi aims to set a global agenda "by means of discourse, performance, and participation."[9]

No doubt, Qaradawi knows his listeners have many other choices in religious programming, from the traditional muftis and shaykhs on a variety of other media to the new media stars, or the "new missionaries," as Galal calls them, like Amr Khaled or Moez Masoud. The latter pose the greatest threat in Qaradawi's mind, because as non-ʿulamāʾ their source of authority comes from their ability to entertain, address religious experience as opposed to legal reasoning, and move audiences to deeper religious commitment. This is the postmodern model that Qaradawi tries to approximate, at least through its more interactive format, but his content and style remain those of an *ʿālim*, whose authority flows from his vast learning and his Al-Azhar pedigree—ironically, a more "modern" distinction and something that Galal sees as a liability within the global discourse of the new media.[10]

It is therefore as an *ʿālim* that Qaradawi has constantly portrayed himself as a spokesperson of Islamic revivalism (al-ṣaḥwa al-islāmiyya),[11] and more specifically as the promoter of a "Middle Road" Islam (al-wasaṭiyya). But it is only since the early 1990s that he has specifically written about legal theory, and in particular about the burgeoning field of the objectives of al-sharīʿa.[12] As he develops these themes, he is careful to acknowledge his debt to Rashid Rida (d. 1935) and Hasan al-Banna (d. 1949).[13] Qaradawi manifestly sees himself as a spokesperson for twentieth- and twenty-first-century political Islam. In light of this, and especially against the backdrop of all the sociological implications of the new media mentioned earlier, this chapter specifically examines how Qaradawi's appropriation of this purposive approach to Islamic jurisprudence enables him to better fulfill his wider agenda—to secure a leading role for the *ʿulamāʾ* in our fast-changing global society.

Qaradawi and the "Purposive Fiqh"

The rich content available in this volume eloquently attests to the popularity and influence of the "Objectives of the Shari'a" movement in Islamic scholarly circles today—a topic I have delved into myself elsewhere.[14] It has only been in the 2000s, however, that Qaradawi has openly hitched his own wagon to this "school,"[15] though he had gradually incorporated elements of this methodology in his writings in the 1990s. Most notably, he was one of the founding directors of the London-based Al-Maqaṣid Research Centre in the Philosophy of Islamic Law, a brainchild and personal project of Sheikh Ahmad Zaki Yamani in 2005.[16] Thirteen other eminent *'ulamā'*, including the influential Muslim Brotherhood author Sheikh Muhammad Salim al-Awa, remain on the Centre's board today. Just the year before, Qaradawi had given the keynote address at a conference in London devoted to this theme. It was not included in the edited volume of conference papers issued by the Maqasid Centre,[17] but rather used by Qaradawi as an introduction to his own volume dedicated to the "Objectives of Shari'a" in 2006.[18]

Not surprisingly,[19] Qaradawi was not invited to take part in the yearly international symposium cosponsored by the Al-Azhar University and the Egyptian Ministry of Religious Affairs in 2010. Ironically, this was to be the last such conference before the 2011 revolution and its theme was "The Purposes of the Islamic Shari'a and Contemporary Issues: Research and Realities." Scholars from over 30 countries participated and the papers were gathered into two volumes.[20] Clearly, the purposes of Shari'a methodology were now in the limelight.

After a brief introduction to the history of this purposive *fiqh* in Islamic legal circles, I will offer some comments on its implications for hermeneutics and epistemology. I will then show how Qaradawi made use of both Ibn Qayyim al-Jawziyya and Abu Ishaq al-Shatibi. Finally, I demonstrate how in incorporating this discourse in the 1990s Qaradawi drew heavily on Rashid Rida, less so on Hasan al-Banna, and thereby strongly identified himself with twentieth-century Islamism or what he calls al-ṣaḥwa al-islāmiyya, or "the Islamic awakening."[21] This in turn will lead us to look behind Qaradawi's adoption of this methodology in light of his career's consistent goals, and finally to wonder about the implications of his epistemology for the future of the *'ulamā'* in our global society.

A Brief Historical and Philosophical Overview

Allow me to introduce the *maqāṣidi* approach as Qaradawi does himself in what I believe is his first attempt to systematize it for his own use[22] in his 1999 book, *Siyāsa al-sharīʿa fī dawʿ nusus al-sharīʿa wa-maqāṣidiha* [Political Governance in Light of the Shariʿa's Texts and Objectives].[23] I will do this in tandem with Muhammad Qasim Zaman, a historian and Islamic law specialist whose research focuses on the issue of authority in contemporary Islam. Zaman began in earnest with his 2002 book, *The ʿulamāʾ in Contemporary Islam: Custodians of Change.*[24] The piece I am drawing from here is a chapter he contributed to the edited book *Public Islam and the Common Good*, "The ʿulamāʾ of Contemporary Islam and Their Conceptions of the Common Good."[25]

Zaman begins by noting that the concept of the common good can be related to "[a] number of doctrines and methods in medieval jurisprudence." He explains:

> In their writings on the principles or foundations of the law (*usul al-fiqh*), medieval jurists often posited five fundamental values as encapsulating the "purposes" of God's law, the shariʿa. These values—religion, life, progeny, property, and rationality—were based not on any explicit listing of their contents in the foundational texts but were derived, the jurists believed, through what Wael Hallaq has characterized as "inductive corroboration." These fundamental values converged on the preservation, within the limits prescribed God [*sic*], of the interests of human beings—their individual and collective good.[26]

What Zaman characterizes as "the individual and collective good" is what the classical jurists called *maṣlaḥa*, usually translated as "human benefit," "welfare," and the like. *Maṣlaḥa*, as the reader of this book knows, was at the heart of much debate in classical Islamic jurisprudence.[27] The first systematic statement about how considerations of *maṣlaḥa* could enrich both legal theory (*uṣūl al-fiqh*) and its practical application (*fiqh*) was made by Abu Hamid al-Ghazali (d. 1111). The earlier five values or the "five necessities" were on the highest level; then came human needs, and finally improvements to human life. Yet as Zaman rightly observes, "because considerations of *maṣlaḥa* usually lacked explicit justifications for themselves in the foundational texts, it was a rather controversial doctrine in medieval jurisprudence."[28] This is why Ghazali was so careful to link any reference to *maṣlaḥa* either to a clear text in the Qurʿan or the authentic Sunna, and if the notion of human benefit was unattached to a text (*maṣlaḥa mursala*), then it had to be tethered to the Islamic legal instrument par excellence, *qiyas* (reasoning by analogy). Bear in mind, Ghazali is, like all the jurists before him, a textualist, that is, one who believes that Islamic jurisprudence (*fiqh*, and the discipline that accords it theological and methodological grounding, uṣūl *al-fiqh*) is based on straightforward textual indications (*adilla*, sing. *dalil*) found in the Qur'an and the Sunna. So before delving further into Qaradawi's work, I open a brief parenthesis about ethical theory.

Maqasid al-shari'a is where theology (and by definition, philosophy) and legal theory meet. Ghazali wanted to make sure that any conception of human good came from revelation, not from human reason. The wider intellectual context of Ghazali's *uṣūl al-fiqh* is played out in two centuries of debates among Muslim scholars over the merits of Greek philosophy in theology and ethics—debates that inevitably impacted the central Islamic discipline of law. The lines of demarcation in the ninth century CE were sharply drawn between the proponents of philosophy and rationalism (the early Mu'tazilites) and the heirs of the first scholars of Islam, the *ahl ḥadith*, or "the students of prophetic traditions," people whose pious outlook was informed and nourished through memorizing the actual words of the Qur'an and the Sunna.[29] So from the beginning, the rationalists clashed with the textualists. This represents, I believe, the eternal tension between reason and revelation in the monotheistic faiths.

This was also at the time when discussions about Aristotle in particular were beginning to feed into the emerging discipline of ethics.[30] By the next century, legal theory was being hammered out in various locations and the textualist camp was becoming more sophisticated through the efforts of ex-Mu'tazilite Abu al-Hassan al-Ash'ari (d. 935). 'Ash'arism, as the new school came to be called, borrowed from the Mu'tazilites their scholastic methodology and some of their ideas, like the rational proof for the existence of God. But Ash'arism too, still considered "Orthodox" Islamic theology for Muslims in general,[31] disagreed with them about the very feasibility of ethics as a discipline.

Ghazali, a loyal Ash'arite whose expert knowledge of philosophy enabled him to forcefully combat the philosophers on their own terms, intentionally tied ethical knowledge to the specific indications (*adilla*) of the sacred texts. This is known as "ethical voluntarism," classically stated by Plato on the lips of Socrates in his Euthyphro Dialogue: a course of action is good only because the gods say it is. Stated otherwise, there is no objective reality in the words "good" or "evil," "justice" or "injustice." The corollary to this position is that human beings cannot access this knowledge outside of divine revelation. The contrasting Mu'tazilite position (which was soon declared heretical by mainstream Sunnism) posited "justice" as an objective norm that even God had to respect—how could he send good people to hell, for instance? Or bad people to heaven? For them, God is not only just (in infinite measure), but the contours of justice are also accessible to human minds.[32] If God commands his creatures to act justly, they reason, then he must have given them some innate knowledge of what a just act looks like apart from what they might learn from revelation. So we have here simultaneously an ontology of objective ethical values and an epistemology that makes them available to human reason.[33] Not surprisingly, the Muʿtazilites were known as "the people of justice and oneness" (*ahl al-ʿadl wa-l-tawḥīd*).[34]

We now return to the issue of the Shariʿa's objectives and how the purposive fiqh appeared. The very notion that God would act for the purpose of achieving a particular end—a central Muʿtazilite affirmation—was controversial for Ashʿarites. First, it seems to impose some limitation on the Almighty, and second, it seems to suggest that the human mind can apprehend that purpose—a nonstarter in Ashʿarite terms. This explains Ghazali's caution about jurists being able to posit any human benefit outside of the revealed texts, which nevertheless seem to indicate the rationale behind at least certain commands. Thus, if intoxication is forbidden specifically during one's ritual prayer, then God must be concerned about the good functioning of a worshipper's mind as he or she is praying. God, then, must want to preserve the integrity of the human mind, and by analogy, anything that impairs the functioning of one's mind should be forbidden—like mind-altering drugs for instance. In medieval terms, the "reason" (*ʿilla*) *behind* the divine command but still *tied to* the texts was the only possible starting point for analogical reasoning (*qiyās*), one of the two reason-based sources of Islamic law.[35]

These considerations notwithstanding, the idea that God's wisdom could be discerned in the Shariʿa was a difficult one to resist. When that was established, it then became much easier to say that human welfare was the purpose behind God's commands and prohibitions. Three Muslim jurists from the late medieval period are most quoted on this issue by the proponents of contemporary purposive jurisprudence: Najm al-Din Al-Tufi (d. 1316), Ibn Qayyim al-Jawziyya (d. 1350), and Abu Ishaq al-Shatibi (d. 1388). Although relatively ignored until the modern era, Tufi has stirred up much controversy of late, as Qaradawi has repeatedly noted, mostly because some have interpreted him as saying that *maṣlaḥa* can even cancel injunctions in the sacred texts. I agree with Zaman's assessment:

> Though Tufi did not always make this explicit, it is clear, Qaradawi says, that *maṣlaḥa* can override indications in the foundational texts only when such indications are not a matter of certainty as to their meaning. When, however, they are, there can be no question but that *maṣlaḥa* must be subordinate to them, and Tufi never asserted otherwise.[36]

Although I do not follow the controversy about Tufi in this chapter, the earlier quote provides a nice introduction to the issues raised by Qaradawi's use of Ibn Qayyim and Shatibi in what follows. Those who see public benefit overriding a clear text have crossed a watershed that Muslim jurists never crossed before (whether Tufi actually did this or not). This is a tipping point where, arguably, reason overtakes revelation—something Qaradawi vehemently rejects. That is indeed the crux of the issue I want to pursue in this chapter.

The Centrality of Ibn Qayyim for Qaradawi's Purposive *Fiqh*

Ibn Qayyim was a disciple of Ibn Taymiyya (d. 1328), both being Hanbali jurists. Although not mentioned by Zaman, Ibn Qayyim is Qaradawi's chief authority in this book on al-sharīʿa-inspired politics (*siyāsa al-sharīʿa*). As a matter of fact, Qaradawi credits him for sparking his own discovery of the *maqāṣidi* perspective. Writing in a later book wholly devoted to this methodology, Qaradawi attributes to Ibn Qayyim's writing the genesis of this idea in his own mind:

> The idea kept coming to me in greater clarity and depth and this word from Ibn Qayyim implanted itself in the depths of my heart: "The shariʿa is built and solidly anchored on the benefits (*maṣlaḥa*) it bestows on humankind. It is altogether justice, altogether mercy, altogether well-being (*maṣlaḥa*), altogether wisdom."[37]

After defining this key term in his introductory chapter of *siyāsa al-sharīʿa* (26–30), Qaradawi asks himself what *al*-siyāsa "meant for our *ʿulamāʾ* of old." It has two meanings, he answers, the first being "the management of people's affairs and earthly concerns by means of religious ordinances... in the stead of God's messenger for the sake of protecting religion and the managing (siyāsa) of this world through it." The second meaning is more specific: "what the imam[38] believes or what rules and decisions he makes, either averting tangible corruption (*fasād*), anticipating future corruption, or resolving a particular problem."[39] Qaradawi goes on to explain that the "rightly guided caliphs" (Muhammad's first four successors ruling in Medina) made all kinds of decisions that fall into that second category in light of the rapidly evolving sociopolitical context.

What is most notable here is that Qaradawi immediately brings up Ibn Qayyim to make one of the central points of this book that "rulers before and during his own time have enacted new laws relative to the state (*qawānīn siyāsiyya*), leaning on their own opinions and inclinations apart from God's law (*al-sharīʿa*), because the jurists (*fuqahāʾ*) had made their task impossible through their own rigidity, slavish imitation of the past (*taqlīd*) and fanatic loyalty to their own school of law."[40] Qaradawi then cites Ibn Qayyim's commentary on another Hanbali jurist, Ibn Aqil (d. 1119), who was one of those *'ulamā'* who restricted the use of political decision making to what may be found in the Shari'a (i.e., the Qur'an and authentic Sunna). Due to this narrow interpretation of *siyāsa al-sharī'a*, Ibn Aqil even states that the caliph Uthman was wrong to have ordered the burning of the Qur'anic manuscripts that did not agree with the version of the Qur'an he had declared authoritative. Thus, Ibn Aqil, like many other *'ulamā'*, by rejecting the consideration of *maṣlaḥa* (human benefit or welfare) in the affairs of state was guilty of giving short shrift both to the real-life conditions of their day and to what the Shari'a actually teaches.[41]

Ibn Qayyim's genius, continues Qaradawi, lay in his analyzing these two extremes in his own day—jurists who were "too narrow," in that they required political decisions to be made according to the sacred texts, and those who were "too wide" in that they "exaggerated" the role of *maṣlaḥa*, and on that basis went against the rulings found in the texts.[42] Then follows this key paraphrase of Ibn Qayyim's view:

> For God—praise be to Him—sent his messengers and revealed his books so that people might conduct [their affairs] with fairness (*qisṭ*), which is justice ('adl), by which the heavens and the earth were put in place. If [rulers] give orders that are just, and this justice shines however [one wishes to investigate it], then that is where you find God's law and his religion. For God—praise be to Him—is more knowledgeable and wise, and more just than to put strict limits on the pathway to justice; how then [could] he forbid that which is more obviously [just] and easier to prove with strong arguments... But God has made his means of legislation manifest: his design (*maqāṣiduhu*) is to establish justice ('adl) among his creatures, to strengthen humankind through fairness (*qisṭ*). Thus, any path that is opened by means of justice and righteousness—that is religion (*dīn*), and not contrary to it.[43]

Notice that the word *maṣlaḥa* does not appear in this short text, but that it is abundantly clear that for Ibn Qayyim "human welfare" is an exact parallel to the ethical norm of justice (*qisṭ* and *'adl* are roughly synonyms). This, by all measures, is a sweeping statement: "the Shari'a is 'designed' by God to "establish justice among his creatures. Thus, any path that is opened by means of justice and righteousness—that is religion." Such a declaration, of course, is vulnerable to a much more liberal application than Qaradawi is willing to accept. Nevertheless, it is a definite break from the literalism of the ultraconservatives whom Qaradawi castigates as wrongly focusing all their attention on the minutae of the texts, as we shall see later.

What is more, this turn away from literalism begs a question relative to Ghazali and, truly, the Ash'arite tradition of which he was a part and likely the most eloquent exponent to this day. As I see it, there is a built-in contradiction, or at least a tension, between the way words like "justice" and "fairness" are applied to God and how they are applied to humans. Here justice and/or righteousness represent objective values human beings can "prove" to one another. So when rulers, as Qaradawi insists Ibn Qayyim is saying, choose justice as a guide for making decisions in areas not covered by the texts, their laws participate in God's higher laws, and therefore, to that extent, their rule is "Shari'a-like." This is, he argues, what *siyāsa al-sharī'a* is, because it comes under God's "purposes" for the world as revealed in the Shari'a. As I said, *maṣlaḥa* and justice are nearly synonymous here: "A just policy [is not] contrary to the rules articulated in the Shari'a, but it agrees with them and is absolutely one with them. We call it a policy (*siyāsa*) that is in tune with your benefit. For it is the justice of God and his messenger that emanates from these orders and rulings."[44]

In the second part of the book (41–97), Qaradawi investigates the use of "opinion" (*ra'y*) in the work of jurisprudence: "The Opinion of the Imam, the Scope of his Purview, and Where He May Apply It."[45] The debate about the appropriate roles of reason and revelation in Islamic law has a long geneology. In essence Qaradawi advances that the early successors of Muhammad, first in Medina and then in Damascus and Baghdad, mostly used their own judgment (or "opinion") to rule the vast territories that had just been won through military conquest. Of course, in matters stipulated by the texts, they obliged, although even there they had to adjust it to new realities, like when the caliph 'Umar changed the Qur'anic regulations on the spoils of war. So in rather meticulous fashion, Qaradawi files through all the caliphs and the major Companions of the Prophet, then through some of the Followers (second generation), in order to give concrete examples of how they used their own judgment. He then moves on to the question of *ra'y* per se. This is when he marshals Ibn Qayyim's expertise once again.

According to Ibn Qayyim, Qaradawi asserts, there are three kinds of "opinion" (*ra'y*). The first kind is controversial and suspect, though it is built on analogical reasoning tied to the sacred texts. But the analogy at stake is often tenuous. Still, we find in the Qur'an that certain laws can be suspended for reasons of duress (*ḍarūra*, e.g., Q. 5: 173, where forbidden foods can be eaten if the alternative is starvation).[46] But Ibn Qayyim wants to make such cases exceptions; his approach remains very cautious—too cautious, in fact, for Qaradawi.[47] The second kind of opinion, as one might expect, is the reprehensible kind, as it is based solely on personal preferences and calculations, with no reference to the texts or even the principles found in the texts. Thus it is baseless as a legal opinion, and of no value (*bāṭil*).[48]

The "praiseworthy" kind of legal opinion for Ibn Qayyim is one of the several categories: (1) that of the Companions or of the next generation (the "Followers"); (2) one based on a commentary of the texts; (3) one that later gains a consensus among the scholars; or (4) one that simply follows the established legal procedures of the Shari'a (*ijtihād al-ra'y fī ḍaw'al-sharī'a*). That last category, of course, is the process Qaradawi maps out later in this book and in all of his specifically legal books. It is the traditional toolbox of the *mujtahid* who performs *ijtihād*—the legal scholar of the *'ulamā'* class who is called upon to provide a legal opinion in order to solve a new problem arising. The following quote is a useful summary of the rightful use of "opinion." Notice the scope given to human reason in the process of "discerning God's law." Note too how crucial the order of the steps is, as is the order of legal tools the *mujtahid* may consult in his challenging task:

> A *mujtahid* may not do without opinion (*ra'y*), no matter how many hadiths or qur'anic texts he has memorized. Nor may he do without it in understanding the texts and in analyzing their legal import in the light of the Shari'a's higher objectives; or in deducing an appropriate ruling when there is no relevant text either in the Qu'ran or the Sunna. [This he will do using the following tools]: analogical reasoning (*qiyās*), or preferrential choice (*istiḥsān*) if analogical reasoning will not work; closing the gate to evil (*sadd al-dharā'i*), or following custom (*'urf*), or presumption of continuity (*istiḥsāb*), or other tools (lit., *adilla*, or "indications" or "proofs") are used when no text can be consulted. He also must follow the path of the Companions in their use of opinion, as they paid close attention to what was required by time, place and circumstance.[49]

It should be clear now that "opinion" here stands in for human reason in the age-old debate about the relative roles of reason and revelation. Humanity, as God's earthly trustee, and particularly at the level of state, is empowered by the Creator to make ethical judgment calls about what are just and fair courses of action.[50] Further, Qaradawi's reliance upon Ibn Qayyim has enabled him to state that, in essence, a text cannot speak for itself much less "dictate" a particular ruling for the jurist confronted with new problems to solve. This is a process of hermeneutics, as opposed to the naïve literal reading of the textualists. Texts have to be read, understood, and their meaning has to be processed by human minds living in particular contexts. I am perhaps going beyond what Qaradawi would say. Still, I would insist, this is the implication of his own reading of Ibn Qayyim.

Qaradawi's Appropriation of Shatibi's "Purposive Fiqh"

The third late medieval jurist who is often quoted—and, I would add, the most quoted by adherents of the *maqāṣid al-sharī'a* approach, Ibn Ishāq al-Shatibi, appears very little in Qaradawi's book *siyāsa al-sharī'a*. Shāṭibī is the great legal mind from Granada who systematized this methodology—a fact, however, that most probably dawned on scholars only over the last few decades.[51] It's also very likely that Qaradawi himself was gradually (re) reading Shatibi in the 1990s. This leads us to his classic 2006 book on the "purposes of Shari'a," *Dirāsa fī maqāṣid al-sharī'a* (A Study of the Shari'a's Purposes).[52] But if the reader is expecting a late-career *magnum* opus on this burgeoning field of Islamic jurisprudence today, he/she would be disappointed. The organizing concept is Qaradawi's decades-long message of *wasaṭiyya*—the "middle road," represented by his own bid to guide the global Muslim *umma* between the two extremes of lax, secularized Islam and the rigid textualist versions of Salafis and others.

So what we have in this 2006 book on *maqāṣid al-sharī'a*, then, is a work in three parts. First come the unyielding textualists ("the new Zahiriyya" school)[53] who only focus on the specific texts (*al-nuṣūs al-juzi'yya*) both in the Qur'an and especially in the Sunna and whose attitudes to religious understanding and practice are characterized by rigidity and obduracy (*jumūd wa-tashaddud*).[54] The second part of the book is devoted to the "New Deniers," those who "cancel the texts in the name of the benefits and the objectives [of Shari'a]."[55] Here, with regard to the Shari'a, the New Mu'tazila[56] have in essence denied the divine origin of the texts by canceling out some of its specific injunctions. Qaradawi, then, takes the role of an inquisitor, though refraining from actually calling them *kuffār* (plural of *kāfir*, unbeliever, or in this case, apostate): "They deify themselves, they deny God's right to legislate for his creatures by allowing that which is forbidden and by forbidding that which is allowed on the basis of their own whims (*bi-ahwāhum*) and window-dressing their own demons. They want people to take them as lords in the place of God."[57]

The last third of the book, unsurprisingly, is the third school with the most material—it's his "Middle School," or "Moderate School" (*al-madrassa al-wasaṭiyya*), those who "master the moderate methodology of the middle umma."[58] It is, no less, the school of the "straight path,... believing in balance and moderation." On the one hand, it doesn't exaggerate in its understanding and application of the specific texts, as do the literalists, but it reads them in light of the general objectives of God's law. On the other hand, it doesn't dismiss the texts as do the negators, but rather affirms them in a balanced way. "It believes that God's statutes have reasons behind them [they are *mu'allila*]; that all of them agree with wisdom, and the reasons are based on a concern for the benefit (*maṣlaḥa*) of the created order."[59]

So what part of this thinking did Qaradawi take from Shatibi? I will argue that it was the interlocking of three crucial components—precisely what in the last section I will say actually erodes any necessary intervention of the *'ulamā'* in twenty-first-century Muslim life. It is the clear demarcation of specific passages from the general texts, the linking of the general texts to the objectives of the law, and finally the method by which those general principles are extracted from the text, that is, by induction, or a kind of "scanning" as Wael Hallaq has pointed out.

Shatibi, writes Hallaq, was laying out principles of legal theory that would give him the necessary ammunition to defeat two extreme camps in his day. On the one end were the Sufis, who allowed people to pick and choose between various legal opinions of the mujtahids of their time, but only if they chose the strictest interpretation. Shatibi adds that the Sufis try to follow the Meccan injunctions as strictly as possible, while discarding the mitigating rules enunciated during the Medinan period (or in the Sunna).[60] On the other end of the spectrum are the jurists, "the more earthly legal scholars who advocated the same view but with the option of choosing the more lenient view." He rebuts their lax approach by reminding them that "religious obligation cannot be devoid of burdensome duties and responsibilities, although they are generally tolerable."[61]

Shatibi's strategy in forging the middle path is to rework a tool handed down to him, which could lead him to a level of juristic certainty that no one could counter. His epistemological weapon turned out to be induction (*istiqrā'*), a legal tool that made its appearance around the fifth/eleventh century and which in the hands of Qarafi, some 200 years later, was elevated to the level of a *dalīl* (a legal indicant). Hallaq explains that "perhaps the most outstanding attestation of the central role of induction appears in Shatibi's theory, which represents a unique and powerful marriage between the expanded notions of public interest and this logical principle."[62]

This "marriage" is effected by using this method of evidential corroboration in tandem with the objectives of the law. Unlike the traditional method corroborating specific injunctions in the Sunna by finding multiple reports (*tawātur lafẓī*) or repeated thematic instances (*tawātur ma'nawī*), this methodology is not focused on the specifics but rather on the general principles. In fact, Shatibi elevates the Qur'an over the Sunna much more than in traditional theology and legal theory—and the general indications of the

Meccan revelation over the Medinan ones. This is because in his search for certainty, the Meccan verses "establish the most general and universal principles, namely, the protection of the right to religion, life, mind, progeny and property."[63] Those, of course, represent the highest level of certainty with regard to the aims of the divine law—the "necessary" level (the *ḍarūriyyāt*, above the *ḥajiyyāt*, or needs, and the *tasḥīniyyāt*, the improvements to human life). This is because these values have been extracted as principles in these verses, and also because they have been culled through the many specific injunctions throughout the rest of the sacred texts.

With this in mind, take a look at what Qaradawi writes at the beginning of his exposition of what the "Middle School" teaches. Notice the same kind of epistemological considerations as in Shatibi, the same focus on the general versus specific rules, and the centrality of the Shari'a's objectives. He has just asserted that the three levels of the *maqāṣidal-sharī'a* are certain. He then adduces his "proof":

> The proof of this is to be found in the way the *sharī'a* is discovered (or "induced": *istiqrā'*) and reflection is given to the texts' indications, both comprehensive and specific ones, and to the general considerations based on the meaning of those texts. This general reading cannot be confirmed [as an overall objective of the shari'a] by a specific injunction but only as indications begin to converge, one added to the other, and so on, with different goals behind them, so that by scanning their totality one thread appears, with all the indications pointing to it. To a certain extent, this is what a general reading produces: decisive generosity and courage in knowing God's pleasure with oneself, and the like. As a result, people do not rely on a specific passage in order to discover the Legislator's purpose for these rules, and never as a specific injunction, but it comes to them through literal meanings and general ones, both unconditional and conditional statements, and specific rulings, in different times, different places, in each and every section of Islamic jurisprudence (*fiqh*), and in each and every area of jurisprudence, so that they gather all the indications of the *sharī'a* into a circle of protection around those rulings, while at the same time paying attention to the linkage of ideas expressed either directly or indirectly.[64]

Yet despite all this fancy methodological footwork, Qaradawi—just like his mentor—cannot extricate himself from the weight of the literalistic hermeneutic that had captured the minds of all Muslim jurists in the premodern era. Although Shatibi didn't subscribe to the Ash'arite theology that denied humans the ability to discern the reasons behind the commands and prohibitions of the texts, "and although he advocated an inductive, not a literal, understanding of the divine sources, he remained, as attested in his fatwas, obdurately loyal to the positive doctrines of his school."[65] Still, Qaradawi often cites Muhammad Rashid Rida as a "jurist" who inspired him in the direction of purposive *fiqh*—the subject of the next section's brief excursus.[66]

Qaradawi's Debt to *Rashid Rida*

The first great reformer of modern Islamic jurisprudence, writes Hallaq, was Muhammad Abduh, though he offered nothing new in legal theory. But he did produce "a theology that was necessary for restructuring and rehabilitating legal ideas." In doing so, Abduh distanced himself from traditional Ash'arism and postulated the power of human reason to discern right from wrong.[67] Yet although he elevated reason, he was still careful to keep reason and revelation as complementary ways of finding God's path; in the final analysis, they could never contradict one another.[68]

Zaman in his earlier mentioned essay on "The "ulamā' of Contemporary Islam" points to Rashid Rida, Abduh's disciple, coauthor, and editor of the *Manār* journal,[69] as the first jurist to seize upon the utility of public benefit (*maṣlaḥa*) as a means for retooling Islamic law in the modern world.[70] This is the central argument of his 1928 work *Yusr al-islām wa-uṣūl al-tashrīʿ al-ʿamm* (The Ease of Islam and the Foundations of General Legislation), which I have analyzed in greater detail elsewhere.[71] Besides being a deliberate "*wasaṭī*" discourse, Ridā's strategy in that book was to amplify "the concept of public interest to such an extent that it would stand on its own as a legal theory and philosophy."[72] But in the end, quips Hallaq after his analysis of Rida's "doctrine," "[it] amounts to a total negation of traditional legal theory."[73] Why such an extreme statement?

Allow me to summarize Hallaq's evaluation of Rida's legal theory with the following points:

1. The Qur'an and the attested Sunna are infallible with regard to matters of worship (*al-ʿibādāt*). On general matters of human experience, however, even the Prophet is known to have erred. This area includes social transactions (*al-muʿmalāt*) which have been defined by the texts, as well as the majority of everyday issues in human society, which fall into the wide category of the permissible. Even past rulings of *fiqh* in these area can be overruled today in the name of public benefit and necessity (*ḍarūra*).

2. Rida in essence dismantles the two traditionally top-tiered "rational foundations" (*uṣūl al-ʿaqliyya*) of Islamic law, analogical reasoning (*qiyās*) and the consensus of the scholars (*ijmāʿ*). Agreeing in part with the Andalusian jurist Ibn Hazm (d. 1064) who forbade any use of analogy, he nevertheless joins Ibn Qayyim in stating that when it clearly promotes *maṣlaḥa*, then *qiyās* is necessary and laudable.[74] As for the use of consensus (*ijmāʿ*), it is now obsolete in view of the fact that Muslim jurists have never truly agreed on important legal issues since the days of the Companions.
3. As for texts in both the Qurʾan and the Sunna that are not absolutely clear (*qaṭʿi al-dalāla*), whatever their traditional interpretation, they can be overriden by considerations of *maṣlaḥa* and *ḍarūra* ("necessity").

These three considerations lead me to agree with Zaman who, leaning on Malcolm Kerr,[75] asserts that Rida cannot hide his own "discomfort with the implications of his own proposals."[76] Here again is the tension between human reason and divine revelation:

> As concerned as he was with demonstrating—and making room for—the responsiveness of the law to changing needs, the case for such responsiveness threatened to make this law appear as the product of human effort, a matter of historical evolution, rather than as a divine blueprint. Rida could not have it both ways; and his discomfort with seeing the divine and sacred dimension of the sharīʿa dissipated by the emphasis on its historical dimension is best illustrated by his polemics against those who seemed to him to emphasize the human and historical dimension of the sharīʿa.[77]

This is the dilemma Qaradawi has faced as well, but unlike Rida, he draws back from such sweeping statements and establishes clear boundaries, as we shall see. But here is how he makes use of Rida in his book about the objectives of the law.

Qaradawi had just enumerated the five "necessary" objectives of the law as laid out by Ghazali and he asks this question: Isn't it possible to define the sharīʿa's objectives in another way? Indeed, he answers, just look at "the moderns and contemporaries" and how "they speak of the objectives of Islam or the Muhammadan message, or the Qurʿan's objectives." For instance, in Rida's *The Muhammadan Inspiration"* we read how he does not deduce the three levels of benefit (*maṣlaḥa*) as did "the mainstream *uṣuliyyūn*" (25). Rather, "he broke down the issue into detail according to the topic with which Islam was dealing, and the greater objectives (*al-maqāṣid al-kubrā*) that the Qur'an fulfills in the life of the *umma*. Rida listed ten objectives for the reformation of humanity (*islāḥ*). Of particular relevance here are numbers 3, 5, 8, and 9: promoting science; getting Muslims to practice their rituals and ethical code more strictly; working for peace and fighting corruption; and "granting women all their humanitarian, religious and civil rights."[78]

Plainly, Rida was thinking globally, yet not just in the perspective of *da'wa* but in the larger framework of global human welfare according to the ethical norms of his day as well. In a previous book, writes Qaradawi,[79] under Islam's objectives he himself had listed five:

1. edifying the righteous person,
2. edifying the righteous family,
3. edifying the righteous society,
4. edifying the righteous umma, and
5. a call [to work] for the good of humanity.[80]

Working out in concentric circles from the individual to all of humanity is one way to look at these objectives. A more telling list comes from the next section, "Circumscribing the [Law's] Objectives into the Five General Ones (*al-kulliyāt*)." Although Qaradawi believes that the five *ḥudūd* punishments can be tied to the five top-tiered objectives first enunciated by Ghazali (a fact that makes them even more binding), he does not see the list as exhaustive. There are other "necessary human benefits" (*al-maṣlaḥa al-ḍarūriyya*). Think of all the ethical values that govern social life (*al-qiyam al-ijtimā'iyya*), he adds, like "freedom, equality, fraternity, solidarity, and human rights." This sounds a lot like Rashid Rida, though now updated to a twenty-first-century context.

Then, in the last third of the book, in the chapter titled "The Central Tenets of the Moderate School," Qaradawi's second point is about "understanding a text in the light of its reasons and contexts (*mulābisātihā*)." His main adversaries here are the "puritans"[81] who want to take every text of the Sunna literally without any regard for its historical context. He reasons, "A deeper scrutiny [of the issue] will show that the ḥadīth are driven by time-specific circumstances so as to meet a perceived benefit (*maṣlaḥa mu'tabira*, or "subjective"), or avoid a particular harm, or solve a problem relative to that time, or they are based on a custom of that day, but which is no longer relevant today."[82] One example has to do with the minimum of gold or silver a person owns that is liable for payment of *zakāt*. Prices fluctuate all the time, argues Qaradawi, and though this is a topic that falls under the rituals of worship, it is certainly different from the rules governing prayer or the fast of Ramadan.

His fourth example is the following ḥadīth: "I am innocent [of the blood] of any Muslim who lives among the associators." Many muftis have understood this to mean Muslims cannot live among non-Muslims and have thereby created great difficulties for Muslims needing to live in Europe, at least for a time, for medical purposes, studies, work, business, fleeing persecution, spreading Islam (*da'wa*), or teaching new Muslims and strengthening them.[83] Then he quotes Rashid Rida, who taught that this ḥadīth was given in the context of Muslims needing to emigrate from non-Muslim lands in order to give support to the Prophet. This, of course, is no longer an issue. Also, this is a ḥadīth with an incomplete chain of transmitters (*mursal*) and that is why Bukhari never included it.[84]

Those who argue this ḥadīth is still valid point to its context. The Prophet had sent some men to Khath'am on a secret mission, but some of them were killed there while they were praying. Muhammad said, "only pay half the blood money on their behalf," since they were too far away to determine exactly what happened. In any case, when emigration (*hijra*) is mandatory, and those who don't emigrate are killed, those are the ones of whom the Prophet said, "I am innocent of their blood." Qaradawi, wielding *qiyās* as a tool, concludes that the text's ruling is tied to its *'illa*—the reason for the original ruling. When that reason no longer applies because of changed circumstances, the ruling itself no longer applies—which means that this hadith (whether reliable or not) is moot today.[85]

All the earlier discourse is that of a jurist taking inspiration from Rida and offering his own legal opinion as a mufti—and not just any mufti. He speaks as the president of the European Council for Fatwa and Research and the International Union of Muslim Scholars—the culmination of a long, illustrious legal career sponsored by, but not limited to, the Qatari royal family. What is also telling in his full-length defense of the purposive jurisprudence is its climax: ten appendices, all fatwas by *'ulamā'* he considers leaders of the wasaṭiyya school of jurisprudence.[86]

Not surprisingly, the first one is by Rashīd Rida, who offers his opinion on Islam and the permissibility of a constitution. Rida argued in the late 1920s that the alternative to a constitution is absolute power, whether of the religious or secular variety, and that for reasons of justice and for the dignity of the umma, power must be limited by a law that people can agree upon. For this reason, he thought, the Turks and Persians were right on this score.[87] Considering the importance of Rida in his book, Qaradawi's choice of his fatwa to open this "Who's Who" of moderate mufis is not surprising. But why use a fatwa on political issues? The importance of politics for

Qaradawi is precisely what will help us discern better what is behind his use of the purposive method.

Qaradawi, Purposive Fiqh, and the Role of the *'ulamā'*

It is significant that Qaradawi, frail as he was, decided to come to Cairo just days after Hosni Mubarak had been ousted by the "January 25 Revolution." The throngs of faithful Muslims[88] in Tahrir Square that Friday, February 18, 2011, the Friday of Victory (*jum'at al-naṣr*), were all sympathetic to Qaradawi's message as a patriot and most of them would also have been supportive of him as a symbol of the Muslim Brotherhood. An indication of how important this was to Qaradawi himself is the publication of a whole book devoted to this appearance: *The January 25 Revolution of the People: Sheikh Qaradawi and the Egyptian Revolution*.[89] This collection of sermons, speeches, and fatwas by Qaradawi—and especially the 80 or so color photographs—clearly serve to emphasize his crucial political role as an *'ālim* with Egyptian roots and an international status.

At one point in the book we read Qaradawi's open letter responding to a fatwa issued by Grand Mufti Ali Gomaa who told people to stay home and no longer demonstrate, mostly because President Mubarak had just issued a list of reforms he promised to undertake. He warned that even "peaceful demonstrations" can lead to chaos (*fitna*). Parents were to forbid their children from attending demonstrations.[90] Qaradawi disagreed with him from the beginning and after much discussion raised this question, "In what should a ruler be obeyed?" His answer was simple: a Muslim ruler is no lord and no god—he can only order his subject in accordance with what his Creator has laid out. As the Prophet said, "Obedience applies only to righteous commands." He quoted another ḥadīth that states that "in the case of wrongdoing there is no paying attention and no obedience." The case of Egypt in 2011, then, is clear-cut for Qaradawi, since the state had ordered the killing of peaceful demonstrators. This is not just sin, it's one of the great sins (*al-kabā'ir*).[91]

This would seem like an ideal culmination of a whole career devoted to the promotion of an activist Islam that in essence "retakes" entire nations from the grip of Western secularist governance and infuses them with the spirit and letter of the Islamic message. Further, this is done in the name of a "moderate" Islam, eschewing both the extremes of the literalists and the vagaries of the "deniers," or the "secularist" Muslims. Coptic Christians are affirmed as citizens of Egypt on par with their Muslim compatriots and therefore democracy and human rights are now seen as Islamic values. Further, as you reflect on the two internal currents Qaradawi aims to refute, notice the similarity of this wasaṭiyya message with the one we discerned both in Shatibi and Rida.[92]

Now how does his recent embrace of the *maqāṣid al-sharīʿa* approach to Islamic legal theory fit into this scheme? Allow me to answer by summarizing some of our findings in the first part.

1. Undoubtedly, as Qaradawi turned to *uṣūl al-fiqh* in the early 1990s, he realized as he read Tufi, Ibn Qayyim, and Shatibi that several elements nicely coalesced to form a comprehensive approach that enabled him to delineate more clearly the middle path between the two extremes: (a) God's law was revealed for the purpose of not just individual welfare in this life and the next but public welfare as well (*maṣlaḥa* in both cases); (b) the clear distinction between specific texts from the general ones and specific injunctions from general principles; (c) the linking of the general texts to the higher purposes of the law; and finally (d) the method of induction (*istiqrāʾ*) by which those broad values are extracted from the text and qualified as "certain."[93]
2. This view of legal theory was coming to prominence all around him at the same time. It was in this sense that I wrote that Qaradawi "hitched his wagon" to a popular movement. But Qaradawi did so as a leader, as his keynote address at the 2004 conference on the *sharīʿa* 's objectives in London amply attests.[94]
3. As an *ʿālim* of the historic "middle path," Qaradawi has consistently aimed at bolstering the role of the *ʿulamāʾ* in twenty-first-century global society—on three levels: (a) his production of knowledge (his own collection of fatwas,[95] his many books on both *fiqh* and usul *al-fiqh*); (b) his institutional presence in the *ʿulamāʾ* establishment;[96] (c) his activism in both social and political causes;[97] and (d) his use of the Internet and satellite TV in order to reinforce the traditional role of the *ʿulamāʾ*, that is, to act as the guardians of Islamic knowledge, religious guides for Muslim peoples, and privileged advisors to rulers.

I have argued elsewhere that his *maqāṣidi* methodology wrought no discernible changes either in his previous convictions or in the content of his fatwas.[98] But let me give one example to illustrate how conservative was Qaradawi's view of the "true" Islamic society. Zaman rightly pointed out how for Qaradawi in a modern society people have lost their traditional ethical moorings. Therefore, Qaradawi urges the imam, or head of state, to legislate discretionary punishments "to curb usury, bribery, usurpation of the rights of the orphan, neglecting prayers, harassment or assaulting of women on the streets, and other evils."[99] As Zaman sees it, "the distinction between sin and crime, between moral and legal infractions, collapses here."[100] In many places of *Dirāsa fī maqāṣid al-sharīʿa*, he also makes it clear that the prescribed punishments in the clear texts (the *ḥudūd*) are "permanent and unchangeable."[101]

What his *maqāṣidi* turn did allow him to do, however, was to rebut the harsh legalism of the literalists by providing a needed softening of their rigid discourse.[102] It also gave him more flexibility to intervene in the political arena following his own convictions, as the case of the Egyptian "revolution" illustrates. Yet that "middle course" is a very relative one, as Gräf and Skovgaard-Petersen rightly point out.[103] With his position on homosexuality, his promotion of the *ḥudūd* and the intervention of a moral police, he seems reactionary and extreme for most Westerners. Yet he seems far too lenient for many conservative Muslims in his politics and advocacy for women's rights. This leads me to my last remark.

Although Qaradawi's turn to the now-popular purposive jurisprudence has not produced any real change with respect to his seminal positions in Islamic jurisprudence, might not his adoption of an ethical theory that moves away from traditional Ashʿarism (ethical voluntarism) and—at least in the areas not mentioned "clearly" in the texts, adopts ethical objectivism with a concomitant epistemology that allows people to discern ethical values—in the direction of rationalism have opened a Pandora's box for those who will follow? The only barrier stemming the tide of a historical contextualization (or even relativization) of revelation is his insistence that clear texts in the Qurʾan are not open for discussion. They apply to all times and climes. But with regard to the body of ḥadīths, he has made some compromises with the traditional hermeneutic. These sayings had a historical context and only the general principles apply today.[104]

If one accepts that the Prophet's judgments about how his community should be ruled in his time can be modified when applied in our changed context, why not the Qurʾan also, many would ask? Several Muslim academics specialized in Islamic law are leading educated Muslims in this direction.[105] But nowhere do we see this in *ʿulamāʾ* circles, even in the West. This is why I contend that patrolling these boundaries seems to be about the protection of a professional guild.

Still, even the conservative International Institute of Islamic Thought (IIIT) has endorsed a rather bold reformist book *Toward Our Reformation* by a non-*ʿālim* on the late economist Mohammad Omar Farooq. The book not only lambasts the abuses and irrational extremes of the *ʿulamāʾ* of both then and now but also castigates their culture of literalism.[106] He also points forward to a new "value orientation" by which the *ʿulamāʾ* would join forces with social scientists and other people conversant with the needs of twenty-first-century societies in order to help Muslims embody the true values of their faith and help change the world for the better. He says, forget about "*maqāṣid al-sharī'a*"; let's talk about "*maqāṣid al-Islam*." This, it seems to me, is a big step away from traditional Islamic jurisprudence. What might this portend?

Clearly, as Zaman rightly argues, the *'ulamā'* will continue to find ways of reinventing themselves whatever future changes our global society deserves. My point in this chapter is that shifting the focus on values rather than on the letter of the law, or moving further away from revelation toward human reason, will likely strengthen the authority of non-*'ulamā'* preachers and Muslim intellectuals and weaken that of the *'ulamā'* in the long run. Qaradawi's turn to the *al-sharī'a*'s purposes may not have helped his cause after all.

Notes

1. See the (incomplete) bibliography provided in Bettina Gräf and Jakob Skovgaard-Petersen, "Introduction," in *Global Mufti: The Phenomenon of Yusuf al-Qaradawi*, ed. Bettina Gräf and Jakob Skovgaard-Petersen (New York: Columbia University Press, 2009), 251–254.
2. Ibid., 2. This is the first full-length book in English on Shaykh Qaradawi. For his connection to the Society of Muslim Brothers, see Husam Tammam's chapter in the same book, "Yusuf al-Qaradawi and the Muslim Brothers: The Nature of a Special Relationship," 55–84.
3. It was his teaching position at the Institute of Islamic Culture at the Al-Azhar University that gave him the opportunity to represent them in Qatar in 1961. There he developed an exceptionally close relationship with the emir of Qatar, Shaykh Khalifa b. Hamad Al Thani who died in 1995. I come back to the significance of his Qatari residence and his role in the "January 25 Revolution."
4. See Alexandre Caeiro and Mahmoud al-Saify, "Qaradawi in Europe, Europe in Qaradawi? The Global Mufti's European Politics," in *Global Mufti*, ed. Gräf and Skovgaard-Petersen, 109–148.
5. I could not find any official website for the ECFR, except one in Arabic (http://e-cfr.org/2013/) for their 23rd International Session, June 25 to June 29, 2013, in Sarajevo, Bosnia. It includes a video link to the final declaration made by its president Yusuf al-Qaradawi on June 29 (accessed August 6, 2013). Based in Dublin, it was founded in 1997 as an initiative of the Federation of Islamic Organizations in Europe (Brussels), which is mostly funded by Arabian Gulf countries.
6. See the IMUS website, http://www.iumsonline.net/en/.
7. Ehab Galal, "Yusuf al-Qaradawi and the New Islamic TV," in *Global Mufti*, ed. Gräf and Skovgaard-Petersen, 149–180, at 150, emphasis his. See also Noah Feldman, "Shari'a and Islamic Democracy in the Age of al-Jazeera,"

in *Shari'a: Islamic Law in the Contemporary Context*, ed. Abbas Madanat and Frank Griffel (Stanford, CA: Stanford University Press), 104–119.

8. Lila Abu-Lughod, *Dramas of Nationhood. The Politics of Television in Egypt* (Cairo: American University Press, 2005); Dale F. Eickelman and Jon W. Anderson, "Redefining Muslim Publics," in *New Media in the Muslim World. The Emerging Public Sphere*, ed. Eickelman and Anderson (Bloomington: Indiana University Press, 1999), 1–18; Dale F. Eickelman and Armando Salvatore, "Muslim Publics," in *Public Islam and the Common Good*, ed. Salvatore and Eickelman (Leiden: Brill, 2006), 1–27. See also Jacob Skovgaard-Petersen, "Yusuf al-Qaradawi and Al-Azhar," in *Global Mufti*, ed. Gräf and Skovgaard-Petersen 27–54.
9. Galal, "Yusuf al-Qaradawi and the New Islamic TV," 164.
10. Ibid., 173.
11. I know of at least three Qaradawi titles with al-ṣaḥwa al-islāmiyya in them, including this one: *Al-ṣaḥwa al-islāmiyya bayna l-ikhtilāf al-mashu'wa-l-tafarruq al-madhmum: dirasa fi fiqh al-ikhtilāf fi daw' al-nusus wa-l-maqasid al-shari'a* [The Islamic Revival between the Permissible Differences and the Reprehensive Disagreements: A Study in the Light of the Sacred Texts and the Purposes of the Shari'a] (Beirut: Al Risala, 2000). Combine that with his emphasis on wasaṭiyya and you find the heart of Qaradawi's message addressed to the global Islamic umma.
12. The previous reference (The Islamic Revival, 1990) is the first title with "the purposes of the Shari'a" in its title. Still, that theme is not a major component of the book. What is even more surprising is that four years later Qaradawi does not even mention purposive jurisprudence in a small book devoted to contemporary *fiqh: fiqh al-ijtihād al-mu'asir bayna al-indibāt wa-l-infirāt* [Contemporary Juristic Reasoning between Discipline and Excess] (Cairo: Dar al-Tawzi' wa-l-Nashr al-Islamiyya, 1994). Human benefit (maṣlaḥa) only comes up in the last of the six "errors" committed by some contemporary jurists according to Qaradawi: "Exaggeration in the Use of maslaḥa, and Even at the Expense of the Texts" (66–86). Besides the usual discourse on the three schools with the middle one being the only valid truly Islamic one (al-wasaṭiyya), what is striking here is that the last section is devoted to refuting Sayyid Qutb's juristic reasoning. His position on contemporary society being apostate (as associated with pre-Islamic Arabian *jahiliyya*) and other related views are extreme, he writes, and "all the thinkers of the Islamic Movement" today repudiate those views (101–132).
13. See later the discussion on Rida's influences on Qaradawi, which he deals with in the next section of the chapter.
14. "A Turn in the Epistemology and Hermeneutics of Twentieth-Century *Usul al-Fiqh*," *Islamic Law and Society* 11:2 (2004), 233–282; "*Maqasid al-Shari'a*: Epistemology and Hermeneutics of Muslim Theologies of Human Rights," *Die Welt des Islams*, 47:2 (2007), 149–187; and the forthcoming "Shaykh al-Qaradawi: Standard Bearer of the New 'Purposive Fiqh,'" in *Comparative Islamic Studies* (forthcoming).

15. I put the word in quotation marks, only because it is nothing like one of the traditional legal schools (*madhāhib*) of traditional Islam. Still, it's a way of thinking that, as I show later, clearly sinks its roots deeply into the soil of the tradition and is becoming more and more a recognizable movement. I would go further: it is arguably the lens through which all Islamic law in the future will be viewed and practiced.
16. The Research Centre was founded as a branch of Sheikh Yamani's Al-Furqan Islamic Heritage Foundation in London (see "The Chairman's Introduction" for more details, at http://www.al-furqan.com/en/al-furqan-foundation/al-maqasid/chairmans-introduction). Yamani is a self-taught *'ālim* with long-reaching political connections, since for many years he was Saudi Arabia's Minister of Petroleum. He is also an ideal bridge between East and West by virtue of his J. D. from Harvard University.
17. (no editors' names given), *Maqasid al-shari'a was qadaya al-'asr: majmu'at* [Purposes of the Islamic Law and Contemporary Issues: A Collection of Papers] (London: Al-Furqan Islamic Heritage Foundation: Al-Maqasid Research Centre in the Philosophy of Islamic Law, 2007).
18. *Maqasid al-shari'a al-islamiyya wa-qadaya al-'asr: buhuth wa-waqa'i'* [A Study of the Shari'a's Purposes: Between the General Purposes and the Specific Texts] (Cairo: Dar al Shuruq, 2006). This textbook becomes the focus of the section later "Qaradawi's Appropriation of Shatibi's 'Purposive Fiqh.'"
19. Qaradawi has always been a critic of the Mubarak regime, though he certainly remained popular with students and faculty at his alma mater, Al-Azhar University.
20. Mahmud Hamdi Zaqzuq, Minister of Awqaf, ed. [The Objectives of the Islamic Shari'a and Contemporary Issues: Research and Realities]. The 22nd General Conference of the Supreme Council of Islamic Affairs, Vol. 1, Cairo, February 22–25, 2010. Cairo: The Supreme Council of Islamic Affairs, Ministry of al-Awqaf, The Arab Republic of Egypt]. Under the Supervion of the President Muhammad Hosni Mubarak.
21. Two books with this phrase in its titles show his preoccupation in the 1980s: *al-Sahwa al-islamiyya bayna l-jumud wa-l-tataruf* [The Islamic Awakening between Rigidity and Extremism] (Cairo: Maktabat Wahba, 1982); *al-Sahwa al-islamiyya wa humum al-watan al-'arabi wa-l-islami* [The Islamic Awakening and the Worries of the Arab and Islamic Nation] (Cairo: Dar al-Shuruq, 1988).
22. His first book on legal theory was in 1993, but only one chapter is devoted to the objectives of the Shari'a: *Madkhal li-dirasat al-shari'a al-islamiyya* [Introduction to the Study of the Islamic Shari'a] (Beirut: Mu'assat al-Risala). A second edition came out in 2001, published by his usual publisher in Cairo, Maktabat al-Wahba. For more details on this, see my article, "Sheikh Yusuf al-Qaradawi: Standard Bearer of the Purposive Fiqh."
23. This was first published in Cairo by his standard publisher, Maktabat al-Wahba, as the fourth volume in the series of books on each of Hasan al-Banna's twenty

principles (uṣūl). To my knowledge, Qaradawi never went beyond this fourth installment. Perhaps he felt that, considering his age, he would not be able to finish the series. Perhaps he was also trying to distance himself from the Muslim Brotherhood a bit more at that stage. In any case, as he explains in the first volume, he had often given lectures on these 20 principles and each one had been recorded on cassette tapes that had widely circulated (*Shumul al-islam*, "The Comprehensiveness of Islam," the longer title being: *Nahwa wihdat fikriyya li-l-'amilin li-l-islam fi daw' sharh 'ilmi mufassil li-l-usul al-'ishrin li-l-shahid Hasan al-Banna'—al-'asl al-awwal shumul al-islam* [Toward the Oneness of Thought for Muslim Activists in the Light of a Detailed and Knowledgeable Explanation of the Martyr Hasan al-Banna's Twenty Principles—The First Principle, The Comprehensiveness of Islam] (Cairo: Maktabat Wahba, 1991).

24. Muhammad Qasim Zaman, *The 'ulamā' in Contemporary Islam: Custodians of Change* (Princeton, NJ: Princeton University Press, 2002).
25. Ed. Armando Salvatore and Dale F. Eickelman (Leiden, The Netherlands: Brill, 2006), 129–155.
26. Ibid., 131.
27. An excellent and succinct historical survey of this concept can be found in Felicitas Opwis, "Islamic Law and Legal Change: The Concept of *Maslaha* in Classical and Contemporary Islamic Legal Theory," in *Shari'a: Islamic Law in the Contemporary Context*, ed. Abbas Amanat and Frank Griffel (Stanford, CA: Stanford University Press, 2007). See my own chapter in that book focused on the modern Moroccan scholar and politician 'Alal al-Fasi who also made a significant contribution to the theory of the Shari'a's purposes ("'Allal al-Fasi: Shari'a as Blueprint for Righteous Global Citizenship," 83–103).
28. Zaman Muhammad, Q., "The 'Ulamā' of Contemporary Islam and Their Conceptions of the Common Good," in *Public Islam and the Common Good*, ed. Armando Salvatore and Dale F. Eickelman (Leiden, The Netherlands: Brill, 2006), 132. Wael B. Hallaq, himself cited by Zaman earlier, dates the appearance of this debate about the public good to the late third century of the Islamic era: "Currently available sources indicate that some time toward the end of the third/ninth century and the beginning of the fourth/tenth, the concept surfaced in legal discourse. The point to be made here is that the doctrine of *maṣlaḥa* evolved from obscure beginnings, to become in the fifth/eleventh century an essential component of *qiyās* and in less than three centuries after Ghazali, it acquired such a prominent status that a whole theoretic was erected around it" (*A History of Islamic Legal Theories: An Introduction to Sunni uæül al-fiqh*, Cambridge, UK: Cambridge University Press, 1997, 132).
29. For a more detailed summary of these early epistemic debates in the first centuries of Islam, see Adis Duderija's first chapter (especially 27–35) in his book, *Constructing a Religiously Ideal "Believer" and "Woman" in Islam: Neo-Traditional Salafi and Progressive Muslims' Methods of Interpretation* (New York: Palgrave Macmillan, 2011). He helpfully teases out the competing hermeneutics and

epistemologies of the *ahl al-Ḥadīth* and *ahl al-Madhahib* (the more rationally inclined legal scholars of the four main legal schools).

30. See Albert Hourani, *Reason and Tradition in Islamic Ethics* (Cambridge, UK: Cambridge University Press, 1985), for a discussion of the relevant issues; and Madjid Fakhry, *Ethical Theories in Islam* (Leiden: E. J. Brill, 1991).
31. Consider the historic effort by the Jordanian crown to gather Muslim scholars and leaders from all schools of thought in 2005, leading them all to sign the Amman Message, which specifically mentions Ash'arism as its official theology (www.ammanmessage.net).
32. I am simplifying almost to the point of distorting a longer discussion I offered in "A Turn in the Epistemology and Hermeneutics of Twentieth-Century *Usul al-Fiqh*," 236–244. A necessary corollary to the "ethical objectivism" of the Mu'tazilites is the human capacity to choose between right and wrong—otherwise, how could God eternally punish an automaton? That would be grossly unjust, they would say.
33. Hallaq puts it this way: "This is the Mu'tazilite tenet that human acts are either good or bad, and the mind, independent of revelation, is capable of determining which act is good and which bad." Then he adds that this position "runs in diametrical opposition to the most fundamental principle of Sunni jurisprudence, namely that God decides on all matters and that the human mind is utterly incompetent to function as a judge of any human act" (*A History of Islamic Legal Theories*, 135).
34. They were people of tawḥīd (unity of God) because they argued against God having any attributes, as those might threaten the status of God as the only eternal One. I argued in my book *Earth, Empire and Sacred Text: Muslims and Christians as Trustees of Creation* (London: Equinox, 2010) that modern Muslim scholars and intellectuals all interpret God's empowering of Adam as his trustee (*khalīfa*) and thereby teaching him "the names of all things" (Q. 2: 30–34) as a mandate for all of humanity to manage the earth in God's stead. As such, humanity is understood by mainstream Muslims (Shia and Sunnis) today as endowed with free will and the capacity to make ethical choices for which they will be held accountable by him on the Last Day. This theological position, also embraced by Qaradawi, is in fact a creative reworking and blending of classical Ash'arism and Mu'tazilism.
35. Analogical reasoning (*qiyās*) is one; the other is the consensus of the scholars (*ijmā'*). The two most authoritative sources, however, are the scriptural ones—Qur'an and Sunna.
36. Zaman, "The 'Ulama of Contemporary Islam," 136. He comments at length on Qaradawi's book *Siyāsa al-sharī'a*, 145–150. The debate about Tufi is clearly a pressing concern to Qaradawi, as he even mentions it in his 3-page Introduction: "And we discussed [in this book] the opinion of the Hanbanli jurist Najm al-Din al-Tufi and the much publicized allegation that he canceled the [sacred] text in the name of *maṣlaḥa*, even to the point of saying that *maṣlaḥa* overrides a decisively clear text (naṣṣ qaṭ'i). The man is innocent of that [error], as we proved it from his own words" (9–10). Since Tufi is regularly used

by the scholars and thinkers more liberal than Qaradawi, this kind of discussion comes up in all of his books on legal issues.

37. Qaradawi, *Dirāsa fi maqāṣid al-sharī'a*, 12 (cf. note 18).
38. Qaradawi explains in the beginning of his book that he means to use the terms *imām*, *walī al-amr*, and *ḥākim* interchangeably. The word I refer to in the next paragraph, which I translate as "rulers," is the plural of *ùäkim*, *ùukkäm*.
39. Qaradawi, *Siyāsa al-sharī'a*, 31.
40. Ibid.
41. Literally, they were guilty of "a limited understanding of the Shari'a and a limited understanding of reality" (Ibid., 32).
42. Ibid., 32–33.
43. Ibid., 33. Qaradawi gives no precise reference for this material, except to say in the previous paragraph that he is referring to Ibn Qayyim's book *I'lam al-muwaqqi'in 'an rabb al-'alamin* [Information for those Who Write about the Lord of the Worlds]. Two exceptions in this chapter: on page 36 he refers to pages 13–19 from Ibn Qayyim's book *al-Turuq al-hukmiyya fi-l-siyasa al-shar'iyya* [The Legal Pathways in Shari'a-Inspired Politics]; and on page 39 he referrences the I'lam al-muwaqqi'in, Vol. 4, 375–379. It is difficult to know whether he is in fact quoting or just paraphrasing.
44. Qaradawi, *Siyāsa al-sharī'a*, 33.
45. This was a key term in the early debates in the late second century between the *ahl al-Ḥadīth* and the emerging *ahl al-ra'y* ("the people of reason-based opinion"). See Duderija's apt discussion of their parting of the ways, with the more rationally inclined applying their hermeneutical and epistemological methods to the Qur'an and Sunna. As opposed to the formers' textually centered models, the latter put greater stock in the human mind *'aql* and its ability to discern ethical principles within the text that then allowed them to find rules of conduct in situations about which the texts were silent (*Constructing a Religiously Ideal "Believer" and "Woman" in Islam*, 29–31).
46. Ibid., 56.
47. Qaradawi later takes Ibn Qayyim to task on this issue, saying that he is being too restrictive here, though he doesn't explain why or give any examples to the contrary. What he does say, however, is that Ibn Qayyim's statement that the legal rulings made by the Companions (and especially the "Rightly Guided Caliphs" as rulers) are still binding on Muslims in his time. Qaradawi brings up a favorite theme here, asserting that their decisions were based on the needs of their own times and circumstances. For that reason, we might have to part ways with some of their secondary rulings (wa-qad nukhalifihim fi ba'd ara'ihim al-juz'iyya), given that legal rulings must be made according to the necessities of each time and place (ibid., 62).
48. Quoting Ibn Qayyim he lists five different types in this category (ibid., 57), but there is no need for us to go into this kind of detail here.
49. Ibid., 62.
50. Qaradawi, as mentioned earlier, rejoins most contemporary jurists and scholars in articulating this kind of ethical objectivism and tying it to the "objectives

of Shari'a." Hallaq sees this as coming more directly from Shatibi, the subject of my next section: "The individual is then God's deputy on earth in that he represents, or ought to represent, God in promoting social welfare through adopting the same intentions that God adopted when He decreed the law" (*A History of Islamic Legal Theories*, 185).

51. Muhammad Khalid Masud's seminal work on Shatibi came out in 1989 (*Islamic Legal Philosophy: A Study of Abu Ishaq al-Shatibi's Life and Thought*, New Delhi: International Islamic Publishers). Hallaq devotes a whole chapter to Shatibi, besides many references to him in other places in his book on legal theory. As I explain later, his greatest contribution according to Hallaq is in the field of epistemology—and in particular his systematic use of induction as a tool focused on the Qur'an. Hallaq writes, "The significance of induction as he put it to use in the service of legal theory does not seem to have been appreciated by posterity. We detect no influence by his theory on later generations" (*A History of Islamic Legal Theories*, 206).
52. Cf. note 18.
53. Here we see Qaradawi's rhetorical skills at work. The label he chooses is that of one of the schools of Islamic law that was later discredited. It had been founded by Andalusian scholar Ibn Hazm (d. 1064) whose reputation is still very good, mostly because of his famous work on comparative theology and a painstaking enumeration of heretical groups. Ibn Hazm was also the eponymous founder of the Âahiriyya school of law, which was best known for its rejection of analogical reasoning. Its name comes from the word "literal" as opposed to "figurative" referring to the meaning of a text. It was largely a reaction against the dominant Maliki school in Spain at the time (Shatibi was a Maliki jurist)—the school that had most emphasized the importance of *maṣlaḥa* until then.
54. Qaradawi, *Dirāsa fi maqāṣid al-sharī'a*, 45. In a footnote on this page, Qaradawi makes it clear who these people are, though the "Salafi" label appears nowhere in the text: "Like many of those leaders from the Salafi tendency, which now has many branches."
55. These people, according to Qaradawi, ignore or neglect the specific texts, even opposing them, in the name of the "general welfare and the wider objectives" (*al-maṣlaḥa al-'amma wa-l-maqāṣid al-kulliyya*). Just as the Mu'tazilaof old denied God's attributes (against the anthropomorphists who gave God a human-like body), these people deny the validity of the texts when it suits them. The Jahmiyya took the same position, but the mainstream Sunni thought took the position of *ithbāt*, or the affirmation of the divine attributes, albeit in a nonphysical sense.
56. These were in the rationalists' camp (along with the Mu'tazila). Their name points to their "denying" that God has any attributes. For if he did, they reasoned, then these could be held up as eternal alongside God himself and thereby threaten the divine unity. The opposite camp "affirmed" the divine attributes (*ithbāt*).
57. Ibid., 87.

58. Ibid., 137.
59. Ibid.
60. He then adds this: "[Shatibi] seems to say that that if the Sufis choose to subject themselves to rigorous piety, so be it. But it is not within their legimate right to impose their will and perception of the law on the community of laymen" (Hallaq, *A History of Islamic Legal Theories*, 204). As we will see later, this group is very similar to today's Salafis, the one "extreme" Qaradawi is eager to refute.
61. Ibid., 203.
62. Ibid., 134.
63. Ibid., 196.
64. Qaradawi, *Dirāsa fi maqāṣid al-sharī'a*, 139–140.
65. Hallaq, *A History of Islamic Legal Theories*, 207–208.
66. Qaradawi's debt to Hasan al-Banna deserves more research. But although he, like other leaders in the Muslim Brotherhood orbit, led a series of talks later recorded on cassette tapes on al-Banna's "twenty principles," he never got further than the fourth in his writings (cf. note 23). The first book in that series dates back to 1991, with a second volume out two years later: *Naḥwā wihdat fikriyya li-l-'amilin li-l-islam* [Toward the Unity of Islamic Activists] *fi daw' sharh 'ilmi mufassil li-l-usul al-'ishrin li-l-shāhid Hasan al-Banna—al-asl al-awwal shumūl al-islam* [In the Light of a Detailed and Scientific Explanation of the Martyr Hasan al-Banna's Twenty Principles] (Cairo: Maktabat al-Wahba).
67. *A History of Islamic Legal Theories*, 212. Hallaq generalizes about modern reformers on this basis: "The value of this theology for modern reformers lies in its emphasis on reason as a source of knowledge without severing reason from religious values. On the basis of this theology Muslims can decide what is best for them without violating the spirit of their religion" (ibid.). As one might suspect, this is not as straightforward as it seems. What if the specific rules laid out by the texts conflict with ethical norms people tend to assume nowadays, like notions of human rights, for example? Qaradawi has never wavered on the *ùudüd* (the five or six specific penalties stipulated by the Qur'an and Sunna).
68. Duderija calls the nineteenth-century reformers "classical modernists," and argues that the moderate islamists (with links to the Muslim Brotherhood) like Muhammad al-Ghazali (1917–1996) and Yusuf al-Qaradawi harken back to some of their ideas (*Constructing a Religiously Ideal 'Believer' and 'Woman' in Islam*, 44–45). Although he doesn't elaborate on it, he does show that his view of Sunna, though anxious to undercut Salafi literalism, remains "completely within the classical Islamic sciences... Sunna is neither epistemologically nor conceptually divorced from the ḥadīth, and the assumptions governing the classical *ulūm ul ḥadīth* sciences are not even addressed" (ibid., 45). Interestingly, Scott Kugle and Stephen Hunt in their study of Qaradawi's pronouncements on homosexuality call him a "neo-traditionalist," that is, someone very much in line with contemporary Salafis. They contend that the terms "islamism" and "fundamentalism" are no longer useful in describing Islamic social movements

and prefer the term "neo-traditional" as an umbrella that covers all the revivalist movements from the jihadis to conservative yet activist types such as Qaradawi, to the Salafis ("Masculinity, Homosexuality, and the Defense of Islam: A Case Study of Yusuf al-Qaradawi's Media Fatwa," in *Religion and Gender*, 2, 2 (2012): 254–279, at 9–13).

69. When Abduh died in 1905, Rida continued as the journal's editor until his own death in 1935. Hasan al-Banna continued editing the journal for several years after that.
70. I disagree with Zaman who writes that "Rida is conspicuously absent from Qaradawi's discussion" ("The 'Ulama of Contemporary Islam," 137). Technically, he is correct in saying that Rida hardly appears in his *Siyāsa al-sharī'a* book. Had he obtained access to Qaradawi's 2006 *Dirāsa fi maqāṣid al-sharī'a*, he would have changed his mind about Qaradawi's attitude toward Rida's work. True, Rida is a bit cavalier for Qaradawi with regard to a ruler's use of *maṣlaḥa* and he ties it down more closely to the sacred texts. Still, Rida for Qaradawi is the great modern pioneer of purposive *fiqh*.
71. "An Epistemological and Hermeneutical Turn," 28–34. More recently I have argued that Qaradawi also found inspiration from Rida for his wasaṭiyya discourse ("Shaykh al-Qaradawi," cf. note 14). Both were targeting the Muslim youth of their time and trying to channel them away from the two extremes of excessive laxity and severity.
72. Hallaq, *A History of Islamic Legal Theories*, 215.
73. Ibid., 219.
74. Ibid., 217.
75. I had drawn heavily on Kerr's groundbreaking work (*Islamic Reform: The Political and Legal Theories of Muhammad Abduh and Rashid Rida*, Berkeley and Los Angeles: University of California Press, 1966) in my essay, "An Epistemological and Hermeneutical Turn." Zaman also mentions Kerr's book as the foundational study on Abduh and Rida.
76. Zaman, "The 'Ulama of Contemporary Islam," 133.
77. Muhammad Qasim Zaman, *Modern Islamic Thought in a Radical Age: Religious Authority and Internal Criticism* (Cambridge: Cambridge University Press, 2012), 113.
78. Qaradawi, *Dirāsa fi maqāṣid al-sharī'a*, 25.
79. Qaradawi, *Madkhal li-ma'rifa al-islam: muqawwimatuh, khasa'isuh, ahdafuh, masadiruh* [Introduction to the Knowledge of Islam: Its Contents, Its Particularities, Its Objectives, Its Sources] (Cairo: Maktabat al-Wahba, 1996).
80. Qaradawi, *Dirāsa fi maqāṣid al-sharī'a*, 27.
81. Expression borrowed from Khaled Abou El Fadl in his 2007 book, *The Great Theft: Wrestling Islam from the Extremists* (HarperOne).
82. Qaradawi, *Dirāsa fi maqāṣid al-sharī'a*, 161.
83. Ibid., 168.
84. Ibid., 169.
85. Ibid., 170.
86. The last two fatwas are his own.

87. Recall, however, that Rida was at the center of the anti-Attarturk movement in the 1920s. He took up his pen and wrote a whole book to oppose what he saw as the secularization of Islam, *al-Khilāfa aw al-imāma al-*'Uzma [The Caliphate, or the Supreme Imamate].
88. There were many Coptic Christians as well and Qaradawi addressed them in his *khuṭba* (Friday sermon). "Even though it is the custom of the Friday preacher to address his audience as 'O Muslims!' I address you today in this square as, 'O Muslims and Copts, O children of Egypt!' This is the day for all of Egypt's children, not one for Muslims only!" The general theme of the sermon was on the necessary and eternal victory of truth and goodness over oppression and evil. With many quotes from the Qur'an Qaradawi framed the revolution as God's victory over Pharoah on behalf of all believers, Christians and Muslims.
89. Yusuf al-Qaradawi, *25 yana'ir sanat 2011 thawrat sha'ab: al-shaykh al-Qaradawi wa-l-thawra al-misriyya. Bayānat wa-khutab wa-fatawā wa-maqalāt wa-suwār* [The 25 January 2011 Revolution of the People: Sheikh Qaradawi and the Egyptian Revolution (Declarations, Sermon, Fatwas, Articles, and Pictures)] (Cairo: Maktabat Wahba, 2012).
90. Qaradawi went public within the first week of the revolt with his support for the demonstrators and the rightness of their cause, as this book amply documents. Using fatwas, Friday sermons, interviews on Al-Jazeera, and declarations published in Egyptian newspapers, Qaradawi openly told Mubarak to resign several times and threw the weight of his authority as "global mufti" born in Egypt urging the masses to flood the streets in peaceful demonstrations. Significantly, the text of the February 3 press release by the International Union of Muslim Scholars does not use the word "revolution" but "blessed uprising." Qaradawi was quick to use it himself, however, even before Mubarak resigned on February 11. He paid homage to the American and French revolutions, but chided them for trying to meddle in the affairs of Arabs today. He addresses France in particular, asking her to stop sabotaging the Tunisian revolution (ibid., 112).
91. Ibid., 143. That said, he issued a fatwa several days after the July 3, 2013 military coup: "Yusuf al-Qaradawi Says in Fatwa Egyptians Should Back Morsy," by Reuters in *The Egypt Independent* (July 6, 2013), accessed November 18, 2013, http://www.egyptindependent.com/news/yusuf-al-qaradawi-says-fatwa-egyptians-should-back-morsy.
92. For more details, see Bettina Gräf, "The Concept of *wasatiyya* in the Work of Yusuf al-Qaradawi," in *Global Mufti*, 213–238.
93. In essence, they reach the top level of certainty in classical Islamic jurisprudence, hereto enjoyed by clear Qur'anic texts and strong ḥadīths (*tawātur*).
94. The opening chapter of *Dirāsa* is actually Qaradawi's keynote address in the 2004 inaugural conference of the London-based Al-Maqasid Research Centre in the Philosophy of Islamic Law led by Shaykh Ahmad Zaki Yamani. The Center was not officially inaugurated until the next year, but the papers presented at this conference were collected in the Center's first publication.
95. He has published three volumes of fatwas so far: *Min hadi 'l-islam; Fatawa mu'asira*, vols. 1–3 (Kuwait: Dar al-Qalam, 1979, 1993, 2002).

96. As mentioned earlier, he was appointed president of two prestigious associations: the European Council for Fatwa and Research and the International Union of Muslim Scholars.
97. Gräf and Skovgaard-Petersen document in the Introduction to their edited volume how for instance in 2006 "Qaradawi was at the forefront of several global Muslim campaigns" (*Global Mufti*, 8). He spearheaded the boycott of Danish goods over the derisive cartoons; he orchestrated the protests over Pope Benedict XVI's ill-fated Regensburg lecture; and when Shia-Sunni relations had gone awry in Iraq he traveled to Iran to mend fences as best he could.
98. "Sheikh Yusuf al-Qaradawi: Standard Bearer of the New Purposive Fiqh."
99. Qaradawi, *Siyāsa al-sharī'a*, 96.
100. Zaman, "The Ulama in Contemporary Islam," 135.
101. Qaradawi, *Dirāsa fi maqāṣid al-sharī'a*, 28, 123, 125, 128–134, 198–199. In this respect, Qaradawi gushes with praise for Saudi Arabia: "Our neighbor is an Arab Islamic state, which in times past was proverbial on account of its chaos and insecurity, to the point that it was said about anyone traveling there for the hajj or 'umra: 'the one going there is lost and the one returning is born!' Yet as soon as King Abd al-Aziz bin Saud (may God have mercy upon him) took power and established the ḥudūd, the situation changed. So a new proverb was minted, all about security and tranquility; so much so, that the months passed and not one hand was cut, thanks to this tenet of Islamic law—even if there are a few shortcomings in other areas" (ibid., 134).
102. The same year his *Siyāsa al-sharī'a* came out he also published a book with almost the same title as Rashid Rida's *Yusr al-islam: Taysir al-fiqh li-l-muslim al-mu'asir fi daw' al-qur'an wa-l-sunna* [Easing Islamic Jurisprudence for the Contemporary Muslim in the Light of the Qur'an and the Sunna, 2 vols] (Cairo: Maktabat al-Wahba, 1999). The *maqāṣid al-sharī'a* are mentioned, but clearly subservient to the overall message of rendering Islamic rulings more flexible. Four more recent books on *fiqh* show little or no change in Qaradawi's long-held positions: the first two are general introductions to his "moderate school" of law: (a) a 55-page introduction to *fiqh* based on a lecture delivered in India to an audience of *'ulama' (Fi l-fiqh wa-l-fatwa wa-l-ijtihād)* [On Jurisprudence, Fatwa and Ijtihād] (Cairo: Maktabat Wahbah, 2011); (b) *Fiqh al-wasaṭiyya al-islamiyya wa-l-tajdīd: ma'alim wa-manārāt* [A Moderate Islamic Jurisprudence and Its Renewal: Signposts and Lighthouses] (Cairo: Dār al-Shurūq, 2010). The other three deal with specific areas: (a) more on politics: *al-Din wa-l-siyāsah: taṣīl wa-radd shubuhāt* [Religion and Politics: Foundations and Answers to Naysayers] (Cairo: Dār al-Shurūq, 2007); (b) a book arguing against extremist fatwas: *al-Fatawa al-shadhda: ma'ayiruha wa-tatbiqatuha wa-asbabuha wa-kayfa nu'alijuha wa-natawaqqaha* [Eccentric Fatwas: Their Characteristics, Nature and Causes, and How We Can Fix and Prevent them] (Cairo: Dār al-Shurūq, 2010); (c) a book weighing in against the jihadis: *Fiqh al-jihād: dirāsah muqārana li-aḥkāmihi wa-falsafatihi fi daw' al-qur'an wa-l-sunna* [The Jurisprudence of

Jihad: A Comparative Study of Its Rulings and Philosophy in the Light of the Qur'an and Sunna] (Cairo: Maktabat Wahbah, 2009); (d) a book on women and family law: *Ḥayāt al-mar'a al-muslima: fi fī iṭār al-ḥudūd al-* al-sharī'a [The Life of a Muslim Woman within the Legal Limits of the Shari'a] (Cairo: Maktabat Wahbah, 2011).

103. Gräf and Skovgaard-Petersen, "Introduction," in *Global Mufti*, 8.
104. Duderija's work rightly underlines the importance of the Sunna in this regard. The "neo-traditionalists" (the Salafis that Qaradawi is targetting) are bound to a ḥadīth-based methodology, by contrast with even the traditional jurists of the various schools of Islamic law who were much more critical in their use of the ḥadīth (see especially 80–82 in *Constructing a Religiously Ideal "Believer" and "Woman" in Islam*).
105. For instance, see Khaled Abou El Fadl, *Speaking in God's Name: Islamic Law, Authority, and Women* (London: Oneworld, 2001); Abdullahi Ahmed An-Naim, *Islam and the Secular State: Negotiating the Future of Shari'a* (Cambridge, MA: Harvard University Press, 2010); and Tariq Ramadan, *Radical Reform: Islamic Ethics and Liberation* (Oxford and New York: Oxford University Press, 2008). Interestingly, Ramadan explicitly uses the *maqāṣidī* approach but draws it to its logical conclusion, unlike Qaradawi. This is what enables him to craft a specifically "European Islamic theology." See also Duderija's last three chapters in his book, *Constructing a Religiously Ideal "Believer" and "Woman" in Islam*, which he devotes to the philosophical, theological, and legal approaches of "Progressive Muslims."
106. *Toward Our Reformation: From Legalism to Value-Oriented Islamic Law and Jurisprudence* (London and Herndon, VA: The International Institute of Islamic Thought, 2011). In my review of his book for the *American Journal of Islamic Social Sciences* I pointed out how ambivalent and ambiguous Farooq's position on Islamic law turns out to be. He confuses *fiqh* and *al-sharī'a*, even saying at one point that "the Shari'ah is essentially a human construct" (ibid., 93). With regard to that he strongly decries the abusive applications of them in many places, but nowhere states clearly whether they should still be applied (or not).

CHAPTER 3

Doha—The Center of Reformist Islam? Considering *Radical Reform* in the Qatar Context: Tariq Ramadan and the Research Center for Islamic Legislation and Ethics (CILE)

David Warren

Introduction: Institutionalizing Radical Reform

In 1993, the Palestinian intellectual Edward W. Said (d. 2003) was invited by the British Broadcasting Corporation to deliver the prestigious "Reith Lectures."[1] During his reflections on the role of the intellectual in civil society, he highlighted the risks of the ever-increasing professionalization of the academy and the subsequent potential for intellectuals' co-option by establishment interests. Comparing the place of the contemporary cultural and social critic to that of an "insurgent," Said argued for his peers' need to continue what Michel Foucault termed "a relentless erudition," while endeavoring to maintain their independence on the basis that, as he put it, "there is something fundamentally unsettling about intellectuals who have neither offices to protect nor territory to consolidate and guard."[2]

The intellectual under discussion in this chapter is of course not the late Said, but Tariq Ramadan, perhaps a comparable figure in terms of public profile. While Said was arguably known first and foremost for his advocacy on behalf of the Palestinian cause, it was primarily in relation to the situation of European Muslims that Ramadan's name first became ubiquitous. In fact, it might be said that in the European, particularly the French, contexts, Ramadan has become a figure of particular anxiety for those popular journalists and commentators who have considered and responded to his various public statements, lectures, and works that addressed the place of European Muslims and Islam within secular, liberal societies.[3] As Andrew F. March points out in several of his detailed discussions and reviews of Ramadan's work, much of this apparent disquiet felt by these European journalistic and politic elites was a result of the apparent difficulty they might have had in categorizing Ramadan as either a threatening "Islamist" in accordance with the legacy of his grandfather Hasan al-Banna (d. 1949) or as a Muslim intellectual more comfortingly uncritical of contemporary European secular liberalism in its varying formulations.[4]

It is Ramadan's 2009 work, *Radical Reform: Islamic Liberation and Ethics*, that this chapter is particularly interested in.[5] While Ramadan initially appeared to achieve a striking coalescence between an Islamic ethical model and a European secular and liberal citizenship, articulated "almost perfectly along the lines of what a Rawlsian or Habermasian liberal might wish for [but derived] *entirely from sources and concepts provided by the classical Islamic legal tradition*,"[6] later, he begins an ambitious articulation of a seemingly original reformist project. Shifting his focus away from European Muslim communities,[7] and looking instead to the Islamic tradition's system of jurisprudence (*fiqh*) as a whole, March interprets Ramadan's work as seeking the displacement or "dissolving" of Islamic law as the source of Muslim behavioral norms. Working primarily through a novel interpretation of the traditional concepts of *maqāṣid al-sharīʿa* and *maṣlaḥa*, this dissolution would appear to be in keeping with a more holistic conception of "ethics (*akhlāq*)," with Islamic law becoming merely a "vanishing mediator."[8]

While Ramadan's "elusive" goals would seem to add to the uneasiness of his detractors and critics, *Radical Reform* presents March too with a certain "puzzle" on the basis that, for all Ramadan's ambition in articulating a truly radical system of Islamic ethics, as will be seen, this is contrasted by a certain timidity when it comes to a more concrete discussion of particular "case studies" in his fourth chapter.[9] March interprets this conundrum in relation to the "Reformer's Dilemma," whereby a would-be reformer's challenge to the foundational shared commitments of a moral community is far more costly in terms of "theological capital" than a more piecemeal approach to altering applied beliefs and practices. This leads March, drawing on Rawl's argument that foundational and metaphysical divisions in a society are so divisive that they should be avoided where necessary, to query why in Ramadan's case the "inverse" appears to be true, that is, "his [Ramadan's] ideas are relatively undemanding on the conscience of the wider Muslim community in terms of the actual norms or behavior he advocates, while very demanding in terms of the reasoning for that behavior."[10] March then elaborates further,

> His [Ramadan's] ecumenical applied ethics seems designed to alienate as few potential constituencies as possible both within the Muslim and non-Muslim populations, or rather, where he does alienate a conservative Muslim conscience it is by reiterating what he argues in his methodological, theological, and attitudinal reflections. All of this leaves one wondering why it is so urgent for him to take the risks he does in areas of theology and method, potentially alienating conservative Muslims. Indeed, this has also fueled the "esoteric" interpretation of Ramadan. Since even in *Radical Reform* Ramadan does not single out [Yusuf al-Qaradawi] for rebuke or finally call for the abolition of the *ḥudūd* punishments.[11]

This apparent puzzle takes us back to the point of the introductory comparison between Said and Ramadan. This was not simply to mouth platitudes, but rather to begin offering a different context in which Ramadan's *Radical Reform* might be considered. The first of these is in relation to the question of religious authority and the subsequent inhibitions such a pursuit entail on the basis that, as Talal Asad theorized, an authoritative discourse is an "achievement between narrator and audience [where] the former cannot speak in total freedom: there are conceptual and institutional conditions that must be attended to if discourses are to be persuasive."[12] Said too noted something similar advocating intellectuals' public role, "Once an intellectual's circle is widened beyond a like group of intellectuals [...] something in the intellectual's vocation is, if not abrogated, then certainly inhibited."[13]

Ramadan's appeals to the authority of the Islamic legal tradition and the "conceptual and institutional conditions" he observes are not the prime subjects of discussion here, but are instead considered in detail as part of the author's doctoral dissertation. Rather, the question posed here is more modest and relates rather to Said's final writings on the role of the intellectual, where he highlighted a further risk in aligning oneself with "centers of civic virtue that forestall deeper kinds of change or critiques of longstanding assumptions" when seeking to engineer lasting change.[14] While in his own wariness of the "imperialism of virtue," Said cited as examples various benevolent multinational organizations such as the Ford Foundation, in siting the Research Center for Islamic Legislation and Ethics (CILE, *markaz dirāsāt al-tashrīʿ al-islāmī wa'l-akhlāq*) in Doha, Ramadan and his cofounder, Jasser Auda, would appear to have chosen a far more formidable backer.[15] This support comes in the form of the fabulously wealthy Qatar Foundation, managed by Sheikha Mozah bint Nasser, arguably the most publically recognizable member of the Qatari royal family and second wife of the former emir of Qatar (who abdicated in favor of his second son in June 2013).

An examination of the early stages of the implementation of Ramadan's reformism in the particular context of Qatar will serve to shed an interesting new light on the project up to this point, and indicating the course it may take in the future. This is in contrast to the more common reading of his work in relation to the European context, and keeping that point in mind, we begin this chapter's analysis with an exploration of the local Qatari context.

The Reform of Islam as Qatari Security Policy and Branding

It has been often remarked that Qatar represents a world of inconsistencies and contradictions. Its tiny local population is dwarfed by large numbers of expatriate workers, most of them young men from the Indian subcontinent, and its truly vast natural gas reserves render it widely ranked as the wealthiest country in the world in terms of gross domestic product per capita.[16] Sharing too with its neighbor Saudi Arabia many of the deeply conservative values associated with the Islamic movement led by Muhammad Ibn 'Abd al-Wahhab (d. 1792, popularly known as Wahhabism), it might seem at first somewhat disingenuous for Doha to be the locale for the siting of Ramadan's project.

While the current, seemingly inexorable, rise of Qatar to its present position of geopolitical influence may well have been fueled by its natural resources, the rulers of the tiny Gulf state appear more than aware of how vulnerable they are on the security front in the face of their giant neighbors, Saudi Arabia, Iraq, and Iran. Ensuring the interest of outside powers, notably the United States and the European Union, in securing Qatar's survival as an independent state has therefore been a key part of the country's security agenda as it has sought to move beyond the Saudi Arabian security umbrella in the wake of the removal of the threat to the north from Saddam Hussein's Iraq (alongside an apparent Saudi Arabian meddling in Qatari internal affairs).[17] It is with this security policy in mind that various observers contextualized Qatar's founding of the media network Al-Jazeera in 1996,[18] alongside its attempts to assert its diplomatic value as a useful mediator in many of the region's conflicts, ranging from Darfur to Afghanistan, to even outright military intervention alongside the NATO during the 2011 Libyan civil war.[19]

The new Qatari emir is Tamim bin Hamad Al Thani, the second son of the aforementioned Sheikha Mozah bint Nasser al-Misnad, whose profile and influence are such that, as Allen Fromherz argues, Sheikha Mozah and her husband, the former emir, operated seemingly as a "dual monarchy." Although power ultimately lay with the former emir Hamad bin Khalifa Al Thani, and now presumably their son, through her control of the Qatar Foundation, Sheikha Mozah al-Misnad has "a large degree of latitude to implement her own vision of cultural and educational development," which the emir can implicitly support "while distancing himself somewhat from the risks associated with such ventures."[20] Fromherz then notes, in a manner recalling Said's earlier cautions,

> What the [former] Emir and his wife, Sheikha Mozah seem to have grasped is that ideas, creativity and intellectual innovation are the greatest untapped resources in the Middle East. The positioning of Qatar as a forum for independent thought in the Middle East, and not simply for material profit as in the Dubai model, is not, of course, simply a selfless act done out of spontaneous benevolence and an idealistic belief in freedom of speech. There is perhaps no better way to subtly tune the ideas that will determine the future of the Arabic and Islamic world than to own the stage upon which those ideas are expressed.[21]

The CILE has been founded under the umbrella of the Qatar Faculty of Islamic Studies (QFIS), from which it receives its funding and is accountable in bureaucratic terms. In the context of the Gulf, John Petersen has emphasized the extent to which "branding has emerged as a state asset to rival geopolitics and traditional considerations of power."[22] Being able to market itself as a center of Islamic reform is useful indeed, and it intersects with the United States' own foreign policy.[23] Turning briefly now to the, albeit limited, existing literature that has set out to examine the local Qatari religious context, it would appear that much has been made of the country's lack of a homegrown scholar class. From a political science perspective, Birol Baskan and Stephen Wright argue that this absence has allowed the Qatari ruling family to govern in a manner similar to the Turkish "secular" model, that is to say, without having to negotiate with formidable religious institutions and elites as in the case of Saudi Arabia,[24] or attempt to forcibly co-opt them, as first occurred in Egypt under Nasser.[25] By contrast, when the first religious institution (*maʿhad dīnī*) was founded in Qatar in 1960, it was under the authority of the Ministry of Education, with not having to implement difficult educational reforms in the face of stiff resistance, introducing the study of secular sciences, mathematics, and so on alongside the Islamic, as had been the experience at Al-Azhar.

However, on taking a closer look, it appears more than a little significant that upon his arrival in 1961 as a veritable exile from Nasserite Egypt, it was a young and little-known Yusuf al-Qaradawi who became the head of this institution.[26] In al-Qaradawi's memoirs he relates his attempts to design the *maʿhad*'s curriculum along the lines that the noted reformist Mustafa al-Maraghi had envisioned for Al-Azhar, steering it away from its sole focus on Hanbali jurisprudence and the Islamic sciences of rhetoric, grammar, and morphology (*balāgha, naḥū, ṣarf*) to instead include an emphasis on foreign languages, science, and math. It was only by gaining a "deep and true understanding of the social reality" (*fiqh al-wāqiʿ*), he argued, an *ʿālim* would be better equipped to understand the challenges of the modern day, ironically Nasser's own premise for reforming Al-Azhar.[27] Portraying himself as the dynamic young reformer in the mold of his predecessors, al-Qaradawi makes much of the obstacles he had to face, apathy among his students, and an unwillingness to accept these changes alongside criticism from the religious elites in Saudi Arabia. A notable incident, al-Qaradawi recalls, was a meeting with the Saudi Arabian Shaykh Muhammad Ibn Ibrahim Al al-Shaykh who,[28] in criticizing the young al-Qaradawi on his first visit to the kingdom in 1963, asked, "So you think that religious students studying these modern sciences aids their study of the religious sciences?" Al-Qaradawi tells the reader, he replied, "But we are forced to do this, how can a student live isolated from his time [...] your eminence knows that the indubitable Ibn al-Qayyim [al-Jawziyya] said 'the true jurist is the one who marries the obligatory with reality.'"[29]

Al-Qaradawi then went on to play a leading role in founding the Sharia Faculty of Qatar University in 1977,[30] of which he became the dean, and he, along with his like-minded peers from the International Union of Muslim Scholars (IUMS, founded in 2004), now dominates the local religious scene.[31] The point of this digression here is to highlight that rather than portraying the Qatari context as representing a virtually blank canvas, on which a scholar like Ramadan might draw on and implement his own reformist project as he sees fit, it is instead more accurate to note the earlier presence of another particular kind of reformism. This refers to al-Qaradawi's own attempts to understand the legacy of earlier Egyptian would-be reformers of Al-Azhar such as Muhammad ʿAbduh, Rashid Rida, Mustafa al-Maraghi, and Mahmud Shaltut.[32]

Tariq Ramadan's Radical Reform: *Between Adaptation and Transformation*

Ramadan and al-Qaradawi are well known to each other, with an apparent shared respect and a limited cooperation in matters related to *fiqh al-aqalliyyāt* (Muslim minority jurisprudence).[33] Writing specifically in relation to the European context and with regard to Muslim minority jurisprudence, while Ramadan notes his esteem for al-Qaradawi and his "profound respect for the man and the scientist," he is also quick to emphasize the limitations of al-Qaradawi's European project.[34] Ramadan refers to *fiqh al-aqalliyyāt* as a "hodge-podge of *fatāwā* thought up like so many accommodations largely in response to arguments from necessity in order to justify a number of legal exemptions to make life less difficult."[35]

While the appearance of a relationship based on mutual respect between Ramadan and al-Qaradawi is considered very controversial in the European context, especially in light of some of Ramadan's broader attempts to renovate the Islamic legal tradition in its entirety in *Radical Reform* and implement this in Doha, his links to al-Qaradawi appear rather advantageous. The Qatari location of the CILE emerges not so much a question of financial necessity as it might have first appeared. In highlighting the key parts of Ramadan's reformist project, even in his earlier more conventional works discussing Muslim European citizenship, the concept of *maqāṣid al-sharī'a* as first articulated by Abu Hamid al-Ghazali proved extremely useful in allowing him to assert the authenticity of his own project and the flexibility of Islam and its legal tradition:

> If Islam is a universal Message, appropriate to all places over all times, then this should be shown, proved, and expressed through a permanent reflection going and coming from the sources to reality and from reality to the sources. This process should be witnessed in every time, everywhere so that the application of the Islamic law remains faithful to the *maqāṣid al-sharī'a* [. . .] One can then see that it is clearly in the name of faithfulness to the Islamic teachings of Sharia and *fiqh* that Muslims can live in the West.[36]

At that point in the development of Ramadan's project, the role of Islamic law and jurisprudence as the determiner of moral norms was very important.[37] In *Radical Reform* however, in beginning to dissolve Islamic law's primacy as a moral mediator, Ramadan's point of departure is to contrast the "adaptation reform" of scholars such as al-Qaradawi, Taha Jabir al-'Alwani, and Ahmad al-Raysuni, as well as presumably his own earlier work, with the need for a new, more radical, "transformation reform." The former then is the kind of renewal that the al-Qaradawi School sought to modernize and renovate in the Islamic jurisprudential structure. The attempt, as they expressed it, was to allow it to provide new answers to the needs (*ḥājāt*) and necessities (*ḍarūrāt*) arising from Muslims' new contexts and situations. This came primarily through a renewed emphasis on the *maṣlaḥa* and *maqāṣid al-sharīʿa*, as discussed elsewhere in this volume. Citing as examples *fiqh al-aqalliyyāt*, especially the "seminal" work of al-Qaradawi and al-ʿAlwani,[38] and the new trend toward "Islamic finance," where "one takes stock of the nature of the capitalistic order, then one adapts to it by creating banking or financial techniques that protect Muslim firms or individuals and by making some transactions more 'Islamic,'" Ramadan argued that such adaptive reform has now reached its historical limits and is clearly no longer capable of providing adequate answers to the issues of the modern day.[39]

With that in mind, the most interesting, indeed radical, part of Ramadan's argument in *Radical Reform* is his positing that the "universe" and the natural world mirror the Qur'an as twin revelations from God. These two "books" are resting in a state of intertextuality with one another for,

> this correspondence between the two books is everywhere present in the Qur'an, which keeps referring to the signs in one or the other of these orders and invites human intelligence to understand the revealed text as well as created nature. The two Universes address and echo each other [...these] are clearly two "revelations" that must imperatively be received, read, interpreted, and understood in their inherent complementarity.[40]

In this new theology, the *maqāṣid al-sharīʿa*, now translated as "the higher objectives and aims of the Way," are now to be derived not solely from the written text, but rather, "it is on the basis of the two Books that it appears necessary to set on inferring, identifying, and categorizing the higher objectives and aims of the Way (*maqāṣid al-sharīʿa*) and thereby determining the theoretical and practical outline of an applied contemporary ethics."[41] Here then, the number of *maqāṣid al-sharīʿa* is expanded far beyond the original five to include the protection of an individual's "*life, dignity, integrity, personal development, health*, and *inner balance*" among many others, to a total of 41 in fact.[42] Indeed, while making this argument, March points out that Ramadan continues to draws on many of legal tradition's jurisprudential maxims (*qawāʿid fiqhiyya*) such as "*akhaff al-ḍararayn* (choose the lesser of two harms)" or "*al-ḍarūra tubīḥ al-maḥẓūrāt* (necessity makes the forbidden permissible)," helping it appear authentic to the extent that March considers it "not hard to imagine an 'adaptation-reform jurist' like al-Qaradawi reasoning in the exact same way."[43] As David Johnston has noted in this volume, conceptualizing new *maqāṣid* is the hallmark of al-Qaradawi's own approach.

If the implications of his reforms were not clear enough, Ramadan affirms that "the point is then to clearly place the two Books, the two Revelations, the text, and the Universe on the same level—as sources of

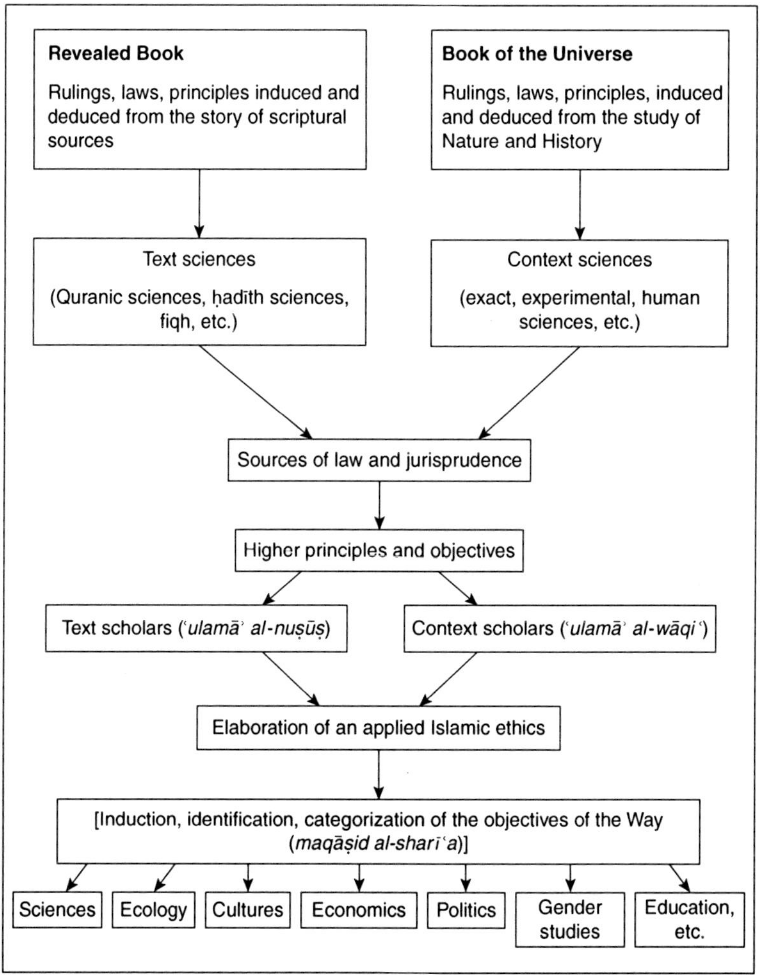

Figure 3.1 Ramadan's illustration of his vision for an applied ethics (Ramadan, *Radical Reform*, 129, Figure 10.1)

law,"[44] or rather that "obligations or forbiddances are not just found in the Qur'an," as the CILE's cofounder, Auda, put it in a later interview with the author.[45] The more practical implications of this new reformism then are that an applied ethics, as opposed to legal norms, must emerge jointly from both the scriptural scholars (*'ulamā' al-nuṣūṣ*) and natural and social scientists (*'ulamā' al-wāqi'*) interacting on an equal footing.[46] As Ramadan puts it, "the Universe, Nature, and the knowledge related to them must assuredly be integrated into the process through which the higher objectives and ethical goals (*al-maqāṣid*) of Islam's general message can be established."[47] This then is what is meant by a desired transformation of the "contents and geography" of *uṣūl al-fiqh* (as illustrated in *Radical Reform*, figure 3.1) in practice, and its progress so far is what is to be explored through a discussion of the CILE's projects in the next section.

Founding the Research Center for Islamic Legislation and Ethics, Doha, 2012

As it appears on the pages of *Radical Reform*, Ramadan's project looks ambitious indeed. In an interview with the author, Ramadan cites himself in agreement with Wael B. Hallaq's argument made in *The Impossible State: Islam, Politics and Modernity's Moral Predicament*, published in 2013. For both Ramadan and Hallaq, it is modernity's "fragmentation of knowledge" into separate spheres (economics, politics, law etc.), and their detachment from one another and from moral responsibility that is the "catastrophe" in need of being addressed.[48] At the same time however, Ramadan has made a clear and sustained effort in attempting to relate his own project back to the Islamic legal tradition when the opportunity presented itself. It will be argued that this permits the more conservative reformers of IUMS based alongside Ramadan and the CILE in Doha to engage with his project to a far greater extent than would otherwise have been possible.

In fact in a manner reminiscent of Ramadan, al-Qaradawi too has engaged in a sustained critique of rival *ulamā'* who have shown an excessive legalism in defining the Sharia as solely "the practical, legislative side of the religion, such as acts of worship and interpersonal transactions (*mu'āmalāt*)," leading to the common collocation "*al-Islām 'Aqīda wa-Sharī'a* (*Islam: Doctrine and Divine Law*)." This legalism misses, in Hallaq's words, the Sharia's "most central phenomenon, the moral impulse."[49] Encouraging a renewed emphasis on *fiqh al-akhlāq* (a deep and true understanding of ethics),[50] al-Qaradawi argues for a more holistic approach to understanding the Sharia as "the whole religion, its doctrines, religious rites, manners, morals, legislations, and interpersonal transactions."[51] A similar sentiment can arguably be seen in Ramadan's translation of Sharia, "On the basis of the root of the word, [Sharia] means 'the way' ('the path leading to the source') and outlines a global conception of creation, existence, death, and the way of life it entails, stemming from a normative reading and an understanding of scriptural sources. It determines 'how to be a Muslim.'"[52] It would be a little inaccurate to emphasize these similarities to too great an extent, for Ramadan's commitment to the Sharia also involves "a mix of individual self-purification and social-democratic politics,"[53] of a manner that al-Qaradawi would not recognize.[54]

Looking to the CILE, the first port of call is its website, CileCenter.org. Its pages in Arabic, English, and French appear to have little difference at first glance (e.g., in contrast to the IUMS website),[55] except in the one noticeable instance where the Arabic homepage makes a much more specific reference to role of "the higher objectives of the Islamic Sharia acting as a beacon to guide [the project]," which is not included with such emphasis in either the English or the French homepage.[56] It is the page discussing the CILE's methodology that is of most interest however with regard to *Radical Reform*. While the CileCenter.org page does not use the legalistic terminology (*ijmāʿ*, *qiyās*, *ʿurf*, *istisḥān*, *istislāḥ*, etc.) that Ramadan argued needed to be reconsidered in light of new realities,[57] the wording of the page still carefully refers back to an ethical tradition within Islam that the reader is told has been neglected. Also emphasized is that the methodology is a work in progress:

> Before [taking] an interest in the study of an applied Islamic ethics (*al-akhlāq al-islāmiyya al-taṭbīqiyya*) [...] There is an urgent need for contemporary Islamic ethics which can only be brought forth by examining Islam's rich and deep scholarly legal tradition and reconnecting that with both correct behavior and the right understanding of the objectives of this very legislation.[58]

Here then, some of the original ambition of *Radical Reform* seems somewhat diminished. There appears to be no mention of positing the universe as an equal revelation alongside the Qur'anic text. Another similar area of caution appears with regard to *Radical Reform* establishing an equivalence between the text scholars (*ʿulamāʾ al-nuṣūṣ*) and natural and social scientists (*ʿulamāʾ al-wāqiʿ*). The Arabic page instead prefers a more qualified reference to an engagement between the *ʿulamāʾ al-sharīʿa* (scholars of the Sharia) and *al-ʿulamāʾ al-mutakhaṣṣiṣīn fī mukhtalif al-majālāt* (scholars specializing in various [scientific] fields).[59] This represents a seemingly median point between the adaptive reform of al-Qaradawi and his peers, who also acknowledge the importance of "specialists (*al-mutakhaṣṣiṣūn*)" who assist the *ulamā'* in coming to a true understanding of the social reality, and echo *Radical Reform* arguing for full equality between scholars of the texts and the natural world as equal *'ulamā'*.[60]

Toward a Methodology of "Applied Ethics"

The most readily implementable sections of *Radical Reform* relate to Ramadan's argument for "a new methodology that precisely aims the enable *fuqahā'* and scientists to work together on specialized, new, open reflection together, and formulate adequate opinions [...] in delicate, but urgent areas."[61] With this in mind, among the CILE's activities that are worth examining more closely are its closed seminars, held four times annually and lasting three consecutive days. These serve to usefully illustrate the current form *Radical Reform*'s implementation is taking, as well as elucidating some of the broader goals of Ramadan's project as a whole.

Each of these seminars is organized around a particular theme, inviting four text scholars and four scientists, with the goal being to find a new methodology in relation to answering specific questions. Najah Nadi Ahmad, a member of CILE's steering committee, explains that this is to avoid the mistakes of the past whereby abstract Muslim reformist theories have apparently been found to be inapplicable in real contexts.[62] The first of these seminars was held between January 4 and 7, 2013, with the discussion theme being health care and bioethics. Those invited to participate alongside Ramadan and Auda most notably were: Ahmad al-Raysuni, Ali al-Qaradaghi, and Abdullah Bin Bayyah on behalf of the "text" scholars and representatives of the IUMS,[63] alongside Tom L. Beauchamp and Anelien Bredenoord as their "context" counterparts.[64]

While this topic might seem particularly appropriate on the basis that health care ethics are often referred to as the quintessential "applied ethics,"[65] it might also appear to be an unusual choice at first, given that of all the fields of modern science, it is in relation to health care and bioethics that Muslim scholars have been most prolific in attempting to articulate an "Islamic" position that is an alternative to the ethics of the "West," since the 1980s in fact.[66] While it is beyond the scope of this chapter to discuss the complexities of this discussion in detail, this trend emerged primarily as a response to the work of Tom L. Beauchamp and James F. Childress who, with their own articulation of the "four principles" of bioethics (respect for individual autonomy, nonmaleficence (do no harm), beneficence, justice) in 1979, essentially founded the modern field of bioethics in the Western academy. It would certainly appear that the emphasis on the importance of their ethical model's "output power" and "practicability" played a role in Ramadan's choice to invite Beauchamp to CILE.[67]

Looking again to the preexisting and contrasting "Islamic" perspective on health care ethics, Sahin Aksoy and Abdurrahman Elmai in fact argue that discussions of ethical principles similar to those of Beauchamp and Childress were occurring as early as the thirteenth century CE.[68] This then developed today into what would already appear to be a rather sophisticated code of ethics that already lays claim to being "Islamic." Abdallah Daar and Ahmed al-Khitamy point to the emergence of a separate Islamic Code of Medical Ethics in 2004, discussing euthanasia, consent, medically advised abortions, organ transplants, dissection of cadavers, and so on, and even included an alternative "Oath of the Muslim Doctor."[69]

Without wishing to essentialize this trend, among the clearest differences between these two positions relates to the question of individual autonomy. While Beauchamp and his colleagues argue for the prime importance of enabling an individual's autonomous action, "rooted in the liberal moral and political tradition of the importance of individual freedom,"[70] the contrasting position emphasizes an "Islamic communitarian ethics," based on concepts found in the legal tradition, such as *shūra* (consultation), that appear to exist in tension with "the dominant principle of autonomy that is based on liberal individualism."[71] This desire to articulate culturally specific ethical models in relation to health care is not unique to Islam and Muslims and can similarly be found in the work of bioethicists based in China, Japan, or the Philippines to name but a few examples. In these contexts too, the prime contrast is an appeal to a certain "communitarianism" rooted in the cultural and religious traditions that are argued to be clearly distinguishable from the individualistic bioethics of the West.[72]

At the same time however, critics have argued for the speciousness of these approaches on the basis that they allow a politics of identity, "cultural difference," and postcolonial resistance to unhelpfully dominate the discussion.[73] It is in this context, then, that Ramadan could be seen to be markedly critical of the advocacy for a distinct and different "Islamic bioethics." It would contradict his own argument that the sciences of the Universe are just as "Islamic" as those of the revealed written text. For Ramadan then, the advocacy of an Islamically distinct bioethics, finance, and so on fails to solve this "problem of the dichotomy and discrepancy between the different Universes of knowledge [...] can there be an 'Islamic' way of operating on hearts or brains surgically or an 'Islamic' method to understanding laws of supply and demand?"[74] Ramadan's criticism of this unhelpful dichotomy between two distinct Western and Islamic ethical frameworks, which Said

Arjomand terms the Islamic "defensive counter-universalism,"[75] has been a common feature in his oeuvre on the basis that,

> [it] tends to define what Islam is, *not* in light of its own principles, but in contrast with what is it *not*, namely Western civilization. If the latter accepts change, evolution, freedom and progress then, *logically*, *reasonably* and *as opposed to it*, Islam does not. Moreover, in their minds, the more one—whether an individual, group or society—refuses change, freedom and progress, the more he or they are genuinely Islamic.[76]

By contrast, then, in his applied ethics Ramadan is clearly looking to overcome this dichotomy in favor of a new form of universalism. This is what Beauchamp has argued for in his own work, proposing that his four bioethical principles operate as an applicable ethical model. As Beauchamp puts it, "More specific rules for health care ethics can be formulated *by reference to* [the four principles], but neither rules nor practical judgments can be straightforwardly *deduced* from [them]."[77] It is in a similar sense, then, that Ramadan's ambitious desire for his ethical model is to not simply react, or adapt, to modern scientific advances and "Islamize" them, but rather to anticipate them. For this to occur, however, it would appear that Islamic jurisprudence's role as the producer of legalistic moral norms should dissolve, or "vanish," in place of applied ethics (though March points out that the terms are used interchangeably at times), and for Ramadan,

> Applied *fiqh* is a field of legal elaboration that can, when separated from the world and its complexities, come to a standstill or turn into thought-establishing atemporal—or rather ahistorical—categories (lawful/unlawful, allowed/forbidden) that shape our thinking and to which what is real is reduced. Any coherent thought, however, aiming at reforming today's world must devise a dynamic *fiqh*, taking into account the time factor, intellectual and social dynamics, and dialectic tensions between higher objectives, universal principles, and historical models: such a *fiqh* should certainly not rigidify normative categories for fear of scientific, social, and human complexities that elude it. Law and jurisprudence related to human and social affairs must set higher objectives and aims and establish the framework of an ethics that determines the stages of mastery and transformation, a *fiqh* that foresees and foretells from the present state of scientific knowledge.[78]

Ramadan desires that his form of ethical universalism should lay claim to being authentically "Islamic" in a novel way—not solely through its formulaic articulation within the conceptual terms and horizons of Islam's tradition, but also in keeping with the equivalence of the Qur'anic text and the natural world as twin revelations. "The text sciences are no more 'Islamic' than the sciences of the Universe" as it were.[79] This "new geography" is to be realized by the CILE explicitly through the "urgent [need] to devise equal-representation, egalitarian, and specialized research and fatwa committees" between those "who are specialized in medicine, economics, and other fields" and the specialists of the texts.[80]

It is in this instance again that the IUMS-*'ulamā'* presence in Doha appears particularly useful to Ramadan in rendering the Qatar context amenable to his project. As noted earlier, al-Qaradawi also emphasized the importance of knowledge produced by non-*'ulamā'* specialists in formulating new legal opinions, which he described as partial *ijtihād* (*ijtihād juz'ī*). This was part of a broader recognition that the issues of the day are too manifold for one individual's expertise alone, leading al-Qaradawi to advocate collective *ijtihād* (*ijtihād jamā'ī*) by which "the endeavours of a team, or an institution, replaces the endeavour of individuals."[81] An example of this in practice can be found in the "adaptive" context of *fiqh al-aqalliyyāt*, with the European Council for Fatwa and Research's controversial fatwa permitting the taking of interest-bearing mortgages and loans on the basis that it now represented a legal necessity (*ḍarūra*). This decision drew on EU sociological and economic research detailing the disadvantages faced by Muslim households and highlighting the negative impact this had on Muslim integration, leading al-Qaradawi to state that "if sociologists and economists have said that Muslim families' possession of residential houses in the West is considered an urgent need for both individuals and the community [. . .] then the need has become a necessity." He also highlighted that "the evaluation of need here is not for the jurists, but the specialists."[82]

As noted however, this form of renewal has proved insufficient in Ramadan's perspective, for it conveys "the idea that *fuqahā'* are compelled—under the pressure of reality to decree [these] *fatāwā*, enabling Muslims to adapt to new realities."[83] Instead, his own methodology envisages natural and social scientists also being considered Islamic scholars, or *'ulamā'*, in their own right, thereby "*shifting the center of gravity of religious and legal authority* in contemporary Muslim societies and communities."[84] An attenuation of the text scholars' privilege to articulate Muslim behavioral norms through *fiqh* and *fatāwā* for "nothing basic legitimates nor justifies such a privilege"[85] is clearly a long-term project and the *'ulamā'* along with "the methodologies set down by [them] throughout the history of the Islamic sciences" still have a role to play according to Ramadan. For the moment however, Ahmad highlights that a key goal of the CILE is to enable the text scholars to perform their current role more effectively and move beyond simply a defensive articulation of what is "Islamic" and what is not in reaction to Western norms.[86] Indeed, the task that Ramadan and the CILE appear to have set themselves is rendered all the more ambitious by the apparent fact that, in the Qatar context certainly, the *'ulamā'* as a scholar class, far from being a conservative obstacle to be moved are rather the ones, and not Ramadan, who are going to articulate and realize his methodology in practice. The CILE is not then meant to be an alternative "*fatwā* center" to rival the *'ulamā'* of the IUMS, nor does Ramadan apparently plan to establish himself as a new authority in Doha. By contrast, Ahmad points out that although "*fatwās* can be very important in how to recommend the applied ethics but he [Ramadan] is trying to stay away from claiming any authority for himself, he is trying to claim their [the *'ulamā'*'s] legitimacy."[87]

However, the extent to which the current group of *'ulamā'* would be willing or able to perform the task expected of them is less clear for, as Ahmad also notes, and as the other essays in this volume will show, "they [the *'ulamā'*] already have stable ideas about how Sharia works."[88] While it would be inappropriate to use examples from the participants' internal discussions at the seminars, since they were intended to be private, 'Ali al-Qaradaghi's own report published on the IUMS English website (though not in Arabic surprisingly) describes how his own involvement in the first seminar was to, as he puts it, "formulate an integrated theory [of an Islamic bioethics] with an Islamic background, completely originating in Islamic philosophy [. . .] with the required open-mindedness to incorporate these four principles into the general objectives of Sharia." Setting aside the substance of al-Qaradaghi's proposals for the moment, what is relevant here is that his understanding of what would be beneficial to Ramadan's project clearly appears to be in keeping with the adaptation reform of al-Qaradawi. Al-Qaradaghi emphasizes then that his contribution was in conceptualizing two new "purposes" for the *maqāṣid* (protection of social security, protection of the security of the just state) alongside the original five as found in the premodern legal tradition.[89]

Similarly, the public contributions of other *'ulamā'* to the CILE would again illustrate their own viewing of Ramadan's project as in keeping with their own work, not only aiding the CILE's reception in Doha but also highlighting the longer-term challenges. As Ahmad similarly remarks, when the *'ulamā'* of IUMS like al-Qaradawi are asked to comment and contribute to questions relating the place of ethics in Islam, they appeared to interpret that as a relatively straightforward question and answered it affirmatively in relation to their own work, rather than as a more foundationally challenging project that aims to entirely transform the model of *fiqh*.[90] For example, in al-Qaradawi's presentation at CILE's first public conference on March 9, he is seen to be articulating a position on ethics that is very clearly in keeping with his own understanding, affirming the importance of ethical values in a holistic understanding of the Sharia, while emphasizing, as would be expected when considering Johnston's earlier chapter, that the Qur'an and the Sunna are to remain the undisputed sources of legislation.[91]

Conclusion

In drawing to a conclusion, while the role of the IUMS *'ulamā'*, their participation and contributions to CILE's project, so far lends a useful legitimacy to its work in the Qatar context, it would also appear to inhibit some of Ramadan's more recent and radical positions, particularly the positing of Universe and Nature as the twin revelations of the Qur'anic text. However, Ramadan's drawing on the *'ulamā'*'s "theological capital"[92] is not solely strategic, but rather the *'ulamā'* as a group appear to have a central role in the eventual realization of Ramadan and the CILE's long-term project. The conviction in Ramadan's mind that, in Ahmad's words, "the legal heritage (*al-turāth*) is an authoritative point of reference (*marja'iyya*)" is also shared by other notable Muslim intellectuals such as Khaled Abou El Fadel, who terms it a "matter of belief and conscience."[93] While other scholars, such as the famous Nasr Hamid Abu Zayd (d. 2010), were vehement critics of the privileged place afforded to the *'ulamā'* and the religious establishment from Abū Hāmid al-Ghazali, onward, for establishing themselves as a barrier between the people and God,[94] Ramadan, by contrast, argues that the Islamic legal tradition "is not frozen into permanent immobility: the essence of 'tradition' is the continued movement in history." This is a position he is clearly attempting to put to the test in arguing that "applied ethics is thus the method a religious, spiritual, or philosophical *tradition* gives itself to think out its *modernity*."[95]

This chapter then has aimed to explore how Ramadan and his colleagues' attempt to realize a new methodology of applied ethics is taking shape in the particular context of Doha. While at first the location appeared to be an enforced logistical and financial necessity, it was also seen to facilitate the CILE's establishment and maintain its links with the structures of a legal tradition that it ultimately aimed to dissolve. That would appear to be a difficult task certainly, rendered all the more so as it also depends upon the more conservative *'ulamā'* with very different understandings of what the project entails. This chapter began with a reference to Said's cautions and, though Ramadan, Auda, and the CILE do not appear to have shied away from discussing potentially controversial issues, such as the living conditions of migrant workers or the Football World Cup, with their Qatari backers,[96] it would be the height of naivety on their part to presume that boundaries are not in place. Even al-Qaradawi himself appears to have realized this of late.[97] While any semblance of a relationship between al-Qaradawi and Ramadan is a source of extreme controversy for the latter in the European context, in Qatar it is quite the opposite not only due to al-Qaradawi's stature and respect for Ramadan's late grandfather, but also due to the fact that the local religious context has been influenced by al-Qaradawi to such an extent as to render it particularly amenable to the CILE project, in its current form at least. In reading and contextualizing Ramadan's *Radical Reform* in relation to Doha and the *'ulamā'* of IUMS, it is argued here, then, that Ramadan's caution in the case studies of *Radical Reform*'s fourth chapter, or his call for a moratorium on the Islamic penal code (*al-ḥudūd*) as it appears in the written text,[98] is because he is not the one who is to make that step. It is to come from within the tradition, which means that it will be the *'ulamā'* themselves who carry out Ramadan's aim to "dissolve the very ambition of religious jurisprudence (the search for God's intended judgments on as many realms of human activity as possible) into an ethical project no longer concerned about even the search for precision, certainty, and authority."[99] Whether they will be able to take such a step remains more than a little unclear, as is the precise future shape of the methodology to which Ramadan aspires. As Ahmad put it, "this process could take years, but if we are successful it will be... amazing."[100]

Notes

1. The "Reith Lectures" are an annual series of six, thirty-minute lectures delivered by an invited speaker and broadcast by the BBC over public radio.
2. Edward W. Said, *Representations of the Intellectual: The 1993 Reith Lectures* (London: Vintage Books, 1994), xviii.
3. See, for just a few example, Caroline Fourest, *Frère Tariq: Discours, stratégie et méthode de Tariq Ramadan* (Paris: B. Grasset, 2004). Paul Landau, *Le sabre et le Coran: Tariq Ramadan et les Freres musulmans a la conquete de l'Europe* (Paris: Rocher, 2005). For an arguably more nuanced journalistic response in that context see Ian Hamel, *La vérité sur Tariq Ramadan: Sa famille, ses réseaux, sa stratégie* (Paris: Favre, 2007).
4. Andrew F. March, "Law as a Vanishing Mediator in the Theological Ethics of Tariq Ramadan," *European Journal of Political Theory*, 11:2 (2011), 177–201; available online at March, "Law as a Vanishing Mediator in the Theological Ethics of Tariq Ramadan," *Islamic Law and Law of the Muslim World Paper* No. 09–84 (2009), 1–41. http://ssrn.com/abstract=1478910 (accessed November 1, 2013).

5. The Arabic translation, *al-Iṣlāḥ al-Jadhrī: al-Akhlāqāt al-Islāmiyya wa'l-Taḥarrur*, appeared two years later. It is, however, of a questionable quality and Ramadan's colleague Najah Nadi Ahmad is currently preparing a new translation.
6. Andrew F. March, "The Post-Legal Ethics of Tariq Ramadan: Persuasion and Performance in *Radical Reform: Islamic Ethics and Liberation*," *Middle East Law & Governance*, 2 (2010), 253–732 (2). Italics in original.
7. See Tariq Ramadan, *To be a European Muslim: A Study of Islamic Sources in the European Context* (Leicester: The Islamic Foundation, 2000); Ramadan, *Muslims in France: The Way Towards Coexistence* (Leicester: The Islamic Foundation, 1999), while the first major work in that context was his, *Les Musulmans dans la Laïcité, responsabilités et droits des musulmans dans les sociétés occidentales* (Lyons: Tawhid, 1994).
8. March, "Law as a Vanishing Mediator."
9. In that section Ramadan discusses six themes: Islamic Ethics and Medical Sciences; Culture and the Arts; Women: Traditions and Liberation; Ecology and Economy; Society, Education, and Power; and Ethics and Universals. In the discussion of female liberation, for example, Ramadan appears very cautious, avoiding the discussion of concrete norms where possible, preferring to emphasize the importance of first "producing a discourse on womanhood that restores the link with meaning rather than single-mindedly focusing on norms." Tariq Ramadan, *Radical Reform: Islamic Liberation & Ethics* (Oxford: Oxford University Press, 2008), 217.
10. March, "The Post-Legal Ethics of Tariq Ramadan," 3–4.
11. Ibid., 3.
12. Talal Asad, *Genealogies of Religion* (Baltimore, MD: John Hopkins University Press, 1993), 210.
13. Said, *Representations of the Intellectual*, 68.
14. Edward W. Said, "The Public Role of Writers and Intellectuals," in Helen Small (ed.), *The Public Intellectual* (Oxford: Blackwell Publishing, 2002), 19–39 (4).
15. Jasser Auda is an Egyptian intellectual whose major work is *Maqasid al-Shariah as Philosophy of Islamic Law: A Systems Approach* (Herndon, VA: International Institute of Islamic Thought, 2007) published later in Arabic under the title, *Maqāṣid al-Sharī'a ka-Falsafa li'l-Tashrī' al-Islāmī: Ru'ya Manẓūmiyya* (Herndon, VA: International Institute of Islamic Thought, 2012). See also Auda, *Fiqh al-Maqāṣid: Ināṭah al-Aḥkām al-Shar'iyya bi-Maqāṣidihā* (Herndon, VA: International Institute of Islamic Thought, 2006). Before moving to Qatar he was based in London and among the founders of the Al-Maqasid Centre, mentioned by David L. Johnston's essay in this volume. Auda was also among the first members of the International Union of Muslim Scholars, his personal website can be found at http://www.jasserauda.net/en/.
16. See, "World Economic Outlook Database," *International Monetary Fund*, http://www.imf.org/external/pubs/ft/weo/2012/01/weodata/index.aspx (accessed 14 November 2013).

17. Saudi Arabia's attempts to influence its neighbor's domestic affairs were most notable in the wake of the 1996 coup that brought the former emir Hamid Al Thani (who recently abdicated in favor of his son Tamim) to power. Saudi Arabian support of a countercoup from the al-Ghafran clan from the al-Murrah tribe led to the dramatic revocation of 6,000 of their members' citizenship *en masse*. Indeed, Qatari fears reportedly extend to that of outright annexation, where the opportunity to present itself with a series of border disputes even resulted in armed clashes between the two states in 1992. Similarly among the documents released by Wikileaks on November 28, 2010, there was a reference to the former prime minister Hamad bin Jassim Al Thani in a meeting with American officials regarding the threat from Iran as their own "hurricane Katrina" saying, "they lie to us, and we lie to them." Allen J. Fromherz, *Qatar: A Modern History* (Washington, DC: Georgetown University Press, 2012), 28, 92–93.
18. Louay Bahry, "The Arab Media Phenomenon: Qatar's Al-Jazeera," *Middle East Policy*, 8:2 (2001), 88–99.
19. Guido Steinberg, "Katar und der Arabische Frühling: Unterstützung für Islamisten und anti-syrische Neuausrichtunag," *Stiftung Wissenschaft und Politik*, February 2012, http://www.swp-berlin.org/fileadmin/contents/products/aktuell/2012A07_sbg.pdf (accessed 1 October 2013).
20. Fromherz, *Qatar*, 27–28.
21. Ibid., 24.
22. Petersen continues, "Assertive branding is necessary for states as well as companies to stand out in the crowd, since they often offer similar products: territory, infrastructure, educated people, and for example in the Gulf almost identical systems of governance." John Peterson, "Qatar and the World: Branding for a Micro-State," *Middle East Journal*, 60:4 (2006), 732–748 (14).
23. Saba Mahmood, "Secularism, Hermeneutics, and Empire: The Politics of Islamic Reformation," *Public Culture* 18:2 (2006), 323–347.
24. Birol Baskan and Stephen Wright, "Seeds of Change: Comparing State-Religion Relations in Qatar and Saudi Arabia," *Arab Studies Quarterly*, 33:2 (2011), 96–111.
25. Malika Zeghal, "Religion and Politics in Egypt: The Ulema of Al-Azhar, Radical Islam, and the State (1952–94)," *International Journal of Middle East Studies*, 31 (1999), 371–399.
26. In his doctoral dissertation examining Qatari religious institutions, Hamed A. Hamed paints a truly dire picture of the quality of local Qatari *imāms* during that period, "until the late fifties of this century, preachers in Qatar were not qualified to perform the duties expected of them. By and large the majority were only able to read and write and therefore lacked the ability to address topics pertaining to problems of Qatari society [... For their Friday sermons], they depended solely on an old book [that contained] fifty-two sermons (*ẖuṭāb*), equal to the number of weeks in the year." Hamed A. Hamed, "Islamic Religion in Qatar During the Twentieth Century: Personnel and Institutions,"

unpublished doctoral dissertation (Manchester, England: University of Manchester, 1993), 120. For al-Qaradawi's own recollections of his shaping of the Qatari religious educational system, see Yusuf al-Qaradawi, *Ibn al-Qarya wa'l-Kuttāb: Malāmiḥ Sīra wa-Masīra*, 4 Vols. (Cairo: Dar al-Shuruq, 2002, 2004, 2006, 2011), 2:333–351. See also, Yusuf Ibrahim al-'Abdallah, *Ta'rīkh al-Ta'līm fi'l-Khalīj al-'Arabī 1913–1971* (Doha: n.p., 2003), especially 305–380; Majahid Khalaf, *al-Qaradawi bayn al-Ikhwān wa'l-Ṣulṭān* (Cairo: Dar al-Jumhuriyya li'l-Sahafa, 2008), 213–239.

27. In 1952, before Nasser's reforms of 1961, after his role as a member of the organizing committee sending Azharite volunteers to fight against the British occupying the Suez Canal came to an end, al-Qaradawi made his own efforts to reform the Al-Azhar curriculum, forming student committees, arranging meetings with senior Shaykhs, and enjoying the support of the then Shaykh al-Azhar Muhammad al-Khadir Husayn (d. 1958). See Yusuf al-Qaradawi, *Risālat al-Azhar bayn al-Ams wa'l-Yawm wa'l-Ghad* (Cairo: Maktabat Wahba, 1984). For a detailed discussion of al-Qaradawi's relationship with the Al-Azhar institution, see Jakob Skovgaard-Petersen, "Yusuf al-Qaradawi and al-Azhar" in Bettina Gräf and Jakob Skovgaard-Peterson (eds.), *Global Mufti: The Phenomenon of Yusuf al-Qaradawi* (London: C. Hurst & Co., 2008), 27–53.
28. Muhammad Ibn Ibrahim Al al-Shaykh (1893–1969) was one of the most influential Saudi *'ulamā'* of the twentieth century, holding key positions such as Grand Mufti, Chief Qadi, president of the Islamic University of Medina, and others. Most significant, however, was his position as head of the new *Dār al-Iftā'* established in 1952. Muhammad al-Atawneh, *Wahhābī Islam Facing the Challenges of Modernity: Dār al-Iftā' in the Modern Saudi State* (Leiden: Brill, 2010), 6.
29. al-Qaradawi, *Ibn al-Qarya wa'l-Kuttāb*, 2: 334–335, 440–442.
30. In relation to this discussion it is also worth briefly contextualizing Mehran Kamrava's point that, on the basis that the majority of the graduates from Qatar's Sharia faculty were females going on to become teachers or employees of Qatari ministries, they would have had only a limited influence on the local religious scene. Although admittedly her impact was felt more strongly outside Qatar, the role of graduates such as Maryam Hasan al-Hajari, a student of al-Qaradawi's who then went on to cofound the website and organization *IslamOnline.net*, which, after its founding in 1997, became arguably the most popular Islamic website online at that time, should not be understated. Mehran Kamrava, "Royal Factionalism and Political Liberalisation in Qatar," *The Middle East Journal*, 63:3 (2009), 401–420 (11). An examination of the role of women in Qatar can be found in Louay Bahry and Phebe Marr, "Qatari Women: A New Generation of Leaders?" *Middle East Policy*, 12 (2005), 104–119, and for a discussion of al-Hajari and the formative influence she ascribed to al-Qaradawi see Bettina Gräf, "IslamOnline.net: Independent, Interactive, Popular," *Arab Media & Society*, (2008), 1–21 (3). For more on *IslamOnline* and its dramatic closure in March 2010, see Mona Abdel-Fadil, "Islam

Offline—Living 'The Message' behind the Screens," *Contemporary Islam*, 7:3 (2013), 283–309; idem., "The Islam-Online Crisis: A Battle of Wasatiyya vs. Salafi Ideologies?" *CyberOrient*, 5:1 (2011), 1–12.

31. For a discussion of the founding and membership of the International Union of Muslim Scholars, see Bettina Gräf, "In Search of a Global Islamic Authority," *ISIM Review* (2005); Muhammad Q. Zaman, *Modern Islamic Thought in a Radical Age: Religious Authority and Internal Criticism* (Cambridge: Cambridge University Press, 2012), 67–68, 152.
32. In the reliance here on al-Qaradawi's own memoirs as the source for his role in designing the curricula in Qatar institutions of religious education, there is undoubtedly the risk of taking for granted a likely overemphasis of own his role. However, for the purposes of this chapter his personal views on the importance of students' ability to engage with social reality are important, rather than precisely was the nature of his contribution to local Qatari religious education. For an overview of these cited figures' reformist projects, see Malcolm H. Kerr, *Islamic Reform: The Political and Legal Theories of Muḥammad 'Abduh and Rashīd Riḍa* (London: Cambridge University Press, 1966); Francine Costet-Tardieu, *Un réformiste à l'université al-Azhar: Œuvre et pensée de Mustafâ al-Marâghî (1881–1945)* (Paris: Karthala, 2005); Kate Zebiri, *Maḥmūd Shaltūt and Islamic Modernism* (Oxford: Clarendon Press, 1993).
33. It is perhaps with such instances in mind a number of studies have sought to consider their work in relation to one another. See, for example, Göran Larsson, "Yusuf al-Qaradawi and Tariq Ramadan on Secularisation: Differences and Similarities," in G. Marranci (ed.), *Muslim Societies and the Challenge of Secularization: An Interdisciplinary Approach* (Dordrecht: Springer, 2010), 47–63; Florian Remien, *Muslime in Europa: Westlicher Staat und islamische Identität: Untersuchung zu Ansätzen von Yusuf al-Qaradawi, Tariq Ramadan und Charles Taylor* (Berlin: EB-Verlag, 2007).
34. Tariq Ramadan and Aziz Zemouri, *Faut-il faire taire Tariq Ramadan?* (Paris: L'Archipel, 2005), 135. See alsoRamadan and Zemouri, "Préface" in Conseil Européen des fatwas et de la recherché (ed.), *Recueil de fatwas: Avis juridiques concernant les musulmans d'Europe* (Lyons: Tawhid, 2001), 9–20.
35. Tariq Ramadan, *Western Muslims and the Future of Islam* (Oxford: Oxford University Press, 2004), 54.
36. Ramadan, *To be a European Muslim*, 93, 171.
37. March, "Law as a Vanishing Mediator," 6–12.
38. Ramadan, *Radical Reform*, 326, footnote 3.
39. Ibid., 30–34.
40. Ibid., 89.
41. Ibid., 136.
42. March, "Law as a Vanishing Mediator," 29. Italics in original.
43. March, "The Post-Legal Ethics of Tariq Ramadan," 11.
44. Ramadan, *Radical Reform*, 89.

45. Interview between the author and Jasser Auda (Doha: Qatar, January 23, 2013).
46. Ramadan distinguishes between natural and social science along the traditional jurisprudential lines of *al-qaṭʿ* and *al-ẓann* (the explicit and the speculative), contrasting the "*sunan al-kawniyya* (laws of the Universe)" that natural scientists discover alongside the more speculative (*ẓannī*) social sciences while noting too that "one cannot, in the social sciences, deny or overlook the presence of constants explaining human behavior patterns." Ramadan, *Radical Reform*, 104–108.
47. Ibid., 4.
48. Skype interview between the author and Tariq Ramadan (May 27, 2014); Wael B. Hallaq, *The Impossible State: Islam, Politics, and Modernity's Moral Predicament* (New York, NY: Columbia University Press, 2013).
49. Wael B. Hallaq, "On Orientalism, Self-Consciousness and History," Islamic Law and Society 18:3 (2011), 387–439 (27).
50. See, for example, Yusuf al-Qaradawi, *Taysīr al-Fiqh li'l-Muslim al-Muʿāṣir* (Cairo: Mu'assasa al-Risala, 2001). I am grateful to Amir Hamad for this reference.
51. Yusuf al-Qaradawi, *Dirāsa fī Fiqh Maqāṣid al-Sharīʿa: Bayna l-Maqāṣid al-Kulliyya wa-l-Nuṣūṣ al-Juz'iyya* (Cairo: Dar al-Shuruq, 2006), 20.
52. Ramadan, *Radical Reform*, 360.
53. March, "Law as a Vanishing Mediator," 21.
54. For Ramadan, a commitment to Sharia means, "On the intimate level, it is working on one's self, mastering one's egoisms and one's violence; on the social level, it is the struggle for greater justice and against various kinds of discrimination, unemployment, and racism; on the political level, it is the defense of civil responsibilities and rights and the promotion of pluralism, freedom of expression, and the democratic processes; on the economic level, it is action against speculation, monopolies, and neocolonialism; on the cultural level, it is the promotion of the arts and forms of expression that respect the dignity of conscience and human values." Ramadan, *Western Muslims and the Future of Islam*, 32.
55. *IUMSonline.net*, http://www.iumsonline.net/ar/ (accessed November 1, 2013).
56. *CileCenter.org*, http://www.cilecenter.org/home-ar (accessed November 1, 2013).
57. Ramadan, *Radical Reform: Islamic Liberation & Ethics*, 120.
58. *CileCenter.org*, http://www.cilecenter.org/areas-of-research-ar/methodology-ar (accessed November 8, 2013).
59. Ibid., http://www.cilecenter.org/about-us-ar/center-activities-ar (accessed November 1, 2013). Despite this apparent caution, as Ramadan points out even granting Natural and Social scientists the rank of *ʿulamāʾ* is a significant change. Ramadan, *Radical Reform*, 131. On returning to the website on November 15, 2013, the terminology appears to have been changed and referring to the *ʿulamāʾ al-sharīʿa wa'l-nuṣūṣ* (scholars of the Sharia and the texts)

and the *'ulamā' al-wāqi' al-mutakhaṣṣiṣīn*. Ibid., http://www.cilecenter.org/about-us-ar/center-activities-ar (accessed November 15, 2013). The interactive aspects of the site are also rather cautious, asking its users to consider questions such as "Where is ethics in the method of determination of the 1st day of Ramadan?" with the four possible answers reading: "[1] In the detection of the crescent new moon by the human eye only; [2] In the astronomical calculations; [3] Both of these methods are acceptable; [4] Decision belongs to the religious authority in the country we live in." Ibid., http://www.cilecenter.org/ (accessed November 1, 2013).

60. Yusuf al-Qaradawi, *al-Ijtihād al-Mu'āṣir bayn al-Inḍibāt wa'l-Infirāṭ* (Cairo: n.p., 1998).
61. Ramadan, *Radical Reform*, 158.
62. Ahmad continues saying, "The ideas have to be formed with the practice, this is one of the issues that is unique to the Center, other Centers just respond to questions, but we are trying to develop the [new] methodologies accompanied by the practice." Skype interview between the author and Najah Nadi Ahmad (November 12, 2013).
63. Ali al-Qaradaghi (b. 1949) is the current general secretary of IUMS while Abdullah Bin Bayyah (b. 1935) is al-Qaradawi's vice-Chairman at IUMS.
64. Other participants included: Abdulsattar Abu Ghuddah of the Islamic Fiqh Academy; Mohammad Ali Albar from King Fahd Centre for Medical Research and Hasan Pasha from King Fahd Armed forces Hospital. *CileCenter.org*, http://www.cilecenter.org/media-center/newsroom/news-details?item=67 (accessed November 1, 2013).
65. Tom L. Beauchamp, "The 'Four Principles' Approach to Healthcare Ethics," in R. E. Ashcroft, A. Dawson, H. Draper, and J. R. McMillan (eds.), *Principles of Healthcare Ethics* (Chichester: John Wiley & Sons, 2006 [1994]), 3–10 (7).
66. The Cilecenter.org website also notes this saying, "Of all the fields, medicine is singular in the great extent to which Muslim scriptural scholars (*fuqahā'*) have been involved and have collaborated with practitioners. Together, they have produced interesting and important legal opinions on issues such as euthanasia, organ transplantation, and cloning." *CileCenter.org*. http://www.cilecenter.org/areas-of-research/medicine-bioethics (accessed November 15, 2013).
67. Tom L. Beauchamp and James F. Childress, *Principles of Biomedical Ethics* (Oxford: Oxford University Press, 2013 [1979]), 354.
68. Sahin Aksoy and Abdurrahman Elmai, "The Core Concepts of the 'Four Principles' of Bioethics as Found in Islamic Tradition," *Medicine and Law*, 21 (2002), 211–224. See also Leigh N. B. Chipman, "The Professional Ethics of Medieval Pharmacists in the Islamic World," *Medicine and Law*, 21 (2002), 321–338.
69. Abdallah Daar and Ahmed al-Khitamy, "Health Care," in Amyn B. Sajoo (ed.), *A Companion to Muslim Ethics* (London: I.B. Tauris, 2010), 119–130 (2). For a description of the Islamic Code of Medical Ethics as adopted by the Islamic Organisation for Medical Sciences (IOMS), see Amyn B. Sajoo, *Muslim Ethics:*

Emerging Vistas (London: I.B. Tauris, 2004), 108–117 and more generally Jonathan E. Brockopp (ed.), *Islamic Ethics of Life: Abortion, War and Euthanasia* (Colombia, SC: University of South Carolina Press, 2002); Farhat Moazam, *Bioethics and Organ Transplantation in a Muslim Society: A Study in Culture, Ethnography, and Religion* (Bloomington: University of Indiana Press, 2006); Frederick M. Denny, *Muslim Medical Ethics: From Theory to Practice* (Colombia, SC: University of South Carolina Press, 2008); Abdulaziz Sachedina, *Islamic Biomedical Ethics: Principles and Applications* (Oxford: Oxford University Press, 2009).

70. Beauchamp, "The 'Four Principles' Approach to Healthcare Ethics," 3–10 (1–2).
71. Abdulaziz Sachedina, "The Search for Islamic Bioethics Principles," in R. E. Ashcroft, A. Dawson, H. Draper, and J. R. McMillan (eds.), *Principles of Healthcare Ethics* (Chichester: John Wiley & Sons, 2006 [1994]), 117–125 (3); Sachedina, *Islamic Biomedical Ethics*, 47. The citation of Sachedina's work here is not intended to be overly reductive, for he also advocates a "distinctly Islamic yet metaculturally communicable and principled deontological-teleological ethics." That position could be read as desiring a similar goal to that of Ramadan, but from a more cautious perspective—an ethical system that is deontologically linked to the Islamic texts but also capable of utilitarianism. Unfortunately however, a detailed analysis of Sachedina's work is outside the scope of this chapter. Ibid., 29.
72. Hyaduki Sakamoto, "The Foundation of a Possible Asian Bioethics," in Ren-Zong Qiu (ed.), *Bioethics: Asian Perspectives: A Quest for Moral Diversity* (Dordrecht: Kluwer Academic Publishers, 2004); Jing-Bao Nie, *Behind the Silence: Chinese Voices on Abortion* (Boulder, CO: Rowman & Littlefield Publishers, 2005); Angeles Alora and Josephine Lumitao (eds.), *Beyond a Western Bioethics* (Washington, DC: Georgetown University Press, 2001).
73. Jing-Bao Nie, "The Speciousness of an Asian Bioethics: Beyond Dichotomizing East and West," in R. E. Ashcroft, A. Dawson, H. Draper, and J. R. McMillan (eds.), *Principles of Healthcare Ethics* (Chichester: John Wiley & Sons, 2006 [1994]), 143–149; Nie, "Is Informed Consent Not Applicable to China? Intellectual Flaws of the Cultural Difference Argument," *Formosa Journal of Medical Humanities*, 2:1–2 (2001), 67–74.
74. Ramadan, *Radical Reform*, 128.
75. Said A. Arjomand, "Islam, Political Change and Globalisation," *Thesis Eleven*, 76:1 (2004), 9–28 (16–19).
76. Ramadan, *To Be a European Muslim*, 55–56. Italics added for emphasis.
77. Beauchamp and Childress prefer to avoid the Hippocratic ethical tradition and arguing for a new approach based on a philosophical querying of varying models of morality. Beauchamp and Childress, *Principles of Biomedical Ethics*, especially Chapters 9 and 10. See also Tom L. Beauchamp, "Comparative Studies: Japan and America," in K. Hoshino (ed.), *Japanese and Western Bioethics: Studies in Moral Diversity* (Dordrecht: Kluwer Academic Publisher, 1997), 25–48. The

quotation is from Beauchamp and Childress, *Principles of Biomedical Ethics*, 2. Italics in original.

78. Ramadan, *Radical Reform*, 131.
79. Ibid., 132.
80. As the website *CileCenter.org* puts it, "CILE will provide the space and opportunity for Muslim scholars of the text/Shari'a and medical scholars to come together to further their current collaboration to developing an Islamic ethical framework which will guide the production of up-to-date and specific solutions to critical questions and contemporary challenges." http://www.cilecenter.org/areas-of-research/medicine-bioethics/medicine-bioethics (accessed November 1, 2013).
81. al-Qaradawi, *al-Ijtihād al-Muʿāṣir*, 50, 103.
82. Yusuf al-Qaradawi, *Fī Fiqh al-Aqalliyyāt al-Muslima: Ḥayāt al-Muslimīn Wasaṭ al-Mujtamaʿāt al-Ukhrā* (Cairo: Dar al-Shuruq, 2001), 45. See also Alexandre Caeiro, "The Social Construction of Sharia: Bank Interest, Home Purchase and Islamic Norms in the West," *Die Welt des Islams*, 44:3 (2004), 351–375.
83. Ramadan *Radical Reform*, 31, 123.
84. Ibid., 124. Italics in original.
85. Ibid., 125.
86. Ramadan, *Western Muslims and the Future of Islam*, 3–4; Skype interview between the author and Najah Nadi Ahmad.
87. Skype interview between the author and Najah Nadi Ahmad.
88. Ibid.
89. *IUMSonline.net*, "Bioethics seminar adopts Qaradaghi's proposal linking them to Shariah purposes," http://www.iumsonline.net/en/default.asp?MenuID=48&contentID=5657 (accessed November 10, 2013).
90. Skype interview between the author and Najah Nadi Ahmad.
91. Yusuf al-Qaradawi, "A Comment on the Relationship Between Ethics and Law in Islam," March 9, 2013, *CileCenter.org*, http://cilecenter.org/media-center/videos# (accessed November 11, 2013).
92. This is March's term. March, "The Post-Legal Ethics of Tariq Ramadan."
93. Khaled Abou El Fadl, *Speaking in God's Name: Islamic Law, Authority and Women* (Oxford: Oneworld, 2001), 31.
94. Nasr Hamid Abu Zayd, *Mafhūm al-Naṣṣ: Dirāsa fī ʿUlūm al-Qurʾān* (Beirut: al-Markaz al-Thaqafi al-ʿArabi, 2000 [1999]), 283–297.
95. Ramadan, *Radical Reform*, 158. Italics in original.
96. *CileCenter.org*, "Issues facing 'Migrant Workers' raised by CILE in public lecture," April 22, 2013, http://www.cilecenter.org/media-center/newsroom/news-details?item=165 (accessed November 1, 2013); Simon Matthey-Doret, Tariq Ramadan, Joël Robert & Philip Meyer, "Qatar, la coupe du monde impossible?," *RTS.ch*, October 4, 2013, http://www.rts.ch/la-1ere/programmes/en-ligne-directe/5245340-qatar-la-coupe-du-monde-impossible-04-10-2013.html (accessed November 1, 2013).

97. For a discussion of the shifting relationship between Yusuf al-Qaradawi, the Qatari royal family and Qatar's foreign policy, see David H. Warren, "The *'Ulamā'* and the Arab Uprising 2011–13: Considering Yusuf al-Qaradawi, the 'Global Mufti,' between the Muslim Brotherhood, the Islamic Legal Tradition & Qatari Foreign Policy," *New Middle Eastern Studies*, 4 (2014), 2–32, http://www.brismes.ac.uk/nmes/wp-content/uploads/2014/03/NMES2014Warren-with-video.pdf.
98. Ramadan, *Radical Reform*, 244–247.
99. March, "Law as a Vanishing Mediator," 32.
100. Skype interview between the author and Najah Nadi Ahmad.

CHAPTER 4

Maqāṣid al-Sharīʿa in Contemporary Shīʿī Jurisprudence

Liyakat Takim

In recent times, there has been a growing awareness of the need to apply the concept of *maqāṣid al-sharīʿa* (aims or objectives of Islamic law) in the derivation of juridical rulings. This need has been felt most acutely among those who advocate revisiting or reinterpreting the *sharīʿa* (Islamic moral-legal law). Interest in the concept of *maqāṣid al-sharīʿa* seems to have been ignited because many Muslim thinkers see it as a hermeneutical tool that can be deployed to resolve some of the major social and political challenges facing the contemporary Muslim world. This chapter explores the role and the significance of the concept of *maqāṣid al-sharīʿa* as a legal-cum-hermeneutical tool in modern Shīʿī legal thought. It also explores the current discourse on reformation in Shīʿī circles.

There has been much debate in Muslim circles regarding reformation in the Muslim world and, more specifically, questions have been posed that include: How can a religion that is believed to be immutable and constant regulate and serve the needs of a changing community? How can a legal system that was formulated over a thousand years ago respond to the requirements of twenty-first-century Muslims? Is there a need for reformation in Islam? If so, where should it begin and in which direction should it proceed? These are some of the most challenging questions facing contemporary scholars of Islam. This chapter examines the question of *maqāṣid al-sharīʿa* and *maṣlaḥa* in Shīʿīsm. Before that, I preface my discussion with a review of reformation in Shīʿī Islam.

Reformation in Contemporary Shī'ī Thought

Within Shī'ī circles, there have been important voices calling for a radical rethinking of the religious tradition. Many of these have emerged after the revolution in Iran in 1979. Some formulations have come from religious intellectuals, such as 'Abdolkarim Soroush, but importantly, others have emerged from within the religious seminaries itself. Scholars such as Ayatullah Sanei (b.1937), Ayatullah Jannati (b.1927), Ayatullah Mohagheg Damad (b. 1946), Hujjatul-Islam Muhsin Sa'idzadeh (b.1956), and Mohsen Kadivar (b.1959) have called for a re-evaluation of traditional juridical pronouncements on many issues. As a matter of fact, in my discussions with some *marāji'*[1] in Qum, Iran, I detected a distinct silent revolution within the seminaries. The views of the *marāji'* are, on many important issues, polarized.

A major feature that reformist thinkers like Ayatullah Sanei, Ayatullah Muhammad Ibrahim Jannati, and Muhammad Husayn Fadlallah (d. 2010) consider is the positioning of the Qur'ān as the primary and the foundational textual source in formulating new legal opinions, empowering reason to uncover the rationale and the wisdom (*'illa*) behind a divine injunction, and taking into account the context of time (*zamān*) and space (*makān*) associated with particular decrees that were legislated. This is evident in the existing legal corpus dealing with issues such as apostasy, status of non-Muslims, and gender justice, many of which contradict the Qur'ānic ethos but are given legal currency primarily on the basis of prophetic traditions (*ḥadīth*), consensus (*ijmā'*), and the science of jurisprudence (*uṣūl al-fiqh*). According to Ayatullah Sanei, this has stultified the onward progression of Islamic legal theory and Islamic law that ought to be harmonious and compatible with the new context and circumstances.[2]

Many Shī'ī scholars lament the fact that current legal treatises (*risāla 'amaliyya*) do not discuss issues that are relevant today. Thus, issues like human rights, *mustahdathāt* (new issues), and sociopolitical issues are largely avoided in these treatises. Instead, more attention is paid to topics like *kurr* (the amount of water that is required to purify an object), details of the distance one has traveled so that one can pray *qaṣr* (shortened prayers), and so on.[3]

Shī'ī scholars have advocated a renewed *ijtihād*[4] keeping in mind the dictates of contemporary times. For example, in his discourse on *ijtihād*, Ayatullah Khumayni urges the theological centers to promote *fiqh* (jurisprudence) in a better form. He states that the seminaries should bear in mind that domestic and foreign problems will not be resolved by presenting impractical theories expressing impractical generalities and views.

By stressing that *ijtihād* should be optimally pursued in the theological centers by the *fuqahā'* and religious scholars, Khumayni hints at the deficiencies of the *ijtihād* prevalent and their inadequacy in meeting the different and complex needs of human communities in the contemporary era. He further states that the modern jurist should always hold the pulse of the community's future reflections and requirements with profound foresight and insight.[5] As Ayatullah Mutahhari poignantly asks, "If a living mujtahid does not respond to modern problems, what is the difference between following a living and a dead [religious authority]?"[6]

Khumayni castigated the jurists for their insistence on abstract principles at the expense of tangible changes in real-life situations. He said that in addition to safeguarding the sanctity and integrity of Islam, their responsibility is to assure that the teachings of Islam are not rendered irrelevant in managing the world of economics, ministry, political, and social relations.

Ayatullah Sanei, too, is of the opinion that there has been a tendency on the part of the jurists to take extreme positions that prevent them from employing the institution of *ijtihād* to resolve challenges confronting Muslims living in the twenty-first century. On one extreme, there are jurists who have sanctified substantive law (*fiqh*) and its principles to such an extent that there is little room for creative re-interpretation. They are oblivious to the fact that the purpose of Islamic law is to provide ease and comfort to people in all ages along with spiritual guidance and not to impose on them difficulty and hardship or rulings that are incompatible with that particular age.[7] The other polarized position is adopted by those who are inattentive to the Islamic legal principles and are eager to satisfy all groups without evaluating whether the positions adopted by them are in harmony with the Islamic principles or not. Sanei proposes a middle ground that accords reverence and respect to Islamic legal principles but at the same time is cognizant that the law must have relevance and be applicable in the present-day context with its special circumstances.[8] This position is akin to the one adopted by the eminent Iranian reformist scholar Dr. Abdolkarim Soroush (b.1945) in the articulation of his theory of expansion and contraction of religious knowledge.[9] He argues that a distinction needs to be made between any religion per se and our understanding of that religion. While the former is, in the view of its beholders, a set of sacred and unchanging truths, the latter is an ever-changing set of personal experiences and publicly accessible ideas and theories that, at any given time, reflects the state of our knowledge. Religious knowledge is theory-laden, time-bound, and context-bound. The ideal of "Islam" is, by definition, something human and this-worldly and as such is being influenced by, among other things, our background knowledge, our place in history and our geographical location, our social, cultural, and political environment, and so on.

Contemporary Reformation in Shī'īsm

Reforms in Shī'īsm have been suggested and enacted in different realms. Here, I will cite just a few examples of reformist thinking in Shī'ī circles. Ayatollah Dr. Seyed Mohammad Bojnourdi, a former member of the Supreme Judicial Council in Iran, maintains that the current method of administering certain Islamic punishments will weaken Islam and present a distorted image of the religion to the world. He proposes that in the execution of Islamic punishments, it would be better to take advantage of the views of psychologists, sociologists, and other experts.[10]

Bojnourdi further states that the criterion in the Islamic penal law is based on the principle of "elimination of obscene deeds." It is not mandatory, he argues, to resort to punishment if someone commits an offense, since the principle in Islam is based on correction and development of mankind. "The life style of the Holy Prophet and Imām 'Ali attest to the fact that at the time of punishment, they would first resort to admonition and guidance in order to lead the convict to repent. In many cases, punishment would be averted if the offender repented."[11] Thus, in many cases of punishment, "if the convict repents prior to the approval of the case by the court, the responsibility of the court to look into the offense would be dropped as well."

Bojnourdi further maintains that if the process for execution of penalty results in the denigration of Islam and causes people, especially the youth, to demean the religion, then the process should be revised so that this does not happen. If certain punishments such as flogging in the public create a negative impression regarding Islam, such a practice should be abandoned. This is because preserving the dignity and prestige of Islam is the prime task, one that has priority over other obligations.

Bojnourdi also states that in 1981–1982, he talked to Ayatullah Khumayni about the issue of *rajm* (stoning). He told Khumayni that under the status quo, *rajm* would cause the weakening of Islam, and it would be used by others as a tool to mock the religion. Not only had *rajm* lost its intended effects, but it had also allowed people to ridicule Islam. Therefore, other options had to be sought in order to substitute it. The Imām went on to inform courts not to issue the verdict of *rajm* but use other options such as the death penalty. Bojnourdi continues, "I even told the Imām that when applying the *rajm*, there is a possibility for the convict to come out of the pitch and escape. If the death penalty were to be enforced, escape would not be possible. I asked what had to be done in that case and the Imām stated that the convict should be guided towards expressing penitence so that he/she would be pardoned."[12]

The Iranian scholar and jurist Ayatullah Mohagheg Damad is also known for his reformist ideas. For example, on the question of slavery, he maintains that laws pertaining to slavery have to be radically reformed. He states that since the international community has agreed to abolish slavery, the institution has disappeared. It is now necessary to conclude that slavery is also forbidden by Islamic law, for the basis of applying the law of slavery has changed. The jurist cannot claim that earlierprisoners of war were enslaved, therefore they must be enslaved today too. Islamic countries have readily signed the international conventions on slavery, and the abolition of slavery is not in any way inconsistent with Islamic law.[13]

Another area of much debate and discussion is regarding the age of puberty for girls. Among Shīʿī jurists, there is much dispute as to when a girl attains puberty. Damad states that the most widely accepted (*mashhūr*) view among scholars is that girls reach puberty at the age of nine. Damad argues, "when all the various opinions are taken into account, one realizes that one is faced with a case of an 'external standard,' since the rulings have been conditioned by climate. Had a petitioner from a certain tribe and another living some distance away come and enquired of the Imām concerning this matter, the answers they received would no doubt have been different. Does this not tell us that puberty should be regarded as consisting of radical changes in the physical development of a young person? One simply cannot compare an Arab girl living in a hot climate with another from the north of Sweden in this respect. The difference is due to the fact that each girl lives in a different part of the world, a girl who lives in Kufa in Iraq might not have reached puberty at the age of nine, quite different from a girl from the Arabian peninsula [*sic*]. Thus the condition of puberty is the actual reaching of the stage of puberty in physical terms; this is what is meant in the Qur'ān by the phrase 'they reached...' (*balaghna*) [2:231–234]. This is the true meaning of the word; it does not refer to the fixed age of nine or, in the case of boys, fourteen."[14]

Another field where there has been much debate is regarding a woman's right to divorce her husband. Perhaps the most revolutionary position is held by the reformist Ayatullah Sanei who states that, "since the subject [women's situation] has changed, the framework of civil laws must change too. Our current laws are in line with the traditional society of the past, whereas these civil laws should be in line with contemporary realities and relations in our own society."[15] Sanei states that, even without a marriage contract, a woman can unilaterally annul a marriage if she feels she cannot live with a man. She can simply annul the marriage without the need for a formal divorce although it is better for her if the *talāq* is recited. "Islam does not say that a woman must stay and put up with her marriage if it is causing her harm—never." The problem, according to Sanei, is that the laws are still in the process of evolution.[16] According to Sanei, in response to a question posed, Khumayni stated that a husband should be persuaded to grant a divorce if his wife seeks it. If he refuses that request, then the divorce can be affected with the permission of a judge.[17]

Shīʿī scholars have also argued that there is a need to expand the scope of their juristic vision and revisit some of the earlier rulings based on the need of the times and the interests of the community. As the sociopolitical situations change, juridical rulings issued must reflect the newer circumstances. For example, Ayatullah Makarim Shirazi (b. 1926) argues that in the past, it was forbidden to sell blood since it was considered to have no monetary value. However, in today's world, blood is a necessity, a valuable commodity that can save lives. So, it is now permissible to sell blood. As an example of how a ruling can change according to time and place, Shirazi quotes Muhammad bin Hassan Al-Tusi's (d. 1067) *fatwa* (religious edict) that it is prohibited to charge for water in winter, whereas it is permissible to do so in the summer. This is because it has value in the summer but not in winter.[18]

Maqāṣid al-Sharīʿa *and Shīʿīsm*

The previous discussion on reformist thinking is intertwined with the discussion on the objectives of law. This is because the purpose of the law is to ensure of well-being of its adherents. As sociopolitical circumstances change, laws have to be revised to ensure that their purposes are not compromised. *Maqāṣid al-sharīʿa*, or the objectives of Islamic law, is an important and yet somewhat neglected discipline of Islamic jurisprudence. Those who advocate this approach view the *sharīʿa* as a vehicle to benefit Muslims, and its laws as designed to protect these benefits. Although Muslims accept that textual injunctions must be treated as expressions of the intentions of the lawgiver, consideration should be given not only to the text but also to its rationale (*ʿilla*) and the purpose of the rulings the text promotes. Thus, although the objectives of the law are rooted in the sacred texts, it is essential to look beyond the particularities of the text and focus on the philosophy and purpose behind its rulings. As such, the *maqāṣid* incorporate a degree of hermeneutics and versatility into the reading of the texts that transcend the vicissitudes of time and space.

The *maqāṣid* did not receive much attention in the early stages of the development of Islamic legal thought, and, as such, represent a later juristic innovation. Even in modern times, many texts on *uṣūl al-fiqh* (Islamic legal theory) do not include a discussion on *maqāṣid al-sharīʿa*. This is probably because rather than engaging in textual and contextual analysis, the apparent meaning of words, and explicating the methodology of reconciling contradictory traditions, the *maqāṣid* are largely concerned with discerning and elucidating the purposes of the law.

Maqāṣid and al-Maṣāliḥ al-Mursala *in Shīʻī Legal Theory*

Due to their close connection, in Shīʻī legal theory, *maqāṣid al-sharīʻa* is generally discussed under the rubric of *maṣlaḥa*. Since the objective of the law (*maqṣad*) is in seeking the interest of the Muslim community, in the works on *uṣūl al-fiqh*, the principle of public good is also referred to as *al-maṣāliḥ al-mursala*, that is, in seeking the benefit of the people in the absence of textual evidence. This suggests that laws can be legislated based on the principle of the public good without any textual proof to support its validity. Moreover, because the purpose of *maṣlaḥa* (being or doing good) is discernible by reason, it has God's approval too, because in Islamic theology, there is a correlation between reason and revelation in matters concerning the common good.[19]

Another reason for this appellation of "public good that is free from textual evidence" is that promoting the public good is rationally derived. It is a positive obligation that requires people to act beneficently whenever possible, and hence, is not in need of scriptural justification. For this reason, *maṣlaḥa* has been admitted as a principle of reasoning to derive new rulings or as a method of suspending earlier rulings out of consideration for the interests and welfare of the community.[20]

The extent to which *maṣlaḥa* can be used to enact legal change depends on a jurist's view regarding the role of reason and revelation in interpreting the law. A jurist who accepts reason as a valid tool in deciding legal matters is more likely to use hermeneutical tools and resort to interpretive activity in determining whether a concrete situation is beneficial or harmful in issuing a ruling.

Shīʻī scholars like Ayatullah Mohammad Fadlallah, Muhsin Kadivar, Mojtahid Shabistari (b.1937), and Mohagheg Damad have argued that there is a need to articulate a jurisprudence that addresses contemporary concerns and issues. They maintain that what is essential to a proper understanding of Islam is not the letter of the text but the spirit of the Qur'ān and the Prophetic traditions. For them, and for many other scholars, there is no single, valid interpretation of the Qur'ān or the *ḥadīth*. Scholars have also argued that changes in the conditions of time and place require a re-examination of laws formulated in the classical period of Islam, the eighth to tenth centuries. Mojtahed Shabistari, a contemporary Iranian scholar, for example, states that a new reading of texts is required, one that goes beyond traditional *fiqh* (Islamic jurisprudence) and *uṣūl* and embraces subjects such as society, history, economics, politics, and psychology.[21] To derive these laws, he states that Muslim thinkers need to construct a comprehensive theory of human nature and social change. Similarly, Saʿidzadeh, a contemporary jurist in Iran, argues that laws pertaining to women and their apparent lack equality with men are products of the Islamic hermeneutical tradition that has favored men. For Saʿidzadeh, such laws are amenable to change based on the needs and interests of the times.[22]

Jurists who argue for the reformulation of Islamic laws also maintain that the interpretations of Islamic revelation were interwoven to the specificity of the times and places. Jurists can only pronounce general principles, not rulings that are to be enforced at all times and places. They also argue that hermeneutical principles such as *maṣlaḥa* allow for a different reading of the classical texts. For the reform-minded jurists, it is essential that Muslims continue to review and revise the law in keeping with the needs and dictates of their changing circumstances.[23]

Maqāṣid and Maṣlaḥa *in Shīʿī Legal Theory*

Muslim jurists have resorted to interpretation in order to apply the sources of the law to the actual legal cases that need to be ruled upon. This interpretive activity includes extending the existing law to new situations and changed circumstances that are not explicitly addressed in the scripture. One of the key principles in this extension is that of *maṣlaḥa*. The application of *maṣlaḥa* rests on a jurist's ability to objectively determine standards of benefit and harm in a society.

A jurist has to also provide justification for any given ruling by appealing to principles and rules that are established in the legal theory. These principles are utilized in all situations about which the *sharīʿa* has neither ruled explicitly nor provided any relevant precedents. In other words, in matters on which the law has not ruled, a legal judgment that falls outside the framework of general rules derived from *maṣlaḥa* is justified based on Qur'ānic verses and traditions that exhort justice and avoidance of wrongdoing. The verse "God commands justice and good deeds" (Q 27:90), and the legal maxim "No harm, no harassment" are rules that flow from the principle of common good.

To be sure, *maṣlaḥa* is based on the notion that the ultimate goal of the *sharīʿa* necessitates doing justice and preserving people's best interests in this world and the next. It is also premised on the view that the intellect is able to determine what is good and that this leads ultimately to the divine intent. However, many Shīʿī jurists have questioned the applicability of a ruling that has been deduced independently of a revealed text based solely on a jurist's assessment of what constitutes the public good. Is it possible to extract the rulings' objectives and evaluative tools based on these texts and formulate general principles and rules that could be employed in future contingencies and situations? Why has the lawgiver not made these objectives and evaluative measures explicitly clear so that there would be no dissent and disagreement? Once objectives that are in consonance with wisdom (*ḥikma*) are discovered, is it possible to prioritize them so that the jurist would know which one to incline toward and favor if there were a clash between any two of them? These are some of the daunting issues discussed by jurists in the works of Islamic legal theory. Due to such misgivings, discussions on *al-maqāṣid* as a science remained on the fringes of the Shī'ī juristic thought that was manifested in the various theories and doctrines of *uṣūl al-fiqh*.[24]

Objections to the Principle of al-Maṣāliḥ al-Mursala

For various reasons, most Shī'ī jurists have not accepted the legal authority of twin concepts of *maqāṣid al-sharī'a* and *maṣlaḥa* since these are considered to be based on practices of the Companions that were not endorsed in the Qur'ān or traditions from the Prophet or Imāms.[25] Other jurists maintain that *maṣlaḥa* cannot be known with certainty based on an inductive reading of the scripture and that since human reason cannot fathom the divine intent, it cannot legislate on behalf of the lawgiver. Discerning and deploying the objectives of the *sharī'a* and the concomitant principle of public good, according to them, is too arbitrary and inductive for a jurist to formulate a response based on his personal assessment of a particular case.[26] For example, Ayatullah Milani (b. 1944), a prominent contemporary scholar in Qum, says that Shī'ī *fuqahā'* (jurists) do not accept *maṣlaḥa* as it is seen as a component of political jurisprudence, which is premised on the interests and needs of the state. Decisions made by reference to *maṣlaḥa* are necessarily based on conjecture, which cannot be relied upon to derive religious ordinances. For him, Shī'ī jurists (*fuqahā'*) do not accept *maṣlaḥa* as it is a law based on the view of the majority.[27]

Some scholars further argue that the analogical deduction founded upon human and divine actions leads to a false notion about God's actions: that they are informed by ends regardless of the means. God does not act in accordance with a good or bad end. God, being omnipotent and omniscient, does not need to evaluate divine acts in terms of their good or bad consequences for humankind. Hence, God is not bound to do the best or the worst for humankind. God simply does what He wishes to do. More pertinently, if one were to believe that God works in the interest of humanity based on public good to protect people from possible harm, the possibility of such speculation and its application in the matter of divine ordinances could lead a jurist to change or commit an error in these ordinances. It is for these reasons that in Shī'ī jurisprudence during the classical age (ninth to eleventh centuries), there is hardly any discussion on this topic. Thus, the *uṣūl* works of prominent Shī'ī figures like Shaykh al-Mufid (d. 1022), Sharif al-Murtada (d. 1044), Muhammad al-Tusi (d. 1067), and 'Allama al-Hilli (d. 1325) have nothing to say about *maqāṣid* or *maṣlaḥa.*

However, some contemporary scholars like Muhammad Taqi al-Hakim (d. 2002) argue that there is nothing to indicate that early Shī'ī jurists completely rejected the idea of seeking what is in the interests of the community. He cautions that the public good principle only applies when one does not have any revelatory proof to establish its validity first.[28] This view is seconded by contemporary Iranian jurist Muhammad Ibrahim al-Jannati who maintains that although *al-maṣālih al-mursala* is admitted as a source of legislation, it cannot be regarded an independent source of law like the Qur'ān or traditions. [29]

Acceptance of Maṣlaḥa *in Shī'īsm*

Contemporary Shī'ī thinkers like Ayatullah Sanei, Shabistari, Kadivar, and Mohagheg Damad believe that the lawgiver has granted recognition to the interests of humanity in the laws of the *sharī'a.* Thus, they rely on the principle of *maṣlaḥa* and other rationally derived rules, such as forestalling harm, when framing new rules to accommodate the needs of a modem society. In their view, the need to respond to people's religious and worldly interests is in accordance with the belief that God's guidance for humanity in Islamic revelation applies to all times and places. This view implies that the laws enacted with regard to the welfare of the community are necessarily mutable. There is an intrinsic relationship between public good and the most effective and just formulation of laws. Thus, certain Islamic legal rulings may change according to the harm or benefit involved.

For instance, Islamic law forbids dismembering a believer's body or removing his/her organs. Thus, any kind of organ transplant is prohibited on religious grounds. However, by invoking the principle of *maṣlaḥa* and contextualizing the reason for its prohibition jurists would be able to override traditions that prohibit organ transplantation on the ground that the benefit accruing from such a procedure to save a life far outweighs that derived by preserving and burying the body in its entirety.

Another example of the acceptance and application of *maṣlaḥa* would be the following. Shī'ī jurists have generally agreed that it is not permissible to work for an unjust ruler. The main reason behind this is not to assist an oppressive or unjust ruler. However, a prominent jurist of the nineteenth century, Shaykh Murtada Ansari (d. 1864), claimed that the theory that justified the permissibility to work for an unjust ruler was *al-qiyām bi-maṣāliḥ al-ʿibād* (undertaking what is in the Muslims' best interests). Ansari quoted an opinion rendered by a sixth/twelfth-century text that read, "Acceptance of an unjust ruler's agency is permitted in [exclusive] occasions where the so called agent would be able restore an entitled individual's violated rights." Ansari then claimed both the consensus of the jurists and the support of the authentication traditions on the validity of such a qualification and argued:

> Prior to invoking such consensus, rational injunctions and reasoning indicate that if the agency of an unjust ruler is prohibited because of its *muḥarramat li-dhātihā* (innate essence), accepting it is [also] permitted. Because there are occasions in which the importance of meeting the best interests and repulsion of detriments outweigh the [subjective status of] being outwardly included among the agents of such ruler.[30]

Ansari also believed that in the interests of Muslims, there are duties whose undertaking does not require permission from the ruler. He argues that the incumbency of certain duties in the realm of the best interests of society is also free from the complexities of juristic debates. [31]

It should also be noted, however, that in the Shīʿī school of law the principles of benefit and harm are determined on the basis of of legal rules (*adilla*) taken from the sacred texts (*nuṣūṣ*). A jurist can decide on the benefit or harm of a rule only when it is rooted in textual sources.[32] Sunnī jurists, on the other hand, have greater scope for determining the purpose of a law; they do not require, as Shīʿī scholars do, that the legal ruling be based on explicit proof in the text. In their view, a jurist can issue a legal ruling regardless of the method used to determine the cause of the ruling and the benefit or harm on which it depends. Thus, they consider methods such as analogy (*qiyās*) and discerning the public interest (*istiṣlāḥ*) as actual sources of law.[33]

After the establishment of the Islamic Republic in Iran, *maṣlaḥa* has found acceptance in some Shīʿī quarters, especially those connected with the government. The discourse on discovering the *ratio-legis* and benefit of a ruling has surfaced in recent times because Iran was confronted with sociopolitical issues that erstwhile Shīʿī jurists did not have to face. Earlier jurists were primarily concerned with guiding people toward moral uprightness and following *sharīʿa* laws in their personal lives rather than with sociopolitical rulings that would lead to the establishment of a just society.

One of the most prominent voices for a revision of traditional *fiqh* (*fiqh-e sunnati*) and an advocate of the principle of *maṣlaḥa* was Ayatullah Khumayni (d. 1989). For Khumayni, the needs of the state and its interests overrode the primary creeds of the *sharī'a*. From 1988 to 1989, he adopted some radical positions on the issues of *maṣlaḥa* and the priority of the interests of the state over even the most fundamental Islamic principles, such as *ḥajj* (pilgrimage to Mecca) and daily prayers. Khumayni not only revived the principle of *maṣlaḥa* but even called for the formation of an expediency council to operate as an arbitration body between the parliament and the guardian council. The new council was called the Council for the Interest of the Islamic Order (*majlis-e takhsis-e maslahat-e nezam-e eslami*). Its mandate was to facilitate the government's implementation of legislation passed by the parliament (*majlis*) without the impediments of the guardian council's oversight.[34]

The commission was entrusted to investigate public welfare to guide policy decisions. Addressing the council, Khumayni stated:

> Honorable gentlemen,
>
> The expediency of the existing order (*maṣlaḥat-e nizām*) is the paramount issue whose neglect may cause the downfall of our precious Islam. Today the world of Islam regards the Islamic Republic of Iran as the best model whereby they may resolve their problems. The expediency of the system is of the highest importance, resisting it may weaken the Islam of the barefooted [wretched] of the earth and will lead to the triumph of American Islam, the Islam of the arrogant and the powerful with the support of the billions of dollars of their domestic and foreign agents [...] The discernment of the *maṣlaḥat* of the system, in my opinion, must be under the supervision of experts who are knowledgeable about specific matters.[35]

Khumayni went further, ruling that all government ordinances are to be classified as part of the primary ordinances and incumbent for all to follow. In other words, state laws were no longer to be treated as secondary ordinances that could be invoked only at times of emergencies or need. In many ways it signaled a revision of the traditional Shī'ī jurisprudence that had only known primary and secondary ordinances. The supreme leader could now legislate Islamic laws and declare them to be legally binding on all believers based on what he deemed to be the interests of the community. The *maṣlaḥa* council could not only override the *sharī'a*, but also suspend it temporarily.[36]

Khumayni also wrote to the council of guardians, advising them on how to overcome many of the issues dealing with governance. He states,

> I subscribe to the widespread *fiqh* that is current amongst the jurists, and the method of *ijtihād* adopted by the late Sahib-i Jawahir (Shaykh Muhammad Hasan Najafi). This type of *fiqh* and *ijtihād* is unavoidable; however, it does not mean that the Islamic *fiqh* is not in need of adapting with the time (*zamān*), rather the factors of time (*zamān*) and place (*makān*) do affect and influence *ijtihād*. Often a situation would have a particular judgment (*ḥukm*) at one time but the same situation on the basis of the fundamental laws that apply on the social, political, and economic spheres would render a different judgment (*ḥukm*).[37]

Khumayni also states that in the interests of the state, it may shut the doors of mosques; it may demolish a mosque or a home tubular road and compensate the owner for his house; the state may unilaterally annul contracts with people if it thinks that the contract threatens the interests of the country and Islam. The state may even temporarily prevent people from going on pilgrimage if it is deemed to be against the interest of the country.[38] By invoking the principle of public interest, any act could be considered necessary for the prevalence of Islam and the implementation of its ordinances. Stated differently, if it is in the interests of the community and to preserve the needs of the state, the government can change any law. Thus, *maslahat-e nezam* or national exigency, is invoked to resolve state-related issues even if they go against traditional *fiqh* rulings. The reasons maybe politically motivated, but to be sure, the ramifications have been felt in Shīʿī jurisprudence.

Other Shīʿī scholars have endorsed not only the need to revise rulings but also to use the principle of *maṣlaḥa*. For example, like Ayatullah Damad and Bojnourdi, Ayatullah Sanei rejects the view that girls attain puberty at the age of nine. He mentions that this age was fixed from Tusi's time onward.[39] Sanei then notes that other scholars, including Tusi, have mentioned ten to be the correct age of puberty. After rejecting the age stipulation, Sanei argues on the basis of hardship and what is in the best interests of the girl. He states that puberty at the age of nine puts a lot of hardship on a girl and that normally, puberty should start when a girl experiences her period, which, depending on various factors, can be at the age of 13. This is in the best interests of the girl since it removes the hardship which an earlier age imposes on her.[40]

Ayatullah Muhammad Husayn Fadlallah (d. 2010) was an important Lebanese cleric who was followed by millions of Shīʿī s throughout the world. He maintains that acts of worship (*'ibādāt*) are constant and are not subject to change. However, he also subscribes to the view that this did not preclude the possibility of understanding the reasons behind the acts. In the realm of human interrelationships, he argues that legal rulings can be modified since it is possible to ascertain the rationale behind a religious ruling by having recourse to the precept's text, contextual evidence or signs, and indications (*qarā'in*).[41]

In Shī'ī legal theory, the principle of *maṣlaḥa* has also been correlated with secondary rulings (*al-aḥkām al-thānawiyya*), those that may be invoked under dire circumstances. This concept has been promoted by many jurists. According to Shaykh Abu al-Qasim 'Ali Doost, a prominent jurist in Qum, secondary rulings can be used to preserve the interests of the people when such a need arises, even if this entails overriding normative laws stated in the classical *fiqh* works. For example, like Bojnourdi, 'Ali Doost states that if a particular form of punishment creates a negative image of Islam, the state can alter that punishment so as to portray a more positive image because this is in the interests of Islam.[42] When two laws conflict, when for example, the laws of privacy conflict with those needed to protect the security of the country, then, 'Ali Doost states that the government has the right to invade and even take over private property. This is called the principle of *aham* and *muhim* (the important and the more important).[43]

Another Iranian jurist, Shaykh Muhammad Jawad Arasta, says that it is essential to discern the objectives of law so as to derive fresh rulings in modern times. Arasta further claims that "there is no proof to substantiate the view that Shī'īs should reject *al-maṣāliḥ al-mursala*. Shī'ī scholars who rejected it in the past did not define or understand the principle correctly."[44] For Arasta, *maṣlaḥa* merely outlines universal *shar'ī* laws, for example, the view that the preservation of life is obligatory. It is up to individual jurists to deploy the principle when the occasion demands it.

However, not all Shī'ī scholars accept the new rulings under the guise of *maṣlaḥa*. Other prominent scholars like Ayatullah Gulpaygani (b.1919) rejected this notion.[45] Jurists like Mohammed Emami Kashani (b.1937), once the Friday Imām (prayer leader) of Tehran, voiced opposition to the principles of *ḍarūra* (necessity) and *maṣlaḥa*, especially when these were seen as opposing the traditional jurisprudential views stated by previous scholars. These would include the state's ability to legislate rulings like labor laws that would be in the state's interests and even revoke a binding contract if it was not in the interests of the state. Jurists were especially perturbed by the powers given to the expediency council. They saw an inherent contradiction between the interests of the state on the one hand and the mandates of Islam on the other.[46] For example Mohammed Yazdi (b.1931), the one-time chief of the judiciary, stated that *maṣlaḥa* means committing acts against the *sharī'a* and against the law in response to necessities of the time.[47]

It was only after the Iranian revolution in 1978–1979 that Shī'ī jurists admitted that the public good principle was an important source for legal-ethical legislation. The relatively late acceptance of *maṣlaḥa* by Shī'ī is because, unlike the Sunnīs, they were a minority and thus did not have to provide practical guidance needed by the government or by the people in everyday dealings.

Maṣlaḥa *and* Maqāṣid *in the View of Two Recent Shī'ī Scholars*

The renewed interest in *maqāṣid* and *maṣlaḥa* among Shī'ī scholars is also seen in the views of two prominent Shī'ī jurists: Ayatullah Mahdi Shams al-Din (d. 2001) and Ayatullah Fadlallah. Mahdi Shams al-Din complains that the social-political dimension of Islamic jurisprudence has not been as emphasized as it should be. This is partly because, due to unfavorable political circumstances, Shī'ī jurists have, in the past, withdrawn themselves from sociopolitical affairs so much so that *fiqh* has been separated from society. Consequently, they have not contributed to the evolution of political and social jurisprudence. Jurists have, instead, immersed themselves in personal issues such as prayers and fasting.[48] He claims that this is a greater problem for Shī'ī scholars than Sunnī jurists since the latter were politically engaged and have developed legal mechanisms and antecedents to assist them in this process. As a result, Shams al-Din argues further that a cleavage had occurred in Shī'ī jurisprudence between the understanding of the law (including its derivation and the processes—*manāhij*) and the *wāqi'* (actual situation). For Shams al-Din, due to the corruption affecting Muslim societies and politics, Shī'ī law has focused primarily on issues affecting the hereafter (*al-mashrū'al-ukhrawi*) and questions of personal salvation. Mahdi Shams al-Din further emphasizes that a jurisprudence that impacts the society in general and people at a personal level is required.[49] In his exposition, he also lays out the principles of *'usr* (hardship) *and al-haraj* (difficulties), which cannot be limited or specified since they are absolute general principles that cannot be revoked.

Sunnī jurists have collectively affirmed that the *aḥkam* (rulings) follow the general principles of *maṣāliḥ* and *mafāsid*—those that promote welfare and prevent corruption in society. The *sharī'a* is concerned with these two key objectives.[50] Shī'ī jurists follow a similar trajectory, but they emphasize that such principles are subject to ethical constructs such as the goodness of an act in itself (*ka-ḥusna al-ḥusn*) or the repulsiveness of oppression (*qubḥ al-ẓulm*). Shams al-Din cites smoking, agriculture, commerce (*tiJara*), or medicine as examples of societal matters whose rulings must be premised on *maṣāliḥ* and *mafāsid*.[51]

These juristic mechanisms—*ka-ḥusna al-ḥusn and qubḥ al-ẓulm*—show that, from the very early period, Shīʿī jurisprudence saw *maṣāliḥ* to be a key component of the objective of the law and the mission of the Prophet. Shams al-Din vehemently argues that the principles of *maṣāliḥ* and *mafāsid* are directly connected to human life and society and that they are applicable to individuals. He also raises the issue of "the wisdom behind the *ḥukm*" as part of the *maqāṣid*. He asks as to how the wisdom of a ruling can be determined and understood. He argues that "wisdom or *ḥikma*" is not an evidentiary tool in the derivation of Islamic law from its sources. Why is this so? Like other Shīʿī scholars, he argues that wisdom is not something consistently understood or a constant, that is, we are not always able to discern the *ḥikma* behind a ruling. Therefore, if the sources do not tell us what the operative wisdom is, can we then derive it on our own? The answer is no, because Shams al-Din distinguishes between two types of *ʿilal-al-ʿilla al mustanbiṭa* (a derived cause which involves the process of *qiyās*) and *al-ʿilla al-manṣūṣa* (a cause that is found in textual sources). He further states that when dealing with the *maqāṣid*, a scholar must be careful not to stray from the textual sources of Islamic law.[52] He bemoans the atomistic nature of Shīʿī law that has been designed by jurists for individuals rather than for communities (*dīn al-afrād wa laysa dīn al-jamāʿa*). According to him, we need a *fiqh* that is connected to the surroundings (*fiqh al-bīʿa*) and whose laws should be derived with social, political, economic, and medical benefits in mind. Furthermore when a *fiqh* is formulated without a clear context or a site of application in mind it becomes *al-tajrīd al-naẓari* (abstract thinking) and the context and place of application is lost. In other words, jurisprudence becomes overly cerebral. Thus, Shams al-Din argues, *fiqh* must be contextual—and its derivation must involve a clear awareness of its application. This approach involves interacting with the spirit of the Qurʾān and the Sunna. It is a problem that plagues contemporary *fiqh* and the *fuqahāʾ*.[53]

He then clearly lays out the problems in the contemporary method of derivation (*istinbāṭ*): The study of *fiqh* is done in an atomistic fashion (*al-fardiyya al-tajziʾiyya*). Juridical discourse is directed at individuals and in doing so jurists lose sight of the message directed to the *umma*. They express the *sharīʿa* in terms of the hereafter, that is, with a focus on the next world. The process of deriving the law is disconnected from the realization of its changing context, that is, where and for whom it will be implemented, and thus it does not interact with *ṭabīʿa* (what is "normal" and what peopled are accustomed to). Observing the *maqāṣid* of the *sharīʿa* is absent in many parts of jurisprudence. Thus, the process of *istinbāṭ* itself does not take into account the broader picture of the public good.[54]

For Shams al-din the process of deriving laws should not be restricted to the derivation of rulings from texts. On the contrary, there must be an understanding of the *wāqi* (actual situation) and a contemplation over it (*tadabaruhu*). This contemplation involves being aware of the relationship between the context and the text and the context and the issues that matter in people's lives. *Ijtihād* will not be proper without contemplating and grappling this contextual relationship.[55] He emphasizes that a jurist must have an overall vision of the law (*al-ru'ya al-kulliyya lil-sharī'a*). He mentions again that the *sharī'a* operates as a complete, integrated structure: it connects various domains such as family life, economics, purity, impurity, and so on, and each system connects to another. The systems are all akin to interconnected bodies. The *mu'āmalāt and 'ibādāt* do not differ in this regard. He goes on to cite more examples of areas in which jurists must develop further understanding and provide contextual *fatāwā*: price fixing, monopolization, or capitalism (*al-iḥtikār*).[56]

To give further credence to his views on *maṣlaḥa*, Shams al-Din then cites from al-Sayyid al-Murtada's *al-Dharī'a*: "Know that the act of worship according to divine legislations follows the *maṣāliḥ* and the legislations are [based on] goodness and grace and *maṣāliḥ*. This is because the Prophet was sent to make us aware of that which is related to our welfare." He further quotes al-Murtada as stating: "Surely the *'ilal* (causes) of the law (*al-shar'*) are separate from the causes of the intellect (*'ilal al-'aql*) because the effective causes of the law follow what is required and [what is conducive to] the welfare [of the people]. The same cannot be stated of that which is based on the reasoning of the intellect (that is *'ilal* based on reason)."[57]

Like Shams al-Din, Ayatullah Fadlallah complains that Shī'ī *fiqh* has focused on personal rather than on social issues. He states that "our works of jurisprudence from the beginning century of compilation, have followed an imitative style insofar as they emphasize individual and particular issues that impact people. They do not follow the method of emphasizing general principles which the law has ruled regarding society except for a few instances."[58] This, in part, is due to the fact that it is largely reliant on the genre of traditions narrated and handed down from the Imāms. These traditions consist primarily of companions asking the Imāms questions pertaining to personal issues. This tendency to focus on the *juz'iyya* (particulars) is because these are areas that impact people most in their lives, that is, the particulars of *fiqh* and its application to specific circumstances of their lives.[59] Another question posed to Fadlallah deals more directly with the *sharī'a* and its overall objectives in deriving the law (*maqāṣid al-kulliyya fī istinbāṭ*). The questioner states that the study of the texts is myopic, at the expense of the broader objectives. Fadlallah is asked, how can a jurist balance a *ḥadīth* that discourages marriage with certain groups of people like Negroes and Kurds keeping in mind the spirit of the *sharī'a*?

He responds that scholars must distinguish between the *ḥarfī* (literal-linguistic approach) and the *'urfī* (customary) understanding of the law. Jurists have not emphasized the latter. He discusses the principle of comparing traditions to the Qur'ān and specifically how scholars may interpret traditions indicating *kirāha* (detesting) in marrying Kurds and Negroes while the Qur'ān clearly states "And We have honoured the children of Adam (17:70)." If a jurist approaches this position from a literalist perspective he would say that the tradition restricts (*takhṣīṣ*) the verse and thus the verse is not applicable to everyone. However, in Fadlallah's view, by approaching it from the *'urfī* perspective one is able to determine that this verse can be used as a principle, thus, any *fatwa* or *ḥadīth* indicating that a certain group of people are inherently deficient would be tantamount to it being against the spirit of the law (*mukhālafan li-rūḥ al-sharī'a*). Fadlallah takes 17:70 to be indicative of the spirit of the *sharī'a* and hence he uses it as an important litmus test in matters of racial-ethnic bias.[60]

Fadlallah's concern in applying the principles of *maqāṣid* and *maṣlaḥa* is evident in another question. He is asked his view regarding the current status of Islamic marital laws and their apparent inequities. For example, if a husband is absent for more than four months due to work and during that time he marries another wife abroad and continues to send financial support to his first wife, it would seem that his first wife has no choice but to stay married to him despite her displeasure. How do the *fatāwā* that allow such behavior accord with the Qur'ānic demand that a husband either live with his wife in accordance with customary norms (*ma'rūf*) or leave her based on *ma'rūf*? He states that there is no doubt that these rulings need to be revised and require further investigation. For instance, a woman's desire (*shahwa*) is greater than that of a man. However, every situation must be examined separately, and patience is needed on both sides. Nevertheless, cases such as these can be solved by recourse to *qā'ida nafī al-haraj* (the principle that averts harm). He then cites 2:185, "Live with them in a kind manner (*bi l-ma'rīf*)." *Ma'rūf* must be understood in its *'urfī* form and thus it must act as a guiding principle over these rulings. In other words, Fadlallah appeals to the common sense and the spirit of the law that states that a marriage must be based upon a common understanding of decency and kindness. Thus, the problem lies with a vast array of jurists who examine texts in an atomistic rather than an *'urfī* manner. This is because their method is imitative (*taqlīdī*) and follows previous interpretations of the *nuṣūṣ*. In many instances, it is the *'urf* that can best determine the normative standards and what is in the best interests of society.[61]

Customary Law and Maṣlaḥa

An important tool that can be utilized in the application of the principle of *maṣlaḥa* is that of the "custom of reasonable persons" (*sīra al-'uqalā'iyya*). The term refers to that which is customarily perceived as reasonable—which is agreed upon by those possessed of reason. *Al-Sīra al-'uqalā'iyya* replaces the need for a written text and becomes a "binding *sunna*" for the community. Although no reported text is essential for the *sīra*, the practice of reasonable people is sufficient proof for a jurist to rule that the lawgiver approbated the practice. It is assumed that all reasonable beings accept and behave according to common norms and values based on a common understanding of right and wrong in the collective interests (*maṣlaḥa*) of society. This being the case, a particular principle can be established by arguing that the pattern of behavior was common to all rational beings, whether they lived in the times of the Imāms or not, and that no objection had been raised by the lawgiver.[62] *Al-Sīra al-'uqalā'iyya* is connected to *maṣlaḥa* because it is assumed that reasonable people will act based on the benefit that accrues to them and harm that is averted.

The source of legal norms for policy matters such as contracts of purchase, rental, and sale, discharge of debts, inheritance, compromise between debtor and creditor (*sulḥ*), limited partnership (*mudaraba*), and so on is based primarily on the custom of reasonable persons. Thus, legal rulings may change according to the harm or benefit involved. The desire to maximize benefit when issuing legal opinions affects the evolution of the legal system.

Maṣlaḥa *and Civil Rules*

The concept of *maṣlaḥa* also plays an important role in legislating civil rules (*al-aḥkām al-wilāyatiyya*). It is to be noted that rulings in Islamic jurisprudence are generally divided into two general categories. The first category consists of fixed rules (*al-aḥkām al-thābita*) that do not change with time and place and are not determined by the government. These are related primarily to matters pertaining to individual worship (prayers, fasting, pilgrimage, etc.). The second category consists of legal rules that are subject to change. These rules depend on some underlying premise ("primary principle"); for instance, rules relating to private property depend on the underlying premise of the right to control one's own wealth. In this example, the principle is expressed in the legal maxim *al-nās muṣallaṭūn 'alā amwālihim* (people have sole authority over their property). The exact determination of rules in this category, in contrast to the first, is left to the discretion of the government, which may either extend or limit them in accordance with the social benefit or harm involved.

As previously noted, if the government deemed that a property entailed some harm to others, those rights could be curtailed, in accordance with the maxim "*lā ḍarar*" no harm [to other parties should result from a ruling]. Another example is the imposition of taxes; in this instance, the ruler or judge might decide that failure to pay taxes causes harm to society, so that payment would become obligatory in order to remove that harm.[63]

Shī'ī scholars cite many other examples of *maṣlaḥa* based on the principles of increasing benefit and reducing harm. For example, if some Muslims were taken prisoners of war and used as human shields, then, are Muslim soldiers allowed to kill innocent Muslims knowing that failure to kill them would enable the enemy to use them and to endanger the entire Muslim village or neighborhood? In such a scenario, Muslim jurists have ruled that it is allowed to kill innocent Muslims for a greater good, that is, to save an entire village or city of Muslims from destruction and from coming to harm.[64]

Shī'ī scholars have argued that there is a need to expand the scope of their juristic vision and revisit some of the earlier rulings based on the need of the times and interests of the community. As the sociopolitical situations change, juridical rulings issued must reflect the newer circumstances. According to the contemporary jurist Ayatullah Mohagheg Damad, since civil rules are variable, Islamic laws must change accordingly. Thus, in our own times, Islamic legal rulings must be reinterpreted based on the principle of harm and benefits and other principles established in *uṣūl al-fiqh*. Stated differently, there is a need to enact laws that are conducive to the welfare of the community even though such laws are not found in earlier texts. Due to such principles, Islamic sacred texts have to be read in different ways.

As an example of the possible reinterpretation of the law, Mohagheg Damad states that in the Qur'ān we encounter the phrase addressed to men concerning their marital life: "Live with them in accordance with that which is recognized as good (*al-ma'rūf*)" (4:19). The Qur'ān indicates that cohabitation in what is perceived as "good" is the foundation of Islamic family law and the foundation of individual laws pertaining to the rights of married women. In the past, when social and economic lives were very different and women were confined to their homes without economic responsibility or the need to earn a living, this Qur'ānic phrase had a particular meaning. Damad asks, "Does cohabitation in accordance with that which is recognized as good have the same connotation today?" In the past, maintenance (*nafaqa*) that was payable to the wife if she was divorced was calculated by jurists at a very low rate. This rate is contingent on the needs of the time.[65]

Mohagheg Damad continues, "If, for instance, one of the Imāms had been asked a thousand years ago about the maintenance due to a woman after divorce, he might have mentioned clothes, dwelling, or food, basing that on the standard of living at that time." Maintenance consisted of something like the fixed payment mentioned earlier. Neither the education of women nor their means of transportation was as important as it is today. Thus, maintenance is an external and not an objective standard. However, "marriage in accordance with that which is recognized as good" is a general legal rule (*ḥukm*) of the *sharīʿa*, and since "times always change and social and economic conditions evolve, the Qur'ān here lays down a standard whose criteria are subject to change."[66] Stated differently, the maintenance of divorced woman must now not only include food and shelter, but also award the wife back pay for housework she has done and other benefits that she had to forgo so as to look after the children. In addition, due to the different roles of women today, the costs of transportation and education must also be taken into account.

Mohagheg Damad further argues that what were once private rights have now become of general or public relevance. Until recently, the concept of labor relations was unknown and the relationship between an employer and employee was conducted entirely on the basis of a contract of hire. That is, a contract was concluded strictly on the basis of hire of labor for wages, with no government oversight. Now, however, the private rights of employer and employee have become public rights. Government intervention has now resulted in labor laws limiting the freedom of both parties. The rationale is that if a worker is allowed to enter into a contract as an agent, he is liable to get himself into a situation in which he eventually becomes disabled and possibly a burden on society. Thus, in the interests of the community, the head of society can intervene and limit the freedom of the parties to conclude a contract. The *maṣlaḥa* of the community dictate that what was at one time considered a private transaction between an employer and employee becomes a public right for all in the civil service.[67]

Conclusion

For a long period, Shīʿī jurists confined their discourse to the text of the revelatory sources and, consequently, did not derive general principles that could be invoked for a variety of other situations by taking into account such factors as contextual indication and any change of circumstances that would have an impact upon defining the subject. To be sure, there is hardly any detailed analysis in the Islamic legal literature of the principles of *ijtihād* or *maṣlaḥa* with regard to newer issues. There is a dearth of analysis of the objectives of *sharī'a* rulings or how jurists arrive at their rulings. This is probably due to the fact that historically, Shī'ī jurists were not required to rule on political *maṣlaḥa* since they were not involved in the political process or decision making of the state.

What constitutes a radical departure in Twelver Shī'ī legal theory is the insistence of contemporary reformers that the litmus test for the validity of the *ḥadīth* reports is Qur'ānic core values and human reason (*'aql*). Any *ḥadīth* citation, no matter how strong its chain of transmission, cannot be accepted as valid if it does not comport with the Qur'ān and the human faculty of reason. Moreover, according to Sanei, a God that categorically denounces and distances himself from injustice and assures His creatures that they need not fear an iota of injustice from Him cannot possibly decree laws that betray his promise.[68]

In the works of contemporary reformists like Ayatollahs Khumayni, Fadlallah, Sanei, and Mohagheg Damad, there is a major epistemological shift in the Twelver Shī'ī legal theory by privileging the Qur'ān, empowering reason as a legitimate source to discover the rationale or *ratio legis* of a legal directive and mindful that legal rulings were issued in a particular context of time (*zamān*) and space (*makān*) and, as such, lack universal applicability for all times and places. Also the jurists are concerned with the objective of a ruling and what is conducive to the welfare of the community or needs of the state. The relationship between ethics and law along with distinguishing features between verses that are of universal and particular import, and taking into account present-day context and circumstances are important hermeneutic devices that are employed by jurists to challenge and revise erstwhile legal rulings.

The reforms that have been discussed in this chapter are important in conveying the view that far from being a static and rigid tradition, there is much discourse within the Muslim community and that the community is attempting to distance itself from the extremist and even archaic articulation of Islam. It is only through such self-critique and an admission of past failings that reformation can generate a fresh understanding of Islamic revelation and Prophetic practices.

Notes

1. The term *marāji'* refers to the most learned juridical authority in the Shī'ī community whose rulings on Islamic law are followed by those who acknowledge him as their source of reference or *marji'*.

2. Yusuf Sanei, *Berabari-ye diyah* (Qum: Mu'assasah-ye farhangi-ye fiqh-e thaqalayn, 2005), 9–12.
3. See Mustafa Ashrafi Shahrudi, "Hamsuy-e fiqh ba tahavvulat va Niyazhay-e Jami-e," in *Ijtihād va Zaman va Makan*, 14 vols. (Qum: Mu'assi Chap va Nashr Uruj, 1995), vol. 1, 119.
4. *Ijtihād* is defined as a jurist's exertion of his mental faculties to arrive at an absolute proof based on the interpretation and application of the authoritative sources of Islamic law: the Qur'ān, the Sunna (Traditions of the Prophet and, in the Shi'i case, Imams), and *ijmā'* (consensus of the scholars). The purpose of the exercise is to arrive at a legal injunction that reflects God's will.
5. The discussion is based on an e-mail received. The lectures of Imam Khumayni were translated by al-Sayyid Muhammad al-Hijazi.
6. Hamid Dabashi, *Theology of Discontent: The Ideological Foundation of the Islamic Revolution in Iran* (London: New York Press, 1993), 164.
7. Sanei, *Berabari-ye diyah*, 9–12.
8. Ibid.
9. Abdokarim Soroush, *Qabz wa bast-e ti'urik-e shari'at: Nazariyyah-ye takamul-e ma'rifat-e dini* (Tehran: Mu'assasah-ye farhangi-ye sirat, 1996).
10. Based on an e-mail I received.
11. Ibid.
12. Ibid.
13. Ayatullah Muhaghegh-Damad, "The Role of Time and Social Welfare in the Modification of Legal Rulings," in *Shi'ite Heritage: Essays on Classical and Modern Traditions*, ed. Lynda Clarke (Binghamton: Global, 2001), 219.
14. Ibid. Ayatullah Bojnourdi also rules along similar lines. See Liyakat Takim, "*Ijtihād* and the Derivation of New Jurisprudence in Contemporary Shī'īsm: The Rulings of Ayatollah Bujnurdi," in *Alternative Islamic Discourses and Religious Authority*, ed. Carool Kersten and Susanna Olsson (Farnham, Ashgate, 2013), 17–34.
15. Ziba Mir-Hosseini, *Islam and Gender: The Religious Debate in Modern Iran* (Princeton, NJ: Princeton University Press, 199), 160.
16. Ibid., 162.
17. Ibid., 165
18. Abd al-Hadi al-Fadhli, *al-Taqlid wa'l ijtihād: Dirasatu'l Fiqhiyya Li-Dhahirati al-Taqlid wa'l ijtihād al-Shari'iyin* (Beirut: Makaz al-Ghadir, 2007), 267–269 quoting Makarim Shirazi, *Anwar al-Usul*, 3:632–668.
19. For a Shi'i critique of *al-maṣāliḥ al-mursala*, see Mustafa Ashrafi Shahrudi, "Hamsuy-e fiqh ba tahavvulat va Niyazhay-e Jami-e," in Ijtihād va Zamān va Makān, 14 vols. (Qum: Mu'assi Chap v Nashr Uruj, 1995), vol. 1, 142–143.
20. Abdulaziz Sachedina, *Islamic Biomedical Ethics: Principles and Applications* (Oxford: Oxford University Press, 2009), 49.
21. Ayatullah Muhammad Mujtahid Shabistari, "Religion, Reason and the New Theology," in *Shi'ite Heritage: Essays on Classical and Modern Traditions*, ed. Lynda Clarke (Binghamton: Global, 2001), 249.

22. Muhammad Qasim Zaman, *The 'Ulama' in Contemporary Islam: Custodians of Change* (Princeton, NJ: Princeton University Press, 2002), 186.
23. See Liyakat Takim, "Revivalism or Reformation: The Reinterpretation of Islamic Law in Modern Times," *American Journal of Islamic Social Sciences*, 25:3 (2008), 61–81.
24. Sachedina, *Islamic Biomedical Ethics*, 49.
25. For a Shi'i understanding of *al-maṣāliḥ al-mursala*, see Ja'far al-Subhani, *Maṣādir al-Fiqh al-Islāmī wa Manābiuhu* (Qum: Mu'assasat al-Imām al-Ṣādiq, 2007), 296–297.
26. See, for example, Ja'far ibn Yahya ibn al-Hasan Muhaqqiq al-Hilli, *Ma'ārij al-Uṣūl* (Qum: Sayyid al-Shuhadā', 1983), 221–223.
27. This observation is based on my conversations with him in August 2011.
28. Muhammad Taqi al-Hakim, *al-Uṣūl al-'Āmma lil Fiqh al-Muqāran* (Beirut: al-Dār Andalus, 1983), 386.
29. See Muhammad Ibrahim Jannati, *Manabi Ijtihād dar didgah-e Madhāhib-e Islāmī* (Tehran: Intishārāti Kayhan, 1991), 336.
30. See Murtada Ansari, *Kitāb al-Makāsib*, 2, 72. Also quoted in Amirhassan Boozari, *Shi'i Jurisprudence and Constitution* (New York: Palgrave Macmillan, 2011), 66.
31. Boozari, *Shi'i Jurisprudence*, 67.
32. Ayatullah Muhaghegh-Damad, "The Role of Time and Social Welfare," 215.
33. Ibid.
34. Behrooz Ghamari-Tabrizi, *Islam and Dissent in Post-Revolutionary Iran* (London: I. B. Tauris, 2008), 86.
35. As quoted in ibid., 146.
36. See Hashemi, *Hoquq-e Asasi-ye Jomhuri-ye Eslami-ye- Iran* (Qum, 1996/1375), 1:211, 213. See also, Said Amir Arjomand, "Authority in Shiism and Constitutional Developments in the Islamic Republic of Iran," in *The Twelver Shi'a in Modern Times*, ed. Rainer Brunner and Werner Ende (Leiden: Brill, 2001), 319.
37. Ayatollah Khumayni, *Sahifehy-i nur* (Tehran: Sazman-i madarik-i farhanghi-ye inqilab-i Islami, 1990), 21–98.
38. Muhammad Jawad Arasta, *Tashkhīs Masleḥa Nizām: Azdidghahe fiqhi-Ḥuqūqi* (Tehran: Intisharat Kanun Andisheh Jawan, 2009), 105.
39. Ayatullah Yusuf Sanei, *Bulūgh al-Banāt* (Qum: Mua'ssis Farhabg-i fiqh al-Thaqalayn, 2003), 28.
40. Ibid., 35–36.
41. Muhammad al-Husayni, ed., *al-Ijtihād wa al-Ḥayāt* (Lebanon: Markaz al-Ghadīr lil-Dirāsat al-Islāmiyya, 1998), 44–45.
42. Based on a personal discussion with him in Qum, September 2011.
43. Abu'l Qasim' Ali Doost, *Fiqh va Maslahat* (Qum: Sazman-i Intisharat Pejushghah Farhang, 2000), 397.
44. Muhammad Jawad Arasta, *Tashkhīs Masleḥa*, 121–122.
45. Behrooz Ghamari-Tabrizi, *Islam and Dissent*, 86–87.

46. Ibid., 153.
47. Ibid.
48. 'Abd al-Jabbar al-Rifa'I, ed., *Maqāṣid al-Sharī'a: Taḥrīr wa Ḥiwār* (Beirut: Dār al-Fikr al-Mu'āṣir, 2002), 17. This work is a collection of interviews and excerpts of writings of a number of scholars regarding *maqāṣid al-shar'īyya*. I am grateful to my research assistant, Vinay Khetia, for sharing his research on this section with me.
49. Ibid., 18.
50. Ibid., 19.
51. Ibid.
52. Ibid., 23.
53. Ibid., 24.
54. Ibid., 23–24.
55. Ibid., 25.
56. Ibid., 27.
57. As cited in ibid., 21. Sharif al-Murtada was one of the foremost Shi'i scholars in the ninth and tenth centuries. Known for his penchant for rationalism, he compiled a number of Shi'i works on theology, jurisprudence, and legal theory.
58. Ibid., 47.
59. Ibid., 46.
60. Ibid., 49–50.
61. Ibid., 60.
62. On this see Liyakat Takim, *The Heirs of the Prophet: Charisma and Religious Authority in Shi'ite Islam* (Albany: State University of New York, 2006), 132–134.
63. Ayatullah Muhaghegh-Damad, "The Role of Time and Social Welfare," 215–216.
64. See Ja'far al-Subhani, *Maṣādir al-Fiqh al-Islāmī*, 297.
65. Ayatullah Muhaghegh-Damad, "The Role of Time and Social Welfare," 218–219.
66. Ibid., 219.
67. Ibid., 220.
68. Ibid., 87.

CHAPTER 5

Maqāṣid or *Sharīʿa*? Secularism, Islamic Reform, and Ethics in Modern Turkey

Aydogan Kars

This chapter elaborates on the role of the *maqāṣid al-sharīʿa* [the higher objectives of Islamic law] in the Islamic reform discussions and movements in modern Turkey. Considering the sustained importance and the pivotal role of the discourse in other Muslim contexts analyzed in this book, I will argue that the Turkish literature on the *maqāṣid al-sharīʿa* appears relatively recent, abstract, academic, and, more significantly, antireformist. This stands in stark contrast to the conventional employment of the *maqāṣid al-sharīʿa* in the service of reform. In the last hundred years or so, the *maqāṣid al-sharīʿa* discourse, however differently understood and conceptualized, was more frequently voiced by a number of different actors as a venue for change rather than what we term "modern reformist projects." Unlike the accepted traditional concepts of "renewal" and "revival" [*tajdīd* and *iṣlāḥ*], reformist projects were viewed as proposals disconnected from and directly attacking the rich traditional legal heritage. In the same vein, a distinguishing feature of one of the most prevalent approaches to the *maqāṣid* discourse in Turkey today is its self-depiction as the authentic conservative voice of the tradition against reformist proposals, and its deep critique of the idea of "reform," understood literally as reshaping religion by declaring the classical Islamic legal heritage as redundant if not an obstacle for meaningful reform. Understanding the specific, local history of *maqāṣid al-sharīʿa* in Turkey involves deconstructing the given meta-narratives and revisiting the seemingly "universal" umbrella concepts such as "reform," "*sharīʿa*," and "Islam," which are usually employed in an uncritical manner. This chapter introduces different and often incompatible conceptions of these terms to explain the intellectual landscapes wherein the contemporary *maqāṣid al-sharīʿa* discussions take place. Insofar as there are many Islams, *sharīʿa*s, approaches to the purposes of law and to the idea of "reform," the implications of the discussions on the *maqāṣid al-sharīʿa* discourse in Turkey are fascinatingly fertile.

Modern Landscapes and the Agents of the Maqāṣid al-Sharīʿa *Debates*

With the exception of few individual efforts, a self-conscious *maqāṣid al-sharīʿa* discourse in Turkey flourished only after the 1950s in the hands of religious scholars and academicians who were born into the secularist-nationalist ideology. The paradigmatic social, legal, and political transformations of the Ottoman Empire (r. 1298–1923), and even of the Republic of Turkey itself, had been mostly completed when this discourse emerged. The primary reasons for the paucity of the legalistic approach to *maqāṣid al-sharīʿa* in this process were (1) the prominence of nonlegal, especially spiritual, conceptions of the purpose of Islam and divine wisdom, (2) the presence and effective employment of alternative legal juristic tools, (3) the emergence of Islamic reform from the discretional legislative power of the ruling elite and its relatively secular space in the hands of the state authority that is practically less reliant on religious discourses to exert power. Firmly grounded on a sustained state theory that gave the agents of reform the powers to intervene and supervise the religious system, and a perennial popular emphasis on the reality of and the wisdom behind the religion more than on its "shell," the *sharīʿa*, it became possible to secularize and modernize the entire political and legal system without addressing the internal legal reformist tools. Instead, the reforms of the late Ottoman Empire were accompanied by a gradual divorce of ethics and law, which created three different conceptions of *sharīʿa*: (1) an ethico-legal conception of the *sharīʿa* that is inseparable from Islam, which is still the prevalent view; (2) *sharīʿa* as an exclusively legal system disconnected from modern times; and (3) *sharīʿa* as an exclusively ethical code redundant to Islam. It is these three conceptualizations of *sharīʿa* that define the rhetorical field wherein the *maqāṣid al-sharīʿa* discourses in Turkey are taking place.

The debates revolving around Islam in contemporary Turkey contain many actors from different ethnic, sectarian, and political groups. These include various Sunni groups and movements (such as various Nurcu groups, most reputably the Gülen movement); Sufi groups, most prominently Naqshbandis who have had followers among noticeable politicians; the Alevis, the estimated number of which is about 15–20 million (15 percent to 25 percent of the entire population); and who have no homogeneous structure or an official mouthpiece; the state Islam officially represented by the Presidency of Religious Affairs [*Diyanet İşleri Başkanlığı*] (PRA) founded in 1924; some individual columnists and lawyers from diverse camps who appear in the media as experts; and an amorphous group of a few thousand academicians employed in the universities, mainly in the divinity faculties. Within the rich spectrum of approaches to Islam in Turkey, however, it has been difficult to write on a key tool of Islamic reform, the *maqāṣid al-sharīʿa*, primarily because of what the word "*sharīʿa*" entails and its sociopolitical connotations in the context of contemporary Turkey. *Sharīʿa*-talk, that is, employing the concept of *sharīʿa* to develop an Islamic discourse in the public space,not only has legal barriers but also is seen by the general Turkish public as an engagement in a retrograde and antisecular political ideology. Many Muslims in Turkey see *sharīʿa* as an unchanging set of legal rulings associated with the premodern Islamic history. *Sharīʿa*, understood as a premodern religion-based legal system, is considered by the official institutions and some Turkish citizens to be inherently against the current legal-political secular ideology that is premised on a legal distinction between the religious and political realms, and is thus officially banned in Turkey. These conceptualizations of *sharīʿa* that reduce it to positive law are problematic because they miss the key, maybe even the existential significance of the term, for many Muslims in Turkey who see "Islam" and "*sharīʿa*" as interchangeable concepts. Respecting the *sharīʿa* as the ultimate guide to life, however, maybe the most common but still is only one interpretation of this polyvalent term. The Turkish society harbors many citizens who explicitly scream "damn the *sharīʿa*" ["*kahrolsun şeriat*"] and still see being Muslim as their primary identity, or at least an important part of their identity. In fact, the more the secularist ideology became transparent especially after the 1950s, the more the legal discursive space opened up for alternative perspectives toward the relationship between secularism and Islam. Still, the vast majority of the population and intellectuals is generally content with the secular constitutional democratic structure of the state. This view is confirmed by empirical studies that show that fewer and fewer people (less than 9 percent of the population with a decreasing ratio) prefer to live in a state governed by *sharīʿa*.[1]

More strikingly, a demand for a politico-legal system that explicitly refers to religion and violates the current secular ideology is seen generally as an attack launched not only on the secular democratic system, but also on *Islam* itself. "Islam," as a category distinct from "*sharī'a*," is understood by the vast majority of the citizens in terms of the "bonding" (identity-based and moral) instead of the "binding" (legal and mandatory) aspects of faith.[2] Importantly, this "bonding" aspect is constantly emphasized by academicians, politicians, religious leaders, and state-based agents of Islam in Turkey. The PRA declarations are the most vivid example of this emphasis. The PRA issues opinion declarations and responds to individual questions via a well-established online system. These responses have no binding status and are always presented as scholarly suggestions and answers based on recommended ethical religious maxims. These values and practices associated with Islam constitute a major source of solidarity in Turkey.[3]

The strong emphasis on being a Muslim (as opposed to the "Islamist" or the "*sharī'a*-ist" [*şeriatçı*]) and the retreat of *sharī'a*-talk are best understood by the long-established ethicalization of Islam throughout the history of Turkey. The agents of this ethicalized approach to *sharī'a*-talk focus more on what can variously be described as the purposes, the "core," "the essence," and "higher objectives" of Islam and less on the positive law-based concept of *sharī'a*.[4] This understanding of Islam, freed from legalistic *sharī'a* refers mainly to ethical maxims and practices related to attain them. According to this view, which is propagated by the state, the majority of the divinity faculty members, various Sufi groups, other Sunni movements, and the Alevis, the main purpose of Islam is the creation of a moral individual and society. It is about human dignity, feeding the poor, showing mercy to others, purifying the soul, and preparing oneself for death and the Day of Judgment.[5] This ethicalized, distinctly nonlegal understanding of Islam is so widespread and well rooted among the majority of religious actors and general population in Turkey that it has striking and immediate consequences for a reformist *maqāṣid al-sharī'a* discourse. The abundant references to the ethical "core," "purpose," or "spirit" of Islam is pivotal to contemporary conceptions of the *maqāṣid al-sharī'a* in modern Turkey. As Weiss points out, the "spirit of law" in the Western sense is more or less the equivalent to what "*maqāṣid al-sharī'a*" means.[6] If there is a popular religious *maqāṣid* discourse, it is evident that at least for many Muslims in contemporary Turkey this discourse refers to an ethicalized Islam with tenuous relationship to, if not a clear separation from, what we could term the "legalistic *sharī'a*." In other words, a prominent contemporary conception of *maqāṣid* in Turkey is *sharī'a* free and secular in legal terms. Islamist countries are criticized to have "*sharī'a* without Islam, since they do not truly understand *the purpose of Islam*."[7] Moreover, legalistic *sharī'a*'s employment in politics, the presentation of Islam as a legal-cum-political ideology, or its mingling with the daily, profane transactions and politics are generally seen as disrespect toward its sacredness and higher purposes.

Based on these diverse conceptions of both *maqāṣid* and *sharīʿa*, I will classify the contemporary *maqāṣid al-sharīʿa* discourses in Turkey under four categories. The first group of columnists, theologians, and academics will be broadly defined as the "traditionalists" or "renewalists" interchangeably, insofar as they define *sharīʿa* as a comprehensive ethical-cum-legal flexible worldview that is capable of renewing itself with its authentic tools, one of which is the *maqāṣid al-sharīʿa*. Thus, it considers itself a part of the long-established renewalist scholarship that existed in classical Islam too. Secularism has a variety of depictions from the traditionalist standpoints ranging from "becoming this-worldly" [*verweltlichung*] to a "lack in religiosity," "pseudo-religion," or even "antireligion." For all of these different and even conflicting standpoints toward secularism, the idea of "*re*-form," understood literally, will represent a radical break from and an attack on traditional Islam advocated by renewalists. The second group is composed of the contemporary academicians who are publishing scholarly books and articles in Turkish devoted to the *maqāṣid al-sharīʿa*. These academic experts distance themselves from popular "reform versus renewal" discussions and controversial debates on various issues pertaining to religion, but produce a highly specialized academic knowledge for readers well versed in classical Islamic jurisprudence [*fiqh*]. A closer analysis of their conceptions of *sharīʿa* and reform will inform us that this dimension of academic *maqāṣid* scholarship aligns itself with the classical framing of the *maqāṣid al-sharīʿa*, divorces itself from the idea of reform, and envisages the *maqāṣid al-sharīʿa* as the embodiment of the continuous, flexible legal tradition as advocated by the renewalists. In that sense, the specialized academicians who write descriptively on the *maqāṣid al-sharīʿa* converge with the much broader and diverse group of traditionalist scholars who criticize the proposals of Islamic reform and deploy the classical idea of "renewal" to defend the continuity and the authenticity of the tradition. The third group is defined as the "revisionist" academicians whose projects are marked by an intellectual concern for establishing a comprehensive and systematic model of interpretation of the Islamic normative sources, which is well informed by the scholarship on post-Enlightenment Western hermeneutics. The final group, the most difficult to define and arguably the most diverse one, regards *sharīʿa* in exclusively legal or ethical terms. In both these cases, the higher purposes of Islam are described to accord with, or even to dictate to, a secular individual and society where religion and politics are separate. The concept of secularism considered from these vantage points is defined in different ways including "the separation of religious and political sphere," "the withdrawal of the religious from the public space," or to refer to performative terms such as being "modern" or "Western." Importantly, however, in each of these conceptualizations of secularism, Islam with its core values is seen to be in perfect harmony with it. Thus, I will refer to this group as the "secularists," and analyze their diverse conceptions of the *maqāṣid al-sharīʿa*. These four categories are to be conceived of as primarily heuristic devices that facilitate conceptual clarity. In reality there is a degree of overlap between them and therefore they are loosely defined.

Renewal and Legal Traditionalism: *Maqāṣid* and *Sharīʿa* versus Reform

For the majority of divinity faculty members and for the PRA, Islam is ethicalized, but it has a binding legal significance as well. Accordingly, the inseparable legal aspect of *sharīʿa* can and should renew itself, and the *maqāṣid al-sharīʿa*, alongside discretionary reasoning [*ijtihād*] and the consideration of utility [*maṣlaḥa*], plays a substantive role in this renewal.[8] Therefore, we describe these scholars broadly as "traditionalists," or "renewalists" since they consciously place themselves in the long-established tradition of *tajdīd*. Taking recourse to the traditional legal methodology [*uṣūl al-fiqh*] concepts and vocabulary, these traditionalist scholars are conversant with the works of al-Qaradawi (b. 1926), Ibn ʿAshur (d. 1973), al-Fasi (d. 1974), Rashid Rida (d. 1935), al-Raysuni (b. 1953), al-ʿAlwani (b. 1935), and other prominent Muslim scholars who wrote extensively on an Islamic reform based on the *maqāṣid al-sharīʿa* principles. This discourse of *maqāṣid*, developed from within the *uṣūl al-fiqh* tradition itself, is very well informed by premodern legal scholarship, and these traditionalist scholars are careful in not employing the *maqāṣid*-oriented approaches in methodologically loose or utilitarian forms.

Hayrettin Karaman (b. 1934), the dissident outspoken critic of the gradually obsolescent Kamalist secularism, is the leading name in this group. As one of the first graduates of the religious high schools that opened in 1949, Karaman writes extensively on Islamic law. Having fundamentally contributed to the study of *maqāṣid al-sharīʿa*, he is regarded as "Turkey's al-Qaradawi."[9] Islam and *sharīʿa* are interchangeable for Karaman because *sharīʿa* with its legal dimension is the natural right of every Muslim. Nevertheless, he recognizes the fact that it would be despotism and injustice to apply Islamic legal rulings to people who do not want to live according to its teachings. The term "secular Muslim" is an oxymoron for Karaman, because *sharīʿa* is both legal and ethical, and secularism is a Western ideology of alienation from the sacred. While he is well informed about the employment of the *maqāṣid al-sharīʿa* discourse by various Islamic reformist intellectuals, Karaman is deeply critical of any idea of "Islamic reform" because religious reformation has an inseparable Lutheran connotation to him.[10] It is inappropriate to be applied to Islam because Islam itself has always had an inherent component of renewal and *ijtihād* the doors of which have always been open.[11] Karaman argues further that the permanent openness of the door of *ijtihād* and the consideration of the *maqāṣid al-sharīʿa* were the key interrelated components of the Islamic legal tradition, both of which are now forgotten and replaced with a static conception of *sharīʿa*. *Maqāṣid al-sharīʿa* embody the immutable purposes of the divine law and simultaneously provide the flexible tool for legal change. Here the delicate balance of the individual precepts [*juz'iyyāt*] and universal principles should be observed in Karaman's view. Appealing to al-Shatibi (d. 1388), Ibn Qayyim al-Jawziyya (d. 1350), al-Qarafi (d. 1285), and many other prominent names of the *maqāṣid al-sharīʿa* discourse, Karaman not only depicts secularization as the alienation of the people from their religious and cultural roots, but also argues that Islam and democracy in their current form in Turkey are incompatible, while an Islamic democracy is possible. On the one hand, he forms the view that an Islam that considers *sharīʿa* as a static legal system should be renewed in the light of the *maqāṣid al-sharīʿa* tradition. On the other hand, Karaman opines that the current democracy implemented in Turkey is nothing but the state oppression of the individual religiosity—a violent and unjust ideology that dramatically presents itself as "religious freedom" and "secularism."[12] Islam does not dictate a certain method of governance, but presents the *maqāṣid al-sharīʿa* that aim to preserve life, religion, reason, progeny, and property. Any governance model that preserves these higher aims with a reference to Islam is legitimate, while the present oppressively secular democracy is far from fulfilling this requirement. At the same time Karaman opposes the employment of the *maqāṣid al-sharīʿa* by apologists or for Westernist purposes. Arguing against the proponents of reform and Westernization, he claims that the West did not preserve the *maqāṣid al-sharīʿa* in the sense that Islam stipulates. The West preserved irreligion (i.e., oppressive secularism) instead of religion; it did not preserve life, reason, property, and the progeny, but only their replica.[13] Coupled with this critique of the West, *maqāṣid al-sharīʿa* is an integral part of Karaman's substantive legal reasoning, which is resolutely antireformist.[14]

Karaman's student Mehmet Erdogan (b. 1956), a professor at Marmara University, and Nihat Dalgın, a professor at Ondokuz Mayıs University, also focus on the dialectical interplay between the *maqāṣid al-sharīʿa* and the literal reading of the sources in their writings. While emphasizing the key role of the *maqāṣid al-sharīʿa* in legal change, both scholars emphasize the strict commitment to the literal reading of the sources, which considerably limits the field of this change. Dalgın's preference for literal reading of *ḥadīth* with singular narration [*aḥad*] over the *maqāṣid al-sharīʿa* takes him away from revisionist or reformist proposals.[15] Thus, Dalgın follows the more conservative views in much-discussed issues such as the right of Muslim women to marry non-Muslim men or women's duty to pray during their periods.[16] Similarly, Erdoğan's emphasis on the strict commitment to the literal reading of the Qur'ān limits the field of legal change. Accordingly, the corporal punishments [*ḥudūd*] are clearly determined and they constitute unchanging aspects of Islamic law. In the same vein, no reference to the *maqāṣid al-sharīʿa* can justify, for example, the abandonment of the traditional veiling injunctions for women; "the injunction of veiling is a universal principle of the Qur'ān that does not change in time and place [except its specifics]."[17]

The rise of a consciously antireformist *maqāṣid al-sharīʿa* discourse with the transition from the last generation of the Ottoman Empire to the children of the Turkish Republic can be best traced by the terminological shift from the influential thinker Said Nursi (d. 1960) to his student Fethullah Gulen (b. 1941). Nursi, the inspiring founder of various movements gathered under the title "Nurculuk," used terms like "divine purposes" [*makasıd-ı ilahiyye*], "masterly purposes" [*makasıd-ı rabbaniyye*], "glorious purposes" [*makasıd-ı subhaniyye*], and "fundamental purposes" [*makasıd-ı esasiyye*] in his corpus. These references to the sacred purposes embody what Weber called "ethical substantive thinking" on the divine, independent of the legally informed *maqāṣid al-sharīʿa* discourse. According to Nursi, there are four key beliefs that embody the divine purpose in imparting the law: testifying the oneness of God, the prophecy, resurrection, and justice.[18] Gulen, Nursi's most prominent student and one of the most influential living Muslims in the globe, uses the same terminology of his master, but he puts these terms now into a context that is informed by the *maqāṣid al-sharīʿa* discourse. He also refers to al-Shatibi in various writings and hints that the arguments he presents can be traced back to al-Shatibi's *maqāṣid al-sharīʿa* theory.[19] Gulen claims that al-Shatibi practiced *ijtihād* based on the *maqāṣid al-sharīʿa* and emphasizes that any procedural, imitative religious study that does not involve the divine *maqāṣid* is in vain. Again, Gulen explicitly distances himself from any reform movement, arguing

> "reform" means to *re*-form something which has been deformed.... Firstly, I never believed that Islam and the principles of my religion have ever been subjected to deformation, alteration, or amendment. Secondly, there is no reform for Islam. Instead, there is *tajdīd*.[20]

Still, Gulen repeatedly states that he propagates neither *tajdīd*, nor *ijtihād*, nor reform and that he is just a follower of Islam, simply a *Muslim*. He is very careful about divorcing himself from any reformist, political, or Islamist discourse. Gulen's conscious dislike of using Islam as a discursive politicized instrument, which was a distinct trait in Nursi's thought as well, indicates an ethicalized approach to Islam from a spiritual perspective. The terminology Gulen uses is less legal than spiritual, as he constantly refers to key terms of popular Islam as well as institutional Sufism. The names he often cites are those of the great Sufi masters like Rumi (d. 1273) and Yunus Emre (d. ca. 1320), instead of those of the jurists. The concept of the *maqāṣid al-sharīʿa*, thus, is not part of any legal reformist discourse for Gulen but the key consideration of a consciously ethicalized traditional worldview supported by substantive reasoning that nourishes from the inseparability of Islam and *sharīʿa* as conceptualized by classical Islamic tradition.

Another prominent follower of Nursi, Metin Karabasoglu (b. 1964) is an intellectual and writer who also argues that the traditional Islamic worldview is threatened by modernist, orientalist, secularist, apologist, or reformist assaults, all of which, consciously or unconsciously appeal to terms, values, and agendas set by others as opposed to the authentic, traditional Islamic ones. These attacks on the tradition, most importantly, do not hesitate to exploit its own classical tools, including the *maqāṣid al-sharīʿa*. In this context Karabasoglu claims that "*maṣlaḥa*... and the *maqāṣid al-sharīʿa* emphasized by al-Shatibi are seriously abused by those contemporary Muslims who are inclined toward secularism."[21] While writers from various camps like Karaman and Karabasoglu are suspicious of the deployment of the *maqāṣid* as they can be misused in the service of secularization, Tahsin Gorgun (b. 1961) presents a different traditionalist perspective to the debate on secularization by playing on its definition. A professor of philosophy at İstanbul 29 Mayıs University, Gorgun argues that the real purpose of the *maqāṣid al-sharīʿa* is to be understood as principles that guarantee a this-worldly life in full integrity with and in the service of the other-worldly purposes. In philosophical terms, the *maqāṣid al-sharīʿa* discourse is

> existence [*varlık*] and the manifestation of existence in this life at the hands of man in the form of life. The *maqāṣid al-sharīʿa* mean that one cannot become a mature Muslim without flourishing in this world. Therefore, one cannot achieve the merits of the afterlife without completing the "necessities," "complementaries," and "embellishments" [*ḍarūriyyāt*, *ḥājiyyāt*, and *taḥsīniyyāt*, i.e., the three classical categories of the *maqāṣid al-sharīʿa*] in every aspect of life. The *maqāṣid al-sharīʿa*

> demand from humans to give this worldly life its due in all of its dimensions, and opposes the institution of asceticism [*ruhbanlık*].[22]

Insofar as the condition of becoming a good Muslim is to become a good this-worldly person, Islam, unlike other religions, does not see "secularism" in the literal sense of "*verweltlichung*" ["becoming this-worldly"; *dünyevileşme*] as a problem, but as a key requirement of perfection. Secularization, according to this approach, is the manifestation of the inner religiosity as actions, principles, and institutions that build a civilization and culture.[23] Thus secularism is not an essential problem for Muslims if we adopt a traditional *maqāṣid*-oriented perspective; *maqāṣid al-sharīʿa* embody the secular requirements in order to attain complete perfection. Accordingly, for Gorgun, the widespread scholarly or *traditionalist* argument against the employment of *maqāṣid al-sharīʿa* in the service of secularization misses the real *traditional* meaning of the *maqāṣid al-sharīʿa* because the common understanding of secularism as negligence of religion, shared by other defendants of the tradition and many others, is a misconception.

Gorgun has alternative traditional conceptions of the *maqāṣid al-sharīʿa* and secularism that depict the two in essential harmony as opposed to their traditionalist dichotomous opposition as well as their reformist juxtapositions. His unique philosophical approach to secularization from the perspective of *maqāṣid al-sharīʿa* is coupled with a deep critique of the modern reformist employment of the *maqāṣid al-sharīʿa* throughout the world. Gorgun argues that the contemporary revival of the *maqāṣid al-sharīʿa* is a colonial modernist project that distorts the fundamental vision of Islam and the role of the *maqāṣid al-sharīʿa* played in classical Islam:

> The nineteenth and twentieth centuries mark a period which pushes knowledge back and puts politics to its center, while Islamic civilization is based on a knowledge-centered [*ilim esaslı*] worldview. Islam presents itself as knowledge.[24]

One of the most important results of this shift at the existential center has been the disappearance of religious sciences, including *fiqh*, and the emergence of various reformist projects that adopt Islam to the new politics-centered formal structure. The *maqāṣid al-sharīʿa* discourse revived in the formalization period of this new worldview is one of the key mechanisms that supplanted the classical religious sciences.[25] In addition to the *maqāṣid*, another very suitable mechanism was the "general principles of law" [*qawāʾid al-kullīyya*], which was employed in the key formalization project of *sharīʿa*, the Mecelle [*Majalla*].[26] *Maqāṣid al-sharīʿa* and *qawāʾid al-kullīyya* were able to serve the new modern, politics-centered formation unlike many classical jurisprudential tools, which gradually wore out becoming irrelevant for the proposals for Islamic reform. A critical reading of the modern employment of the *maqāṣid al-sharī'a* in the service of the rising world order and an emphasis on the positive significance of the classical *maqāṣid al-sharī'a* for secularization are Gorgun's original contributions to the *maqāṣid* debates in Turkey.

The bonding decrees of the PRA also apply the *maqāṣid al-sharī'a* in the service of the classical tradition of *tajdīd* and against reform. This is clearly evident in the case of their views on insurance. The PRA commission explains first the general principle that it follows when determining the legal status of insurance:

> Insurance is a contract that did not exist in the time of the Prophet or in the classical sources of *fiqh* but later in the modern ages. Therefore the legal status of insurance can be identified in the orientation of the *maqāṣid* of religion and the general principles of the sacred sources [*naṣṣ*].[27]

The PRA uses the *maqāṣid al-sharī'a* as a way of following public utility in unprecedented cases that cannot be solved with a direct reference to the sacred sources. Thus, *maqāṣid al-sharī'a* is equated with the *maṣlaḥa*, which plays an important role for the PRA in determining the legal status of organ transplantation as well.[28] Importantly, however, in line with the classical tradition, the PRA does not use the *maqāṣid al-sharī'a* to settle controversies about devotional matters [*'ibādāt*] and limits it with unprecedented cases to the field of civil transactions [*mu'amalat*]. Clear examples are regarding daily prayers in one's native language or women's prayers in private without veiling, none of which are approved by the PRA. It forms the view that the *'ibādāt* elements of the Islamic tradition have their wisdom [*ḥikma*], purposes, and reasons of legislation as well as forms, requirements, and pillars, and these forms cannot change. For example, the reformist proposal of stunning the animal using electric current instead of the traditional method of slaughtering (i.e., slitting the throat) violates a pillar of the ritual sacrifice. Similarly, one cannot fulfill the *'ibāda* of sacrifice by donation, and one should not present two different devotional matters of donation and sacrifice as alternatives on the basis of their intention, because the form of these devotional matters are explicit in the sources and they have different purposes of legislation.[29]

In summary, the scholars who work on *maqāṣid al sharī'a* concept from within the classical tradition of *uṣūl al-fiqh* are seen as predominantly far from being reformists. Indeed, they generally distance themselves from the idea of reform or actively criticize it. They underline the classical inseparability of ethics from law, both of which are embodied by the flexible *sharīʿa*, and place themselves in the tradition of renewal. Therefore, the *maqāṣid al-sharīʿa* in Turkey often operates as the voice of tradition against reformist projects that are generally considered to threaten the authentic legal heritage.

The Specialized *Maqāṣid al-Sharīʿa* Scholarship: Theory without Reform

There is a large volume of academic writing in Turkish on the *maqāṣid al-sharīʿa* discourse. Innumerable masters and doctoral theses are written on the discourse, its classical architects, and its modern implementations. These academic studies are informed by the non-Turkish literature, especially writings by great modern reformists such as Ibn ʿAshur, al-Qaradawi, Rashīd Rida, and Fazlur Rahman (d. 1988). Arguments expressed in the academia are systematic and comprehensive, demonstrating that the current state of worldwide scholarship on *maqāṣid al-sharīʿa* literature is closely followed by the Turkish academia.

A leading name of the academic *maqāṣid al-sharīʿa* scholarship is Ahmet Yaman (b. 1967), a professor of Islamic law at Akdeniz University. He recently edited a world-class comprehensive monograph in Turkish on the *maqāṣid al-sharīʿa* to which 16 scholars contributed.[30] The book is designed to become a reference source in the field; thus, it is mainly historical and descriptive in nature introducing the history of the *maqāṣid al-sharīʿa* discourse, its representatives, and its functions. Yaman as well as his students, such as Rahmi Telkenaroglu (b. 1975), a professor of Islamic law at Gumushane University, frame the *maqāṣid al-sharīʿa* in terms of *ijtihād* directed toward the discovery and analysis of the ratio legis [*ʿilla*].[31] According to Yaman, *ijtihād* and *maqāṣid* are two indispensable and interdependent concepts of *uṣūl al-fiqh*. The legal change depends on *ijtihād*, which should take the *maqāṣid al-sharīʿa* as its normative reference point, while the direction of this change is evaluated on the basis of the divine *maqāṣid*.[32] Yunus Vehbi Yavuz (b. 1944), an emeritus professor of Islamic law at Uludag University, argues along the same lines asserting that "all *ijtihād* methods in *uṣūl al-fiqh* aim to understand the *maqāṣid* of Islam. The fundamental underlying element is purpose [*maqṣid*]. The *maqṣid* is to attain *maṣlaḥa*."[33] Accordingly, all rulings in the Qur'ān are directed toward the utility of the individual and the society as a whole.[34] A contributor to Yaman's book, Abdurrahman Haçkalı (b. 1970), a professor of Islamic law at Rize University, joins Yaman, Telkenaroglu, and Yavuz in framing the *maqāṣid al-sharīʿa* primarily in terms of *ijtihād*. Yaman accepts this pivotal role played by the *maqāṣid al-sharīʿa* in connecting *ijtihād* to *maṣlaḥa*, but he claims that the concept of *maqāṣid* is also present in the employment of juristic preference [*istiḥsān*], which is a *maqāṣid*-oriented type of exegesis.[35] In other words, *maqāṣid*-oriented *ijtihād* and teleological [*ghāʾī*] exegesis are identical. This key role assumed by the concept of *maqāṣid al-sharīʿa* in determining the direction of *ijtihād* and exegesis gives it an immense power. Yaman points to two significant threats in the application of this powerful tool. First, the determination of the *maqāṣid* exclusively by the exegete might lead to unwarranted subjectivism, while its determination on the basis of an imitative, passive reading ends up with inflexible literalism.[36] Second, Yaman points to the danger of absolutization inherent in the human effort to access the absolute divine intention. Citing al-Shatibi, Yaman claims that "talking in the name of God and arriving at judgments about the purposes and aims of verses can engender great dangers.... And God knows best."[37] Hence, individual jurists might not understand the divine *maqāṣid* and may misuse it. God-consciousness [*taqwā*] of the heart and the supervision of the tradition, consensus [*ijmāʿ*], embody in Yaman's view the remedy to both threats. Understanding, in Qur'ānic language is an act of the heart, and a God-conscious heart will respect essence of the Qur'ān in interpreting it. Besides, *ijmāʿ*—the embodiment of the valid tradition for Yaman—simultaneously preserves the flexibility of law and protects it from relativistic tendencies.[38]

Another contributor in Yaman's monograph, Ali Pekcan (b. 1965) is one of the most devoted and productive scholars of *maqāṣid al-sharīʿa* in Turkey. Working as a professor of Islamic law at the Selçuk Center for Higher Religious Education, his doctoral dissertation and published works focus directly on the *maqāṣid al-sharīʿa*. In addition, he teaches a "*maqāṣid theory*" course at the Selçuk Center. Pekcan also published a very comprehensive bibliography composed of more than two hundred books written in Arabic, English, or Turkish since the 1910s that focus on the *maqāṣid al-sharīʿa*. Pekcan's writings, similar to those of Yaman and Haçkalı, are primarily descriptive and aim to introduce the historical development of the *maqāṣid al-sharīʿa* discourse, its central role in contemporary reform movements, its classical fathers, modern spokespersons, and their scholarship.[39]

While the academic *maqāṣid al-sharīʿa* scholarship in Turkish is rigorous, the scarcity of works elaborating the practical problems of the *maqāṣid al-sharīʿa* theory points to its abstractness. As such, a number of questions remain mostly unanswered: How does one keep the hierarchy of various higher purposes? How does one transcend the limits of the exterior of the *naṣṣ* from within the *maqāṣid al-sharīʿa* tradition? How do the *maqāṣid* translate into concrete legal terms today? Where, for example, can human rights,[40] LGBTQIA rights, environmental ethics, or animal welfare be placed in the classical classification of the *maqāṣid al-sharīʿa*?[41] Under what circumstances can essential needs turn into complementary necessities? How can we avoid the problem of what Sherman Jackson calls "false universalism," that is the common practice of applying generalized rules to all Muslims in the world independent of their specific circumstances and contexts?[42] These questions are extensively discussed in other languages and countries and display that this scholarship, unlike the one in Turkish, is serious about considering the *maqāṣid al-sharīʿa* as a concrete option of legal reform. In contrast, as already noted, the scholarship on the *maqāṣid al-sharīʿa* in Turkey is abstract, because the idea of and the practical need for an Islamic reform in legal terms are simply absent or considered as irrelevant if not inappropriate.

However, once we scratch below the surface we will discover that the academic writing on the *maqāṣid al-sharīʿa*, regardless of its abstract nature, tends to align itself closely with the traditionalists. The very presence of the *maqāṣid al-sharīʿa* is seen as the inherently flexible, dynamic capacity of the legal tradition, and *re*-form, understood literally, is considered as an attack launched on its continuity.[43] In that sense they are part of the renewalist tradition, which limits the application of the *maqāṣid al-sharīʿa* to those injunctions that fall within the scope of the explicit *naṣṣ* and the field of civil transactions. For example, Yaman is very clear that traditional veiling is an inviolable injunction honored by the *naṣṣ* as well as the *ijmāʿ*.[44] Similarly, he criticizes the reformist proposals, such as fulfilling the devotional matter of sacrifice by donation, altering the form of the ritual prayers, or fornication in the guise of "sexual freedom."[45] In the same vein, Pekcan seems content with the traditional definition of abortion as murder.[46] He also favors the traditional classification of the five necessary goals [*ḍarūriyyāt*], as against its modern alternatives, that is replacing them with the preservation of reason, freedom, and justice as suggested by prominent Egyptian scholar Nasr Abu Zayd (d. 2010).[47] Therefore, the specialized academic writing on the *maqāṣid al-sharīʿa* opposes reformist proposals and envisages the *maqāṣid al-sharīʿa* discourse as an important expression of the legal tradition perpetually renewable while preserving its higher purposes. The *maqāṣid* scholars in the Turkish academia closely follow the premodern *maqāṣid al sharīʿa* literature, and their writings are inclose conversation with it.

Maqāṣid al-Sharīʿa in the Revisionist Perspective

There is also a diverse group of scholars who use the *maqāṣid al-sharīʿa* discourse as integral to their broader arguments for the construction of a novel

Qur'ān-sunna hermeneutics. These scholars are often referred to in the literature as "revisionists" rather than reformists. This position is advocated by Körner who argues

> [these scholars'] effort to use insights so far not connected to Qur'an hermeneutics, their own frequent thematizing of method, their willingness to experiment with new approaches, and their consciousness of doing something relevant to the whole of Islam seem to justify the word "revisionist," instead of "reformist."[48]

The most visible aspect of the revisionist arguments is the fundamental role they assign to decidedly post-Enlightenment hermeneutics in the understanding of the Qur'ān and sunna. According to these scholars, a sustained critique of the traditional scholarly methodology of reading the sacred sources is pivotal because the modern problems of Muslims are primarily hermeneutical. The absence of a sustained interpretive methodology in Islamic sciences is the diagnosis of this basic problem, and the *maqāṣid al-sharīʿa* is among the many tools that can function in the construction of a new methodology of interpretation of the sacred sources.

The "Ankara School" is the most well-known group of scholars who employ the *maqāṣid* in the service of broader hermeneutical revisionist proposals. Mehmet Paçacı (b. 1959), a leading member of the school and one of the most influential academicians in the divinity faculties, envisages a revisionist Qur'ān hermeneutics with an appeal to the German hermeneutical tradition. In Paçacı's writings, we find references to al-Shatibi and the *maqāṣid al-sharīʿa* coupled together with discussions on and references to Schleiermacher, Dilthey, Heidegger, and, especially, Gadamer. Paçacı diagnoses the absence of a comprehensive hermeneutical methodology mainly due to the inability of the classical *uṣūl al-fiqh* science to incorporate modern sources of knowledge. In this context, Paçacı opines that *fiqh*, which originally means "understanding," rendered the nature of the Qur'ān as primarily a legalistic text, especially under the influence of al-Shafiʿi (d. 820), thereby disconnecting the Qur'ān from its fundamental ethical principles in accordance with which the reader will transcend the literal meaning [*ẓāhir*] of the *naṣṣ* and understand his/her own self [*nafs*].[49] Paçacı argues further that the classical tools of *fiqh* like *istiḥsān* that would permit less philologically dominant interpretations of the Qur'ān and sunna were attacked by al-Shafiʿi and later jurists, while scholars like al-Shatibi used *istiḥsān* and inductive corroboration [*istiqrā'*] to derive universal ethical principles from individual precepts. In the latter approach, legal injunctions are determined in accordance with the ultimate ethical principles [*maqāṣid*] of the Qur'ān and the telos of the reasoning is the achievement of the highest good.[50] Paçacı considers that *maṣlaḥa* is an extra-Qur'ānic source that al-Shatibi derived from lived experiences. Here, Paçacı cites three classical categories of the *maqāṣid al-sharī'a* in order to substantiate his argument that *maṣlaḥa* allowed al-Shatibi go beyond the surface of the text.[51] *Maqāṣid al-sharī'a*'s role in the proposal of Paçacı is to find the ethical principles in the Qur'ān that will provide us with a hierarchy of values to be followed in our lives. In this context, he asserts that mistaking or equating the literal application of Qur'ānic injunctions with the higher values that are supposed to guide them is nothing but blindness from an ethical perspective and a drifting away from the spirit of the Qur'ān.[52] Challenging the view of the Qur'ān as a book of laws, Paçacı argues that the scripture serves primarily as a guide to ethical divine purposes. Echoing Abu Zayd and citing Ismail al-Faruqi (d. 1986), he even proposes to go beyond the classical classification of the *maqāṣid* in favor of ethics. In this context he asserts:

> We need today to improve the classical model [of *maqāṣid al-sharī'a*], or even to produce new models. It is possible to criticize al-Shatibi as he placed ethics into the lowest level in his *maqāṣid* theory [i.e., to the category of *taḥsīniyyāt*].... The significant task of Muslims [today] is to re-determine the value content of the Qur'an systematically.[53]

Paçacı's *maqāṣid*-oriented approach does not operate within a legal or reformist framework, but he applies it to strengthen his broader hermeneutical and ethical program. *Maqāṣid al-sharī'a* is called for by scholars as a guide not only to establish a revisionary exegetical methodology, but even more frequently to construct a new *ḥadīth* methodology. Mehmet Görmez (b. 1959), the current president (2010–) of the PRA and a respected *ḥadīth* scholar with close connections to the Ankara School, refers to *maqāṣid al-sharī'a* in his various works as a guide for a new *ḥadīth* methodology. Görmez argues that

> [in the classical *ḥadīth* scholarship] a methodology to understand and interpret the *ḥadīth* and *sunna* did not emerge; moreover, the method of understanding developed by *uṣūl al-fiqh*, which was appealed as to fill this gap of methodology, was not satisfactory.[54]

The construction of such a methodology consists of three dimensions according to Görmez. The first one is the reconstruction of the *ḥadīth* sciences by re-asking what their main purposes and scope are as well as revisiting their subcategories. Second, the *ḥadīth* scholarship would and should systematically benefit from modern semiology and hermeneutics.[55] Finally, the priorities of *uṣūl al-fiqh* have to be reconsidered. Modifying the order of priorities of the higher principles, which are employed by the method of understanding embraced by the *uṣūl al-fiqh*, can make the *uṣūl al-fiqh* a method applicable to *ḥadīth* sciences. It is the *maqāṣid al-sharīʿa* developed by al-Juwayni (d. 1085), al-Ghazali (d. 1111), al-Rāzī (d. 1210), and al-Shatibi that will ground this prioritization of the values and the determination of the universal principles of *ḥadīth*.[56] In this three-tiered proposal of the current president of the PRA, the construction of a methodology for *ḥadīth* sciences is fundamentally dependent on the *maqāṣid al-sharīʿa* insofar as it is still *uṣūl al-fiqh* that will provide the backbone of the new methodology for *ḥadīth* sciences.

A similar proposal of an "alternative *ḥadīth* methodology" with a revisionist approach to *ḥadīth* is proposed by another *ḥadīth* professor at Ankara University, Hayri Kırbaşoğlu (b. 1954). *Maqāṣid al-sharīʿa* plays a subsidiary role in his main project, and his critique of the classical *ḥadīth* methodology is similar to that of Görmez. Unlike Görmez, Kırbaşoğlu frames "*sunna*" as interchangeable with the concept "Islam," with references to al-Qaradawi, Fazlur Rahman, and al-Shatibi. *Sunna* is not limited to the letter [*lafẓ*], but it is the spirit, wisdom, and purpose behind it explicated in the Qur'ān. Kırbaşoğlu argues that

> we have to seriously consider the view that *sunna* is an interpretation and implementation of the Qur'an, and *sunna* roots in the Qur'an. The origins of this view regress back to 'Ā'isha (d. 678) [a wife of the Prophet and a religious scholar] and it was systematized by al-Shatibi.... *Sunna* should be conceived as an opening of the Qur'an to life.[57]

Sunna is a worldview [*weltanschauung*] composed of principles organizing the individual, the society, and the universe, and the task of the believer is to determine the purposes and higher aims that shaped the *sunna* and *ḥadīth*.[58] Thus, a broader hermeneutical approach to *sunna* and *ḥadīth* that considers the *maqāṣid al-sharīʿa* is needed. With their calls for a unified hermeneutical methodology based on a *maqāṣid*-oriented *ijtihād*, the scholars of the Ankara School present a coherent, comprehensive revisionist proposal.

In these "revisionist" proposals, *maqāṣid al-sharīʿa* discourse plays a subsidiary role in wider theological, hermeneutical, or philosophical agendas, all of which give primacy to ethics instead of law. References to the higher purposes of law thus do not operate as an independent discourse or as a tool of an Islamic legal reform. Instead, *maqāṣid al-sharīʿa* is called for as an authentic traditional tool of legal change that has a secondary role in the formation of an *ijtihād*-centered ethical idea of renewal, and an auxiliary role in the construction of a novel hermeneutical methodology.

Reform at the Expense of the Tradition: *Maqāṣid* versus *Sharīʿa*

A popular approach to *sharīʿa* clearly separates it from "Islam" and divorces ethics from law, thereby creating a variety of possible conceptions of the *maqāṣid*. On the one hand *sharīʿa*, for many Muslims in Turkey, is about legal, enforceable laws. The purposes of Islam, on the other hand, are understood to be far beyond these legal and political implementations and more related to higher ethical principles and spirituality. *Maqāṣid*, from this widespread view, transcends the legalistic *sharīʿa* or simply makes it irrelevant to Islam altogether. Therefore, in order to be a Muslim, one does not need to even ponder on what *sharīʿa* is, while the purposes of religion are very clear to all people, be they religious or nonreligious. It is important to note that the concept of *sharīʿa* is not necessarily conceptualized as legal or retrograde for all who subscribe to the divorce of ethics from law. For some of them *sharīʿa* is exclusively ethical, and thus has no legal or binding content. Being Muslim for them means to follow the *sharīʿa*, which has no legal bearing. Alevis and various Sufi groups fit in this group. Most of their members are explicitly secular both in legal-political and performative terms, and they see this as an important requirement of being a contemporary Muslim. The content of their ethicalized Islam, that is, human dignity, helping the needy, striving to become a better person, and purifying the soul, is clearly driven by well-rooted spiritual ideals and terminology. *Sharīʿa* is thus associated with the exterior aspect of Islam, but its reality, kernel, or truth is far beyond and is hierarchically superior to it. These various ethical conceptions of "the higher objectives of Islam" or "divine wisdom" are nourished by Sufism and popular Islam, and leave little room for an alternative, legal discourse of reform. Ideas cease to be reformist when they are based on *sharīʿa* talk.

Mehmet Dağ (b. 1943), an emeritus professor of theology at Ondokuz Mayıs University, uses the *maqāṣid* in such a perspective. His argument is uninformed by the traditional *maqāṣid al-sharīʿa* discourse, and it nourishes itself from a primarily ethical understanding of the purpose of *sharīʿa*:

> Social and political rulings vary in time and society; thus they are valid only in these circumstances. Thus, the Qur'an does not have a purpose of ruling or regulating every society with such rulings. The real purpose of the Qur'an... is to improve people ethically.[59]

Dağ claims that the need today is for neither renewal nor reform, but rather for the reconstruction of a positivist, scientific mind-set.[60] Islam has nothing to contribute to the modern epistemology, and its primary aim and purpose is in regulating faith and ethics. For example, regarding the specific question of veiling, Dağ claims that the *purpose* of the Qur'ān is not to regulate the outer appearance of people, but to obtain internal purity and chastity.[61]

A small group of scholars separate *sharīʿa* and Islam by employing the *uṣūl al-fiqh*. For these scholars, secular democracy is an inherently Islamic system because one arrives at secular modernity as one follows the purposes of the Islamic law. Among these scholars, Yaşar Nuri Ozturk (b. 1945) is the only scholar who consciously bases his project on the *maqāṣid al-sharīʿa*. He is an emeritus professor at İstanbul University, a lawyer, a columnist, and a politician who regularly appears in the media. Ozturk's main argument is that *sharīʿa*, as distinct from Islam, is conflated by both the divinity scholars and the traditionalists with *fiqh*, which is full of inconsistencies and contains many unqur'ānic injunctions.[62] Well-versed in the *uṣūl al-fiqh*, Ozturk uses the *maqāṣid al-sharīʿa* discourse to emphasize the real nature of religion, which is more profound than its legal aspects. Accordingly, legalistic classical *sharīʿa* is the way of yesterday. It is secularism, according to Ozturk, that preserves the values and purposes of the divine revelation by preventing the institutionalization of religion as the official hegemonic power.[63] Secularism for Ozturk is a worldview and a legal-political system based on it that treats everybody equally independent of their religious commitments and this principle of justice is a core value of the Qur'ān. Qur'ān not only condones secularism, but stipulates it. Secularism is therefore a key requirement of being a mature contemporary Muslim. Thus, Ozturk further argues that Islam is against religious hegemony and emanates from the option to choose freely as the Qur'ān emphasizes and as scholars like al-Shatibi remind us. Based on his theory of *maqāṣid al-sharīʿa* he comes up with some controversial views regarding specific matters pertaining to the religious practices. For example, Ozturk famously argues that the higher objective of ritual sacrifice is to feed the poor, and that there are better, non-bloody ways to fulfill this objective.[64] Daily prayers are *intended* to be a dialogue with the divine, thus they can be performed in the native language and in forms looser than they are depicted by scholars. Merging daily prayers [*jamʿ*] under necessary conditions is also permissible, citing al-Shatibi.[65] In terms of veiling, Ozturk opines that the Qur'an and *sunna* are also much more lenient than they are described by these so-called religious authorities.[66] Against the "disgusting and unIslamic tyranny" of religious experts over religion, Ozturk perpetually defends what he calls the "Qur'anic Islam," thereby giving a radical primacy to the encounter with the scripture over *fiqh* and the traditional institutions, and asserts emphatically that Islam is *purely* Qur'ān.[67]

Ozturk's *maqāṣid*-oriented perspective conflicts not only with traditionalist scholars, but also with prevalent *maqāṣid* scholarship and the PRA, which limit the employment of the *maqāṣid* to unprecedented cases exclusively in the *mu'āmalāt*. On the one hand, his critics accuse him of being a "reformist," while Ozturk consistently defines himself as a renewer [*mujaddid*] *reconstructing* and *renewing* Islam on the basis of its sacred scripture, as opposed to a reformist who notoriously works in a paradigm "imported from the West."[68] Like the traditionalist voices that are critical of his ideas, Ozturk refuses to be categorized as a "reformist" and speaks out against reform in favor of traditional renewal. Extending the application of the *maqāṣid al-sharī'a* to the *'ibādāt* is one of these critiques as in the case of animal sacrifice or praying in one's native language. The use of *maṣlaḥa* and the *maqāṣid al-sharī'a* to transgress the explicit, "literal" reading of the *naṣṣ*, such as in the case of veiling, is another accusation aimed at him. Ultrasecularists, on the other hand, accuse him of not understanding the real grounds of secularism that essentially cannot be reconciled with religiosity.[69]

Conclusions

Contemporary Turkey has inherited very strong, long-lasting, nonlegal (or sometimes even anti-legal) traditions of thinking on the higher purposes of Islam and the wisdom behind the sacred law. The prevalent idea that these purposes are beyond the legal discourses hindered the emergence of the conceptual, ethical, theological, and political habitat for the higher purposes as a legally conscious tool of Islamic reform faithful to the spirit of the sacred sources. The presence of alternative tools of legal change within *uṣūl al-fiqh*, such as *ijtihād*, *ijmā'*, customary law [*'urf*], and *maṣlaḥa* also played a significant role in the reform process. Along with the traditional legal-cum-ethical conception of the *sharī'a*, two already present conceptions that divorce ethics from *nomos* gained strength accompanying the reforms of the late Ottoman Empire. *Sharī'a* began to be seen either as an ethical guide to life without any legal content, or as an exclusively legal system separate from Islam that needs to be reformed or to be dropped altogether. Insofar as the concept of "reform" is concerned, it is predominantly conceptualized as a foreign intervention and a threat to the classical heritage. Therefore, the *maqāṣid al-sharī'a* concept is not employed to support an Islamic reform proposal in such a sense. Instead, it is the concept of "renewal" that is accepted to express the authentic change in the inherently flexible and ethical legal tradition. The traditionalist scholars who are the most conversant with the *uṣūl al-fiqh* employ the *maqāṣid al-sharī'a* to vocalize the tradition and traditional renewal as opposed to reform, whereas revisionist scholars employ the *maqāṣid al-sharī'a* to buttress their wider hermeneutical projects and to build an encompassing *ijtihād*-based methodology of Islamic sciences. Finally, the secularist scholars come closest to a legally conscious Islamic reform via a *maqāṣid*-oriented reasoning, as their proposals come closer to a *sharī'a*-free Islam.

Notes

Acknowledgments: I am grateful to Adis Duderija for helping me with patience, kindness, and wisdom in thinking through how the paper should be organized. I am solely responsible for any errors.

1. Binnaz Toprak and Ali Çarkoğlu, *Religion, Society and Politics in a Changing Turkey*, trans. Çiğdem Aksoy Fromm, ed. Jenny Sanders (Tesev, 2006), 81.
2. Hakan Yavuz, "Islam without Shari'a?" in *Shari'a Politics*, ed. Robert Hefner (Bloomington: Indiana University Press, 2011), 149.
3. Ibid., 164–165.
4. Ibid., 152.
5. Ibid.
6. Bernard Weiss, *The Spirit of Islamic Law* (Athens: University of Georgia Press, 1998), 56–58.
7. Yavuz, "Islam without Shari'a?" 173–174 (emphasis mine).
8. I follow Atif Ahmad in translating *maṣlaḥa* as "utility" instead of "good," which evokes Aristotelian themes that are "not relevant to the Islamic context and tend to disorient rather than guide the reader" (Ahmad Atif Ahmad, *Structural Interrelations of Theory and Practice in Islamic Law* (Brill, 2006), 142).
9. Yavuz, "Islam without Shari'a?" 166–167.
10. Hayrettin Karaman, *İslam'ın Işığında Günün Meseleleri*, vol. 2 (İz Yayıncılık, 2003), 82–83.
11. Hayrettin Karaman, *Yeni Gelişmeler Karşısında İslam Hukuku*, 2nd ed. (İklim Yayınları, 1987), 50–54.
12. Hayrettin Karaman, "Laikliğin Tarifi (3)," *Yeni Şafak*, October 27, 2006.
13. Hayrettin Karaman, "Batı ve İslami Maksatlar," *Yeni Şafak*, October 6, 2011.
14. For the parallel traditionalist account of Husnu Aktas (b. 1950) (penname Yusuf Kerimoglu), whose writings appear in the ultraconservative journal *Misak* that he owns, see Yusuf Kerimoglu, *Fıkhi Meseleler* (Ölçü Yayınları, 1987), 109–124.
15. Nihat Dalgın, "Özel Günlerdeki Kadınların İbadeti," *İslam Hukuku Araştırmaları Dergisi*, 9 (2007), 387.
16. Nihat Dalgın, "İslam Hukuku Açısından Müslüman Bayanın Ehl-i Kitap Erkekle Evliliği," *İslam Hukuku Dergisi*, 2 (2003), 131–156.
17. Mehmet Erdoğan, *İslam Hukukunda Ahkamın Değişmesi* (MÜİFV, 1990), 55.

18. Bediüzzaman Said Nursi, *Risale-i Nur Külliyatı: Kaynaklı, İndeksli, Lügatli*, II vols (YeniAsya, 1994), 1159–1160, 1848–1850.
19. "Fethullah Gülen Bir Reformist Midir?," Fethullah Gülen, last modified January 26, 2012 (accessed June 17, 2013), http://tr.fgulen.com/content/view/20201/5/.
20. "Fethullah Gülen Bir Reformist Midir?"
21. "Bediüzzaman'ı Anlamak Üzerine," Metin Karabasoglu (accessed June 17, 2013), http://www.cevaplar.org/index.php?content_view=3676&ctgr_id=138.
22. Tahsin Gorgun, "Dünyevileşme ve Makasıd," *Din ve Hayat*, 3 (2011), 14–15.
23. Ibid., "Dünyevileşme ve Makasıd," 14–15.
24. Tahsin Gorgun, "Siyasallaşan Dünyada Dini İlimlerin Değişen Statüleri" (paper presented at *Türkiye'de İslamcılık Düşüncesi Sempozyumu*, Istanbul, May 17–19, 2013).
25. Gorgun, "Siyasallaşan Dünyada Dini İlimlerin Değişen Statüleri."
26. Ibid. One of the most important Islamic reform projects of the nineteenth century was the codification of *sharīʿa* in 1869–1876 with Majalla, which was effective until its abrogation in 1926.
27. "Diyanet Kurul Kararları, 2005," PRA (accessed June 17, 2013), http://www.diyanet.gov.tr/turkish/dy/KurulDetay.aspx?ID=1134.
28. "Diyanet Kurul Kararları, 1980," PRA (accessed June 17, 2013), http://www.diyanet.gov.tr/turkish/dy/KurulDetay.aspx?ID=3.
29. "Diyanet Kurul Kararları, 2000," PRA (accessed June 17, 2013), http://www.diyanet.gov.tr/turkish/dy/KurulDetay.aspx?ID=8.
30. Ahmet Yaman, ed., *Makasıd ve İctihad* (Yediveren Yayınları, 2002).
31. Rahmi Telkenaroglu, "Makasıd İctihadına Dayanan Külli Kaideler," *Usul*, 10 (2008), 39.
32. Yaman, *Makasıd ve İctihad*, 11, 178.
33. Yunus Vehbi Yavuz, "Maksadi Yorum," *İHD*, 8 (2006), 41.
34. Yunus Vehbi Yavuz, "Kur'an Hükümlerinin Amaçları" (Bursa, 1988), 1–33.
35. Yaman, *Makasıd ve İctihad*, 180.
36. Ibid., 185–190.
37. Ibid., 224–225. Yaman here points out that the *maqāṣid al-sharīʿa* is prone to the constant danger, in el Fadl's words, of calling the "authority of the Author (God) to justify the despotism of the reader. A human being can only represent his or her efforts in search of this truth.... And, God knows best." Khaled Abou El Fadl, "Islamic Authority," in *New Directions in Islamic Thought*, ed. Karl Vogt et al. (I.B. Tauris, 2009), 129.
38. Ahmet Yaman, "Dinin Kaynağı Ben Miyim," *Timetürk*, August 17, 2011. Still, one has to be very careful about not absolutizing the *ijmāʿ* for Yaman (Ahmet Yaman, "İslam Hukuk Mirasını Algılama ve Uygulama Yöntemi Üzerine," *Divan*, 13 (2002/2), 309–310).
39. Ali Pekcan, *İslam Hukukunda Gaye Problemi*, 2nd ed. (Ek Kitap, 2012).
40. For the first steps of applying the *maqāṣid al-sharīʿa* as the key for an authentic Islamic human rights, see Recep Ardoğan, "İslam'da İnsan Haklarının Teolojik

Değeri" (paper presented at İnsan Haklarında Yeni Arayışlar Sempozyumu, May 27–29, 2006), 277–304.
41. See Mohammad Hashim Kamali, *Maqasid al-Shari'ah Made Simple* (IAIS, Malaysia, 2008), 11–15.
42. Sherman Jackson, "Literalism, Empiricism, and Induction," *Michigan State Law Review* (2006), 1479–1480.
43. See, for example, Yunus Vehbi Yavuz, "Dindarlıkta Reform," *Habervaktim*, February 22, 2009.
44. Ahmet Yaman, "Nasdan Olguya Başörtüsü," *EskiYeni*, 8 (2008), 103–108.
45. Yaman, *Makasıd ve İctihad*, 187–190.
46. Pekcan, *İslam Hukukunda Gaye Problemi*, 191–192.
47. Ibid., 156–157, 308, 406.
48. Felix Korner, *Revisionist Koran Hermeneutics in Contemporary Turkish University Theology* (Ergon Verlag, 2005), 60.
49. See Mehmet Pacacı, *Kur'an ve Ben Ne Kadar Tarihseliz?* (Ankara Okulu, 2000), 34.
50. Pacacı, *Kur'an ve Ben*, 48, 65.
51. Ibid., 49–50.
52. Ibid., 50–51.
53. Ibid., 50. For a parallel *maqāṣid*-oriented proposal of a new hermeneutical methodology in line with Abu Zayd, see Mustafa İslamoğlu, "Lafız, Mana, Maksat," *Yeni Şafak*, April 8, 2000.
54. Mehmet Gormez, "Sünnet ve Hadis'in Anlaşılması ve Yorumlanmasında Metodoloji Sorunu," *Journal of Islamic Research*, 10 (1997), 35.
55. Ibid., 35–39.
56. Ibid., 38.
57. Hayri Kırbasoglu, *İslam Düşüncesinde Sünnet. Eleştirel Bir Yaklaşım* (Ankara Okulu, 2001), 238–239. Traditionalists are very critical of this definition of *sunna*. See, for example, Hayrettin Karaman, "Maksat İslam'ı Kuşa Çevirmek Değilse," *Altınoluk*, 114 (1995), 41–44.
58. Kırbasoglu, *İslam Düşüncesinde Sünnet*, 89–90, 111–116.
59. Mehmet Dag, "İslam'da Örtünme Üzerine," *İslam İlimleri Enstitüsü*, 5 (1982), 191.
60. Mehmet Dag, "İslam Dininde Reform, Ama Nasıl?" *Cumhuriyet*, October 4, 2004, 2.
61. Dag, "İslamda Örtünme Üzerine," 190. Mehmet Erdoğan's direct attack on Dağ's ethicalizing view on the veiling for women on the basis of the *maqāṣid al-sharīʻa* displays the tension between the conflicting conceptualizations of the divine purposes (Erdoğan, *İslam Hukukunda Ahkamın Değişmesi*, 55).
62. Yaşar Nuri Ozturk, *Kur'an Verileri Açısından Laiklik* (Yeni Boyut, 2003), 45.
63. Yaşar Nuri Ozturk, *Din ve Fıtrat (Yaradılış)*, 2nd ed. (Yeni Boyut, 1992), 33–34.
64. Yaşar Nuri Ozturk, *İslam Nasıl Yozlaştırıldı?* (Yeni Boyut, 2000), 407. This *maqāṣid*-oriented argument has been attacked not only by the traditionalists,

but also by the PRA and the *maqāṣid* scholars who follow the traditional line such as Yaman (see, e.g., Yaman, *Makasid ve Ictihad*, 187).

65. Yaşar Nuri Ozturk, *Kur'an Uyarıyor (Tevhid Mücadelesi)*, 4th ed. (Yeni Boyut, 1999), 52.
66. Yaşar Nuri Ozturk, *Kur'an'ı Anlamaya Doğru*, 10th ed. (Yeni Boyut, 1999), 237–239.
67. Yaşar Nuri Ozturk, *İslam'ı Anlamaya Doğru*, 3rd ed. (Yeni Boyut, 1997), 165. Interestingly, this privileged role given to the Qur'ān was a key mark of the classical *maqāṣid al-sharī'a* scholars as well. Hallaq argues that this overemphasis on the Qur'ān was the main reason why the *maqāṣid al-sharī'a* discourse did not fit into the highly complex intricate legal theory (see Felicitas Opwis, *Maslaha and the Purpose of the Law* (Brill, 2010), 331).
68. Ozturk, *İslam'ı Anlamaya Doğru*, 164–165; Ozturk, *Kur'an Uyarıyor*, 202–204.
69. Yasin Ceylan, a philosophy professor at the Middle East Technical University, unites these two critiques in his reading of Ozturk ("Yaşar Nuri Ozturk'ün Misyonu," Yasin Ceylan (accessed June 17, 2013), http://www.phil.metu.edu.tr/yceylan/works/ysr-nr-ztrk.html).

CHAPTER 6

Maṣlaḥa and Rachid al-Ghannushi's Reformist Project

Karim Sadek

Introduction

Maṣlaḥa, or human interest and well-being, as the embodiment of *maqāṣid al-sharīʿa* (the higher objectives of Islamic law) is one of the principles in *uṣūl al-fiqh* (the origins or fundamentals of jurisprudence) that entered Islamic legal theory as early as the tenth century.[1] In the modern period, there has been an increasing reliance on *maṣlaḥa* as a tool for legal change,[2] and, as this volume demonstrates, a wide range of contemporary Islamic reformists have resorted to a *maqāṣidi* (purposive) approach to find solutions internal to Islam for a variety of challenges that Muslims face. In this respect, Rachid al-Ghannushi, the Tunisian Islamic thinker and leader of *ḥizb al-nahda* (The Renaissance Party), is no exception. To be sure, there is a great deal of diversity in how Islamic thinkers and jurists have understood *maqāṣid al-sharīʿa* and how they have incorporated *maṣlaḥa* in their overall legal, ethical, social, and political theories. In this chapter I critically assess Ghannushi's employment of *maṣlaḥa* in his sociopolitical reformist project.

Ghannushi's thought and politics have been well respected and widely debated in Islamic and non-Islamic circles, both inside and outside the Arab world, and he is considered to be representative of a contemporary trend in Islamic revivalist thought and movements.[3] Ghannushi's dissident activity has chiefly been against an oppressive Tunisian state that systematically excluded Islamists from social and political life and his demand was for public inclusion. Today, however, *ḥizb al-nahda* is at the center of Tunisian social and political life. Does this mean that Ghannushi's contribution has become obsolete? I do not think so. There is a wider intellectual project in Ghannushi's work that goes beyond the Tunisian borders and the demand for public inclusion. The concern of that project is to enter modernity via the doors of Islam. In this context, the following statement is instructive: "Islamists today seek genuine modernity, one that emanates from within, one that is in response to local needs and that is in conformity with local culture and value system."[4] This more ambitious project, which Ghannushi articulates in his theoretical model of the Islamic state, is my main concern in the following pages. It is thus worth noting that this chapter approaches Ghannushi as a political thinker who has something to say on the relation between state, society, and religion, rather than as an activist or a politician.

In his theoretical model of the Islamic state, Ghannushi attempts to negotiate a delicate marriage between a conception of the state that is characteristically Islamic and the demands of democracy, human rights, and pluralism. Further, Ghannushi conducts this negotiation with an awareness of the backdrop against which it takes place, namely, an authoritarian postcolonial rule and a series of successes and failures in Islamic revivalist thought and experience. While the challenges obstructing this marriage are thorny and multifaceted, they should not blind us from appreciating the significance of carrying out the task at hand. After all, the success of such a marriage stands a chance to simultaneously address the worry that many Muslims have over the survival of Islamic identity in the modern world and that many other Muslims and non-Muslims have regarding Islam's alleged undemocratic and exclusionist nature. In what follows, I focus on one item from that negotiation assignment: Can the Islamic state respect the freedom and equality of all its citizens while maintaining that *sharīʿa* is the highest legislative authority? Ghannushi answers in the positive and in doing so he relies on *maqāṣid al-sharīʿa* as the framework for an Islamic scheme of human rights on the basis of which he argues that the Islamic state perceives and treats all its citizens as free and equal agents. Ghannushi's political model, as I show here, succeeds in providing Islamic grounds for the treatment of all citizens as equals and for granting them the freedom to exercise, express, and defend their religions and worldviews more generally. I argue, however, that when we switch from the perspective of the state (i.e., how the state perceives and treats its citizens) to the perspective of citizens (i.e., how citizens perceive the state, its foundations, laws, and policies), the freedom and equality Ghannushi aims to achieve are ultimately undermined due to his attempt at preserving the Islamic character of the state by granting *sharīʿa* the highest legislative authority. This does not necessarily imply the failure of Ghannushi's project, and I shall suggest a *maṣlaḥa*-inspired way out for his political model.

In the next section, "Ghannushi's Reformist Project," I reconstruct Ghannushi's reformist project while paying special attention to his reformist strategy and vision. Critical of a Western hegemonic discourse, and of an Islamic movement wedded to an idealized past, Ghannushi calls for a reinterpretation of Islamic principles and values in light of the challenges Muslims face in their everyday social realities. In the process of such reinterpretation, Ghannushi adopts a *maqāṣidi* approach to *sharīʿa* as the embodiment of God's message expressed in *al-naṣṣ* (Qur'ān and Sunna). In the section "Ghannushi's Employment of maqāṣid al-sharīʿa and maṣlaḥa," I lay out two instances in which Ghannushi employs *maqāṣid al-sharīʿa* for the service of his project. In the first instance, Ghannushi justifies the religious duty of Muslims in political participation while living under non-Islamic regimes on the basis of enhancing the higher purposes of Islamic law.[5] In the second instance, Ghannushi employs *maqāṣid al-sharīʿa* as the framework for, and limits on, an Islamic scheme of human rights. The rights he defends in that scheme, particularly the right to religious freedom, play a crucial role in arguing that the model of the Islamic state he defends, which in turn could serve as a guiding ideal for the Islamic movement and for Muslims to aspire to and seek to achieve, respects all its citizens as free and equal agents. This is important for Ghannushi's reformist project since in order for his conception of the Islamic state to be plausible and for it to take social roots, it has to account for the concerns of Muslims living in the modern world, which, among other things, relate to freedom and equality. By way of critically assessing the success of Ghannushi's reliance on *maqāṣid al-sharīʿa* as the framework for, and limits on, human rights in his reformist project, I focus on non-Muslim citizens as a test case for equality and freedom in the Islamic state. In the section "Acknowledging the Islamic Character of the State," I argue that non-Muslims would rightly feel they are second-class citizens in the Islamic state as conceptualized by Ghannushi—hence, undermining the freedom and equality his model aims to achieve. In the final section "That without Which Life Would Be Ruined," I conclude with a *maṣlaḥa*-inspired modification on Ghannushi's political model.

Ghannushi's Reformist Project

Like other Islamic reformists before him, Ghannushi is dissatisfied with the status quo of Muslim societies. The solution for him, and again like many of his predecessors, lies in Islam and the application of *sharīʿa*. The question is how to conceive of *sharīʿa* and its application,[6] and the answer clarifies the reform project under consideration.

First, on Ghannushi's view, the application of *sharīʿa* does not imply a wholesale rejection of Western notions, ideals, and achievements. In fact, according to Ghannushi, in the absence of an Islamic state, secular democracy is the second best alternative.[7] As far as Islam's relation to the West is concerned, Ghannushi neither rejects nor indiscriminately adopts Western models of democracy and modernity. Fundamentally, what Ghannushi rejects is the blind acceptance of the Western secular perspective and its guiding assumptions as setting the criteria for success in determining whether and how Islam can join modernity and be democratic.[8] One of the difficulties Islam in the modern period is facing, Ghannushi contends, results not from Muslims deviating from the path of *sharīʿa*, but from Muslims increasingly resisting the authority of *sharīʿa*,that is, becoming less accepting of *sharīʿa's* authority. Ghannushi traces this resistance to the modern secular Western perspective, which conceives of the human being as independent from its creator, and consequently requires Muslims to adapt the understanding of their religion accordingly in order for them to join modernity.[9] Doing so, however, contradicts the very basis of Islam's God-dependent view of the human being. At the foundation of the Islamic perspective, Ghannushi maintains, lies the claim that the human being is the vicegerent of God on earth.[10]

It is important to clarify that by *sharīʿa* Ghannushi is not referring to any particular set of legalistic rulings derived from *al-naṣṣ* but to the divine message as embodied in *al-naṣṣ* and the worldview it expresses.[11] In the introduction to his main work, *al-ḥurriyyāt al-'amma fi al-dawla al-islāmiyya*, Ghannushi defines *sharīʿa* as the "fixed fundamentals" as we find them in the Qur'ān and the Sunna, and these "mean nothing more than the clearly stated and uncontroversial rulings in the Qur'ān, as well as the clear rulings in the Sunna that is soundly transmitted."[12] Further on in that same work, Ghannushi elaborates that *sharīʿa* "is not a summation of rigid texts, neither is it articulated in a final manner, nor is it a legalistic document that identified a ruling for every act and state. Rather, there is plenty of room for interpretation, specification, addition, and renewal through the use of individual and collective *ijtihād*."[13]

Second, the application of *sharīʿa*, according to Ghannushi, does not imply the application of another era's interpretations of Islamic principles and values. Ghannushi identifies the main challenge that faces the Islamic movement when he asks: "How can we [the Islamic movement] live in this modern world while preserving our Islam?"[14] While he acknowledges the different achievements of the Islamic movement, he is critical of its inability to understand and connect with the everyday realities of Muslims as social members. For instance, Ghannushi traces the failures of the Islamic movement in appealing to the working class and to women on its inability to connect to the difficulties they face in their respective social realities.[15] Ghannushi continues to blame such inability on a way of thinking that remains wedded to a rather archaic understanding of Islam, by which he means Islamic principles and values that applied to former Muslim social realities do not cater to the modern realities that Muslims are living in. His attack here is directed to what he calls the "idealistic" or "utopian" frame of mind that characterizes a large part of the Islamic movement. As a result of operating with such mind-set, the Muslim of today "gets infected with a disability to understand her own reality and embracing its evolutions, moving forces, and latent potentials."[16]

With this critical attitude Ghannushi is both open to borrowing from the West without letting it set the rules of the game and capable of embracing the Islamic movement's aim of bringing social change through the application of *sharīʿa* without rigidly holding on to an idealized past. The way out for Muslim societies implies neither a wholesale rejection of Western notions, ideals, and achievements, nor the dogmatic application of an outdated understanding of Islamic principles and values. Instead, Ghannushi calls for a renewed process of reinterpretation of *sharīʿa* as embodied in *al-naṣṣ* in a way that is sensitive and answers to the realities of Muslims' everyday lives in the modern period.

Other than this critical attitude, Ghannushi's reformist project stands out in its method for achieving social change. Although for Ghannushi establishing an Islamic state is required for a proper and full realization of Islam, political reform falls last in the priorities of his reformist project. The priority, instead, goes to reforming the individual and the community.[17] Ghannushi gives priority to the social over the political, and this is manifest in more than one way in his reformist project. He advocates political change through social change and he targets social interests, which "must be put before anything else."[18] Further, as evident in the quote as follows, he seeks to achieve social change through persuasion rather than through violence:

> It has been proven that what is achieved socially is more permanent and better than what is achieved politically. Modern experience has taught us that things achieved through the state are quick but short-lived, because they depend on force. But what is done through social activity lasts, because it depends on persuasion. Humans do not like to be forced.[19]

Ghannushi's reformist method is not based only on prudential considerations, however. He argues that society is the foundation for legitimate political authority. "We, the Tunisian Islamists, value human dignity and civil liberties, accept that popular will is the source of political legitimacy and believe in pluralism and in the alteration of power through free elections."[20] This is not to say, however, that social activism is a mere means to the end of political power. Ghannushi writes: "Government is a small part of the institutions of civil society. It is there to support and strengthen society. There must be more institutions of civil society, enough so that the people don't need the state."[21] Thus, not only is social work more effective than politics, but also the role of politics—specifically, the government—is to serve society to the point where the people become independent from it. Hence, even if political power is achieved, social activism should not subside. With Ghannushi's reformist strategy in mind, let us turn to the basic features of his reformist vision, the Islamic state as a political model for an Islamic society.

The fundamental core of Islamic political philosophy is the vicegerency theory: the human being is God's vicegerent on earth.[22] On the basis of this theory, Ghannushi derives the two sources of authority in the Islamic state: *al-naṣṣ* and *shūra*.[23] *Al-naṣṣ*, on the one hand, embodies God's law, *sharīʿa*, which is overarching, unquestionable, and eternal. *Shūra*, on the other hand, is "the spinal cord of the *umma*'s authority in establishing political rule on the basis of participation, cooperation, and responsibility."[24] The Islamic state is thus the "state of God and the people, the state of *al-naṣṣ* and *shūra*."[25] Ghannushi sets two criteria that defines the Islamic government:

1. Supreme legislative authority is for the *shariʿa*. That is the revealed law of Islam, which transcends all laws. Within this context, it is the responsibility of scholars to deduce detailed laws and regulations to be used as guidelines by judges. The head of the Islamic state is the leader of the executive body entrusted with the responsibility of implementing such laws and regulations.
2. Political power belongs to the community (*umma*), which should adopt a form of *shura*, which is a system of mandatory consultation.[26]

Although Ghannushi does not sufficiently elaborate on the connection between the scholars' interpretations of *al-naṣṣ* and the state's legislative body, it should be noted that the connection is tight and somehow built into the structure of the Islamic government. This connection is important and will play a role in the argument later (see sections "Acknowledging the Islamic Character of the State" and "That without Which Life Would Be Ruined"). Turning to *shūra*, as a principle rather than a particular form of governance,[27] Ghannushi includes elections, deliberative processes, and "any allowed path [i.e., not in contradiction with *al-naṣṣ*] that can indicate or show who gets the trust of the *umma*."[28] Other than the set of mechanisms for democratic will formation, decision making, and opinion giving, *shūra* takes the form of a basic principle underlying everyday social interaction in the Islamic state, which Ghannushi refers to in terms of "habits of *shūra*" and a shuristic "way of life."[29] Having said that, one should ask, how are divine and human authority related? In this regard, Ghannushi writes: "Transforming the Book into an *umma* is the essence of the mission of *'ulamā'*, and it is a mission that goes beyond individual efforts."[30] Thus, the function of *ijtihād* is to bridge the gap between the universal general (i.e., the directives of *al-naṣṣ*) and the concrete particular (i.e., everyday human life).[31] Now, given the changing nature of social life, *ijtihād* must be flexible. *Ijtihād* is also revisable and fallible since it could never reach the epistemic status of certainty.[32] Finally, Ghannushi maintains that although jurists have the authority and responsibility to derive rulings from *al-naṣṣ*, they have no authority to impose their interpretations on Muslims:

> While respecting its *'ulama*, an Islamic society does not lose its freedom of choice. The *'ulama* interpret religion in their capacity as *mujtahidin* [plural of *mujtahid*—jurist] not as representatives of some kind of an official establishment that monopolises speaking in the name of God or interpreting his revelation. What the *'ulama* suggest is no more than their understanding, or their *ijtihad*, a proposal submitted to the community, which has the final word in accepting or rejecting [. . .]. An *ijtihad* that is accepted by the majority is usually adopted, though on most matters there could be more than one *ijtihad*. In this case people subscribe to the *ijtihad* they feel more comfortable with.[33]

Thus, the community has a role to play in order for the essence of the mission of the *'ulamā'* to be completed, that is, in order for the Book to be transformed into an *umma*. Hence, the success (but not the validity) of juristic interpretations cannot be determined independently from the subjects for whom they are made and through whom they are to take shape and get implemented—otherwise, how could the Book be transformed into an *umma*?[34] *Ijtihād*, then, according to Ghannushi is flexible, fallible, and includes, though in different ways, the Muslim community and not only the jurists.

The Islamic state is then the "state of God and the people, the state of *al-naṣṣ* and *shūra*."[35] While *al-naṣṣ* represents divine authority, *shūra* represents human authority, and the Islamic state is to combine both sources of authority. In fact, the whole point of the Islamic state, its raison d'être, is "to realize *sharī'a*, to instantiate the absolute in the course of history, and to connect the divine with the human. . . ."[36] Hence, the jurists, who are considered the experts on *al-naṣṣ* are to transform the "Book into an *umma*"[37] and in that process all members of the Muslim community have a role to play. While jurists determine the validity of interpretations, Muslims determine the success of interpretations. We can then say that the Islamic state is to facilitate, enhance, and protect the proper application of *sharīʿa* as embodied in *al-naṣṣ* to diverse and changing human circumstances. Ghannushi gives an important role to *maqāṣid al-sharīʿa* and *maṣlaḥa* in that ongoing process of *sharīʿa* application by arguing that jurists must have the purposes of *sharīʿa* in mind when legislating and must also be keen on making sure that their understanding of *sharīʿa* does in fact serve these purposes.[38] There is then a clear way in which the very function of the Islamic state incorporates *maqāṣid al-sharīʿa* and *maṣlaḥa*. Before I move to a more detailed explanation of the role *maqāṣid al-sharīʿa* and *maṣlaḥa* in Ghannushi's reformist project, let me conclude this section by noting that Ghannushi distinguishes between "Islamic legitimacy" and "political legitimacy." Islamic legitimacy requires abiding to God's commands.[39] While political legitimacy requires the acceptance of the ruled, expressing the will of the ruled, and taking care of the interests of the ruled.[40] The Islamic state as the state of *al-naṣṣ* and *shūra* is supposed to satisfy both kinds of legitimacy. First, it satisfies Islamic legitimacy in its commitment to *al-naṣṣ*. Second, it satisfies political legitimacy in its commitment to *shūra*, hence, to popular sovereignty and the will and interest of the people.[41]

Ghannushi's Employment of maqāṣid al-sharīʿa and maṣlaḥa

The history of *maṣlaḥa* and *maqāṣid al-sharīʿa*, as this volume testifies, is rich, complex, and has evolved in several stages.[42] The basic idea, however, is simple. The purpose of divine revelation is the improvement and attainment of human interest and well-being in this life and the hereafter. As the purpose of the *sharīʿa* embodied in *al-naṣṣ, maṣlaḥa* has been used by jurists and *ʿulamāʾ* in different ways. It has been used as a guiding principle in the procedure of deriving laws by analogy (*qiyās*) when applying a text to a situation that is not covered by *al-naṣṣ*. *Maṣlaḥa* has also been used in a more substantive way as a validity test for already derived legal rulings. Further, and most significantly, *maṣlaḥa* has been used to override textual rulings—to adapt the text.[43] Opwis summarizes that for deriving laws and/or for checking the validity of laws, *maṣlaḥa* functioned as "a tool of finding new law when the authoritative texts are silent and adapting existing law when circumstances call for it."[44] *Maṣlaḥa* is then a key legal tool for both widening the scope of application and revising Islamic law. Classical jurists who have capitalized on the principle of *maṣlaḥa* to expand or adapt al-naṣṣ have also set restrictions on its application. There is a wide variety in the scope and justification of such restrictions, but in all cases *maṣlaḥa* does not unqualifiedly take precedence over the text. Commenting on the variety of ways restrictions on *maṣlaḥa* took shape, Opwis writes:

> The extent to which a jurist permitted textual rulings to be superseded by appeal to the purpose of the law, either in form of unattested *maṣlaḥas* or legal precepts, varies greatly. At one end of the spectrum we find Ibn Taymiyya who held that the human intellect cannot comprehend God's will and, hence, cannot evaluate situations merely by looking at the *maṣlaḥa* involved. *Maṣlaḥa* has no priority over the revealed texts simply by being intended by the Lawgiver. Without taking recourse to the texts, a jurist's decision was invalid. Located at the other extreme is al-Ṭūfī. He saw in *maṣlaḥa* a method to unify the Muslim community and, hence, permitted its application widely in the sphere of customs and civil transactions.[45]

Ghannushi's own use of *maṣlaḥa* and *maqāṣid al-sharīʿa* draws on the views of Abu Ishaq al-Shatibi, the fourteenth-century Andalusian jurist, who "found the principle of *maṣlaḥa* to be the essential point at which all the enquiries about the nature and purpose of legal obligation, social and legal change, and the method of legal reasoning converge. At the same time this principle also provides the basis of the unity that underlies the diversity of rules in Islamic law."[46] Shatibi's work on *maqāṣid al-sharīʿa* and *maṣlaḥa* is considered to have "provided jurists with a comprehensive system to extend and adapt the law to new circumstances."[47] Yet, and like other classical jurists, Shatibi puts restrictions on the application of *maṣlaḥa*. He

> did not consider *maṣlaḥa* to be weightier in every instance. Exempted were those particular rulings that constituted legal licenses (*rukhaṣ*) or specifications (*takhṣīṣāt*). In addition, considerations of *maṣlaḥa* had no bearing on acts of worship (*ʿibādāt*), acts that happened or could have happened during the lifetime of the Prophet and that received a ruling, and the continuous practice of the early Islamic community. Any other act may be judged according to the *maṣlaḥa* it entails under particular circumstances, which, of course, varies by place, time, and person.[48]

Based on a thorough study of *al-naṣṣ*, the tradition of Islamic jurisprudence, and considering the different experiences of the applications of jurisprudence and the state of human knowledge, Shatibi established the basic guidelines of the *maqāṣidī* school.[49] Quoting Shatibi, Ghannushi writes: "From our exploration of the *shari`a*, we have concluded that it was only set up to serve the interests of man."[50] In Ghannushi's own words, according to *maqāṣid al-sharī'a* "religion was revealed only to fulfill and protect the needs and interests of mankind in this life and the hereafter, as a general framework for tackling new problems with the Muslim society."[51] As for the definition of *maṣlaḥa*, Ghannushi summarizes Shatibi's categorization of the requirements of *maṣlaḥa*:[52]

> He [Shāṭibī] categorizes them into "essential requirements" without which life would be ruined; these include the protection of faith, of life, of progeny, of wealth and mind. Then he spoke of the "special requirements" without which man would be in distress and hardship. They include the requirement to enjoy lawful and good things in life. Finally, he spoke of "ameliorative requirements" whose absence would not seriously undermine life. These include the various manners related for instance to eating and drinking, etc.[53]

Ghannushi uses this categorization as the general framework within which all the details of religion are to be subsumed, and "all new problems in the lives not only of Muslims but of all humanity, can find proper solutions that guarantee the fulfillment of their requirements."[54] With that in mind, let us take a look at a particular context in which Ghannushi employs *maṣlaḥa* to adapt God's law and accommodate for the needs of Muslims. The example illustrates the extent to which Ghannushi takes *sharī'a* to have "room for interpretation, specification, addition, and renewal through the use of individual and collective *ijtihād*."[55]

Ghannushi affirms that it is the duty of every Muslim to work toward establishing the Islamic state, where *sharī'a*, as divine law, has the highest legislative authority and "political power belongs to the community (*umma*), which should adopt a form of *shūra*, which is a system of mandatory consultation."[56] When this ideal, however, is not attainable what should Muslims do both in the context of forming a majority or a minority, if they are bound to live in a non-Islamic regime? By way of addressing this question, Ghannushi draws on *maṣlaḥa* to justify a religious duty for Muslims' participation and power sharing in such regimes. He writes:

> Power-sharing in a Muslim or a non-Muslim environment becomes a necessity in order to lay the foundations of the social order. This power-sharing may not necessarily be based on Islamic *sharī'a* law. However, it

> must be based on an important foundation of the Islamic government, namely *shūra*, or the authority of the *umma*, so as to prevent the evils of dictatorship, foreign domination, or local anarchy. Such a process of power sharing may also aim to achieve a national or humanistic interest such as independence, development, social solidarity, civil liberties, human rights, political pluralism, independence of the judiciary, freedom of the press, or liberty for mosques and Islamic activities.[57]

The participation of Muslims in non-Islamic regimes, including forming alliances with the non-religious and secularists, is justified when considering that it involves promoting the interest ofand man and preventing harm, that is *maṣlaḥa*. This is a case in point where given Muslims' reality, Ghannushi relies on *maṣlaḥa* as the purpose of *sharīʿa* to find a solution internal to Islam for Muslims. In that sense and to that extent, we can say that the employment of *maqāṣid al-sharīʿa* has served Ghannushi well. With *maṣlaḥa*, as a legal tool, the literality of *al-naṣṣ* could be transcended in a systematic way. The jurist has at his disposal a tool for interpreting, applying, and revising the text, and it is a tool that is independent from the literality of the text. To show or deny *maṣlaḥa*, one could provide rational arguments whose convincing powers are independent from the literality of *al-naṣṣ*, and from the intricacies of the Islamic legal tradition. What counts as conducive or inimical to *maṣlaḥa* is subject to human discernment and the sociocultural background of the context in question. As Opwis puts it:

> In the final analysis, what attains *maṣlaḥa* and averts harm is—as al-Shatibi's thought shows—determined by human estimation. Acceptable harm is known by custom and convention not by religious law. Human evaluation of what constitutes hardship is decisive in determining the believer's religious responsibility to obey God's laws.[58]

Other than accommodating for Muslims living under non-Islamic regimes, Ghannushi employs *maqāṣid al-sharīʿa* and *maṣlaḥa* to set the framework for, and limits on, human rights. Ghannushi starts his discussion of human rights in Islam by grounding them on the vicegerency thesis.[59] "The human being in Islam is the vicegerent of God, and that trusteeship—the Islamic *sharīʿa*—includes a set of rights and duties."[60] As such, humans have the responsibility and duty to honor and protect those rights, which also implies that human rights enjoy a sanctity that forbids any party, parliament, or ruler to misuse, modify, or violate them.[61] Ghannushi continues to state that since Islam aims to guide and protect the interests of people in this life and the hereafter, it is only natural to "consider these interests as the general framework within which the behavior of individuals, as well as the exercise of public and private liberties, get organized."[62] Expectedly, Ghannushi refers to Shatibi's understanding of *maṣlaḥa* as the embodiment of *maqāṣid al-sharī'a* to spell out these human interests and hence the framework of his Islamic scheme of human rights. With this general framework in place, Ghannushi proceeds to discuss different human rights.

Starting with religious freedom, Ghannushi argues that all individuals in an Islamic society have the right to choose their religion away from any pressure or coercion. This freedom is the result of humans' God-given responsibility and agency.[63] Drawing the implications of religious freedom, Ghannushi argues that equality is the basis of interaction in the Islamic society and that all individuals are to enjoy the freedom to exercise, express, and defend their religion and beliefs more generally, including atheistic ones.[64] The basic idea here is that Islamic society is open to all creeds and points of views including atheistic ones.[65] The point of such inclusion is to reflect Islam's respect for all human beings as equal and free agents irrespective of creed, color, ethnicity, and so on. Consequently, the Islamic state, which grows out of an Islamic society, is to respect and protect that openness and diversity. All citizens are equal in the eyes of the state, with respect to duties and rights, be they Muslims or not.[66] Just as Muslims enjoy the freedom to exercise, express, and defend their religion, so do non-Muslims. While keeping this in mind, it must be noted that the Islamic state is also committed to *al-naṣṣ*, to preserving the Islamic identity and protecting the Islamic character of the state, which in turn puts restrictions on both equality and freedom.

Ghannushi clarifies that equal treatment does not necessarily imply nondifferential treatment. Sometimes, treating citizens equally requires treating them differently.[67] In Ghannushi's view, differential treatment is justified only when it relates to matters of creed. All citizens enjoy equal rights and duties "except in what is required by their differences in creed."[68] For instance, Ghannushi illustrates, prohibiting the non-Muslim from drinking alcohol is unfair, just as prohibiting the Muslim to get a divorce is unfair.[69] Similarly, Ghannushi argues that in order to preserve the Islamic identity of the state, certain political and legal positions (e.g., being the head of the state) are restricted to Muslims.[70] These restrictions, however, are not to affect the public recognition of group identities. Ghannushi's efforts to accommodate non-Muslims in the Islamic state come to the fore when we look at the implications of accepting someone's creed. Crucially, Ghannushi notes that to accept someone's creed implies acknowledging their right to defend it and to show its advantages over, and the disadvantages of, what differs from it. That is why he allows non-Muslim citizens to preach to Muslims and attempt to persuade them to join their creed. Citizens of all faiths are welcome to engage in public debates, to defend their views, criticize others, and so on.[71] Further, and most interestingly, Ghannushi maintains that if such openness in public debates undermine Muslims' faith, then "the only solution for those Muslims lies in deepening their faith, or raising these challenges to their scholars,"[72] and that the only way to challenge such debates is to develop and provide stronger and more cogent arguments.[73] Thus, Ghannushi's political model recognizes all groups by securing opportunity for each group to express its identity in public. Further, Ghannushi does not put any obstacles that prevent that opportunity from turning into an active exercise of those groups' right to political self-determination. Rather, he leaves the door wide open for non-Muslims to organize themselves in the way they see fit in order to guarantee their survival and to defend their existence. This is most explicit in his views on political parties in the Islamic state. Non-Muslims can form political parties and don't even need a license to do so, nor to establish newspapers, magazines, and other forms of expression.[74] Ghannushi also gives political parties, be they Muslim or not, a crucial role. They are the organizers of civil society. The organizing role of political parties in the Islamic state, or any state for that matter, according to Ghannushi, is fundamental. If society is not organized, the principles of *shūra* and of doing good and forbidding wrong remain slogans lacking the mechanisms that allow it to become a power to check and control the power that represents it.[75]

This does not mean, however, that citizens of the Islamic state can do and say what they want. There are restrictions on freedoms as well. These restrictions are articulated in terms of *maṣlaḥa* as representing *maqāṣid al-sharīʿa*. Ghannushi writes: "*maqāṣid al-sharīʿa* provide the Muslim with a scale to weigh his behavior, a ranking of values that arranges in different degrees the directives of Islam, be they big or small, as well as guidance for his freedom and a limit for his rights and duties."[76] Ghannushi continues to assert that with regard to any matter, as long as the individual is operating within the boundaries of public interest and social well-being no one is to object, protest, or oppose his behavior. But, transgressing these boundaries "count as a violation that should be stopped and contained."[77] *Maṣlaḥa*, whose interpretation determine the understanding of public interest, sets the boundaries within which individual human rights are to operate. Ghannushi is explicit about the limits on equality and on the freedom to exercise, express, and defend one's religion and beliefs. The terminologies he uses include: "the requirements of the general system or social identity and the higher values that society abides by";[78] "general opinion... of the majority";[79] "the feelings of the majority";[80] and "respecting the general morals of dialogue."[81] What all these have in common is that they refer in one way or another to Islam as the identity that characterizes the society that the Islamic state is to serve and protect.

Acknowledging the Islamic Character of the State

The Islamic state's commitment to *al-naṣṣ*, to preserving the Islamic identity and protecting the Islamic character of the state is absolutely crucial. The question I want to address now is whether the equality and freedom of non-Muslim citizens in the Islamic state get curtailed in the name of preserving the Islamic character of the state? I focus on non-Muslim citizens only as a test case for equality and freedom in Ghannushi's political model. The main citizenship requirement that Ghannushi has for non-Muslims is that they must pay their allegiance to the Islamic state, that is, acknowledge, and commit to, the Islamic character of the state.[82] By adopting the citizens' perspective (i.e., how they look at the state, its foundations, and laws), I systematically unpack that requirement and argue that there is an inequality built into the political system that puts non-Muslims under the mercy of their Muslim compatriots. In this way, there is an implicit unfairness in Ghannushi's political model that undermines its commitment to freedom and equality.

Let me start by asking, what exactly is the object of the requirement that non-Muslims must acknowledge and commit to the Islamic character of the state? Ghannushi separates between the form and the content of a political arrangement and contends that it is the latter rather than the former that characterizes and differentiates one political arrangement from another. The difference between the Islamic state and Western secular democratic states, for instance, is in the content only and not in mechanisms such as elections, polls, the parliament, rotating power, and so on. It is the content (i.e., the set of assumptions, values, and principles) within which these mechanisms operate and are supposed to serve that characterizes a political arrangement.[83] Thus, if non-Muslims are to acknowledge the Islamic character of the state they must acknowledge the content that characterizes the Islamic state. As the state of *al-naṣṣ* and *shūra*, the content is provided by *al-naṣṣ* rather than by *shūra*, since there is nothing characteristically Islamic about the mechanisms of *shūra*, and the habits of *shūra* operate on the social rather than the political level. So, the object of non-Muslim's commitment is *al-naṣṣ*.

But what does such a commitment imply? It does mean that non-Muslims must acknowledge and commit to *al-naṣṣ* as the source of absolute truth and validity, since that would be asking non-Muslims to join the

Islamic faith, which is in contradiction with the Islamic state's acceptance of different creeds and worldviews including atheistic ones. To his credit, Ghannushi shows sensitivity in this matter when he takes into consideration non-Muslim citizens' perspective and confirms that non-Muslims, unlike Muslims, are not required nor expected to accept the validity of *sharīʿa* as embodied in *al-naṣṣ*.[84] He writes: "*sharīʿa* for them [non-Muslim citizens] is nothing more than a law that organizes the political community [the citizenry]."[85] We can then infer that, for Ghannushi to say that non-Muslims must acknowledge the Islamic character of the state is to say that they must acknowledge *al-naṣṣ* as the source of the law that organizes the dealings among citizens as well as the interaction between citizens and the state, and nothing more. Muslims perceive the law that organizes the citizenry as the expression of divine law. As such, and from the perspective of Muslim citizens, the state, along with its foundations and laws, is an expression of their faith, identity, and self-understanding.

It is unfortunate that Ghannushi does not elaborate on the difference between how Muslims and non-Muslims perceive the state, its laws, and so on, since that would have clarified the meaning of the requirement he puts on non-Muslim citizenship. By way of moving our discussion forward and preserving the political legitimacy of the Islamic state,[86] we could interpret these different perceptions of the state in terms of an overlapping consensus, to use John Rawls's term.[87] That is, different social constituencies adopt and abide by *sharīʿa* each for their own reasons. To the extent that such an overlapping consensus can be achieved, Ghannushi would be able to maintain that the content that characterizes the Islamic state is provided by *al-naṣṣ*, and that all citizens are committed to *al-naṣṣ* (though each for their own reasons), without undermining the Islamic state's commitment to accept different worldviews and be pluralistic. Unfortunately, however, this does not work for the following reasons.

Why would non-Muslims accept *al-naṣṣ* as the source of the law? Ghannushi needs to make a case to the effect that non-Muslims would have reasons internal to their own worldviews on the basis of which they would accept *al-naṣṣ* to be the source of the organizing law. But, neither does Ghannushi make the case, nor is it clear that such a case can be made. After all, *al-naṣṣ* makes substantive prescriptions about the world, our place in it, and how we should behave. Different creeds and worldviews differ and disagree precisely on such substantive prescriptions. In all plausibility, non-Muslims would have reasons not to commit to *al-naṣṣ* as the source of the organizing law, and they might very well have alternative sources for the organizing law. The flaw in Ghannushi's view on this matter is that he seems to think that it makes sense from the perspective of non-Muslim citizens to acknowledge and commit to *sharī'a* as "nothing more than a law that organizes the political community," in total separation from *sharī'a* as an expression of a particular and substantive worldview.

There is yet another problematic aspect in requiring non-Muslims to acknowledge and commit to *al-naṣṣ* as the source of the law that organizes the citizenry. What does it, effectively speaking, mean to say that *al-naṣṣ* is the source of the law in the Islamic state? After all, *al-naṣṣ* is a text, and non-Muslims should be concerned with the authority that can derive the laws they are expected to abide by. This concern directly connects with public interest as setting the limits on human rights in the Islamic state. *Maqāṣid al-sharī'a* are the higher purposes of Islamic law as embodied in *al-naṣṣ*. For Ghannushi, these purposes are defined in terms *maṣlaḥa*. The understanding of these requirements determines the understanding of public interest in the Islamic state, which sets the boundaries of individual freedoms. The non-Muslims' concern with the authority that can derive laws from *al-naṣṣ* blends in with a concern about the authority that can determine the requirements of *maṣlaḥa*.

We already saw that the reference to *al-naṣṣ* in the political context should be understood as a reference to an entire structure and process constituted of *al-naṣṣ*, the jurists (who determine the validity of interpretations), and the Islamic community (which determines the success of juristic interpretations)—call it "*ijtihād* system"—that take us from the absolute general to the concrete particular. In effect, it is human interpretations of *al-naṣṣ* that political power in the Islamic state must be in line with or, at least, not in contradiction with. Further, and crucially, all members of the Islamic community play an important, though different, role in these interpretations. Hence, acknowledging *al-naṣṣ* as the source of law implies accepting the interpretive outcome of the *ijtihād* system to be law. But why would non-Muslims make and uphold such a commitment? Would it be fair to ask them to do so? While a flexible, fallible, and inclusive *ijtihād* is better than having one person or a small group of people determine the law, it is not good enough for non-Muslim citizens. After all, and unlike their Muslim compatriots, they have little say in determining the success of interpretations. The ability of non-Muslims to determine the success of interpretations is at best an indirect and convoluted. Muslim social members have a direct impact on the process of *ijtihād* since they are to determine the success (but not the validity) of juristic interpretations. These Muslim citizens themselves live in society along with non-Muslim citizens and thus can see and sense the impact of different juristic interpretations on them. This in turn might affect Muslim citizen's judgments regarding the success of these interpretations. In short, non-Muslim citizens can affect the success of *ijtihād* only by being part of the social context of Muslim citizens. Such a chain of influence is deficient and by itself unacceptable to non-Muslims. Non-Muslims would always and rightly feel under the mercy of Muslims in the Islamic state. Further, and crucially, being and feeling in such a subordinate position is not merely the result of being the minority in an Islamic society, but is systemic. The fact that the Islamic state is a Muslim majority state does not justify the category of a second-class citizenship. There is a built-in inequality and unfairness that must be addressed to the extent that Ghannushi wants to rescue a robust understanding of equal citizenship, political parties' pluralism, and religious freedom in the Islamic state.

In summing up, by unpacking Ghannushi's requirement that non-Muslims must pay allegiance to the state and acknowledge its Islamic character, we see how that requirement undermines the claim that all citizens in the Islamic state are treated as equal free agents. By imposing limits on human rights that are directly and structurally determined by the Islamic community (*ijtihād* system), equality, freedom, and party pluralism are more decorative than substantive. How emancipatory and meaningful is the claim that groups can form political parties to organize themselves, make political demands, and defend their worldviews in public debates, if their demands and the way they can express their identities and interests are directly and systemically regulated and controlled by Islamic criteria they do not endorse and cannot even influence how they are understood? From the perspective of non-Muslims, law in the Islamic state is not in their service but in the service of their supposed-to-be-equal Muslim compatriots. They would rightly feel like second-class citizens under the mercy of Muslims. While the Islamic state aims at perceiving and treating non-Muslims as equal free agents, in effect it does not.

That "without Which Life Would Be Ruined"

Where does this leave us? If the argument in the previous section is convincing then, in order for Ghannushi to uphold his commitment to equal citizenship (along with its implications on pluralism, freedom, and equality), he needs to either let go of the requirement that non-Muslims must acknowledge the Islamic character of the state or give an alternative reading of that requirement. Given that paying allegiance to the state is what citizens of any state are required to do, and that in the Islamic state that has to be cached in terms of the Islamic character of the state, this requirement is here to stay. We are left with finding an alternative reading of that requirement.

In the previous section, we considered reaching an overlapping consensus on *al-naṣṣ* as the source of the law that organizes the citizenry. That failed, however, for more than one reason. *Al-naṣṣ* represents a distinct view on the world, has substantive prescriptions, and belongs to a particular worldview. Furthermore, we saw that on Ghannushi's conceptualization of the Islamic state, acknowledging *al-naṣṣ* as the ultimate legislative authority effectively implies acknowledging that the *ijtihād* system is granted an inherent and direct role in determining state law in the Islamic state. Significantly, part of what the *ijtihād* system determines is public interest, and hence the boundaries within which individual human rights (including the limits on equality, on freedom of conscience, and on public debates) are to operate. All that contributed to the previous section's argument based on Ghannushi's model of the Islamic state is that non-Muslims would in effect be second-class citizens.

Maṣlaḥa, as a legal tool, cannot help in addressing this difficulty. *Maṣlaḥa* allows jurists to systematically transcend the literality of *al-naṣṣ*, and because its determination depends on the human context and situation, its potential to expand and change Islamic law is almost boundless. The scope within which *maṣlaḥa* as a legal tool is to work, however, is in finding solutions internal to Islam for Muslims. Yet the challenge I have raised in the previous section goes beyond that scope. As long as we are interested in developing a social and political ideal that is Islamic and that answers to the concerns of modern times, we need to find solutions internal to Islam for *all* citizens (not only for Muslim citizens).

By way of concluding, I want to capitalize on an aspect in *maqāṣid al-sharīʿa* and *maṣlaḥa* to make use of it outside the established Islamic legal theory parameters in order to address the problem at hand. What I have in mind is the formal aspect of the essential requirements of *maṣlaḥa*. Those requirements depict spheres of human life "without which life would be ruined." My suggestion is that Ghannushi's model of the Islamic state can significantly benefit if it sought to achieve an overlapping consensus on items "without which life would be ruined," instead of *al-naṣṣ*. Those could include the five essentials of *maṣlaḥa*—the protection of faith, life, progeny, wealth, and mind—but there is no in principal reason not to go beyond them. By following this suggestion, Ghannushi could address my criticism of the previous section. With the suggested modification on the object of the overlapping consensus, two main benefits are achieved. First, it becomes more reasonable and plausible to expect and achieve the overlapping consensus, and hence attain political legitimacy in the Islamic state. Second, there is enough distance created between the religious system and the realm of politics and state law that will allow his model to reclaim its achievements with regard to equality and freedom.[88]

If we conceive of items, "without which life would be ruined," in their abstract forms—that is, as concepts that call for specification and concretization—no particular view of the world gets attached to them. The input of worldviews is mostly apparent on the level of substantiating those items. It is thus more reasonable to achieve an overlapping consensus over such concepts, in their abstract forms, rather than in achieving the same over *al-naṣṣ*. While it is true that achieving this objective in this way is rather doubtful—as a result of the needed abstraction to achieve the overlapping consensus—it can nevertheless provide a common umbrella within which disagreement can take place. Each religion and worldview would have its own specification, or family of specifications, of those items and they are to convince their contenders of the value and importance of these particular specifications. To be sure, for Muslims the normative validity of these items is boosted, respected, and abided by because they represent a dimension of the purpose of *al-naṣṣ*. Muslims would articulate and specify them against their broader understanding of *al-naṣṣ*. *Al-naṣṣ* will remain the general background against which Muslims understand human interest. There is no doubt that Muslims will disagree on what these items include and how to substantiate them. This diversity and pluralism is internal to the Muslim community, and it is up to Muslims to contest and debate their differences in these regards. What Muslims should not do, however, is to consider the outcome of their debates to be legitimate for the entire political community, that is, for Muslim and non-Muslims citizens of the Islamic state. Muslims do not have a monopoly on how to understand human interest, and how to specify and concretize items without which life would be ruined. Other religions and worldviews also have something to say in this regard and they are to specify and concretize these items in accordance with their own understanding of the world and their place in it. In such an overlapping consensus, non-Muslims would have to acknowledge these items without which life would be ruined as the framework within which the law that organizes the citizenry gets articulated, though they would not have to acknowledge (unlike Muslims) that the normative validity and the way these items get specified are derived from *al-naṣṣ*. By giving structural superiority to the *ijtihād* system in determining how public interest is to be specified and concretized, Ghannushi's political model effectively institutionalizes a monopoly on determining public interest, and that is a violation of non-Muslims as equal free agents. The *ijtihād* system would have its own specifications of what the different items of the overlapping consensus mean, but these specifications are not to be confused with those items understood abstractly, nor are they to be confused with why that framework has normative validity for Muslims. Of course, given that in the Islamic state Muslims are the majority, it might remain true that the *ijtihād* system in the Islamic state would have the upper hand in determining how those items get specified, but that would no more be built into the system. Instead, it would merely be the result of Muslims being a majority in that society. This is a fundamental difference.

Basically, the modification I am suggesting is that instead of using *maṣlaḥa* as a tool in Islamic legal theory, we can use items without which life would be ruined as a set of abstract concepts/requirements over which an overlapping consensus can be achieved, and within which the contestations over specifying and concretizing public interest, as well as of state law and public policies, take place. The implication of the modification I am suggesting is that instead of conceiving of the Islamic state as a political arrangement that is in charge of maintaining the commitment to *al-naṣṣ*, we conceive of the Islamic state as a political arrangement that allows the Islamic community to take charge of maintaining the commitment to *al-naṣṣ*, without building in the very structure of the state any privileged status for Muslims. Interestingly, modifying Ghannushi's model in this way is more in line with Ghannushi's own reformist strategy where the social takes priority over the political, his minimalist conception of the government, the role he gives to an active and organized civil society, and his understanding of *shūra* in terms of habits and a way of life on a prepolitical social level. In both models, before and after the modification, *al-naṣṣ*—as in the interpretive outcomes of the *ijtihād* system as a whole—sets the limit on state law, on political outcomes and policies, and on the specifications of public interest. The difference lies in how such limits get set. Before the modification, it is structurally encoded so to speak. After the modification, it is in the hands of Muslims as active social members. We saw that Ghannushi defined *shūra* as "the spinal cord of the *umma*'s authority in establishing political rule on the basis of participation, cooperation, and responsibility."[89] What the suggested modification fundamentally calls for is an Islamic community whose members are to behave on the basis of "participation, cooperation, and responsibility," to keep the "spinal cord of the *umma*'s authority" erect and active in establishing its delegated authority in establishing God's rule on earth. Yet none of this should be systematically encoded. Instead it should take shape and expression through the mechanisms of *shūra*, that is, through the democratic procedures of will formation, opinion giving, and decision making.

Notes

1. See Wael Hallaq, *A History of Islamic Legal Theories: An Introduction to Sunnī Uṣūl al-Fiqh* (Cambridge, UK: Cambridge University Press, 1997); Felicitas Opwis, *Maṣlaḥa and the Purposes of Law* (Leiden: Brill, 2010); and Muhammad Khalid Masud, *Islamic Legal Philosophy: a Study of Abū Iṣḥāq al-Shatibi's Life and Thought* (Delhi: International Islamic Publishers, 1989).
2. Felicitas Opwis, "Maṣlaḥa in Contemporary Islamic Legal Theory," *Islamic Law and Society*, 12, 2.
3. See, for example, John Esposito and John Voll, *Makers of Contemporary Islam* (Oxford: Oxford University Press, 2001); Ibrahim, M. Abu-Rabi', *Contemporary Arab Thought: Studies in Post-1967* (London: Pluto Press, 2004); and Azzam Tamimi, *Rachid Ghannuchi: A Democrat within Islamism* (New York: Oxford University Press, 2001).
4. Rachid al-Ghannushi, "Secularism in the Arab Maghreb," in *Islam and Secularism in the Middle East*, ed. John Esposito and Azzam Tamimi (New York: New York University Press, 2000), 100.
5. Rachid al-Ghannushi, "Participation in Non-Islamic Government," in *Liberal Islam: A Sourcebook*, ed. Charles Kruzman (New York, Oxford: Oxford University Press, 1998).
6. For a brief description of the changes in the understanding of *sharī'a* see, Frank Griffel's "Introduction," in *Sharī'a: Islamic Law in the Contemporary Context*, ed. Abbas Amanat and Frank Griffel (Stanford, CA: Stanford University Press, 2007).
7. Ghannushi, "Secularism," 123.
8. See, for instance, Rachid al-Ghannushi, *Muqārabāt fi al-'lmaniyya wa al-mujtama' al-madanī*, Dar and Mujtahid lil-nashir wa al-tawzi', 2011, 23. All translations are the author's.
9. Al-Ghannushi, Rāchid., *al-ḥurriyyāt al-'amma fi al-dawla al-islāmiyya*, 1st ed. (Beirut: Markaz Dirasat al-Wihdah al-`Arabiyah, 1993), 100.
10. Ghannushi, *al-ḥurriyyāt*, 97.
11. Ghannushi clearly distinguishes between *sharī'a* as divine revelation, and *fiqh* (jurisprudence) as human interpretation. For instance, Ghannushi writes: "Considering Islamic *sharī'a* a revelation that reveals absolute divine justice and mercy—and that is different from *fiqh* [jurisprudence] which is a human interpretation—it is impossible to imagine the tiniest contradiction between it and the law of reason or humanistic values, or the real interest of the human being that experience attests for it." Ghannushi, *Muqārabāt*, 52. For the place of the community in legislation and understanding *sharī'a*, see Ghannushi, *al-ḥurriyyāt*, 119–121.
12. Rachid al-Ghannushi, *al-ḥurriyyāt al-'amma fi al-dawla al-islāmiyya*, 1st ed. (Beirut: Markaz Dirasat al-Wihdah al-`Arabiyah, 1993), 25.
13. Ghannushi, *al-ḥurriyyāt*, 120–121.
14. Rachid al-Ghannushi, *al-ḥaraka al-islāmiyya wa mas'lat al-taghyyir*, dar al-mujtahid lil-nashir wa al-tawzi', matba'at Tunis al-'ola, 2011, 119.

15. Ibid., 44–46.
16. Ibid., 43.
17. Ghannushi, *al-ḥaraka*, 42. Also, "Islamic Movements: Self-Criticism and Reconsideration." Online article: http://www.islamonline.net/english/Contemporary/2002/05/Article16.shtml; Available in *Palestine Times*, no. 94, April 1999; and *Middle East Affairs Journal*, Vol. 3(1–2), Winter/Spring 1997.
18. Ghannushi, "Islamic Movements," 2.
19. Ibid., 2.
20. Ghannushi, "Secularism," 100.
21. Ghannushi, "Islamic Movements," 2.
22. Ghannushi, *al-ḥurriyyāt*, 97.
23. Ghannushi, *al-ḥurriyyāt*, 98.
24. Ghannushi, *al-ḥurriyyāt*, 109.
25. Ghannushi, *al-ḥurriyyāt*, 148.
26. Ghannushi, "Participation," 91.
27. Although Islam did not specify the shape and form that *shūra* can take, making it a matter of controversy and debate, it did assert "that public affairs be managed through *shūra*," Ghannushi, *al-ḥurriyyāt*, 125.
28. Ghannushi, *al-ḥurriyyāt*, 125.
29. Ghannushi writes "*shūra* is not merely a style in managing political matters... but is a way of life that springs from the general vicegerency of humans, the primacy of the collective over the individual, and considering the individual to be weak on his own but strong with his brother, and mistaken on his own but enlightened towards his best with his brother," Ghannushi, *al-ḥurriyyāt*, 190–191.
30. Ghannushi, *al-ḥurriyyāt*, 297.
31. There is an unbridgeable gap between God's law and all actual human attempts to understand, interpret, and apply it. For a discussion of this issue in the Islamic context, see Adis Duderija, *Constructing Religiously Ideal, 'Believer,' and 'Muslim Woman,' in Islam: Neo-Traditional Salafi and Progressive Muslim Methods of Interpretation* (New York: Palgrave, 2011).
32. Ghannushi writes: "Perfection is not in the particulars, but in the generalities," Ghannushi, *al-ḥurriyyāt*, 101. That is, *al-naṣṣ* is general and perfect while human interpretations are particular and imperfect. "What the *'ulama* suggest is no more than their understanding, or their *ijtihad*" (Ghannushi, "Secularism," 114). *Ijtihād*, as the product of human effort, is always an approximation and it never reaches the epistemic status of certainty. Ghannushi explicitly states that human knowledge is always deficient and lacking. See, Ghannushi, *al-ḥurriyyāt*, 119. This human deficiency, however, according to Ghannushi, can be minimized when Muslims act as a community, that is, collective deliberation and action has an epistemic value. Although Ghannushi is not clear as to whether this epistemic value could in fact reach absolute certainty, it would be inconsistent for him to say so. That would not only undermine his claim that human knowledge is "deficient and lacking," but it would contradict other

claims he makes such as the claim that "perfection is not in the particulars, but in the generalities," Ghannushi, *al-ḥurriyyāt*, 101.

33. Ghannushi, "Secularism," 113–114.
34. Ghannushi description of current schools of jurisprudence as "societal projects" is telling: schools of *ijtihād* are "societal projects that materialize out of the interaction of Islam with specific social and cultural conditions. Once these conditions change, the school would have to accommodate them. A failure to do so would inevitably cost an intractable school of jurisprudence its hold on the public, who might opt for another, and are free to do so," Ghannushi, "Secularism," 114.
35. Ghannushi, *al-ḥurriyyāt*, 148.
36. Ibid., 104.
37. Ibid., 297.
38. Rachid al-Ghannushi, *ḥiwarat* (London: Khalil Media Service, 1992), 138.
39. Ghannushi, *al-ḥurriyyāt*, 101.
40. Ibid., 101, footnote 32.
41. All the people, not only Muslims. To be sure, we cannot expect that the will and interests of the entire body of citizens (each and every citizen, the different groups or political parties, or whichever way you divide the citizenry) will be catered for. But we should not accept (and Ghannushi would agree) that, by definition, only the will and interests of some of the people would be catered for.
42. Also see, Felicitas Opwis, *Maṣlaḥa*; Masud, *Islamic Legal Philosophy*; and Hallaq, *A History*.
43. For a classification of the different ways *maṣlaḥa* has been used and incorporated into legal theory in the middle period of Islam please see, Opwis, "Maṣlaḥa"; Masud, *Islamic Legal Philosophy*, Chapter 4; and, Ahmad al-Raysuni, *Imam Al-Shatibi's Theory of the Higher Objectives and Intents of Islamic Law*, The International Institute of Islamic Thought, 2005, Chapter 1.
44. Opwis, *Maṣlaḥa*, 2.
45. Opwis, *Maṣlaḥa*, 348. In the case of Shāṭibī, for example, Opwis says that he "did not consider *maṣlaḥa* to be weightier in every instance. Exempted were those particular rulings that constituted legal licenses (rukas) or specifications (takhsisat). In addition, considerations of *maṣlaḥa* had no bearing on acts of worship ('ibadat), acts that happened or could have happened during the lifetime of the Prophet and that received a ruling, and the continuous practice of the early Islamic community. Any other act may be judged according to the *maṣlaḥa* it entails under particular circumstances, which, of course, varies by place, time, and person," Opwis, "Maṣlaḥa," 196.
46. Masud, *Islamic Legal Philosophy*, 318.
47. Opwis, "Maṣlaḥa," 196. It is also worth noting that "*maqāṣid* and *maṣlaḥa* become interchangeable terms in reference to obligation in Shāṭibī's discussion of *maṣlaḥa*." Masud, *Islamic Legal Philosophy*, 225.
48. Ibid.

49. Ghannushi, "Participation," 90.
50. Ibid.
51. Ibid., 91.
52. In his categorization of *maṣlaḥa*, Shāṭibī like most scholars follows Abu Hamid Muḥammad al-Ghazali's categorization. For Ghazālī's conception and use of *maṣlaḥa* see Hallaq, *A History*, 88–90, and Masud, *Islamic Legal Philosophy*, 152–160.
53. Ghannushi, "Participation," 91.
54. Ibid.
55. Ghannushi, *al-ḥurriyyāt*, 120.
56. Ghannushi, "Participation," 91.
57. Ibid., 92.
58. Opwis, *Maṣlaḥa*, 351.
59. Ghannushi, *al-ḥurriyyāt*, 37–38.
60. Ibid., 42.
61. Ibid., 41–42.
62. Ibid., 43.
63. Ibid., 44.
64. Ibid., 44–48. Ghannushi also discusses apostasy and other rights including social and economic rights, see Ghannushi, *al-ḥurriyyāt*, 48–68. In this chapter, I focus on equality and freedom of conscious.
65. Rachid al-Ghannushi, *ḥuqūq al-muwāṭana: waḍʿiyyat ghair al-muslim fi-l-mujtamʿ al-islāmi*, maṭbaʿat tūnis qarṭāj. November 1989, 19, 20, 27.
66. Ghannushi, *al-ḥurriyyāt*, 46 and *ḥuqūq*, 20, 27.
67. Ghannushi, *ḥuqūq*, 40.
68. Ibid.
69. Ibid.
70. For more on Ghannushi's position on citizenship, see Adullah Saeed, "Rethinking Citizenship Rights of Non-Muslims in an Islamic State: Rachid Ghannushi's Contribution to the Evolving Debate," *Islam and Christian-Muslim Relations*, 10:3, 1999. For a more general treatment of citizenship form an Islamic perspective see Mohammad Hashim Kamali, "Citizenship: An Islamic Perspective," *Journal of Islamic Law and Culture*, 11:2, 121–153. That said, I should note that Ghannushi seems to have somewhat retracted from the claim that certain posts are restricted to Muslims in his "Freedom Comes First," http://www.onislam.net/english/shariah/contemporary-issues/human-conditions-and-social-context/420536-freedom-comes-first.html.
71. Ghannushi, *al-ḥurriyyāt*, 47, 292. Ghannushi, *ḥuqūq*, 37.
72. Ghannushi, *al-ḥurriyyāt*, 48.
73. Ibid., 47–48.
74. Ibid., 300.
75. Ibid., 297.
76. Ibid., 43.
77. Ibid., 43.

78. Ibid., 46.
79. Ibid., 47.
80. Ibid.
81. Ibid., 294.
82. Ghannushi, *al-ḥurriyyāt*, 291, and *ḥuqūq*, 40, 41.
83. Ghannushi, *al-ḥurriyyāt*, 77, 88, 321.
84. It is worth noting here that adopting the citizens' perspective, a key move of this section's argument, is neither ad-hoc nor an imposition on Ghannushi's political thought. Further, given what I said on Ghannushi's reformist project in the section "Ghannushi's Reformist Project," we should infer that citizens' perspective has in fact a central place in Ghannushi's overall reformist critical attitude, strategy, and vision. Thus, the critique I am providing is an internal critique. That is, it is a critique that is based on the internal inconsistency of Ghannushi's political thought, rather than on some standards external to his thought that he does not accept.
85. Ghannushi, *al-ḥurriyyāt*, 105.
86. Recall the distinction between "Islamic legitimacy" and "political legitimacy," in the section "Ghannushi's Reformist Project." Islamic legitimacy, on the one hand, requires abiding to God's commands. Political legitimacy, on the other hand, requires the acceptance of the ruled, expressing the will of the ruled, and taking care of the interests of the ruled. The Islamic state as the state of *al-naṣṣ* and *shūra* is supposed to satisfy both kinds of legitimacy. First, it satisfies Islamic legitimacy in its commitment to *al-naṣṣ*. Second, it satisfies political legitimacy in its commitment to *shūra* hence, to popular sovereignty and the will and interest of the people.
87. John Rawls, *Political Liberalism* (New York: Columbia University Press, 2005).
88. I want to emphasize here that what is of relevance is not the specific items that constitute the five essentials, but the category of "essential requirements" itself, that is, that "without which life would be ruined." Ghannushi, "participation," 91. What exactly is to be included under "essential requirements" could be debated and is subject to change over time. These changes, however, do not affect the point I am making.
89. Ghannushi, *al-ḥurriyyāt*, 109.

CHAPTER 7

On Reading Shāṭibī in Rabat and Tunis

Ebrahim Moosa

The ethical turn in Islamic jurisprudence known as the "*maqāṣidī* turn" has captured the imagination of many twentieth- and twenty-first-century practitioners and writers on Islamic law. Few places can rival debates related to "the purposes of the Sharī'a" than North African thinkers, scholars, and philosophers who have spilt much ink on this topic for more than a century in order to provide blueprints for the reconstruction and reform of Muslim moral philosophy. From Muḥammad al-Tahir bin 'Ashur (1879–1973) of Tunisia to 'Allah al-Fassi (1910–1974) of Morocco in the nineteenth and twentieth centuries, to the contemporary Aḥmad al-Raysuni (b. 1953) and several others, there have been scholars who voiced their opinion and support for this new trend of reading Islamic law. But the debate on the purposes of the Sharī'a has also enjoyed a trans-regional dimension as thinkers from Egypt, Syria, Iraq, Lebanon, and from the Indo-Pakistan subcontinent periodically weighed in along with scholars based in Europe and North America whose voices approve, disapprove, or exhibit caution on this trend. Recently, however, philosophers have engaged Shāṭibī too, and this chapter will address their take on the topic.

Shāṭibī's book *Al-Muwāfaqāt fi uṣūl al-Sharī'ah, The Reconciliation of the Fundamentals of the Sharī'ah*, according to some accounts, was brought to the attention of the larger reading public by the Egyptian reformer Muḥammad 'Abduh. The latter was intrigued to discover scholars at the Zaytuna mosque-university in Tunis reading such an interesting book. 'Abduh was so impressed by the innovative thinking of the fourteenth-century jurist from Granada in Muslim Spain, Abu Ishaq al-Shatibi (d. 1388), that he personally carried a copy to Cairo. One of 'Abduh's disciples, Dr. 'Abd Allah Daraz, a graduate of the Al-Azhar who undertook graduate studies at the Sorbonne in Paris, edited and published *Muwāfaqāt*, a task that posthumously allowed Shāṭibī to emerge from the shadows of obscurity.

Due to Shāṭibī's own lofty scruples and ascetic qualities, he made many enemies during his lifetime. But his legacy outlived his critics and he continues to transfix and inspire a global Muslim scholarly audience. His detailed elucidation of the theory of knowledge underlying a value-based approach to law found some echo with the needs of modern Muslims. Not only does a burgeoning scholarship now adorn Shāṭibī's name but also some Muslims view him as an unclaimed "renewer" of the spirit of the times (*mujaddid*) whose ideas found a fit with modern projects of social, intellectual, and religious reform (*iṣlāḥ*) in Muslim thought.

Not only jurists but also philosophers at Muḥammad V University in the city of Rabat, Morocco, have shown interest in Shāṭibī's writings. He features in a two-decade-old spirited debate among North African scholars on the reconstruction of Muslim thought, especially the philosophical, historical, and religious dimensions of how to renovate and energize a complex Muslim legacy and tradition (*turath*). Their efforts have yielded uncanny insights and sparked earnest debates in scholarly circles around the Arab and Islamic world. While some orthodox scholars (*ulamā'*) regularly apply Shāṭibī's insights in their rulings, how contemporary Muslim philosophers rework Shāṭibī's ideas has been less well studied.

A good place to begin with is Muḥammad 'Abid al-Jabiri (d. 2010), a philosopher-historian trained at Muḥammad V University, whose writings spawned a minor canon of philosophical literature. His influential quartet generically called *Critique of Arabic Reason—Naqd al-aql al-arabi* include titles such as the *Formation of Arabic Reason-Takwin al-Aql al-Arabi*, *Construction of Arabic Reason—Binyat al-aql al-arabi*, *Arabic Political Reason-al-Aql al-Siyasi al-Arabi*, *Arabic Ethical Reasoning—al-Aql al-akhlaqi al-arabi*. Challenging some of Jābirī's ideas is the Sorbonne-trained Taha 'Abd al-Rahman, a leading Moroccan philosopher of language and ethics who also taught at the same university where Jābirī spent his career.[1]

Of the two philosophers, Jābirī was for a long time the premier pan-Arab intellectual interlocutor who penned lengthy tomes that analyzed the crisis of Arabo-Islamic thought. Jābirī engages in meta-critique and invested a herculean effort in order to deconstruct the epistemological foundations of Arabo-Islamic thought. He is now famed for identifying and explaining how three forms of reasoning became embedded in Muslim culture and thought over the centuries. In his hierarchical scheme, demonstrative reason (*burhān*) of the philosophers is at the top of the pyramid. This is the kind of reason he favored and wished had prevailed in Muslim thought for it contained, in his view, the seeds for a flourishing Muslim civilization. To his great regret it was largely explicatory reasoning (*bayān*) that prevailed in the Muslim discursive tradition. *Bayān* to Jābirī's mind was a reductive, mechanical, and a form of closed hermeneutical reasoning that was made popular by legions of Muslim jurists, theologians, and grammarians. To Jābirī's mind, mystical intuition (*'irfān*), the kind of reasoning advanced by mystics and some philosophers, was the most damaging to the construction of Islamic thought and society. He was relentless in his critique of Persian philosophical, theological, and mystical influences that in his view fatally wounded Arabic thought.

In Jābirī's view, Shāṭibī was among a quartet of exemplary scholars who tried to reconstruct the epistemological edifice of Arabo-Islamic thought on stronger rational foundations. Given Jābirī's preference for demonstrative rational arguments he enthusiastically identified with his heroes from Muslim Spain, in what he called the "Andalusian resurgence." The reader will not miss a certain regional bias in the analysis given the proximity of Muslim Spain to the Islamic West, the Maghrib. The quartet was the jurist Ibn Hazm, the jurist, theologian and philosopher Ibn Rushd, the grammarian and legal theorist Shāṭibī, and the polymath and historian Ibn Khaldun.[2] What all four shared in common, argued Jābirī, was an epistemological edifice marked by the influence of Ibn Hazm and Ibn Rushd, what he called the "Hazm-Rushdi effect."[3] Each one of his four exemplars attempted to refurbish their respective disciplines by overhauling the knowledge foundations and epistemology in order to find more convincing arguments. So, for instance, Ibn Hazm labored on the law front just as Ibn Rushd during his time crafted a new rational theology, while Shāṭibī remade legal theory, and Ibn Khaldun rewrote history, all striving to craft a better rational foundation for the discipline they engaged.[4] These thinkers from the Islamic West especially, says Jābirī, preferred demonstrative rationality (*burhān*) drawing on Ibn Rushd's clarion call and epitomized in his statement: "Whoever dismissed causation has also dismissed knowledge."[5]

Just as Ibn Hazm unleashed his fusillade of frustration at the unreliable deductive reasoning (*bayān*) favored by the jurists who preceded him, so did Shāṭibī also express his frustration at the absence of categorical foundations in the discipline of legal theory. Shāṭibī was in search of what he called the "universal postulates of the Sharī'a." Shāṭibī was in awe of arguments supported by natural reason, not Greek modes of reason. With that desideratum in mind, he reconfigured Muslim legal theory (*uṣūl al-fiqh*) by building on the work of predecessors, but crafting an elegant theory of moral purposes (*maqāṣid*) of the law. Shāṭibī attempted to displace the hermeneutical deductive reasoning of the previous jurists by seeking out modes of reasoning and replacing them with modes of reasoning he deemed to be universal principles. However, Jābirī had to concede that both Ibn Hazm and Shāṭibī were not entirely averse to the closed system of deductive reasoning prevalent among jurists; otherwise their work would not have made sense to their colleagues during their time. In other words, while they did engage in deductive reasoning in Islamic law, they nevertheless aspired to displace it with something better as part of a work in progress.

Yet, Jābirī's four exemplary thinkers were distinctive from their peers insofar as they tried to bridge the closed hermeneutic or explicatory reasoning (*bayān*) of the jurist-theologians with the demonstrative reasoning (*burhān*) of the philosophers. Why were these thinkers so keen to keep knowledge of religion within the bounds of the reasonable? One can speculate. Perhaps, they thought knowledge had to sustain ethical postulates, which could best be attained with persuasive forms of reasoning. Jābirī does not comment whether in his view the pioneers of the Andalusian resurgence succeeded in making an impact on displacing explicatory reasoning or modifying it. The answer must be in negative since explicatory reasoning has prevailed in subsequent centuries.

Furthermore, Jābirī's polarized thinking of pitting the Muslim West (Maghrib) against the Muslim East (Mashriq) is exaggerated and is prefigured to produce a Western/Maghribi triumphalism.[6] It is a rather hollow triumphalism if one were to take the story of the jurisprudence of moral purposes (maqāṣid) championed by Shāṭibī as an example. While Jābirī does acknowledge the contribution of Juwayni, Ghazālī, and later 'Izz al-Din Ibn 'Abd al-Salam to the jurisprudence of moral purposes, which finally culminated in the writing of Shāṭibī, it is ironic that Jābirī hardly gives any significant credit to the early influences.[7] All of those thinkers come from the Muslim East and their epistemic frameworks are found to be poisoned by deductive reasoning and Eastern mysticism. While he credits Ibn Rushd and Ibn Hazm for being the new inspiration to Western Islam, Shāṭibī hardly refers to Ibn Rushd, save once, but he made copious references to Juwayni and Ghazālī. This is not meant to be polemical but to give some push-back to Jābirī's questionable and sometimes excessive claims.

Yet, it will be an error not to acknowledge Shāṭibī's genius and originality in reconstructing the jurisprudence of moral purposes on a grand scale. Shāṭibī's major goal was to put Muslim jurisprudence on a sound epistemological foundation. His strategy was to rinse out all extraneous debates that were unrelated to jurisprudence proper and to craft sound epistemological principles based on certainty.

Another Moroccan scholar, the philosopher Taha 'Abd al-Rahman, continues Jābirī's fascination with Shāṭibī, albeit in a slightly different register.[8] If Jābirī viewed Shāṭibī as pushing juristic thought in the direction of demonstrative reason, then 'Abd al-Rahman reads Shāṭibī's main contribution to be in the realm of epistemological coherence of Arabo-Islamic thought. Shāṭibī, in 'Abd al-Rahman's view, draws on sources internal to the Muslim tradition, yet he is not closed off from external promptings in order to design a more robust epistemological framework. 'Abd al-Rahman calls Shāṭibī's effort an "internal epistemological imbrication—interconnectedness or meshing" (*al-tadākhul al-ma'rifi al-dākhilī*).[9] He identifies two kinds of epistemological imbrication or meshing: trivial (*ibtidhālī*) and procedural (*ijrā'ī*).[10] Shāṭibī's own words best illustrate his rejection of trivial epistemological imbrication. "Any topic discussed in legal theory (uṣūl al-fiqh) that does not serve as a basis for the [generation] of secondary rules (*furū' fiqhīya*) or [advancing] an excellence of the revealed law (adab shar'iyya) or assists in these matters, then its place [in the genre] of legal theory is futile."[11] So Shāṭibī streamlines legal theory, which is Muslim moral theory proper, and excludes all that he deemed extraneous debates, such as matters dealing with language, grammar, logic, and philosophy from consideration in legal theory.

'Abd al-Rahman favors Shāṭibī's knowledge project because it boosts a cumulative epistemology. Shāṭibī's innovation is to argue that individual verses of the Qur'ān or reports from the Prophet might only amount to probable strength in epistemic authority. But if these verses and reports are bundled cumulatively, their reading can indeed result in epistemological certainty. In order to achieve this goal, Shāṭibī developed a fine-grained hermeneutic. So he collected a variety of strands of prophetic reports (ḥadīth) on a particular topic in order to eliminate, evaluate, and weigh the cumulative message of the collection of reports. This allowed him to assess the total package of teaching and then adjudicate it as certain or in varying degrees of uncertainty. Similarly, Qur'ānic verses, Shāṭibī argues, should be viewed in a spectrum of Meccan and Madinan verses; the former represent universal claims whereas the latter are elaborations and refinements of the Meccan verses. Similarly, Shāṭibī works from certain cultural assumptions of culture and language that supported the Muslim revelation in history.

Among contemporary scholars, Abdurrahman is perhaps one of the first to do a fairly rigorous and at times radical re-reading of Shāṭibī's project of the moral purposes of the law and offers several methodological interventions.

Re-Reading Shāṭibī: Taha 'Abd al-Rahman

Theorists of Islamic law, experts in uṣūl al-fiqh, have devoted considerable time, energy, and resources in order to grasp the rules, assessments, and judgments of the law known as *aḥkām*, 'Abd al-Rahman complains. But, he argues, they have rarely paid attention to what it means to call something the purposes of the Sharī'a.[12] His re-reading of Shāṭibī and intervention centers around four critical points. 'Abd al-Rahman views:

1. The discourses of "moral purposes" (maqāṣid) as Muslim moral discourse proper (*'ilm al-akhlāq al-islāmī*).[13]
2. Muslim morals are constitutive of three distinctive but interlocking subtheories of "moral purposes."
3. Some theories of "moral purposes" are in need of correction and rehabilitation.
4. The Sharī'a rules (*aḥkām shar'īya*) take as their grounds the moral dimensions embedded in duty-based (*fiqhī*) rules, just as the duty-based rules in turn also direct the moral dimensions. In other words, he believes that a dialogic relationship is operative.

Redefining Purposes (maqāṣid) as Moral Values

Morals not only determine human actions, in 'Abd al-Rahman's view, they also have implications for one's existence (*wujūd*) or identity (*huwīya*), two terms that are used interchangeably in classical and postclassical Muslim discourses.[14] All human conduct is either attached to a virtuous or debased moral value that either elevates or degrades the moral agent, respectively. Even mental acts do elevate and denigrate the moral agent. What distinguishes a human from a beast is not the capacity of reason or the mind, also evident in a lesser form in quadrupeds, but by the *moral* capacity that humans possess, he argues.[15]

The current definitions for the "study of moral purposes," 'Abd al-Rahman points out, are tautological. The proper goal of the law, he argues, is not to secure a benefit (maṣlaḥa) of the law since the real moral purpose is to secure "righteousness" (*ṣalāḥ*). So when one claims to seek knowledge of "moral purposes" then one is actually examining two things: what benefits humans will attain in this world and also what they will attain in the afterlife. In other words, seeking the moral purposes means exploring the multiple ways human beings can attain worldly good as well as other-worldly good. It is wrongly understood, he argues, that benefits are the goal. The real objective is to follow modes of "right conduct" (*maslak* pl. *masālik*).

Why? Because servitude to God is only attained through right conduct. In reality, 'Abd al-Rahman says, to put it differently, to seek knowledge of the moral purposes of the law is actually to seek knowledge of righteousness. So *righteousness* is the primary moral value and centerpiece of morality, which is synonymous to "the good" or "happiness," except that "righteousness" surpasses the notion of "the good" in one sense; righteousness is intimately connected with right conduct, whereas "the good" plainly might not require accompanying conduct.

Need for Three Theories Related to Moral Purposes

'Abd al-Rahman's innovation is his proposal for the deepening and refinement of Muslim moral theory. He derives this insight from his inquiry and lexicographical exploration of the plurivocal sense of the term "purpose" (*maqṣad*). This forms the grounds for his three complementary theories undergirding Muslim moral knowledge as derived from discussions on the moral purposes of the law. To be clear, on deriving semiotic meanings about "purpose," 'Abd al-Rahman's approach is not unprecedented. The eleventh-century Shafi`i jurist al-Juwayni had already discussed these linguistic registers in his writings.[16] 'Abd al-Rahman utilizes some of these insights in order to provide a new ethical and moral framework.

First, the word "purpose" (*maqṣad*) has the sense of "outcome" (*maqṣūd*) as in when we say: "the outcome of the statement." Here 'Abd al-Rahman conceives the outcome to mean the requisite "action." For this reason moral knowledge must also deepen one's reflection on a theory of action.

Second, "purpose" can also mean the "intention," which in turn signifies the emotional content. Without emotional or intentional content a statement can be rendered nonsense. Following Shāṭibī's lead, 'Abd al-Rahman proposes that one has to be in a position to decipher the intention of the Lawgiver (God) as well as get a sense of the required intention the moral subject *ought* to display. For this reason, 'Abd al-Rahman says that moral theory should have an elaborate theoretical exploration of intention so that intention and sincerity of a moral agent, in other words the normative aspects, can be subject to adjudication.

Third, "purpose" can also mean the desired "end." As in, "the end the speaker aims at in his statement and wishes to realize it." He explains that in the sense of "end" the word "purpose" means "value" (*qima*), signifying the value-based aspect of the theory of moral purposes. For without a value dimension, a moral claim can be fruitless. So in this sense, if someone says "moral purposes of the Sharī'a-*maqāṣid al-Sharī'a*" then it could also mean, says 'Abd al-Rahman, values of the Sharī'a. Experts in theoretical jurisprudence also use the term *maṣlaḥa* in a moral sense. Somewhat idiosyncratically, he points out the term "maṣlaḥa" can also be used in the sense of "improving or making better a person's life," which is identical to the function the word "value" plays in moral deliberation.[17] Furthermore, he explains, knowledge of the moral purposes of the law also requires some theorization of values. Sharī'a values operate on concepts of "innate nature" (*fiṭra*) and "improvement" (*iṣlāḥ*) and can therefore not be ignored.

Acts, intention, and value are three indispensable elements that will deepen the theorization of Muslim moral theory. An act ought to be related to its intent; and intentions target certain values provided by moral theory. No moral action is free from intention and no intention is free from a value. 'Abd al-Rahman then places these theories in a hierarchical relationship where value enjoys prominence, followed by intention, which is succeeded by action. The theory of value, in his view, enjoys primacy. He explains why he differs from traditional scholars, contemporary and past ones in this matter. The cardinal error of traditional scholars was not to distinguish between the various linguistic registers in the term *maqṣad* such as "outcome," "intent," and "end." Failure to recognize these differences caused them to miss significant consequences. Hence, traditional scholars gave priority to making *actions* the driving element, followed by intention and, lastly, they gave a place to the role of values. In 'Abd al-Rahman's view, such a move inverted the pyramid.

But he also wants to change the orientation and approach crafted by the classical tradition of duty-based ethics, called *fiqh*. Definitions of *fiqh* place the ethical emphasis on the adjudication of human acts seeking to make them comply in an obligatory sense to some acts or to make them abstain from certain acts. *Fiqh* gives Muslim ethics a legal tonality. 'Abd al-Rahman believes that the traditional jurists have failed to pay attention to the moral and ethical apparatus underlying the system of duty-based ethics. Drawing on arguments available in the writings of Shāṭibī, he argues that there are suggestive and nuanced linguistic clues to reach a moral purpose (*maqṣūd*). There are multiple layers of complexity in the architecture of the theory of moral purposes such as identifying an act, intention, and value that need separate consideration and to which traditional jurists were inattentive. A moral agent "gains access" (*tawassul*) to an act at the lowest rung of a three-step hierarchy. This is followed by intention as the moral agent's "subtle means" (*taḥayyul*-as in legal stratagems) pitched to the second rung of the three-step hierarchy, and finally, values do the "mediation" (*tadharru'*) to reach the apex.

'Abd al-Rahman also makes a plea for a greater concordance between causal reasoning and teleological reasoning in moral philosophy. Most juristic discussions allow causal reasoning (*al-ta'līl al-sababī*) to be guided by teleological reasoning (*ta'līl al-ghā'ī*), yet they are not consistent in attaining this objective. He pleads for greater consistency in order for legal causes to conform to the underlying wisdom and reasoning of the rules.

He also draws attention to another area of confusion among traditional scholars. Often scholars, in his view, are inattentive to the different forms of reasoning at work in ethical and moral judgments. For instance, if one can rationally discern the descriptions for certain rules provided by the divine legislator, then, surely reason provides an "explanation" (*mufassir*) for specific acts and practices. On other occasions reason can fathom the ends and values embedded in the rules, when it becomes "directive" (*tawjīhī*) and hence one can grasp the normative criteria involved when rules are applied to specific human acts. 'Abd al-Rahman points out how scholars often missed the difference between "explanatory and descriptive reasoning" and "directive and normative reasoning." This only adds to the confusion in moral and ethical thought.

'Abd al-Rahman points out how the hierarchy of moral purposes labeled as "necessary" (*ḍarūrī*), "required" (*ḥājī*), and "refinement (*taḥsīnī*) were arrayed in diminishing order of importance and were associated with "priority" (*i'tibār*), "caution" (*iḥtiyāt*), and excellence (*makārim*), respectively.[18] This arrangement, in his view, was erroneous and requires serious revision and correction. The "necessary" category was unusually restricted to the five primary purposes, listed as the preservation of religion, life, reason, property, and offspring. If these values were arrived at by way of induction, he explains, then surely they will be fungible as changes in human existence occur over time. Similarly, in the "refinement" category, "excellence in character" is viewed as some kind of afterthought. In 'Abd al-Rahman's view, traditional classification needed serious attention. In summary, he says, values cannot be reduced to a small number; the difference in values should be ranked in terms of their moral and ethical strength; "excellence in character" is a norm that should be integrated in all rungs of the hierarchy of moral purposes.

Reconfiguring Values

'Abd al-Rahman proposes some ideas for a new configuration of values. One category is what he describes as organic value or the values of beneficence and malevolence. We experience pleasure when we are beneficiaries of a good thing and we experience displeasure with pain. Under this broad category, the traditional values of moral purposes listed as the preservation of religion, life, health, family, and property can easily be scaled as values of beneficence and malevolence. But such a category would contain a more descriptive typology. Another category he devises includes rational values or aesthetic values of beauty and ugliness. These are rational and psychological values that coincide with experiences of happiness and sadness. The third category he designs are spiritual values or values of the good and the detestable. The moral values associated with the latter are happiness when being a beneficiary of the good and wretchedness when one experiences something that is corrosive.

The traditional method of interpreting Islamic law, 'Abd al-Rahman points out, gave priority to the material aspect of life instead of the spiritual dimension. It went so far that one could reasonably mistake the Sharī'a as being as material as the materiality of reason, when in fact, the Sharī'a only had a "relation" to materiality. In 'Abd al-Rahman's revised hierarchy, only those values that enabled human beings to realize their humanity would enjoy preeminence. So spiritual values or values that help discern good and bad enjoy the highest rank because they promote excellence in a human being and make him or her recognize his or her servitude to God.[19] Rational or aesthetic values come next, followed by values that help discern between benefit and harm.

Relationship between Law and Morality

'Abd al-Rahman insists that Sharī'a rules must perfect their dialogical relationship so that "the legal aspect" (*al-wajh al-qānūnī*) synchronizes with the "moral aspect" (*al-wajh al-akhlāqī*). He seems to accept *fiqh* as positive law and therefore it functions as law (*qanūn*).[20]

The moral aspect consists of three elements, namely, value, intention, and action. Each of these, in turn, corresponds to deeper metaphysical propositions and psychological dimensions. For instance, values are intrinsically related to an innate human nature (*fiṭra*). Intention in this moral construction is intimately tied to the notion of sincerity, which he describes as "a divine secret located in the hearts of humans."[21] Finally, actions are firmly embedded in revealed rules, and they enable humans to ascend to higher levels of moral advancement.

The "legal aspect" consists of three elements or parts, namely, the directive of the rule, the ratio of the rule, and the case. The first part is the directive of the rule (*jihat al-ḥukm*), the legal value associated with the discourse of the lawgiver, whether it is obligatory (*ījāb*), prohibitory (*taḥrīm*), or permissible/indifferent (*mubāḥ*). The second part is the ratio of the rule (*'illa al-ḥukm or ratio legis*), the descriptive aspect that serves as the grounds for the lawgiver to make it the *cause* for a particular direction. The third part is the content subordinate to the rule (*al-maḍmūn al-maḥkūm 'alayhi*), namely, the descriptive "case" involving the action of the one who is morally obligated by the directive legal value.

The "act" in the legal construction, he explains, is crucially different from the "act" in the moral construction of moral discourse. An "act" is stripped of any legal value in the law, where it is correctly described as a "case," whereas an "act" in moral discourse is always linked to a moral directive as well as a value.

So the legal face regulates the external or formal aspects of the *legal subject* whereas the moral face deals with the interior subjectivity of the *moral subject*. The same act can be both legal-*fiqhī* as well as moral (and vice versa), since both law and morality aspire to the same end: to realize one's humanity in the service of God. This mutual dialectic of practice and reflection retains the integrity of each in order to keep the law from becoming stagnant and keeps both dimensions honest. 'Abd al-Rahman is particularly concerned about the polarization of literalist partisanship versus esoteric partisanship resulting from what he calls "the great textual sedition" (*al-fitna al-naṣṣīya al-kubra*).[22] He thinks obsession with the literal text of tradition and regarding it as paramount above all other considerations is deeply problematic. Instead, he calls for balance and invites for the careful observation of both the legal and moral components of rules and regulations.

In summation, 'Abd al-Rahman invites scholars to pay attention to method in the study of morals in contemporary Islam as well as to understand its complexities and deepen the theorization of this subject. He urges for a closer theoretical and practical relationship between law and morality while simultaneously correcting some aspects of the traditional framework in order to make it more robust. The downside of 'Abd al-Rahman's theory is that it is highly abstract and theoretical with little demonstration of how this would apply in practical terms, a task I suspect he would leave to others to accomplish.

If the theory of the moral purposes of law has enjoyed a warm response from a variety of quarters, it has also received very little critical appraisal. However, a prominent contemporary Tunisian philosopher has been bold enough to offer critique as we shall see next.

Abū Ya'rab al-Marzuqi

Abū Ya'rab al-Marzuqi is a French-trained Tunisian philosopher. He was nominated to his country's postrevolutionary parliament by the Renaissance party but resigned more than a year later in frustration. Marzūqī writes extensively about politics, law, and philosophy but his impenetrable style makes it hard to understand him clearly. Drawing extensively from classical authors including Ghazālī, Ibn Taymiyya, and especially Ibn Khaldun, he often provides a critical perspective against secularists (*'almāniyūn*) as well as against "authentics" (*aṣlāniyūn*), his code for Islamic fundamentalists in search of an elusive authenticity. Both camps, secular and fundamentalists, he complains allege he belongs to the other side. Fundamentalists call him a secularist and the secularists suspect him to be an Islamist, charges that he advertises as a badge of honor. Yet, he comes across as an *enfant terrible* of contemporary Arabic philosophy taking unpopular positions and raising difficult questions.

He is, however, among the few contemporary Muslim thinkers who believe contemporary Islamic thought must take knowledge in the humanities, social sciences, science, and aesthetics seriously for without these insights the possibility of creative thought is doomed from the word go. He is unsparing in his criticism of the scholars of Islam, especially the *ulamā'*, who do not fulfill their ethical commitments to Islamic learning. Like many modern scholars, Marzūqī takes the Qur'ān as an ontological starting point as did Malik Bennabi (d. 1973), Muḥammad Iqbal (d. 1938), and Fazlur Rahman to mention but a few before him. Humanity is in a state of loss (*khusr*), a term Marzūqī draws from the exegesis of the Qur'ān. This condition of loss can only be remedied by acts of humanity such as repeatedly offering counsel in order to strive to attain the truth and to persevere with patience in times of adversity. Humanity, in his view, has a purpose, namely, to grow and flourish in practices of truth-seeking and mutual caring.

What is characteristic of Marzūqī's thought is that he at least takes the time to subject some of the strongest and most popular currents of contemporary Islamic thought to radical critique. One area he addresses is Islamic law and he subjects it to strong philosophical critique. The vaunted and increasingly popular moral purposes (*maqāṣidī*) approach to Sharī'a is a topic Marzūqī views as extremely problematic and as the very antithesis of revelation.

In his own words, he writes:

> The outcome of a purposive exegesis is to effectively repeal a heavenly legislation (*tashrī' samāwī*) at its roots and to return to a posture of pure political instrumentalism in matters of private and public rights. So claims of moral purposes (*maqāṣid*) logically and historically only goes back to assert legislative instrumentalism that in turn relies only on calculating worldly interests, nothing else... There is no third possibility [i.e., no difference] between [first] a heavenly norm-making process (*al-tashrī' al-samāwī*) that incorporates afterworldly interests by way of

devotional practices (*ta'abbudīyan*) and where the latter are made subservient to worldly interests by way of social transactions (*ta'āmulan*), and, [the second] is a secular norm-making process principally based on calculating worldly interests, nothing else. Every claim that purports that a transcendent norm-making process in history is not a religious one, is nothing but self-deception, for it claims to have absolute knowledge which [in turn] elevates a natural contractual right philosophically-speaking, to the level of a sacred contractual right, religiously-speaking: that is true atheistic humanism.[23]

Denouncing the moral purposes of the law thesis, Marzūqī resorts to arguments of history and philosophy where elements of Zahiri nominalism also raise its head. The *aporia* (insoluble problem) in his view is this: in Islam, there is an end to revelation and hence there is no need for humans, especially for the jurists (*fuqahā'*) to act as pseudo legislators.[24] Echoing some of Ibn Hazm's criticism without attributing to the Andalusian scholar, Marzūqī argues for a total fealty to the Qur'ānic teachings. According to the Qur'ān, mortals as individuals are denied the liberty to extend the logic of the revelation. Only in a tradition where revelation was continuous could one anticipate a situation where the law was repeatedly updated in order to end any contradiction that might exist between a text and a changing context. Such scenarios are thinkable in what he calls extreme Shi'ism where a jurist acts on behalf of a hidden leader (*imām*) or in an institution like a church in Christianity, but not in a version of Sunni Islam as he imagines it. In his view, the error of Sunni Muslim jurists was to pretend to make rules as if they were recipients of ongoing revelation when in fact they were not awarded any such a privilege. In his words, they are accustomed to trade in a "corrupt revelation" (*waḥy fāsid*).[25]

Muslim jurists, going back centuries, in his view, "abducted the legislative process" and continued to devise new Sharī'a rules even when revelation had ended. They either extended the ambit of revelation via analogy and interpretation or they delimited the revelatory legislation by allowing the purposes of the law to trump all other forms of reasoning.[26] The jurists, he charged, played loose and fast with the revealed texts (*nuṣūṣ*) to effectively keep a mode of revelation going when it in fact there was none!

But where he introduces a radical idea is in his argument that ongoing normative work must take place in the voice of the Muslim community, with their participation and consent. He does not apportion any exclusive legislative role for the jurists apart from enforcing existing rule. The obligation to make rules rightfully belongs to the community of Muslims (*umma*). To pretend that revelation was continuous was theologically egregious in

Marzūqī's view. It was damaging in many respects, of which at least two propositions deserve mention. First, it denies the end of revelation criterion by pretending that revelation is continuous by means of juristic hermeneutics. Second, it denies the infallibility of the Muslim community as promised by the Prophet. In other words, what Muslims as a community accomplish via an informed consensus receives divine blessings, grace, and infallibility for what they view as beautiful and good was also good in the eyes of God, according to tradition.

Marzūqī's main theological objection to the moral purposes of the Sharīʿa theory is directed at the assumption that human beings can definitively know God's purposes. Only one who has omniscience can make such a claim, which would be preposterous.[27] Furthermore, Marzūqī says it ironically appears that humans need these benefits (*maṣāliḥ*) and moral purposes after God had created them. He taunts that it will appear odd for God to create human beings and then attempt to equip them with the requisite benefits. In an attempt to rebut some of Marzūqī's charges, the late Shaykh Saʿid Ramaḍān al-Buti (d. 2013) of Syria argued that the moral purposes were conditional and tied to God's revealed law and were not tied to the creation of humans. The symposium of essays between Marzūqī and al-Buti on the problematic of renewing legal theory deserves separate and closer attention and study.

But Marzūqī's main point is that Islamic law cannot really function outside the viable social context of political society. Governance and the political community should, in his view, remedy much of what Muslim jurists are trying to address *via* the theory of the moral purposes of the Sharīʿa. Political community involves all people within the Muslim polity. Without a viable political community, it is almost certain that Sharīʿa and its multiple discourses and value systems will be perverted and distorted. Therefore, he raises objections. His major fear is that religious morals and values will be distorted by the contingencies of politics. He wishes to preserve the sacred law and keep it tied to its designed function, namely to keep humans within a mode of divinely prescribed practices in a defined number of issues. All further contingencies not addressed by the divine revelation fall on humans to resolve and find answers to, but they are not authorized to extend the voice of God by means of analogy.

Conclusion

The growing interest in the purposes of the Sharīʿa in modern times is quite understandable. One reason for its growth is that traditional Sharīʿa research is still very much in the grip of Muslim traditionalists who are caught up in the *minutiae* of fiqh literature with little innovation, creativity, and engagement with the social reality in which Muslims live. The Sharīʿa approach is a utilitarian one that allows jurists and practitioners to bypass some elements of the traditional fiqh model of the Sharīʿa by offering a big-picture approach to God's purposes. Yet, the question arises: Will the existing tradition of fiqh have to be euthanized out of existence by the moral purposes of the Sharīʿa approach? A large part of the Qur'ān and ḥadīth materials were wedded to a very detailed hermeneutic tradition where the divine intentions were extended to new contingencies in the various law schools. Marzūqī vehemently objects to this process while ʿAbd al-Rahman thinks that there are ways in which the same method can serve as a resource for ethics and morality as well as calibrate the law. The key question to be addressed is this: How does the big-picture version of the Sharīʿa relate to the traditional practice of Islamic law? Will one eclipse the other over time?

Notes

1. Taha ʿAbd al-Rahman, *Tajdīd Al-Manhaj Fī Taqwīm Al-Turāth*, 3rd ed. (Casablanca: al-Markaz al-Thaqāfī, 1994).
2. Muḥammad ʿĀbid al-Jabiri and Mohammed `Abed, al-Jabri, *Arab-Islamic Philosophy: A Contemporary Critique*, trans. Aziz Abbassi (Austin, TX: Center for Middle Eastern Studies, University of Texas at Austin, 1999), 63–107.
3. Muḥammad ʿĀbid al-Jabiri, *Binyat Al-ʿaql Al-ʿarabī : Dirāsah Taḥlīlīyah Naqdīyah Li-Nuẓum Al-Maʿrifah Fī Al-Thaqāfah Al-ʿarabīyah*, 6th ed., Naqd Al-ʿaql Al-ʿarabī 2 (Beirut: Markaz Dirāsāt al-Waḥdah al-ʿArabiyah, 1986), 536.
4. Muḥammad ʿĀbid al-Jābiri, *Al-ʿaql Al-Akhlāqī Al-ʿarabī: Dirāsa Taḥlīlīya Naqdīya Li Nazm Al-Qiyam Fīal-Thaqāfa Al-ʿarabīya* (Beirut: Markaz Dirāsāt al-Waḥda al-ʿArabīya, 2001), 598; al-Jabiri, *Binyat*, 536.
5. al-Jabiri, *Binyat*, 536.
6. For a critique of Jābirī see Jurj Tarabishi, *Waḥdat Al-ʿaql Al-ʿarabī Al-Islāmī*, al-Ṭabʿah, 1st ed., Naqd Naqd Al-ʿaql Al-ʿarabī (Beirut: Dār al-Sāqī, 2002).
7. See ʿAbd al-Majīd al-Ṣughayyar, *Al-Fikṛ Al-Uṣūlī Wa-Ishkālīyat Al-Sulṭa Al-ʿIlmīya Fī Al-Islām:Qirāʾat Fī Nashʾat ʿIlm Al-Uṣūl Wa-Maqāṣid Al-Sharīʿa*, 1st ed. (Beirut: Dār al-Muntakhab al-ʿArabī, 1994), 494, footnote 31.
8. ʿAbd al-Rahman, *Tajdīd Al-Manhaj Fī Taqwīm Al-Turāth*, 93.
9. Ibid.
10. Ibid., 94.
11. Abū Isḥāq al-Shatibi, *Al-Muwāfaqāt Fī Uṣūl Al-Sharīʿa*, ed. Abd Allah Daraz, 4 vols (Beirut: Dār al-Maʿrifa, n.d.), 1:42.
12. Taha ʿAbd al-Rahman, "Mashrūʿ Tajdīd ʿIlmī Li Mabḥath Maqāṣid Al-Sharīʿa," *al-Muslim al-muʿāṣir: special issue, maqāṣid al-sharīʿ* 26:103 (1422/2002), 41.
13. Although ʿAbd al-Rahman does discuss the difference between ethics and moral, he does not really clarify whether he accepts the distinction; therefore,

I have translated akhlāq as morals, see *Su'āl Al-Akhlāq: Musāhama Fī Al-Naqd Al-Akhlāqī Lil-Ḥadātha Al-Gharbīya*, al-Ṭab'ah, 1st ed. (Casablanca: al-Markaz al-Thaqāfī al-'Arabī, 2000), 17–24.

14. Muḥammad 'Alī (A'lā) al-Tahānawī and (ed.) Rafīq al-'Ajam, *Mawsū'a Kashshāf Iṣṭilāḥāt Al-Funūn Wa Al-'ulūm*, 2 vols. (Beirut: Maktaba Lubnan, 1996), 2:1745–1746.
15. Taha 'Abd al-Rahman, *al-Muslim al-mu'āṣir*, 42.
16. See 'Abd al-Malik ibn 'Abd Allāh Imām al-Ḥaramayn al-Juwayni and 'Abd al-'Azim Dīb, *Al-Burhān Fī Uṣūl Al-Fiqh:Makhṭūṭ Yunsharu Li-Awwal Marrah*, al-Ṭab'ah 1st ed., 2 vols, Maktabat Imām Al-Ḥaramayn (Doha: Ṭubi'a 'ala nafaqat Khalīfah ibn Ḥamad āl-Thānī, 1399).
17. 'Abd al-Rahman, "Mashrū'," 45.
18. Ibid., 50.
19. Ibid., 53.
20. Ibid., 54–56.
21. Ibid., 54.
22. Ibid., 57.
23. Abū Ya'rub al-Marzuqi and Muḥammad Sa'īd Ramaḍān al-Buti, *Ishkālīyat Tajdīd Uṣūl Al-Fiqh* (Damascus: Dār al-Fikr, 2006), 98.
24. Ibid., 21.
25. Ibid., 22.
26. Ibid.
27. Ibid., 92–93.

CHAPTER 8

Maqāṣid al-Sharīʿa, Gender Non-patriarchal Qurʾān-Sunna Hermeneutics, and the Reformation of Muslim Family Law

Adis Duderija

Introduction

This chapter attempts to systematically employ the insights from maqāṣid-oriented approaches to Islamic law and gender non-patriarchal Qurʾān hermeneutics in providing a novel gender-symmetrical reinterpretation of Muslim family laws.[1]

To do so, I first outline the gender differences in rights and duties between men and women in classical Islamic law and examine the reasons for these. Second, I provide examples of classical and modern patriarchal interpretations of Qurʾānic verses 4:34 and 2:228, which are the lynchpins upon which patriarchal interpretations of Muslim family law are based. Third, I briefly discuss the interpretational assumptions that underlie these interpretations. Fourth, I provide Qurʾān and ḥadīth evidence on the basis of which new maqāṣid relevant to a gender-just reconstruction of Muslim family law. Fifth, I discuss how the recent discourses on gender-just Qurʾānic hermeneutics are already utilizing some of this evidence but not linking it to that of the maqāṣid. Sixth, I develop a model of interpretation and outline how a discursive synthesis between maqāṣid approaches to Islamic law and non-patriarchal Qurʾānic hermeneutics can bring about a gender-just interpretation of Muslim family law.

As mentioned earlier, there is a dearth of studies that employ the maqāṣid-based approach in arguing for gender symmetry–based reforms in Muslim family law. The only study the author is aware of that links the concept of maqāṣid al-sharīʿa with such a Muslim family law reform is the article by Hashim Kamali.[2] Kamali laments the fact that the existing rulings in the al-sharīʿa pertaining to women and family law were not sufficiently informed by and grounded in the maqāṣid-based approach to Islamic law, which, in itself, has been methodologically undertheorized and marginalized in the overall Islamic legal theory. Although not directly engaging with the concept of maqāṣid in the concept of Muslim family law reform in the article, Kamali does take methodological recourse to several principles from the Qurʾān and the Sunna to argue for gender equality in Muslim family law. These include: the idea that the Qurʾānic outlook is supportive of moral autonomy of individuals; the employment of the Qurʾānic formula promotes good and forbids evil; and the Qurʾānic concepts of al-ʾadl (justice), qisṭ (equity), iḥsan (moral excellence), raḥmah (mercy), and moderation (wasaṭiyya). He argues that these Qurʾānic ethical norms must be reflected in the legal rulings of al-sharīʿa in matters pertaining to gender issues including marital and family life. He also refers to the juristic principle of takhayyur (selection of ideas among different existing legal schools, which are most women "emanticipatory") and istiḥsan (juristic preference) as methodological principles that could be employed for the development of more gender-just Muslim family law. With reference to the concept of maqāṣid al-sharīʿa, he concludes the article with this recommendation:

> Reform measures and adjustment of existing fiqh rules pertaining to family welfare and women should take their cue from the broader guidelines of the Qurʾān and Sunna on fairness, human dignity, and justice. These and other principles of broader import should not be overshadowed by technical details, customary, and historical constrains[3].

While the work of Kamali has made some important contributions to the issue of reform of Muslim family laws from a maqāṣid perspective, this chapter aims to build further on his efforts.

Gender Differences in Terms of Rights and Duties in Classical Islamic Law and Reasons for the Same

In order to have a better understanding of the nature of Muslim family law, we need to keep in mind that classical Islamic law contains a number of gender-specific rights, duties, and norms pertaining not only to the legal sphere but also to that of the political/governmental, educational, ritual, juridical, and general personal conduct.[4] Most of these gender differences can be traced back to a particular understanding of female- and male sexuality–based on the majority of the classical jurists' subscription to the thesis of "gender complementarity" (also known as gender dualism), which states that women, unlike men, are highly emotional beings with weak and easily befuddled or, according to some, deficient rational faculties.[5] The first assumption that governs the traditional or premodern views of the female and the male sexuality is their essential difference. According to this view sexuality is a crucial marker, but not the only one,[6] of the construction of masculinity and femininity. These sexual differences are said to be based on biological and mental functions and capacities that strongly differentiate the sexes as embodied in the idea of gender dualism, considering the female nature to be derivative vis-à-vis the male, whose superiority is both ontological and sociomoral. The female body is, furthermore, considered as sexually and morally corrupting. Men are conceptualized as having an insatiable sexual desire aroused by the very sight, smell, or voice of a woman, thereby distracting and diverting energy from their important religious and other public duties. Furthermore, the premodern views of women are posited on (an artificial) split between body and mind, sexuality and spirituality. The category of the female gender is constructed primarily in sexual terms. Women are identified with the "irreligious" realm of sexual passion, as repositories of all "lower" aspects of human nature, the very antithesis of the "illuminated" sphere of male (religious) knowledge and who are considered the sole bearers of religious authority. Women and their active sexuality are conceptualized and constructed as sources of sociomoral chaos, embodiments of seduction, and a threat to a healthy social order. All of this necessitates the need to regulate female sexual instinct by "external precautionary safeguards" such as veiling, seclusion, gender segregation, and constant surveillance. The highly gender-differentiated nature of classical Islamic law in general affects the nature of Muslim family law, particularly because these gender-based differences also apply to the rights and duties of husbands and wives by, for example, restricting the wife's mobility or control over her sex organs (more on this later) but not that of the husband's.

This aspect of classical Islamic law is also premised upon a certain interpretational model (manhaj) of the Qurʾān and the Sunna, whose patriarchal interpretational implications have been documented elsewhere.[7] For the purposes of this chapter, I merely outline its main delineating features: a philologically centered interpretational orientation (i.e., various philological sciences and their role in the process of derivation of meaning are Qurʾān's most decisive and hermeneutically powerful interpretational tools);

a "voluntarist-traditionalist" view of the relationship between reason and revelation, law, morality and ontology, which manifests itself in the idea that revelation is the only objective standard in discerning ethical values of good and bad; a belief in the fixed, stable nature of the meaning of the Qur'ānic text residing in totality in the mind of its originator, whose will is discoverable in principle (hermeneutical approach known as "textual intentionalism"), and hence a marginalization of the role of the interpreter in the process of deriving meaning; a decontextualization and marginalization of the Qur'ānic revelationary background for the purposes of its interpretation; a textual segmentalism or lack of a thematic approach to interpretation; a largely ḥadīth-dependent concept of the Sunna, which conflates the principles of the Sunna and the ḥadīth; and lastly an approach with a relative lack of purposive (maqāṣid) and ethico-religious values[8] to the Qur'ānic hermeneutics occupying the highest position in the overall manhaj, one that is informed by contemporary understandings of justice and fairness.

Examples of Classical and Modern Patriarchal Interpretations of the Quran

It is on the basis of gender-dualism reasoning and manhaj described earlier that Qur'ānic verses such as 4:34 and 2:228, the lynchpins of classical highly gender-asymmetrical Muslim family law, have been interpreted in patriarchal ways. However, there are other Qur'ānic and juristic concepts that have also been employed to construct more gender-asymmetrical Muslim family laws and I briefly discuss the most important of them.

The first one is the concept of *wilāya*. In the context of classical Islamic law, *wilāya* is defined as "an authority granted to a person over the affairs of another by virtue of which acts undertaken on behalf of such other person, without his consent, are assigned legal effects."[9] It is not employed as such in the Qur'ān (where it primarily means mutual support or help and cooperation as in 9:7).[10] In the context of Muslim family law, it denotes the guardianship of the husband over the wife and children (female until marriage and male until age of majority). The concept of *wilāya* is itself embedded in the larger concept of Islamic law of marriage being considered a contract (*al-aqd*) containing an element of ownership (*milk*) that gives rise to gender-differentiated rights and duties of husband and wife.[11] The concept of wilāya is very important in the construction of asymmetrical interpretations of Muslim family law because on its basis women are, generally speaking, denied the freedom to contract marriage independently of their male kin, have control over their mobility (decisions regarding a married woman's mobility are in the hands of her husband because of the fact that Muslim marriage law makes a link between the wife's duty to be sexually available to her husband at his complete discretion with that of the husband's duty to her maintenance. In the case of a nonmarried woman her movements are controlled by her father or other male kin).[12] The concept of *wilāya* is mentioned only in an isolated (aḥad) ḥadith such as "there is no marriage contract without a walī"[13] (bride's male kin representative who gives her in marriage to the groom with or without her consent).[14] Because of the classical manhaj described here, it has found its way into Muslim family law.

Other important juristic concepts that have shaped the formulation of Muslim family laws that need mentioning include *isma* (husband's/father's authority over wife and children), ṭalāq (unilateral right of the husband to divorce his wife), *tamkin* and *nafaqa* (wife's sexual submission in marriage in exchange for her right to shelter, food, and clothing), *ta'a* (wife's obedience), and *nushuz* (wife's recalcitrance or rebellion). Due to space constraints, I am not able to discuss these concepts at length. What I want to highlight is that all of these concepts are embedded in the same gender-duality theories and interpretations of the Qurʾān and the Sunna described earlier, which have almost single-handedly shaped the formulation of Muslim family laws by classical Muslim jurists.

In what follows I first provide quotes of two representative examples of both classical and modern patriarchal interpretations of 4:34, one by a male and the other by a female exegete foregrounding the issue of men's custodianship (qawwāmun) of women, men's faḍḍala (preference) over women, and men having a degree (*darajāt*) higher over women and employing them as central concepts in the construction of patriarchal and asymmetrical Muslim family laws.

For example, the classical Sunni tafsīr of the verse 4:34 by Jar Allah Al-Zamakhshari (d. 1143/1144) is representative of the majority view of the classical Qurʾānic interpretations of this (and its sister verse 2:228) gender-dualism-informed manhaj. In relation to 4:34, he comments:

> Men are the commanders [of right] and forbidders [of wrong], just as a governor guides the people. The "some" in *some of them* refers to all men and all women. It means that men are only in control over women because God made some of them superior, and those are men, to others, and they are women. This is proof that governance is only merited by superiority (*tafdīl*), not by dominance, an overbearing attitude, or subjugation. Concerning the superiority of men over women, the exegetes mention rationality (*'aql*), good judgment (*hazm*), determination, strength, writing—for the majority of men—horsemanship, archery, that men are prophets, learned (*'ulamā'*), have the duties of the greater

> and lesser imamate, *jihād*, call to prayer, the Friday sermon, seclusion in the mosque (*i'tikāf*), saying the prayers during the holidays (*takbīrāt al-tashrīq*), according to Abū Hanīfa they witness cases of injury or death (*hudūd* and *qisās*), they have more shares in inheritance, bloodwit (*himāla*), pronouncement of an oath 50 times which establishes guilt or innocence in cases of murder (*qasāma*), authority in marriage, divorce, and taking back the wife after a revocable divorce, a greater number of spouses, lineage passing through the male line, and they have beards and turban.[15]

Muhammad Husein Tabatabai (d. 1981)

Tabatabai,[16] a renowned contemporary neo-traditionalist Shi'i scholar, in his commentary of 2:228 writes as follows:

> The natural law of society says that all members of society should be treated equally, they should have as much rights as they have obligations. At the same time it decrees that every individual's personal perfection and attributes must be recognized. The rule's authority, the people's subordination, the scholar's knowledge, the illiterate person's ignorance, all must be weighed in the scale of their usefulness for, and, effort on, society; and with that recognition everyone should be given his proper right. The same principle was applied by Islam concerning the rights and obligations of woman. It gave her as much right upon her husband as it ordained upon her for the husband. At the same time, it preserved her rightful value and place in her union with the man and in this area, Islam found that men have a right a degree above women.[17]

Commentating on 4:34 in relation to qiwāma, he is of the view that qiwāma is not a specific rule for a husband's conduct in relation to his wife but a general statement that applies to society at large. Men are collectively speaking the maintainers of women. He forms the view that the verse "refers to the natural characteristics of men who have stronger rationality than women, and are stronger in bearing difficulties and in performing heavy tasks" and that women are to confine themselves to the management of domestic affairs and bringing up children.[18]

Zainab al Ghazali (d. 2005)

Al Ghazali, the Al-Azhar educated neo-traditionalist scholar, in her commentary of 4:34 argues that men have responsibility over women and that men have the right to leadership in the family. This, however, does not remove women's sovereignty (wilāya) in her house and her being the commander (amira), administering freely her husband's affairs in order to protect the interests of the family and the intactness of its unity. She forms the view that the basis of qiwāma is responsibility (masʿuliya) in the sense that the man is entrusted with providing for his wife and children. Al Ghazali also asserts that the wife is the one in charge of the family (wilāyatu amri-hi) within the home. She is responsible before God for the soundness of her husband and her children. All of this does not arise without the women surrendering readily with love and obedience to God and (understanding) that man's qiwāma over her is a source of justice and is for her benefit. This is because qiwāma demands from man the best treatment and equity (insāf) concerning her in every matter whereof she is in need of any service. He is also responsible for protecting her dignity, her honor, and her humanity because with his sovereignty (wilāyati-hi) over his wife, she becomes the trust in his hands.[19]

In all of these cited exegetical evidence we see how, in addition to the mahaj aspect, adhering to the thesis of gender dualism—often expressed in the language of the "natural" (i.e., God-determined) qualities of the sexes (physically strong vs. physically weak; rational vs. highly emotional) or in terms of certain socioculturally contingent views on in/appropriate male/female functions (giver or recipient of dowry, financial maintainer, or recipient of material support) and behavior (nature of male vs. female sexualities)—has resulted in the construction of the patriarchal Qur'ānic exegesis of 4:34 and 2:228.

Are alternative non-patriarchal interpretations of the Qur'ān and the Sunna possible on the basis of which we can formulate gender-symmetrical Muslim family laws? We move to these questions next.

Deriving New Maqāṣid in Relation to Muslim Family Law

As outlined earlier, the classical Muslim family law (and its modern endorsements) has been formulated primarily on the basis of foregrounding concepts of men's qiwāma, taf ḍīl, ta'a, and wilāya over women to construct a highly gender-differentiated and rigid Muslim family law. These laws have strong gender-rights imbalances, generally favoring husbands as in, for example, the case of divorce and child custody, and the wife's male kin in the case of inheritance. Since the Qur'ān and ḥadīth contain specific injunctions pertaining to many aspects of what later, on the basis of the manahij outlined earlier, became classical Muslim family laws, these imbalances were not addressed as they were considered to be immutable aspects and in harmony with the Will of the Just and Divine Legislator. Therefore, these laws were considered by classical Muslim jurists as essentially and principally the most just laws there can possibly be. However, as it will become evident later the Qur'ānic and juristic concepts employed by classical Muslim scholarship to formulate highly asymmetrical Muslim family laws are by no means the only concepts upon which these laws can be constructed. Moreover, recent scholarship has identified that different interpretational models of the Qur'ān and the Sunna can yield very different results, the Qur'ān in relation to issues such as the normative nature and purpose of marriage and the kind of relationships that govern the interaction between the spouses.[20] In other words, there is nothing inevitable about patriarchal interpretations of the Qur'ān and the Sunna and, as this part of this chapter aims to show, it is perfectly possible to identify a number of new maqāṣid relevant to Muslim family law on the basis of which gender-symmetrical Muslim family law can be constructed. In this context it is important to emphasize that, although occurring in the Qur'ān and the Sunna, these newly identified maqāṣid, and the interpretational manahij and the assumptions underpinning them, are not just simply a lost treasure finally recovered, but also a product of the "human rights era consciousness" (the concepts of gender non-patriarchalism and gender justice being its fundamental elements) adopted on the part of the interpreter, which acts as a lens through which the Qur'ān and the Sunna are interpreted. This argument is further reinforced by the fact that the very nature of interpretation is such that it is always tainted by the intellectual, moral, educational, cultural, and contextual milieus in which communities of interpretation (i.e., groups of interpreters sharing certain factors that influence the outcome of the process of interpretation, e.g., such as those mentioned in this sentence) of the Qur'ān and the Sunna are embedded.

New Maqāṣid Relevant to Muslim Family Law

While the traditional Muslim scholarship has extensively relied on the earlier mentioned juristic concepts to construct highly gender asymmetrical Muslim family laws, these concepts are by no means the only or, for that matter, the most relevant and/or readily apparent concepts that can be deduced from the Qur'ān and the Sunna. Indeed, traditional scholarship has excluded, consciously or unconsciously, many other relevant concepts that can be employed for the construction of a much more gender-symmetrical Muslim family law. In this section, I explore the possibility of deriving alternative relevant concepts from the Qur'ān and the Sunna that could be employed for such a purpose. I would like to start this section with a quote from Kecia Ali, a leading progressive-minded contemporary scholar, who in the context of discussing the possibilities of reform of marriage laws recognizes clearly this potential:

> Our contemporary recognition that the traditional scheme of marriage law is compromised beyond repair liberates us to pursue a new jurisprudence, one based on assumptions that do not liken women to slaves or marriage to purchase [as traditional jurisprudence does]. A marriage law that foregrounds the mutual protectorship of men and women (Q 9:71) rather than male providership (Q 4:34), or that focuses on the cooperation and harmony of the spouses inherent in the *Qur'ānic* declaration that spouses are garments for one another, can represent a starting point for a new jurisprudence of marriage. The result will be a closer—but still only human, and therefore fallible—approximation of divinely revealed *al-sharīʿa* than what currently exists.[21]

There are a number of relevant verses in the Qur'ān and the ḥadīth on the basis of which new maqāṣid can be identified and with reference to which gender-just Muslim family law can be constructed. The new maqāṣid that are *directly* relevant to reformulation of Muslim family law would include the following: raḥma, muwadda, and sakīna, that is, mercy (or compassion), love, harmony (or tranquillity), sameness/equality, and intimate closeness.

They can be identified in the following Qur'ānic verses and ḥadīth:

> 30:21
>
> Another of His signs is that He created spouses from among yourselves for you to live with in tranquillity (sakīna): He ordained love (muwadda) and kindness (raḥma) between you. There truly are signs in this for those who reflect. (258).
>
> 7:189
>
> It is He who created you all from one soul, and from it made its mate so that he might find comfort (yaskun) in her (108).
>
> 2:187
>
> You [believers] are permitted to lie with your wives during the night of the fast: they are [close] as garments to you, as you are to them (21).
>
> ḥadīth:
>
> "The best of you are those who behave best to their wives."
>
> "The more civil and kind a Muslim is to his wife, the more perfect in faith he is."[22]
>
> "Women are but sisters (or twin halves) of Men."[23]

The values that are inherent in these Qur'ānic verses and ḥadīth can be employed as legal indicant (adilla) describing the normative nature of spousal relationship. From these we can derive new maqāṣid specific to Muslim family law and the concept of marriage in particular.[24] It is my contention, clearly unlike what the majority of classical jurists thought, that these values cannot be meaningfully fulfilled in the context of a gender-hierarchical and highly differentiated relationship present in the classical Muslim family law as outlined earlier. However, one problem with this argument is that these new maqāṣid cannot be legally enforced since most of them operate at the level of feeling and emotions. Although this is true on the basis of these new maqāṣid, as well as those outlined later, we can question the strong legal asymmetries arising from the highly gender-hierarchical and differentiated nature of legally enforceable aspects of Muslim family law that are based on patriarchy and an androcentric worldview.

At this junction it is important to note, however, that the majority of ḥadīth pertaining to the relationship between husbands and wives are patriarchal and at times male chauvinistic in nature.[25] Maqāṣid approaches would consider women-"friendly" ḥadīth[26] to be more in accordance with the objectives of the Qur'ān and the Sunna, even if they are less "authentic" according to classical ḥadīth sciences (*ulūm* ul ḥadīth), because women-friendly ḥadīth are more closely aligned with the values underpinning the maqāṣid. To question the normative nature of these ḥadīth, one could also resort to the existing mechanisms within classical ḥadīth studies pertaining to reconciliation of contradictory ḥadīth (ta'arud) but through the new maqāṣid interpretive lens as outlined in the previous sentence. Also conceptual, epistemological, and hermeneutical differentiation of the Sunna and the ḥadīth is another mechanism through which the normative character of these ḥadīth can be questioned.[27]

Further maqāṣid of relevance to the reformulation of classical Muslim family law can be derived from either non-gender-specific or specifically female-gender-inclusive Qur'ānic concepts of: khilāfa (vicerency), *taqwā* (God consciousness), *ma'ruf* (doing what is commonly known to be good), equality in creation and human worth/honor (*karama*), *wilāya* (mutual support or companionship), and *qisṭ* (justice).[28] These central Qur'ānic concepts are employed either directly or indirectly in the Qur'ānin the context of gender or spousal relationships as well as in the context of regulating the relationship between the Creator and the created, as well as in general human social intercourses.[29] As such they would be applicable to the realm of family life as well, which is a significant and integral part of both.

I shall turn to these in more detail in the context of discussing recent works on gender non-patriarchal Qur'ānic hermeneutics in the next section.

From these verses and others in a similar fashion, we can deduce or derive the earlier mentioned new maqāṣid on the basis of which gender just and non-patriarchal Muslim family law can be erected. As I mentioned in "Introduction," the non-patriarchal hermeneutics of the Qur'ān have already been developed by several predominantly female Muslim scholars. However, these discussions have not been linked to the discourses pertaining to the maqāṣid al-sharī'a in any systematic fashion. This is what follows in the rest of this chapter.

Objectives based Non-patriarchal Qur'ān-Sunna Hermeneutics

I define non-patriarchal Qur'ān-Sunna hermeneutics as a body of scholarship that advocates for gender equality and women's full legal rights from *within* the Islamic epistemic and methodological framework by systematically deriving and justifying these rights on the basis of a particular conceptualization and interpretation of the inherited Muslim traditions (turath), especially its primary fountainheads, the Qur'ān and the Sunna. Here two most noteworthy contributions are those by Amina Wadud and Asma Barlas. In what follows I am not focusing on the actual interpretational models employed by Wadud and Barlas.[30] Instead, I discuss the arguments they use with special reference to the new maqāṣid concepts identified in the last part of the previous section and how we can utilize the same when developing a novel manhaj of the Qur'ān and the Sunna, which can pave the way to formulation of gender-symmetrical Muslim family laws.

Wadud constructs her gender non-patriarchal Qur'ānic hermeneutics on the basis of gender-neutral or inclusive concepts in the Qur'ān, including islām (defined as an act of voluntary "engaged surrender"), which is enabled through the concept of khilāfa (moral agency) and taqwā, all of which operate under the umbrella of Qur'ānic concept of tawḥīd, or what she terms the "tawḥīdic paradigm."

Let us start by discussing what Wadud understands by tawḥīdic paradigm[31] and see how she links it to other concepts such as khilāfa and taqwā. The first thing we need to note in this context is that she does not consider tawḥīd to be a purely theological concept but also an ethical one with concrete sociopolitical implications and relevance. Tawḥīd for Wadud "is the operating principle of equilibrium and cosmic harmony... [*T*]*awḥid* relates to relationships and developments within the social and political realms, emphasizing the unity of all human creatures beneath one Creator."[32] The only distinction between people is on the basis of *taqwā* (Q 49:13) and hence the primacy of social justice, with the objective of eradicating all barriers to discrimination, and here specifically, is on the basis of gender.[33] She forms the view that if human beings are truly created to be God's trustees [khilāfa] on earth (Q 2:30), then the purpose of this human agency is to work in harmony with God's purposes of justice and equity. "Being *khalifah* is equivalent to fulfilling one's human destiny as moral agent, whose responsibility is to participate in upholding the harmony of the universe."[34] So the Qur'ānic concept of khalifa or human agency in Wadud's thinking is not restricted to that of the male. It is a means of acquiring taqwā by being just and doing good deeds on earth, which, in turn, by definition implies establishing human relationships of equality, including in the context of marriage.

In arguing against patriarchy and patriarchal understandings of Islam, she furthermore asserts the following:

> To go beyond these attitudes and structures of inequality we have to move towards reforms that acknowledge the equal significance of women's creation, women's ways of thinking and being, and their equal responsibility in judgement. We can do this by establishing a system of social justice that practices muwada, relations of reciprocity, and equality between men and women. This system would acknowledge both men and women as competent contributors in both the private and public spheres of activity. Such a system would encourage women and men to excel in whatever that do and would not restrict them to one sphere over another. The basis of this reciprocity is central in islam under the rubric of tawḥīd.[35]

Wadud use the values of reciprocity and symmetry in Quran 33:35 and 30:21 as an additional tool for establishing gender-symmetrical Muslim family laws and relationships that are not based on domination (as in the case of classical Muslim family law and gender relations) but on cooperation and partnership.

She also uses the theological meaning of God's tawḥīd to argue for equality of human relationships by arguing that the tawḥīd implies that the only ontologically hierarchical relationship is that between the Creator and the creation and that hierarchical relationships between genders would constitute shirk.[36] In this context, she asserts the following:

> Since God is the highest conceptual aspect of all, then no person can be greater than another person, especially for mere reasons of gender, race, class, nationality, etc. The *tawḥīdic* paradigm then acts as a basic theoretical principle for removing gender asymmetry, which is a kind of satanic logic or *shirk*, positing priority or superiority to men. Instead, women and men must occupy a relationship of horizontal reciprocity, maintaining the highest place for God in His/Her/Its uniqueness.[37]

Barlas's non-patriarchal Qurʾānic hermeneutics are in several ways similar to that of Wadud (e.g., with their focus on the nature of "Godhead" and discussions surrounding the meaning and nature of tawḥīd and khilāfa and their implications for gender relationships) although some differences exist (e.g., Barlas's focus is on "liberating" Qurʾān from patriarchal readings although she recognizes that patriarchal readings are also legitimate while Wadud's directs her attention to demonstrate that the Qurʾān, "properly" or "correctly" interpreted, is advocating gender justice and equality). Barlas's[38] work purports to restore what the author views as the Qurʾānic basis of gender equality in Islam by freeing the Qurʾān from the patriarchal nature of its classical and some modern exegesis (or as Barlas would argue *eisegesis*). She does so systematically on both historical and hermeneutical grounds. Here I highlight how her anti-patriarchal Qurʾān hermeneutics can be employed for the purposes of the earlier identified new gender non-patriarchal maqāṣid.

Barlas develops a systematic "anti-patriarchal Qurʾānic hermeneutic of liberation" to argue that the Qurʾāncan be:

1. read in sexually non-patriarchal manner (in the sense that "the Qurʾān considers sex as irrelevant to moral agency") and
2. moreover, that it is anti-patriarchal in nature.

Barlas links ontology with hermeneutics to argue that the Qurʾānic God as manifest in God's self-disclosure does not advocate any of the patriarchal dimensions as found in her definition.[39] Moreover, on this account, Barlas argues that the Qurʾān can be seen as anti-patriarchal because it insists on God's sovereignty. This is important because the way humans conceptualize God has important implications for humanity's own moral, social, and sexual self-worth and relationships. She asserts the following in this context:

> When sacred knowledge is used to engender or sexualize God (humanize or anthropomorphize God) as male, it also underwrites male privilege since men acquire power from "the fact that the source of ultimate value is often described in anthropomorphic images as Father or King." Indeed, feminists believe that it is the "exclusively masculine symbolism for God, for the notion of divine 'incarnation' in human nature, and for the human relationship to God" that reinforces sexual oppression. (Daly,[40] 1973, 4)[41]

Furthermore, she maintains that "not only does Islamic monotheism [tawḥīd], properly understood, serve to liberate women from the tyranny of male rule, but, by privileging the rights of God, it dislocates rule by the father as well as theories of male sovereignty, which are at the roots of women's oppression."[42] The importance of the Qur'ānic concept of tawḥīd for nonhierarchical gender relationships is also highlighted in this passage:

> The single most essential aspect of God's Self-Disclosure in the Qur'ān is that God is One, hence Indivisible; this principle of Divine Unity (Tawḥīd) extends to the idea that God is Incomparable, hence Unrepresentable. Both separately and together, these doctrines preclude associating forebears, partners, or progeny with God, or misrepresenting God as father, son, husband, or male.[43]

Similar to Wadud, Barlas considers that one important implication of this concept of tawḥīd is that gender-hierarchical relationships in patriarchal societies systematically privileging males by awarding them higher degree of agency or moral or human worth are tantamount to shirk or idolatry that manifest themselves concretely at the societal level in classical Muslim tradition's understanding of the concepts of men's qiwāma, tafḍīl, darajāt, or wilāya. This is so because they undermine the concept of tawḥīd by transferring the indivisible God's Sovereignty onto males.

Barlas also discusses the idea of khilāfa, arguing that this concept, in the way it is employed in the Qur'ān, is not contingent on sex and while being a relational term (human as representatives of God and acting as His trustees) it does not imply that certain humans are viceregents over others or more specifically that males enjoy the status of ẖilafa over women.[44] In this context, she remarks, "There is thus no reason to assume that only males are vice-regents on earth, much less vice-regents over women."[45] She concludes by saying that on the Qur'ānic concepts such as tawḥīd and khilāfa it is possible to reject gender dualisms and binaries and develop interpretations of Islamic tradition founded on the complete equality and humanity of women and men.[46]

So in summary of this section, we can conclude that Qur'ānic hermeneutics as exemplified by Wadud and Barlas employ concepts such as tawḥīd, taqwā, muwada, and khilāfa in order to argue for gender non-patriarchal understandings of the Qur'ān. It is my contention that we can employ and incorporate these discussions into discourses pertaining to maqāṣid approaches to Islamic law to strengthen the case for gender-nonpatriarchal Muslim family law.

In the rest of this section, I would like to show how this can be done by outlining an interpretational model that synthesizes a maqāṣid-based approach and gender non-patriarchal Qur'ānic hermeneutics for reformation of Muslim family law. It consists of ontological, methodological, and broader hermeneutical dimensions as outlined next.

The ontological dimension is based on the tawḥīdic paradigm/God's self-disclosure of incomparibility and unrepresentedness argument as espoused by Wadud and Barlas. It implies that the only hierarchical relationship is between God/Allah and the creation and that all kinds of relationships between humans (this includes relationships between genders in and outside of context of marriage and family life) by default according to the Qur'ānic conceptualization of God are based on non-patriarchalism/equality and reciprocity (see figure 8.1).

The methodological dimension of gender non-patriarchal Muslim family law can be pictorially represented as in figure 8.2:

1. Circle—the concept of gender non-patriarchal maqāṣid al nikaḥ on the basis of relevant Qur'ānic concepts (see point 2) is deduced.
2. Single arrows—pointing to the circle represent Qur'ānic concepts from which the gender-egalitarian/just maqāṣid al nikaḥ is derived: *muwada* (1), *raḥmah* (2), *wilāya* (3), *sakīna* (4), *taqwā* (5), khilāfa (6), *ma'ruf/munkar* (7), *karama* (8), and *iḥsān* (9).
3. Double arrows—represent the idea of interconnectedness of all Qur'ānic concepts whereby the Qur'ānic text is conceived as being weblike within which ideas/concepts are interwoven and are relational in nature. The identification and/or the arrival at a proper Qur'ānic *value* or its "comprehensive constant" (*ṭabitan kulliyan*) is achieved through this thematic search for all the relevant Qur'ānic concepts (i.e., *keywords underpinning its weltanschauung*) that converge to engender a larger Qur'ānic *value* by the method of corroborative induction (*istiqrā'*). The eventual uncovering of the ṭabitan

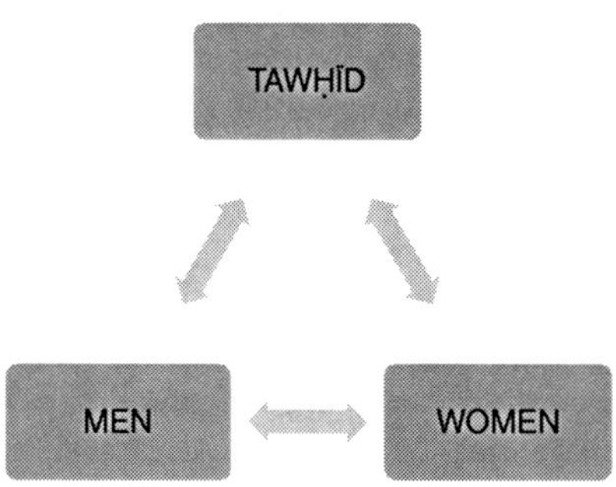

Figure 8.1 Ontological dimension of nonpatriarchal Muslim family laws

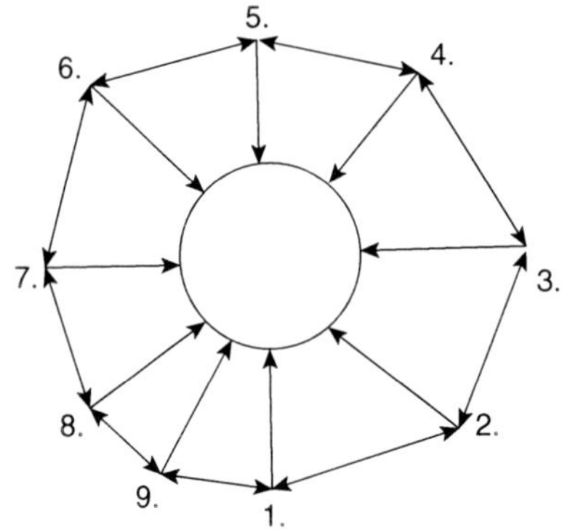

Figure 8.2 Methodological dimension of nonpatriarchal Muslim family laws

> kulliyan would, in turn, be the aim or the objective (qaṣd) of the reading/interpreting process. So the Qur'ānic concepts labeled 1–9 would according to this manhaj yield the underlying objectives of Qur'ānic texts, which would give rise to the identification of a Qur'ānic ethical *value*,[47] namely, in this case, that of non-patriarchy. The patriarchal elements in the Qur'ān, such as those in verses 2:223, 2:228, and 4:34, are rather isolated and peripheral, and unlike the concepts identified in figure 8.2 they do not repeatedly occur in the Qur'ān; hence they cannot be identified as ṭabitan kulliyan as per methodology identified above and therefore are not considered to have a Qur'ānic value.

The broader hermeneutical principles upon which the concept of maqāṣid is based consist of the following elements (figure 8.3):

1. Comprehensive contextualization.

By comprehensive contextualization I mean investigating, in a methodical manner, the role of context in shaping of content of the Qur'ān and its worldview. For this, we need to recognize the Qur'ān's orientation toward the assumed operational discourse that manifests itself in the Qur'ānic content and is reflected in grammatical and syntactical structures employed in its language. This Qur'ānically assumed operational discourse must be seen as often reflecting the prevalent religious, cultural, social, political, and economic situation of its direct audience, its first community of listeners, and participants upon which the dialogical nature of the Qur'ān's discourse is premised. This nature of Qur'ānic discourse has been noted by several Muslims scholars. Abu Zayd, for example, considers that Qur'ānic discourse reflects the dialectical relationship between the Qur'ān and the reality of the early Muslim community. Achrati elsewhere argues that the oral-based

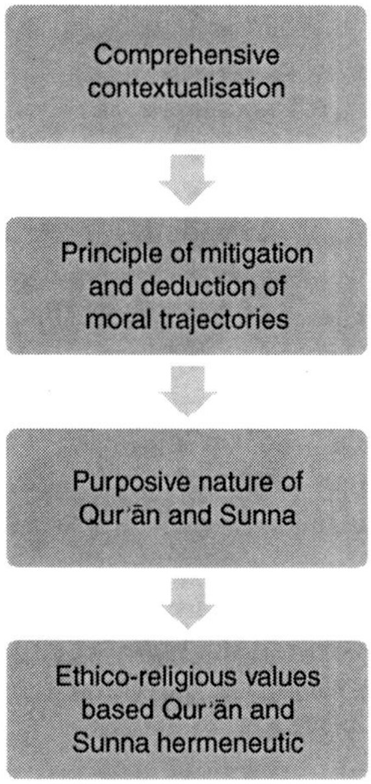

Figure 8.3 Broader hermeneutical mechanism on which the concept of maqāṣid in the Qurʾān and Sunna is based

culture of the Arab Bedouins strongly influenced the character and the nature of Qurʾānic discourse. This dialectical and symbiotic nature of the Qurʾān and its relationship with its first listeners is, in turn, based upon Qurʾān's essential orality. The hermeneutical importance of this idea of Qurʾān's recognition of the prior knowledge and mentality resident among its first audience has important hermeneutical implications as I will demonstrate in relation to the issue of ṭalāq.[48]

We can apply comprehensive contextualization to the Qurʾānic concept of ṭalāq by noting that one the most evident assumptions evident in a majority of the passages in the Qurʾān that have sociolegal import is the existence of an all-embracing patriarchy[49] existing in its historically revelatory milieu and reflected in the structure and the content of the Qurʾān itself.[50] a husband's right to unilateral dissolution of marriage is one aspect of this patriarchal milieu. According to Schacht:

> The right to a one-sided dissolution of a marriage belonged to the man exclusively, among the pre-Islamic Arabs. Long before Muḥammad, this *ṭalāq was* in general use among the Arabs and meant the immediate definite abandonment by the man of all rights over his wife, which he could insist upon as a result of his marriage.[51]

At the philological level, this patriarchal revelation context is evident in the Qur'ānic injunctions that are exclusively directed at men in matters pertaining to divorce and marriage. For example, the Qur'ān (65: 1–2) [52] instructs the Prophet that if the *men* divorce their women (*ṭalāqtumu nisā'*) they should allow women to reside in their marital home during their *'idda* and then instructs *men* to keep or stay with their *wives* in dignity or you divorce them in kindness and dignity.[53] In the premodern Qur'ānic commentary (*tafsīr*) literature that I consulted (Al-Suyuti, Ibn 'Abbas, Al-Qurtubi, Ibn Kathir, Al-Wahidi, and others) on this verse, it is evident that all of the exegetes (*mufassirūn*) considered that the unilateral right of men to divorce their wives was a "pregiven" and "natural" order of things and did not problematize it at all apart from emphasizing that although the verse addresses the Prophet it also speaks to all the male believers (*mu'minūn*). Instead, the *mufassirūn* either focused on the discussions surrounding the 'idda and/or the proper treatment of one's wife during this time and provided the circumstances for the revelation of the verse (e.g., the Prophet's divorcing of his elderly wife Hafza or Abd Allah Ibn 'Umar divorcing his wife when she had her menses).[54]

What I wish to highlight is that this Qur'ānic verse (and others I discussed elsewhere)[55] *presupposes* the existence of a social and cultural order that confers the right to enter into marriage [contract], divorce, physical punishment, disciplining, and even possession of women (as in case of slavery and female concubinage) solely to men, the reality of which is assumed, acknowledged, and addressed by the Qur'ān. However, does this necessarily imply that the Qur'ān endorses the same powers to men or does it attempt to mitigate and limit them? To answer this question, we take recourse to the next hermeneutical principle namely that of mitigation and deduction of moral trajectories.

2. Principle of mitigation and deduction of moral trajectories.

The process of comprehensive contextualization, in turn, points to the mitigatory nature of the Qur'ān and Sunna in relation to its sociolegal dimensions, especially those concerning women. On the basis of this mitigatory nature of the Qur'ān and Sunna, the principle of moral trajectories is deduced, which stipulates that the Qur'ān and Sunna teachings were pointing to certain directions as ideals to be attained in the future, which were not possible at the time of the Revelation due to the mentality and the level of civilization of the immediate audience. In other words, the Qur'ān and the Sunna are purposive in nature, that is, they pointed toward certain objectives or higher intentions.

The principles of mitigation and moral trajectories can be applied to the issue of the Qur'ān's concept of divorce too. Among others, Abou El Fadl has observed the existence of the mitigating effect of Qurʾānic verses concerning the sociolegal rights of women by asserting that these Qurʾānic verses were performing the function of "protecting women from the power of men [they] already possess[ed] by the virtue of the customs and practices of the society in which Islam was revealed."[56] Similarly, elsewhere he asserts:

> The thorough and fair-minded researcher would observe that behind every single Qurʾānic revelation regarding women was an effort to protect the women from exploitative situations and from situations in which they are treated inequitably. In studying the Qurʾān it becomes clear that the Qurʾān is educating Muslims how to make incremental but lasting improvements in the condition of women that can only be described as progressive for their time and place.[57]

Wadud develops this type of argument further with the employment of the hermeneutical principle of Qurʾānic moral trajectories pertaining to women through what she terms "textual development" in the Qurʾān. By textual development, Wadud wishes to alert the reader/interpreter to be sensitive to how Qurʾānic text establishes new moral, social, and political trajectories that go beyond the literal and concrete meaning and searches for the underlying rationale (*ratio*) or objective/aim[58]:

> The notion of new moral trajectories leads Wadud to take a hermeneutical recourse to ethical principles such as equality, justice and human rights as being constitutive of the Qurʾānic ultimate aims as well as being its hermeneutically most powerful principles of interpretation.

Fletcher similarly states that the "Prophet's mission is not correctly indicated by reified content of Islamic Law but rather by the direction of his reforms," and more specifically to issues pertaining to women, "Prophet's message with respect to the Arab sunna must be clearly understood to benefit women and to reform the existing practices extremely prejudicial to women."[59]

Furthermore, according to scholars such as Abu Zayd and Souaiaia, and based on the semantical and historical analyses of these verses, it would be safe to assert that all of the Qurʾānic injunctions pertaining to family issues aim to limit the rights of men that existed in the patriarchal and tribal-based social, economic, cultural, and political reality of the Qurʾānic revelational milieu, rather than to stipulate absolute rules and regulations.[60] Additionally, all of the Qurʾānic and Sunna injunctions pertaining to the rights of women had a mitigating effect on the basis of which we could deduce certain moral trajectories such as fairness and equality of rights as argued in the works of Wadud mentioned earlier.[61]

But is this mitigating process an end in itself or just a means to an end?

3. Purposive nature of the Qur'ān and the Sunna and Islamic law/philosophy

The existence of moral trajectories points to another hermeneutical mechanism in the Qur'ān and Sunna, namely their purposive nature. By purposive nature of the ethico-legal teachings of the Qur'ān and Sunna (as systematized in Islamic law and its philosophy), I mean that the primary function of Islamic law and the most fundamental element in its methodological philosophy is based upon a realization and fulfillment of its purposes (maqāṣid) which, in turn, are identified on the basis of a legal theory methodology that hermeneutically privileges an ethico-religious values-based approach to the interpretation of the Qur'ān and Sunna.

In the context of Qur'ān and Sunna injunctions pertaining to Muslim family laws, we could argue that if the principle of the Qur'ānic textual assumption of certain patriarchal practices prevalent in its milieu such as ṭalāq and their subsequent mitigation on the basis of other relevant Qur'ānic verses was recognized as a hermeneutical tool giving rise to the idea of extrapolation of moral trajectories, this would contribute toward the development of a purposive or maqāṣid-based Qur'ān-Sunna hermeneutic and maqāṣid-oriented Islamic legal theory philosophy. So the Qur'ānic reflection of divorce practices in its historical milieu would not be considered as representing a Qur'ānic *value* (in the sense developed earlier) but the Qur'ān's mitigating and limiting concern would lead to the extrapolation of a moral trajectory pointing toward fairness and equality/symmetry of rights as its ideals. These, in turn, would be identified as *the* actual Qur'ānic *values*. The idea of values brings us to the final hermeneutical mechanism, namely that of ethico-religious values–based hermeneutic of the Qur'ān and the Sunna.

4. Ethico-religious values–based hermeneutic of the Qur'ān and the Sunna.

This is a hermeneutical method that stipulates that the actual nature and character of the Qur'ān-*Sunna* discourse is hermeneutically best served and privileges its own interpretation on the basis of certain ethico-religious principles such as justice, righteousness, equality, etc. understood in ethically objectivist terms. By ethically objectivist terms I mean that values such as what are considered as ethically "good" or "repugnant" are discoverable and recognized by reason independent of revelation (here recourse to the

Qur'ānic principle of fiṭra could be taken) and are subject of evolution in concert with civilisational progress.

This is exactly what Abu Zayd argues when suggesting that all the legal injunctions in the Qur'ān[62] are to be hermeneutically interpreted so that they are in accordance with the hermeneutically most powerful *Qur'ānic* value of justice, which is one of the values that the Qur'ān *initiated* rather than reflected. In relation to *ṭalāq*, this would translate into the argument that because our contemporary notions of Qur'ānic justice are in conflict with gender-based legal asymmetries and unjust ethical implications inherent in *ṭalāq*, the concept of *ṭalāq* would not be considered as part of Qur'ān-Sunna teachings because it goes against the larger Qur'ān-Sunna *values determined on the basis of the methodology outlined above.*

Conclusion

The main concern of this chapter was to highlight the significance of making a synthesis between and incorporate the contemporary discussions on maqāṣid al-sharī'a and gender non-patriarchal Qur'ānic hermeneutics as important hermeneutical tools that can engender a gender-just Muslim family law. It was argued that on the basis of contemporary maqāṣid approaches and gender non-patriarchal Qur'ānic hermeneutics that new maqāṣid pertaining to Muslim family law can be derived. Moreover, I attempted to outline a model of interpretation that can demonstrate that this synthesis can both, account for the patriarchal nature of the classical manahij of the Qur'ān and the Sunna as not being inevitable as well as provide an important foundation, in addition to other hermeneutical methods, for the engendering of gender-just Muslim family law.

Notes

1. I will use the phrases non-patriarchal and gender symmetrical interchangeably. By gender symmetrical, I wish to convey that idea that Muslim family laws as formulated by classical Muslim jurists are based on gender-differentiation arguments assigning unchanging and sharply distinct gender roles to men and women that are seen to be "God-given" and therefore "just." These classically formulated Muslim family laws, in turn, gave rise to rigid highly gender-asymmetrical rights and duties and this aspect of Muslim law needs to be reformed. On why the term gender equality or justice is problematic in this sense see, A. Emon, "The Paradox of Equality and the Politics of Difference: Gender Equality, Islamic Law and the Modern Muslim State," in *Gender and Equality in Muslim Family Law: Justice and Ethics in the Islamic Legal Tradition*,

in Z. Mir-Hosseini, Kari Vogts, Lena Larsen, and Christian Moe (New York: I. B. Tauris, 2011), 237–258.

2. Hashim Kamali, "Islamic Family Law Reform: Problems and Prospects," *Islam and Civilisational Renewal*, 3 (2011), 37–52; cf. Sayed Sikandar Haneef "Treatment of Recalcitrant Wife in Islamic Law: The Need for a Purposive Juridical Construct," *Global Jurist*, 12 (2012), n.p. Ramadan discusses in general terms women "liberation" and how maqāṣid and maṣlaḥa-based arguments can be useful in achieving it but falls short of actually developing specific arguments for Muslim family law reforms based on these insights. T. Ramadan, *Radical Reform: Islamic Ethics and Liberation* (Oxford: Oxford University Press, 2009), 212–218.
3. Kamali, "Islamic Family Law Reform," 51.
4. For details see Amineh Mahallati, "Women in Traditional Sharīa: A List of Differences between Men and Women in Islamic Tradition," *Journal of Islamic Law and Culture*, 12 (2010), 1–9.
5. This is reflected in medieval dictionary of the Arabic language written by Ibn Manzur who in his entry on ra'y, he defines it as "well considered opinion, mental perception, and sound judgment." He, however, applies this description to some males only because he considers that women in general could not possess ra'y. See http://www.baheth.info/all.jsp?term=%D8%B1%D8%A7%D9%8A#0. For some of these views in the tafsīr literature, see Karen Bauer, "Room for Interpretation: Qur'ānic Exegesis and Gender," PhD dissertation (Princeton, NJ: Princeton University, 2008).
6. They extend to other realms of what it means to be a woman and a man. For example, Al-Ghazali relates that the fourth caliph Ali (d. 661) and the first Shi'i Imam as having said the following: "The worst characteristics of men constitute the best characteristics of women; namely, stinginess, pride and cowardice. For if a woman is stingy, she will preserve her own and her husband's possessions; if she is proud, she will refrain from loose and improper words to everyone; and if she is cowardly, she will dread everything and will therefore not go ut of her house and will avoid [a] compromising situation for the fear of her husband." Imam Al Ghazali, *Marriage and Sexuality in Islam*, trans. Madelaine Farah (Kuala Lumpur: Islamic Book Trust, 2012), 78.
7. Adis Duderija, *Constructing A Religiously Ideal 'Believer' and 'Woman' in Islam: Neo-Traditional Salafi and Progressive Muslim Methods of Interpretation (manahij)* (New York: Palgrave, 2011), 69–85.
8. This phrase will be explained in the main text later.
9. Imran Nyazee, *Outlines of Islamic Jurisprudence* (Lahore: Advanced Legal Studies Institute, 2000), 225.
10. Other meanings we find in the Qur'ān that come under the same semantic field in relation to human beings (in contrast with Attributes of God) include: ally (5:51; 5:81; 4:1440; master (with reference to Satan 7:30), defender of rights (17:33), watcher over someone's interest (2:282). For an excellent recent discussion of the classical doctrine of wilāya and the kind of interpretational and legal

reasoning it is based on, see Kh. Masud, "Gender Equality and the Doctrine of Wilāya," in *Gender and Equality in Muslim Family Law: Justice and Ethics in the Islamic Legal Tradition*, ed. Z. Mir-Hosseini, Kari Vogts, Lena Larsen, and Christian Moe (New York: I.B. Tauris, 2013), 127–152, 132.

11. On this, see Kecia Ali, *Marriage and Islam in Early Islam* (Cambridge, MA: Harvard University Press, 2010).
12. Ibid.
13. Ibn Majah, *Sunan Ibn Majah* (Riyadh: Dar al Salam, 2000), Hadith Ibn Abbas no. 1880, 2589; Abu Da'ud, Sunan Abi Da'ud (Riyadh: Dar al Salam, 2000), Hadith, Aisha, no. 2083. As noted by Masud, these two hadith are cited more frequently by classical jurists who argue for necessity of guardianship in marriage rather than other hadith that do not. Masud, "Gender Equality and the Doctrine of Wilāya," 135.
14. Dien, Mawil Y. Izzi; Walker, P. E. "Wilāya (a.)," *EI* (2nd ed.).
15. Jar Allāh Mahmud b. 'Umar, Al-Zamakhshari, *Al-Kashshāf*, ed. Ahmad b. al-Munir al-Iskandari, Beirut, Dār al-Kitāb al-'Arabī, 1965, vol. 1, 505. Cited in and translated by Karen Bauer, "Room for Interpretation," 137.
16. Muhammad Tabatabai, *Tafsir Al Mizan*, http://www.shiasource.com/al-mizan/.
17. Ibid.
18. Muhammad Tabatabai, *Tafsir Al Mizan*, trans. Sayyid Saeed Akhtar Rizvi (Teheran: World Organisation for Islamic Services, 1990), vol. 8, 220.
19. Zainab Al Ghazali, *Nazarāt fi kitāb Allah* (Cairo: Dar Ash Shuruq, 1994), Vol. 1, 297.
20. Duderija, *Constructing a Religiously Ideal "Believer" and "Woman" in Islam.*
21. Kecia Ali, "Progressive Muslims and Muslim Jurisprudence: The Necessity for Critical Engagement with Marriage and Divorce Law," in *Progressive Muslims: On Justice, Gender and Pluralism*, ed. O. Safi (Oxford: Oneworld, 2003), 163–189.
22. Found in Ibn Al-Athir, *Jami' al Usul* (Cairo, 1969), vol. 4, 414, no. 1977.
23. For a list of women "friendly" (or better said those having emincipatory potential for women if seen in their historical context) hadith, see http://one-islam.org/sahih_muhammad/sahih_Women.htm (accessed February 3, 2012).
24. Attia, in his comprehensive treatment of the theory of maqāṣid, identified mawadda, raḥma, and sakīna as concepts on the basis of which the intent of Islamic law in the realm of the family, which he describes as achieving harmony, affection, and compassion, can be formulated. However, he does not employ this intent to argue for non-patriarchal reform of Muslim family laws and essentially upholds the traditional understanding of these laws. Gamal E. Attia, *Towards Realisation of the Higher Intents of Islamic Law—Maqāṣid Al Shari'ah—A Functional Approach*, trans. Nancy Robers (Kuala Lumpur: IIIT, 2010), 126–127.
25. On several examples of these patriarchal ḥadīth, see Aid Al Qarni, *How to Become the Happiest Woman on Earth* (London: Al Firdous, 2006). On criticism of the authenticity and employment of these hadith in contemporary

neo-conservative Muslim thought, see Khaled Abou El Fadl, *Speaking in God's Name: Muslim Law, Authority and Women* (Oxford: Oneworld, 2003).

26. That is, those ḥadīth that can have emancipator or women-affirmative potential if evaluated in their historical context.
27. Duderija, *Constructing A Religiously Ideal "Believer" and "Woman" in Islam.*
28. See, for example, 49:13; 4:1; 16:97; 33:35; 9:71–72; 2:30; 17:70; 33:72; 65:2, 2:236–237, 65:6.
29. I have separated these two realms for clarification purposes only. In actual fact the Qurʿān does not make such a neat distinction between the two if at all.
30. See, on this, Duderija, *Constructing a Religiously Ideal "Believer" and "Woman" in Islam.*
31. Amina Wadud coined the term "the *tawhidic paradigm*" in her *Inside the Gender Jihad.* Amina Wadud, *Inside the Gender Jihad: Women's Reform in Islam* (Oxford: Oneworld, 2006), 24.
32. Ibid., 28.
33. Ibid., 185.
34. Ibid., 34.
35. Amina Wadud, "Islam beyond Patriarchy through Gender Inclusive Qurʿanic Analysis," in ed. Zaina Anwar, *Wanted: Equality and Justice in Muslim Family* (Kuala Lumpur: Sisters in Islam, 2009), 103–104.
36. Ibid., 104–109.
37. Amina Wadud, foreword to Issue in *International Feminist Journal of Politics,* "Engaging *Tawhid* in Islam and Feminisms," 10 (2008): 437.
38. Asma Barlas, *Believing Women in Islam: Unreading Patriarchal Interpretations of the Qurʿān* (Austin, TX: University of Texas Press, 2002).
39. Defined as "father-rule and/or a politics of male privilege based in theories of sexual differentiation." Barlas, *Believing Women in Islam*, 93.
40. Mary Daly, *Beyond God the Father: Toward a Philosophy of Women's Liberation* (Boston, MA: Beacon Press, 1973).
41. Barlas, *Believing Women in Islam*, 94.
42. Ibid., 205.
43. Ibid., 95.
44. Ibid., 106.
45. Ibid., 107.
46. Ibid., 108.
47. And hence also is the Sunna ethical value/objective as the Qurʿan and the Sunna are organically linked without contradicting each other. For more on this nature of the Qurʿan-Sunna hermeneutics that incorporates but goes beyond classical discussions, see Adis Duderija, "A Paradigm Shift in Assessing/Evaluating the Value and Significance of Hadīth in Islamic Thought: From ʿulūmu-l-isnād/rijāl to *uṣūl al-fiqh*," *Arab Law Quarterly*, 23 (2009), 195–206.
48. Adis Duderija, "The Case study of Patriarchy and Slavery: The Hermeneutical Importance of Qurʿānic Assumptions in the Development of a Values-Based

and Purposive Oriented Qurān-Sunna Hermeneutic," *Hawwa*, 11 (2013), 58–87.

49. There are many definitions of patriarchy but in our case we shall define it as control/rule of fathers/men over women at each/or some levels of society (e.g., family, public life in terms of socially acceptable norms and behaviors), law (e.g., family law), and politics (men having ultimate decision-making powers in running a society and having their work considered as more valuable than that of women).
50. Which does not imply that Qurʿān is necessary or in essence a patriarchal text. In fact, the Qurʿān can sustain multiple interpretations, some of which can be seen as being anti-patriarchal. For example, Barlas, *Believing Women in Islam*.
51. Schacht, J. and A. Layish, "Ṭalāḳ (a.)." *Encyclopaedia of Islam*, 2nd ed. Ed. P. Bearman, Th. Bianquis, C. E. Bosworth, E. van Donzel, and W. P. Heinrichs (Brill Online. University of Melbourne, January 18, 2012).
52. Y. Ali's translation of the Qurʿān is used here.
53. O Prophet! When ye do divorce women, divorce them at their prescribed periods, and count (accurately), their prescribed periods: And fear Allah your Lord: and turn them not out of their houses, nor shall they (themselves) leave (65:1). Thus when they fulfil their term appointed, either take them back on equitable terms or part with them on equitable terms (65:2).
54. These commentaries are available here: http://mosshaf.com/web/.
55. Duderija, "The Case study of Patriarchy and Slavery."
56. Khaled Abou El-Fadl, "The Pearls of Beauty," in *A Search for Beauty in Islam: The Conference of the Books* (Lanham: University of America Press, 2001), 275.
57. Khaled Abou El-Fadl, *The Great Theft: Wrestling Islam from the Extremists* (New York: Harper Collins, 2005), 262.
58. Amina Wadud, *Qurān and Woman: Rereading the Sacred Text from a Woman's Perspective*, 2nd ed. (Oxford: Oxford University Press, 1999), ix, 7.
59. Madeleine Fletcher, "How Can We Understand Islamic Law Today?" *Journal of Islam and Christian–Muslim Relations*, 17 (2006), 163, 165.
60. Duderija, "The Case Study of Patriarchy and Slavery."
61. Verses such as 2:227; 2; 230; and 4:35 that address both parties in marriage suggest that there was "an incremental empowerment of women" scheme unfolding in the Qurān. El-Fadl, "The Pearls of Beauty," 275.
62. These legal injunctions mentioned in the Qurʿān, according to Abu Zayd, ought not to be considered to actually be Qurʿānic. The only purely or solely Qurʿānic values are those that have been *initiated* by the Qurʿān. He also adds that based on this criterion, none of the Qurʿānic injunctions pertaining to punishments (*hudūd*), inheritance, or divorce laws (i.e., those that differentiate on the basis of gender or social status in general) are Qurʿānic or divine imperative as they were not initially established by the Qurʿān; rather, they reflect the historical and cultural norms within which the Qurʿān was revealed and initially operated. The Qurʿān initially operated within this context, argues Abu Zayd

further, in order that its immediate addressees would "get" or comprehend its ultimate message, which is theological and moral in nature. Elevating this historical aspect of the Qur'ān to divine status or at the expense of the divine and perennial Qur'ānic values such as justice, argues Abu Zayd, would violate the actual Word of God. H. Nasr, Abu Zayd, "The Nexus of Theory and Practice," in *The New Voices of Islam-Rethinking Politics and Modernity, A Reader*, ed. Mehran Kamvara (Berkeley and Los Angeles: University of California Press, 2006), 154–167.

CHAPTER 9

A Case Study of Patriarchy and Slavery: The Hermeneutical Importance of Qur'ānic Assumptions in the Development of a Values-Based and Purposive Qur'ān-Sunna Hermeneutic

Adis Duderija

Introduction

When engaging in the process of developing a Qur'ānic hermeneutic[1] and Islamic legal theory (*usūl ul-fiqh*), generations upon generations of Islamic legal theorists (*usuliyyūn*), jurists (fuqahā'), and exegetes (*mufassirūn*) have *primarily* concerned themselves with questions of what the Qur'ān has to *say* on a particular issue or theme but not what the Qur'ān tacitly assumes to be normative as understood by its direct audience and as evident in the Qur'ān's content. They did not fully recognize the interpretational implications of the Qur'ānic presuppositions present in its discourse, especially in relation to developing a Qur'ānic hermeneutic and Islamic legal theory whose most powerful hermeneutical tool would entail an ethico-religious values– and purposive (*maqāṣid*)[2]-based approach to interpretation of the Qur'ān and the Sunna and the purposive nature of Islamic law and its philosophy.[3] By an ethico-religious values–based approach, I mean a broader hermeneutical method that stipulates that the actual nature and character of the Qur'ān-Sunna discourse is hermeneutically best served and privileges its own interpretation on the basis of certain principles such as justice, righteousness, and equality, as based on the ethically objective nature of these values.[4] By the purposive nature of Islamic law and its philosophy, I mean that the primary function of Islamic law and the most fundamental element in its methodology is based upon a realization and fulfillment of its purposes (*maqāsiḍ*) which, in turn, is identified on the basis of a legal theory methodology that hermeneutically privileges an ethico-religious values–based approach to the interpretation of the Qur'ān and Sunna mentioned earlier. The ethico-religious values– and *maqāṣid*-based approaches to Islamic legal philosophy and Qur'ānic hermeneutics, therefore, are very closely interrelated. As noted by Kamali, they are derived from the idea that the laws and the teachings of the Qur'ān and Sunna, both in the realm of *mu'malāt* (civil transactions) and the *'ibādāt* (rituals) are, in essence, goal oriented and rational (*ta'lilī*) in nature. [5]

I argue that the development of any Islamic legal theory (and, therefore, Qur'ānic hermeneutics) must recognize that the Qur'ān does not provide an organized, ahistorical, and comprehensive system of universal ethics that can be simply retrieved or discovered but that some principles of universalist ethics/morality can be deduced or derived on the basis of the Qur'ān's "comprehensive contextualization" and a view that Islamic law and its philosophy are essentially purposive in nature. By comprehensive contextualization I mean investigating, in a methodical manner, the role of context in shaping of the very content of the Qur'ān and its worldview. For this to take place, we need to recognize the Qur'ān's orientation toward the assumed operational discourse of its revelational context that manifests itself in its content and is reflected in the grammatical and syntactical structures employed in its language. This Qur'ānically assumed operational discourse must be seen as often reflecting the prevalent religious, cultural, social, political, and economic situation of its direct audience, its community of listeners, and participants, upon which a dialogical nature of the Qur'ān's discourse is premised.[6]

It is the task of this chapter to argue that the development of a new Qur'ān-Sunna hermeneutic and therefore Islamic legal theory that hermeneutically privileges an ethico-religious values and purposive (*maqāsiḍ*) approaches to a Qur'ānic interpretation has a potential to engender a more gender egalitarian or gender just Islamic legal theory.

This is not to reduce the task of the entire edifice of Qur'ān-Sunna hermeneutics to that of the potential discovery of Qur'ānic intentionality since this intentionality-driven hermeneutics is hermeneutically derived, as I have shown elsewhere,[7] on the basis of a particular broader Qur'ān-

Sunna hermeneutic. This hermeneutic includes what I term "comprehensive contextualization," a particular view of the nature of language and revelation that considers Qur'ān, for interpretational purposes, as a socioculturally produced text, a thematic/holistic approach to interpretation of Qur'ān and ḥadīth textual indicants based on the principle corroborative induction (*istiqrā'*) that views texts as interwoven weblike sets of ideas, a reader-oriented determinacy of meaning hermeneutics,[8] the endorsement of the objective nature of ethical values in revelation and epistemological,[9] methodological,[10] and hermeneutical[11] divorcing of the Sunna from ḥadīth.

Additionally, in the first section of this chapter I discuss one reason why I consider the classical Islamic scholarship failed to develop this approach, namely, a hermeneutical shift from a dialogical Qur'ān-Sunna hermeneutic to that of a Sunna-ḥadīth episteme.

At the outset, it is to be acknowledged that some modern Muslim and non-Muslim scholars have alluded to what Qur'ān assumes to be normative by its direct recipients when developing their models of Qur'ānic interpretation and/or Islamic legal theory.[12] For example, Moosa maintains that the Qur'ān without its direct recipient audience would cease to be the Qur'ān.[13] Achrati elsewhere argues that the oral-based culture of the Arab bedouins strongly influenced the character and the nature of the Qur'ānic discourse.[14] Similarly, Abu Zayd considers that the Qur'ānic discourse reflects the dialectical relationship between the Qur'ān and the reality of the early Muslim community.[15] Soroush goes even further by asserting that the experiential, evolutionary, and dialogical nature of the prophetic experience had a very significant impact on the nature and the content of the revelation itself.[16] Neuwirth has similarly noted that the social concerns and theological questions of the Qur'ān's first listeners permeate it and are reflected in its content.[17] Halverson concurs with this by stating that the Qur'ān not only addresses its first audience not only in the particular language that they spoke but also the world in which they lived.[18] In similar fashion, Wright perceptively remarks that

> the Qur'ān reaches out allusively not simply for the purposes of shaking hands with members of its audience, but to activate the power of a prior knowledge it recognizes as resident among them.[19]

This dialectical nature of the Qur'ān in turn is based upon its essential orality and has important hermeneutical implications.[20]

None of these studies explicitly investigated the relationship between the dialogical nature of the Qur'ānic discourse and the development of an Islamic legal theory whose most powerful hermeneutical tool is an ethico-religious values– and purposive-based approach to its interpretation.[21] Additionally, there are no existing studies that examine how the change in the hermeneutical relationship and hierarchy between the Qur'ān and Sunna, Sunna and ḥadīth, and therefore the Qur'ān and ḥadīth bodies of knowledge as formulated by the preclassical and that of the classical Islamic scholarship influenced the Islamic scholarship on Islamic legal theory. In other words, the question why the Qur'ān has the content it does, including various suppositions embedded in its content, and to what extent did the given context shape and determine its content has not been systematically explored.

Prior to discussing some of the assumptions evident in the Qur'ānic content and their interpretational implications, a brief discussion of the preclassical and classical hermeneutical hierarchy governing the hermeneutical relationship between the Qur'ān, Sunna, and ḥadīth bodies of knowledge requires some elaboration. This enables us to understand the shift from an understanding of a revelation based on an oral, symbiotic, reason inclusive, ethically objective, values-oriented relationship between the Qur'ān and Sunna bodies of knowledge that existed during the formative period of Islamic thought[22] to that of a textually and ḥadīth-dependent, largely reason deductive (i.e., syllogistic or analogical reason), nonvalues-based approach. Additionally, the knowledge of the mechanisms responsible for the earlier process itself marginalized, if not obstructed, the importance of the recognition of Qur'ānic assumptions as evident in its content and their hermeneutical function as "pointers" to a development of a Qur'ānic hermeneutic and Islamic legal theory founded on a purposive ethico-religious values–based approach as its most hermeneutically privileged interpretational mechanism. We will first discuss the nature of the hermeneutical relationship between Qur'ān and Sunna and then between Sunna and ḥadīth. Since the classical definition of the concept of Sunna conceptually conflates the ḥadīth and Sunna bodies of knowledge,[23] we will also discuss the implications this has on the overall Qur'ānic hermeneutic.

The Preclassical and Classical Views on the Nature of the Hermeneutical Relationship between the Qur'ān and Sunna Bodies of Knowledge

The postformative, classical Islamic scholarship engendered a largely ḥadīth-based Qur'ān–Sunna hermeneutic[24] hermeneutically marginalizing the importance of the various assumptions evident in the Qur'ānic text pertaining to issues relating to ethics, morality, sociocultural norms, and gender relations to name but a few. This markedly affected the methodological and epistemological parameters within which Qur'ānic interpretation operated as well as the methodological and epistemological tools that governed its hermeneutic.[25] The recent works of Souaiaia have convincingly demonstrated that oral traditions and precedents originating from the generations of Companions and Successors were, however, instrumental in imparting, assigning, and fixing particular meaning/s to the written sources such as the Qur'ān and Sunna and were embodied in classical jurisprudential doctrines such as abrogation (*nash*), *'adl*, and the practice of the regency of living scholar (*marja'yya*) in Shi'ism.[26] I do not dispute this fact but merely wish to emphasize the point that the Islamic legal theory, as a result of what I call the process of traditionalization of the Islamic thought and the ḥadīthtification of Sunna,[27] was framed and constrained by a progressively increasing written body of knowledge, mainly in the form of prophetic reports that were conflated with the concept of Sunna and, as described later, changed the nature and the hermeneutical character of the Qur'ān-Sunna discourse.

During the preclassical period of Islamic thought, the concept of Sunna was organically linked to that of the Qur'ān and was not considered as an independent entity.[28] This coupling of the Qur'ān and Sunna was based on two premises. First, it was based on the principle of the *Deutungsbeduerftigkeit* of the Qur'ān (i.e., its need of/for interpretation) on whose basis its *distinct* ethico-moral (*ahlāq*), law (*fiqh*), and creedal (*'aqīda*) teachings are to be deduced and contrasted against the prevalent sociocultural values, worldview assumptions, and norms governing pre-Qur'ānic Arabia. Second, it was based on the need for the practical manifestation of certain Qur'ānic injunctions that are to be carried out in action (*'amal*) but were not described in detail in the Qur'ān (e.g., how to perform prayer, hajj, ablution, etc.). We refer to these as ritual-based (*'ibāda*) or practice-based (*'amal*) components of the Qur'ānic worldview. Therefore, the function and scope of the Sunna would involve a practical embodiment of the Qur'ānic *'aqīda*, *akhlāq*, *fiqh*, and *'amal*/*'ibāda*[29] that permeate the Qur'ān in the form of the phrase 'Obey Allah *and* His Messenger.'

This hermeneutically intimate relationship is also noted by Sachedina who avers that

> Explication of the divine intention of the revelation was among the functions that the Qur'ān assigned to the Prophet. The Prophet functioned as the projection of the divine message embodied in the Qur'ān. He was the living commentary of the Qur'ān, inextricately related to the revelatory text. Without the Prophet the Qur'ān was incomprehensible, just as without the Qur'ān the Prophet was no prophet at all.[30]

The nature of this conceptually and hermeneutically symbiotic Qur'ān-Sunna relationship can also be gleaned from Graham who maintains that

> It appears [that] for the Companions and the early Followers of the Prophet, the divine activity manifested in the mission of Muhammad was a unitary reality in which the divine word, the prophetic guidance, and even the example and witness of all who participated in the sacred history of the Prophet's time, were all perceived as complementary, integral aspects of a single phenomenon.[31]

Similarly, in his investigation of an early Hanafi jurist, Isa b. Aban (d. 221/836), Bedir asserts that at this time the hierarchy of Qur'ān and Sunna was not yet clear.[32] This unity of the "prophetic-revelatory event," to use Graham's phrase, has from the very beginning and throughout the first one hundred and fifty years of the formative Islamic thought reflected the early Muslim understanding of the function, nature, scope, and the relationship between the Qur'ān and Sunna.[33] This interdependent, symbiotic relationship between the Qur'ān and Sunna, therefore, seems to have enjoyed widespread acceptability in early Islam.

Therefore, the Qur'ān and Sunna bodies of knowledge existed in what we describe as a symbiotic or organically linked relationship. We refer to this relationship between Qur'ān and Sunna discourses as a Qur'ān-Sunna dynamic to highlight this conceptual,[34] epistemological,[35] and hermeneutical[36] interdependence between the Qur'ān and Sunna concepts.

Apart from their symbiotic relationship, there were a number of other characteristics that defined the nature of the Qur'ān and Sunna during this preclassical period. One such delineating feature was that both concepts were primarily understood as being ethico-religious in nature. A number of Muslim scholars have argued for the predominantly ethico-religious character of the Qur'ān and Qur'ānic legislative dimension based on its overriding concern for the moral conduct of humans[37] that translated itself into prophetic activity emphasizing a person's moral responsibility and God consciousness rather than positive law formulation.[38] This nature and the character of the Qur'ānic revelation including its legislative element, embodied by the Prophet, was geared toward certain underlying legislative norms based on certain ethico-religious purposes and objectives.[39] In this context, it should come to us as no surprise that one of the ways the concept of Sunna was understood and conceptualized even in the second century Hijri was as a *righteous practice* of Muslims in general (*as-Sunna al-'adīla; jarāt al-Sunna*).[40]

In addition to the ethico-moral nature of the Qur'ān and Sunna, their interpretation was considered to be reason inclusive and the nature of ethical values in these bodies of knowledge was generally considered to be objective. For example, modern scholars of Muslim tradition such as Hourani maintain that the Qur'ān cannot be said to completely disregard the value of *'aql* (inherent human reason) in forming ethical judgments, while Reinhart asserts that "the Qur'ānic message time and again appeals to impartial knowledge that confirms the Qur'ānic summons."[41] Moreover, Reinhart argues that *'aql*'s explicit Qur'ānic endorsement in recognizing God's existence, Unity, and Grandeur is considered to favor its implicit usage in the realms of ethics and morality.[42] Furthermore, Hourani is of the view that

> Qur'ān and Muhammad both display a common sense attitude and that we should not expect either of them to claim that for every ethical judgement he makes a man must consult a book or a scholar, or work out an analogy when the book or scholar give no direct answer to the Problem.[43]

In his exhaustive investigation of the moral world of the Qur'ān, Draz echoes this view by concluding that, as per the Qur'ānic moral worldview the human consciousness is prior to Revelation and is capable of divorcing right from wrong without it.[44] A further argument that gives credence to the objective nature of ethical values in the Qur'ān refers to its assumptions regarding the meaning and the usage of moral principles. In the famous Qur'ānic maxim of enjoying the good (*ma'rūf*) and forbidding the evil (*munkar*), which forms the basis for political governance of a Muslim state, El-Fadl argues that *ma'rūf* means that which is commonly known to be good. "Goodness, in the Qur'ānic discourse, is part of what one may call a lived reality—it is a product of human experience, and constructed normative understandings."[45]

A final characteristic that influenced the nature of the Qur'ān-Sunna relationship in preclassical Islam was the Qur'ān's essential discursive, oral, and rhetorical nature.[46] According to Abu Zayd, "Qur'ān was an outcome of dialogue, debate, augment, acceptance and rejection, both with the pre-Islamic norms, practices, and culture, and with its own previous assessments, presuppositions and assertions."[47] Sunna reflects this discursive nature of the Qur'ān itself and is, therefore, apart from its *'ibāda* element, an ethico-religious, dynamic, but not a reified, textually fixed concept.

Apart from these considerations pertaining to the nature and character of the Qur'ān and Sunna and their relationship, as convincingly demonstrated by Souaiaia, interpretative strategies that were based on the primacy of oral-based sources permitted an epistemologically and methodologically more flexible and fluid interpretive framework that often authorized interpretations of the Qur'ānic enunciations contradictory to its literal meaning and based on the principle of the Qur'ān's (and Sunna's) overall purpose and objective/s (*qaṣd/maqāṣid*) or that of social expediency (maṣlaḥa).[48] For example, Islamic law pertaining to inheritance often diverges from explicit Qur'ānic enunciations based on these considerations. Several well-known jurisprudential decisions made by the second caliph 'Umar Al Khattab (d. 644) that contradicted the literal Qur'ānic injunctions of the practice of the Prophet are also suggestive of the nature of the Qur'ān-Sunna as described earlier.[49] Table 9.1 presents a summary of the discussion so far.

During the classical period of Islamic thought, however, the process of traditionalization of the Islamic thought and the "ḥadīthtification" of Sunna[50] changed the nature of the hermeneutical relationship between the Qur'ān and Sunna bodies of knowledge as summarized in table 9.2. By "ḥadīthification" of Sunna, I mean that the written ḥadīth body of knowledge came to be seen by some Muslim scholars, mainly belonging to the

Table 9.1 The hermeneutical relationship between the Qur'ān and the Sunna and the Qur'ān and the ḥadīth bodies of knowledge during the preclassical and classical periods of Islamic thought

Body of knowledge: Qur'ān	*Preclassical or formative period (up to third century Hijrah)*	*Classical or postformative period*
Nature character/ aspects[a]	Ethico-religious, principles, and value-oriented; values based on ethical objectivism principle, law a minor component, reason inclusive, oral discourse	Law-based, edified, largely reason-exclusive, values based on ethical voluntarism, textual
Nature of transmission	Predominantly oral	Predominantly written
Epistemological validity	*Mutawātir*	Mutawātir
Hermeneutical relationship with Sunna	Symbiotic, interdependent, non-ḥadīth-based, based on ethico-religious values and certain ethically objectivist values/principles	Largely ḥadīth based, Qur'ān and Sunna conceptually different bodies of knowledge
Hermeneutical relationship with ḥadīth	Divorced conceptually, methodologically, and epistemologically	ḥadīth as primary hermeneutical, methodological, and exegetical tool

[a] As above, the Qur'ān and Sunna bodies of knowledge consist of four aspects: *'aqīda, ahlaq, fiqh*, and *'amal/ibāda*.

Table 9.2 The hermeneutical relationship between the Sunna and the Qur'ān and Sunna and the ḥadīth bodies of knowledge during the preclassical and classical periods of Islamic thought[a]

Body of knowledge: Sunna[b]	*Preclassical or formative period (up to third century Hijrah)*	*Classical or postformative period*
Nature/character	Ethico-religious, principles, and value-oriented; values based on ethical objectivism principle, law a minor component, reason inclusive, not restricted to the authority of the Prophet only but also to Companions or to certain abstract principles such as justice	Law-based, edified, largely reason-exclusive, values based on ethical voluntarism, largely restricted to the authority of the Prophet only
Nature of transmission	Oral and written	Primarily written
Epistemological validity	*Mutawātir*[c]	ḥadīth-based, therefore primarily aḥad[d]
Hermeneutical relationship with Qur'ān	Symbiotic, interdependent, non-ḥadīth based	ḥadīth-based, Qur'ān and Sunna conceptually different bodies of knowledge, breaking of symbiotic relationship
Hermeneutical relationship with ḥadīth	Divorced conceptually, methodologically, and epistemologically	ḥadīth as primary hermeneutical and exegetical tool, conceptually conflated, methodologically and epistemologically dependent on ḥadīth[e]

[a] Based on Duderija, "Evolution of the Concept of Sunna."

[b] Since based on a symbiotic relationship with the Qur'ān same as for Qur'ānic body of knowledge as outlined in the main text earlier.

[c] *'Amal* or practice-based Sunna that includes the *'ibādāt* such as prayer and hajj. Non-*amal* aspects of Sunna are based on a particular Qur'ānic hermeneutic.

[d] This would exclude the concept of Sunna among some Hanafi and Maliki jurists belonging to their respective *madhadhib*. See note 51.

[e] Ibid.

Shafi'i and Habali madhahib, as epistemologically Sunna's only vehicle of transmission/embodiment. By ḥadīthification of Sunna, I also refer to the process of the development of a ḥadīth-dependent methodology of derivation of Sunna, that is, the view that emerged among some Muslim scholars that the Sunna compliance (or otherwise) of certain legal, ethical or theological practices, values, or norms is and can only be determined by sifting through numerous narratives reportedly going back to the time of the Prophet Muhammad via a sound chain of narrators (*isnād*).

I define traditionalization of Islamic thought as those social, political, and jurisprudential mechanisms that, throughout the second century of Hijri, contributed to

- the continued growth and proliferation of ḥadīth,
- the increased perceived importance given to ḥadīth at the cost of the ethico-moral and *'amal*-based concept of Sunna,
- the articulation of practically and other nonverbally[51] based Sunna into individual sound ḥadith,
- the increased application of ḥadīth in Qur'ānic and Sunnaic sciences such as *uṣūl-ul-din*, *tafsīr*, *uṣūl-ul-fiqh*, and *uṣūl-as-Sunna*, and
- the development of *hierarchical, semi-contextualist* legal hermeneutical models that were entirely textually based (i.e., based on Qur'ān and ḥadith) and marginalization of nontextually based epistemologico-methodological tools of Sunna (and Qur'ān) such as the notions of *ra'y, istiḥsān*, and *ijtihād* or the view that Sunna was conceptually coterminous with certain ethical values or principles such as justice or righteous conduct including the expression *Sunna al-'adīla* that was employed by Muslims in the second century Hijri.[52]

Resultantly, the nature and the character of the Qur'ān and Sunna were increasingly legalistic, edified, and the nature of the ethical values was based on the principle of ethical voluntarism rather than on objectivism. Other changes that occurred in the classical period will be discussed later in the context of the ḥadīth body of knowledge.

The Preclassical and Classical Views of the Nature of the Hermeneutical Relationship between the ḥadīth and Sunna and the ḥadīth and Qur'ān Bodies of Knowledge

During the *tadwīn* period, the process of "ḥadīthtification" of Sunna was taking place, which further contributed to the traditionalization of Islamic thought. In the pre-*tadwīn* era, Sunna was understood to exist in what I termed a hermeneutically symbiotic relationship with the Qur'ān and was conceptually (i.e., epistemologically, methodologically, and hermeneutically) divorced from ḥadīth. With the process of conceptual conflation of ḥadith and Sunna among some Muslim scholars (excluding some Hanafī and Malikī jurists),[53] the nature of the hermeneutical relationship between the Qur'ān and Sunna and Sunna and ḥadith bodies of knowledge changed. As a result of this process the nature and the character of the Qur'ān and Sunna also changed and they became increasingly legalistic and edified. Importantly, this phenomenon also changed the way the nature of the Qur'ān-Sunna ethical values was understood, shifting from the one based on ethical voluntarism to one based on ethical objectivism.[54] Additionally, having been increasingly (but not entirely) conflated with the concept of a sound ḥadith, the concept of Sunna changed both epistemologically and methodologically, and the concept of a sound ḥadith was considered the main vehicle of Sunna's transmission and embodiment among some Muslim scholars.[55]

Four main factors seemed to have provided the impetus for the forces of traditionalization and the process of "ḥadīthification" of Sunna in the second half of the firstcentury hijri. They included the following:

- A general, widespread perception that the expanding Muslim empire would become organically detached from the Qur'ānic and Sunnaic teachings, creating a need for a systematic development of Islamic thought, especially law;
- The partisan tensions that emerged within the nascent Muslim community that brought serious schisms based on conflicting claims regarding successorship to Prophet's political authority;
- Certain theological controversies prevalent at the time; and
- A gradual transition from oral to written-based transmission of knowledge.[56]

These trends resulted, first, in the concept of Sunna being increasingly clad in the mantle of a written-based, predominantly purely prophetic Sunna, and, second, in the development of more stringent mechanisms in establishing the soundness of written-based Sunna, especially in terms of the mode of its transmission, that is, *ulūm-ul-isnād*, which further contributed to the ḥadīthification of Sunna by (supposedly) by making it more sound.[57] Having been conflated with the concept of a sound ḥadīth, the concept of Sunna changed in several ways as summarized in Table 9.3.

Importantly, the hermeneutically interdependent and symbiotic relationship between the Qur'ān and Sunna was severed as the Qur'ān, and therefore

Table 9.3 The hermeneutical relationship between the ḥadīth body of knowledge and the Qur'ān and Sunna during the preclassical and classical periods of Islamic thought[a]

Body of knowledge: ḥadīth	*Preclassical or formative period (up to third century Hijri)*	*Classical or postformative period*
Nature/character	Politically motivated, *awāil*/anecdotes put in circulation by qusāss, tarḥīb wa targhīb genre	All comprehensive, no distinction between ethico-moral and legal; law based, edified, largely reason-exclusive, values based on ethical voluntarism, largely restricted to the authority of the Prophet only
Nature of transmission[b]	Oral and written	Primarily written
Epistemological validity	*Mutawātir*	ḥadīth-based, therefore primarily *aḥad*
Hermeneutical relationship with Qur'ān	Divorced conceptually, methodologically, and epistemologically	ḥadīth-based, Qur'ān and Sunna conceptually different bodies of knowledge, ḥadith as primary hermeneutical and exegetical tool therefore the breaking of the symbiotic relationship between Qur'ān and Sunna
Hermeneutical relationship with Sunna	Divorced conceptually, methodologically, and epistemologically	ḥadīth as it is the only vehicle of perpetuation/embodiment and transmission, conceptually conflated, methodologically and epistemologically dependent on ḥadīth[c]

[a]This would exclude the concept of Sunna among some Hanafī and Malikī jurists belonging to their respective *madhadhib*. See note 51.
[b]As based on work by Souaiaia cited in notes 20 and 21.
[c]Again, exception would be some Hanafī and Malikī scholars. See note 47.

Islamic legal theory, became increasingly hermeneutically dependent upon the ḥadīth body of knowledge. This changed the nature and the character of the Qur'ān (and Sunna) bodies of knowledge, the way its/their worldview was conceptualized, and, most significantly for the purposes of this chapter, the way in which the interpreters approached the Qur'ānic, for the purposes of its interpretation. Namely, these processes shifted the interpreters' focus away from the actual text, its dialogical and purposive nature,[58] and the assumptions governing its revelational context to that of interpreting it through the lens of extra-Qur'ānic sources of knowledge, mainly in the form of ḥadīth.[59] This is one reason why I consider that the classical Islamic legal theory did not sufficiently examine the importance of textual presuppositions evident in the Qur'ānic discourse as they manifest themselves in its actual text and what the hermeneutical implications of these suppositions are.[60]

More specifically, in relation to issues surrounding the role and status of women in Muslim societies, which is one of our case studies to be discussed later, other factors that contributed to at times androcentric and at times very patriarchal interpretations of the Qur'ān and Sunna, apart from the methodological and hermeneutical mechanisms mentioned earlier, include the nature of interpretative communities (namely, overwhelmingly male community of interpreters operating within an androcentric/patriarchal sociocultural and historical context) and the nature of political and sexual power during the formative period of Islam.[61] Since these have been discussed in some detail in other studies, they will not be elaborated upon here.[62]

The aim of the rest of this chapter is to identify some of these assumptions present in the Qur'ānic discourse and the implications they have on the development of a Qur'ānic, hermeneutic, and Islamic legal theory whose most hermeneutically powerful mechanisms is an ethico-religious values–and purposive-based approach to interpretation.

Before these presuppositions are considered, a few preliminary remarks as to how they manifest themselves in the Qur'ānic text are necessary.

Qur'ānic Textual Assumptions and Their Hermeneutical Implications

As we shall see, manifestations of Qur'ānic assumptions are evident in their usage (to its direct audiences) of familiar concepts (e.g., Sunna, Allah), people's stories/people (e.g., story of various prophets such as Lut, Noah, Abraham, etc.[63]), beliefs (e.g., angels, scriptures, etc.), ethical terms (e.g., *ma'rūf, sharr, ḥasan*), and the use of particular words/phrases/grammatical/philological constructs (e.g., the primary Qur'ānic addressees are assumed to be male, and hence the believers are primarily addressed as *mu'minūn*, i.e., second person plural *male*)[64]. Halverson aptly summarizes the reason for this:

> The Qur'ān employs a set of existing religious ideas, themes, and concepts, or what some scholars refer to as an existing body of "religious knowledge," while simultaneously extracting and modifying certain

> elements necessary to successfully transfer these characters and traditional narratives into the service of the text and reinforce its fundamental precepts (e.g., *al-tawḥīd*).[65]

In order to make a better sense of these assumptions, we shall categorize them into two groups, namely, sociocultural and ethico-moral.

Sociocultural Suppositions—The Case of Patriarchy

One of the most evident assumptions evident in a majority of the passages in the Qur'ān is the existence of an all-embracing patriarchy[66] existing in its historically revelatory milieu.[67] The husband's right to unilateral dissolution of marriage, known as ṭalāq, is one aspect of this patriarchal milieu. According to Joseph Schacht:

> The right to a one-sided dissolution of a marriage belonged to the man exclusively, among the pre-Islamic Arabs. Long before Muḥammad, this *ṭalāq was* in general use among the Arabs and meant the immediate definite abandonment by the man of all rights over his wife, which he could insist upon as a result of his marriage.[68]

At the philological level this patriarchal revelation context is evident in the Qur'ānic injunctions that are exclusively directed at men in matters pertaining to divorce and marriage. For example, Qur'ān[69] (65:1–2) instructs the Prophet that if the *men* divorce their women (*ṭalāqtumu nisā'*) they should allow women to reside in their marital home during their *'idda* (waiting period), and then instructs "*men* to keep or stay with their *wives* in dignity or you divorce them in kindness and dignity."[70] In the premodern Qur'ānic commentary (*tafsīr*) literature that I consulted (Suyuti, Ibn 'Abbas, Al Qurtubi, At- Tabari, Al-Zamakhshari, Ibn Kathir, and Al-Wahidi) on this verse, it is evident that all of the exegetes (*mufassirūn*) considered that the unilateral right of men to divorce their wives was a "pregiven" and the "natural" order of things and did not problematize it at all apart from emphasizing that although the verse addresses the Prophet it also speaks to all the male believers (*mu'minūn*). Instead, they focused on the discussions surrounding the 'idda and/or proper wife's treatment during this time and provided the circumstance for the revelation of the verse (e.g., Prophet's divorcing of Hafza or 'Abd Allah Ibn 'Umar divorcing his wife when she had menses).[71]

Qur'ān (2:230) stipulates that if a *man* divorces a woman (*fa inn ṭalāq-ha*) irrevocably, a man cannot remarry her until she is married to another.[72] As in the case of *tafsīr* of 65:1, discussed above the same premodern exegetes who this verse simply assumes the validity of unilateral *ṭalāq* being the sole prerogative of men and clarifies that in this case that *fa inna ṭalāqa-ha* means the third divorce after which the husband cannot remarry the same woman prior to her marrying another man and having sexual intercourse with him and waiting for the *'idda* period to be completed. Some also document the occasions (*asbāb*) of the revelation about a woman who was divorced by her husband and married another man and wished to return to her first previous husband.

Again, in 33:49 the *male* believers are told that if they married believing women and then divorced them (*ṭalāqtumuhunna*) before touching them, they do not need to count the *'idda*.[73] As far as *tāfāsīr* go, the same analysis applies to this verse as in the case of 65:1 and 2:230 earlier. Namely, the consideration of a husband's unilateral right to divorce is assumed.

Similarly, in 2:236 *men* (masculine second person plural—*ṭalāqtumu nisā'*) are, when divorcing women before consummating marriage, told to bestow gifts upon them.[74]

It seems that, at least in these instances,[75] decisions pertaining to both men and women in relation to divorce and related matters have been surrendered entirely to men and that women play only a derivative and nonautonomous role.

The famous *qawwama* (4:34)[76] and its "sister" verse (2:228)[77] that bestows upon men a qualified degree (darajāt) over women based on the male's socially privileged role of breadwinners including the right to physically punish (*daraba*)[78] recalcitrant (*nushuz*)[79] women can be considered as another aspect of the patriarchal revelational milieu mirrored in the Qur'ān at the level of sociocultural rights/rules. The same would also apply to the inheritance verses in *surat-ul-Nisā'* which stipulate unequal shares/proportions to men and women (in favor of men)[80] or the tribal practice of taking the women and children of defeated tribes as spoils of war that is indirectly referred to in the Qur'ān and was the practice at the time of the Prophet.

What I wish to highlight for the purposes of the present chapter is that all of the earlier examples presuppose the existence of a social and cultural order that confers the right to enter into marriage (contract), divorce, physically punish, discipline, and even possess women (as in the case of slavery—as shall be demonstrated later) solely to men, the reality of which is assumed, acknowledged, and addressed by the Qur'ān. However, does this necessarily mean that the Qur'ān endorses the same powers to men or does it attempt to mitigate and limit them?

If we examine carefully the stated verses pertaining to divorce or marriage matters in general, as El-Fadl astutely observes, they all were performing the function of "protecting women from the power of men [they] already possess[ed] by the virtue of the customs and practices of the society in which Islam was revealed."[81] Abu Zayd furthermore argues that based on the semantical and historical analyses of these verses, it would be safe to assert that the primary aim of the Qur'ānic injunctions is to limit the rights of men that existed in the patriarchal and tribal-based social, economic, cultural, and political reality of the Qur'ānic revelational milieu, rather than to stipulate absolute inheritance portions.[82] Additionally, El-Fadl argues that Qur'ānic verses 65:6[83] and 2:229[84] could be used to argue for this mitigating effect of Qur'ānic injunctions.[85] The same mitigating effect applies to the concept of Sunna.[86] But is this mitigating process an end in itself or just a means to a more just end?

If this principle of Qur'ānic textual assumption of certain patriarchal practices prevalent in its milieu and their subsequent mitigation on the basis of other relevant Qur'ānic verses is recognized as a hermeneutical tool on the basis of which a moral trajectory could be extrapolated, it would contribute toward the development of an ethico-religious values– and purposive-based Qur'ānic hermeneutic. This is exactly what Abu Zayd argues when suggesting that all the legal injunctions in the Qur'ān[87] are to be hermeneutically interpreted so that they are in accordance with the hermeneutically most powerful *Qur'ānic* value of justice. In this context, the words of Al-Alwani, who makes the following observation in relation to the question of female witnesses in the Qur'ān, are instructive:

> By establishing a role for women in the witnessing of transactions, even though at the time of revelation they had little to do with such matters, the Qur'ān seeks to give concrete form to the idea of women as participant... The objective is to end the traditional perception by including them, among such are acceptable to you as witness'... the matter of witnessing served merely as a means to an end or a practical way of establishing the concept of gender equality.[88]

This concept of a moral trajectory was not used as a hermeneutical tool of the highest order by the majority of classical Islamic interpreters of the Qur'ān and legal theorists because the interpretational or hermeneutical implications of these presuppositions embedded within the Qur'ānic text were not fully acknowledged and applied hermeneutically. However, as perceptively recognized by a young Tunisian thinker Shaykh Tahir Al Haddad (d. 1935),

> there is no textual evidence or proof that suggests that what had gradually been achieved in the life of the prophet, is the final goal after which

> there is no further purpose; as long as those matters that are connected with gradualism continue to present difficulties then it is appropriate to eliminate such hardship.[89]

One of the reasons for this hermeneutical "failure" of classical Islamic scholarship forms the subject matter of this very chapter, namely, the shift from a dialogical, symbiotic, and ethico-religious and purposive nature of early Qur'ān-Sunna hermeneutic to that of its Sunna-ḥadīth episteme.[90] This resulted in the formulation and subsequent canonization of a legal and sociocultural tradition based primarily on a ḥadīth-based Qur'ān-Sunna hermeneutic that contained several misogynist and gender discriminative practices clearly disadvantaging Muslim women.[91] In the context of discussing the penal code (*ḥudūd*) as it appears in the Qur'ān Abu Zayd makes exactly this point by averring:

> Through my research and study I have concluded that the Qur'ānic objectives that jurists long ago agreed upon were deduced from the penal code alive and well during the seventh century on the Arabian Peninsula. The objectives were not deduced from looking at the paradigm of the entire Qur'ān.[92]

Ethical/Moral Assumptions—The Case of Free Individuals versus Slaves' Social Stratification

Although slavery is a social ill, repugnance for it is certainly moral in nature. The existence of slavery (including female sex slavery and female concubinage) is another sociocultural reality that the Qur'ān assumes as culturally accepted as evident in, for example, *Sura An-Nisā'*.[93]

In pre-Qur'ānic Arabia, it was a common practice that masters (almost exclusively male) would force their (female) concubines into prostitution and would not set them free if they (i.e., the concubines) wanted to get married in order to live more "honorable" lives. Qur'ān's response toward this practice was to make moral appeals to slave owners (exclusively men, e.g., 4:25) in order to limit these abuses and alleviate/mitigate the unfavorable/miserable conditions. Acknowledging the different mentality and conditions under which slaves were brought up and lived, a set of punishments were instituted by the Qur'ān (4:25) for slave owners in addition to a set of social and behavioral norms.[94] Indeed, the entire edifice of the subsequent Islamic law and its legal theory was based on the notion of what Azam terms "differentiated and hierarchical ethico-moral and legal subjectivity," with the free Muslim man at the top and the slave woman at the bottom.[95]

It is commonly known that the practice of setting slaves free was one way in which the Qur'ān sanctioned the expiation of one's sins. Furthermore, the Qur'ān consistently highlights the importance of kind and gentle treatment of slaves. Moreover, the Prophet's example andinstructions for proper conduct when dealing with slaves were in complete accordance with these Qur'ānic instructions.[96] Thus based on the earlier Qur'ān-Sunna indicants the *mitigating effect* of the Qur'ān-Sunna attitude becomes evident again.

Given the overall evidence and attitude of the Qur'ān and Sunna toward slavery, it could be easily argued, as it was in the case of patriarchy, that the moral trajectory taken by the Qur'ān-Sunna attitude warrants the complete eradication of slavery and thus the obliteration of separate moral standards/normative behavior for free and enslaved human beings.

Again for the hermeneutical shift from preclassical to classical Islam, just like in the case of issues related to male-female gender dynamics, the mitigating effect of the Qur'ān–Sunna *élan* premised upon the recognition of the hermeneutical implications of the ethico-moral acceptance of slavery in the Qur'ānic revelatory milieu was not fully recognized as a legitimate hermeneutical tool that could lay the path toward an ethico-religious values– and purposive-based approaches to Qur'ān-Sunna hermeneutics.[97]This, in turn, translated itself in the field of Islamic law and legal theory. Indeed, as Azam argues, despite what "may have been the liberatory intent of the Qur'ān and the Prophetic example (Sunna) the fact [remains] that Islamic Law legitimizes the pre-Islamic view that human being in an abstract sense—occupies a dual space as both a person and property, subject and object, owner and commodity."[98]

Conclusion

In summary, one important component in developing an ethico-religious values– and purposive-based Qur'ānic hermeneutic and, therefore, that of Islamic legal theory, is taking into account the Qur'ānic presuppositions evident in its text/content as well as the preclassical nature of the Qur'ān-Sunna discourse based on their hermeneutically symbiotic, dialogical, ethico-religious, and purposive-based nature. As demonstrated in the case of some aspects of male–female gender dynamics and slavery, the Qur'ān-Sunna mitigating effect would seem to suggest that the deeply embedded contextual patriarchal and slavery practices not only do *not* form the inherent components of their worldview but also that the overall Qur'ān-Sunna principles premised on the alleviation of unjust practices at the time of the Prophet mitigated these practices and paved the way toward their complete abolition in the future. However, these practices and norms were often, and in many of its aspects still are, considered by some Muslims as an integral and essential part of the Qur'ān-Sunna normative worldview. In this context the purpose of this chapter was to emphasize that it is important to recognize that one of the reasons for the development and the continued embeddedness of this view was a result of a particular hermeneutical hierarchy and relationship between the Qur'ān, Sunna, and ḥadīth bodies of knowledge that was formulated during the classical period of Islamic thought.[99] Attempts to interpret the Qur'ān-Sunna indicants in the light of a different hermeneutic or to develop an Islamic legal theory that is more in tune with the preclassical Islamic thought premised on the hermeneutical primacy of an ethico-religious values– and purposive-based approaches to Qur'ān-Sunna hermeneutics are fiercely resisted by certain schools of thought within the Islamic tradition and are considered as undermining the very foundational pillars of an Islamic *Weltanschauung as they conceptualize it.* In the final analyses these approaches, however, in this author's mind, not only betray the preclassical understanding of the nature of the Qur'ān–Sunna but also restrict the inherently polysemic character of the Qur'ānic text, and therefore the Islamic legal theory, to its medieval interpretational possibilities, which are based on, among others, patriarchal and slavery-condoning values, norms, and practices.

Notes

This chapter with the same title was first published in *Hawwa*, 11 (2013): 58–87. http://booksandjournals.brillonline.com/content/journals/10.1163/15692086-12341239. I would like to thank the publisher, Brill, for allowing me to republish it for the purposes of this edited volume.

1. According to the leading Western theoretician of hermeneutics of the twentieth century Hans-Georg Gadamer, hermeneutics is "the classical discipline concerned with the art of understanding texts." Hans-Georg Gadamer, *Truth and Method*, 2nd rev. ed., trans. rev. Joel Weinsheimer and Donald G. Marshall (London: Continuum, 2004), 164. As such hermeneutical theories deal with "1.) nature of a text; 2.) what it means to understand a text; and 3.) how understanding and interpretation are determined by the presuppositions and beliefs (the horizon) of the audience to which the text is being interpreted." Van A. Harvey, "Hermeneutics," *Encyclopedia of Religion*, ed. Lindsay Jones, Vol. 6, 2nd ed. (Detroit: Macmillan Reference USA, 2005), 3930–3936, 3930. In the context of religion, hermeneutics refers to the study of the interpretation of sacred texts, especially texts in the areas of theology and law. H. A. Virkler, *Hermeneutics: Principles and Processes of Biblical Interpretation* (Grand Rapids, MI: Baker Book House, 1981). Hermeneutics is, therefore, a process comprising "both the understanding of the rules of exegesis and the epistemology of

understanding—the study of the construction of meaning in the past and their relationship to the construction of meanings in the present." Duncun. S. Ferguson, *Biblical Hermeneutics: An Introduction* (Atlanta: John Knox Press, 1986).

2. In other words I subscribe to the view that the author of the Qur'ān structured revelatory texts in such a way that its texts have intended meanings that, in principle, are discoverable rationally. In the context of the Islamic tradition on this, see Hashim Kamali, "Maqasid Al Shari'ah and Ijtihad as Instruments of Civilisational Renewal: A Methodological Perspective," *Islam and Civilisational Renewal*, 2 (2010): 245–271. Kamali on page 250 gives the following examples from the Qur'ān that support this view: the purpose of law of retaliation is preservation of life (2:179); the underlying objective of jihad is to fight injustice (22:39); the aims of performing prayers (*salat*) are to repel evil and immorality (29:45); the payment of the compulsory alms tax is to prevent circulation of wealth among only the rich (59:7). On the appropriateness of interpreting sacred texts in terms of authorial-intent discourse in the Christian tradition, T. Longman, "Literary Approaches to Biblical Interpretation," in *Foundations of Contemporary Interpretation*, ed. Philips Long et al. (Grand Rapids, MI: Zondervan Publishing House, 1996). See Nicolas, Wolterstorff, *Divine Discourse: Philosophical Reflections on the Claim That God Speaks* (Cambridge: Cambridge University Press, 1995). In the context of the Islamic tradition, see Kamali, "Maqasid Al Shari'ah and Ijtihad."
3. Jasser Auda, *Maqasid Al-Shariah as Philosophy of Islamic Law* (London: International Institute for Islamic Thought, 2008).
4. This theory is known as ethical objectivism, according to which there are real qualities or relations of acts that make them right, independent of opinions of people or Revelation. This is to be contrasted with ethical subjectivism, according to which ethical value terms mean only what is approved or disapproved, commanded, or forbidden by God. In terms of legal theory (*uṣūl-ul-fiqh*), this would translate into a view that all ethico-moral and legal rules must ultimately be derived from prescriptions enunciated by God. George Hourani, "Ethical Presuppositions of the Qur'ān," *Muslim World*, 70 (1980): 1–28.
5. The Qur'ānic evidence Kamali provides for the *ta'lil* nature of the Qur'ān and its laws are reference to the proclamation on just retaliation (*qisās*) that "in qisas there is (saving of) life for you, you men of understanding" (Q 2:179); the prohibition of wine-drinking and gambling being premised on the rationale of preventing "hostility and rancor" among people and interference with the remembrance of God (Q 5:91). Legal alms and charities are levied in order to prevent the concentration of wealth among the rich (Q 57:7). With reference even to the prophethood of Muhammad, "We have not sent thee but a mercy to mankind" (Q 21:10). Mercy *in* this verse and communication (Q 5:92) and warning *in* other places (Q 22:49), Hashim Kamali, "Fiqh and Adaptation to Social Reality," *The Muslim World*, 86 (1996): 76.
6. For a further discussion of "comprehensive contextualisation," see chapter 8 in this volume.

7. See Adis Duderija, *Constructing a Religiously Ideal "Believer" and "Women" in Islam: Neo-Traditional Salafi and Progressive Muslim Methods of Interpretation* (New York: Palgrave Macmillan, 2011).
8. Which highlights the important role of the reader in determining or helping produce meaning. In contrast to that of the text or the author and her intention.
9. By epistemological divorcing, I mean that Sunna and ḥadīth are considered to have been perpetuated by different mechanisms having different epistemological values.
10. By methodological divorcing, I mean that the compliance of certain theological, legal, or ethical values, norms, or principles with Sunna did not need to be determined by sifting through numerous narratives reportedly going back to the time of the Prophet Muhammad via a sound chain of narrators (*isnād*).
11. By hermeneutical divorcing, I mean the distinction made in the function and role Sunna and ḥadīth played in the overall theory of interpretation with respect to the Qur'ān.
12. See, for example, Khaled Abou El-Fadl, *Speaking in God's Name: Islamic Law, Authority and Women* (Oxford: Oneworld, 2001); Amina Wadud, *Qur'ān and Woman—Rereading the Sacred Text from a Woman's Perspective*, 2nd ed. (Oxford: Oxford University Press, 1999); Nasir Abu Zayd, *Re-Thinking the Qur'ān—Towards a Humanistic Hermeneutic* (Utrecht: Humanities University Press, 2004); Fazrul Rahman, *Islam and Modernity: The Transformation of an Intellectual Tradition* (Chicago: Chicago University Press, 1982); Hasan Hanafi, *Islam in the Modern World*, Vol. 2 (Heliopolis: Dar Al Kebaa, 2000); Asma Barlas, *Believing Women in Islam: Unreading Patriarchal Interpretations of the Qur'ān* (Austin: University of Texas Press, 2002).
13. Ebrahim Moosa, "The Debt and Burdens of Critical Islam," in *Progressive Muslims: On Social Justice, Gender and Pluralism*, ed. O. Safi (Oxford: Oneworld, 2003), 111–128.
14. Achmed, Achrati, "Arabic, Qur'ānic Speech and Postmodern Language: What the Qur'ān Simply Says," *Arabica*, 54 (2008): 161–203.
15. Hamid Nasir Abu Zayd, "The Qur'ān: God and Man in Communication," unpublished paper available http://www.let.leidenuniv.nl/forum/01_1/onderzoek/lecture.pdf.
16. Abdul Kareem Soroush, *The Expansion of Prophetic Experience: Essays on Historicity, Contingency and Plurality in Religion*, trans. N. Mobasser, edited with an analytical introduction by F. Jahanbakhsh (Leiden: Brill, 2009), 3–13, 63–90.
17. Angelika Neuwirth, "Two Faces of the Qur'ān: Qur'ān and Mushaf," *Oral Tradition*, 25 (2010): 144.
18. Jeffrey Halverson, *Theology and Creed in Sunni Islam: The Muslim Brotherhood, Asharism and Political Sunnism* (New York: Palgrave Macmillan, 2010), 134.
19. Peter, M. Wright, "Modern Qur'ānic Hermeneutics" (PhD dissertation, Chapell Hill, 2008), 155.
20. Neuwirth, "Two Faces of the Qur'ān," 144.

21. An exception to this would be Hamid Nasir Abu Zayd, "The Nexus of Theory and Practice," in *The New Voices of Islam-Rethinking Politics and Modernity, A Reader*, ed. M. Kamvara (Berkeley and Los Angeles: University of California Press, 2006), 153–176. He argues that the value of "justice" embedded in the overall Qur'ānic worldview ought to be considered as its most hermeneutically privileged tool. See also Ahmad Souaiaia, *Contesting Justice: Women, Islam, Law, and Society* (New York: SUNY, 2008), 115. On the importance of these assumptions and the literary devices in the Qur'ānic text employed in relation to understanding the nature of the Qur'ān and the development of its hermeneutic, see Wright, "Modern Qur'ānic Hermeneutics."
22. For this, see Duderija, *Constructing a Religiously Ideal "Believer" and "Women" in Islam.*
23. For a discussion of a classical definition of Sunna and the implications it has on the nature of hermeneutical relationship between the Qur'ān and Sunna and Sunna and ḥadīth bodies of knowledge, see Adis Duderija, "A Paradigm Shift in Assessing/Evaluating the Value and Significance of hadith in Islamic thought—From ulūm-ul-hadith to *uṣūl-ul-fiqh*," *Arab Law Quarterly*, 23 (2009): 195–206.
24. See Duderija, *Constructing a Religiously Ideal "Believer" and "Woman" in Islam.*
25. Ibid.
26. Ahmed Souaiaia, *The Function of Orality in Islamic Law and Practices: Verbalizing Meaning* (New York: Edwin Mellen Press, 2006).
27. Explained in the main text later.
28. Adis Duderija, "The Evolution in the Concept of Sunna during the First Four Generations of Muslims in Relation to the Development of the Concept of an Sound Hadith as Based on Recent Western Scholarship," *Arab Law Quarterly* 26, no. 4 (2012): 393–437. Also see our discussion later.
29. Adis Duderija, "Toward a Methodology of the Nature and the Scope of the Concept of Sunna," *Arab Law Quarterly* 21, no. 3 (2007): 269–280. The practical embodiment of the Qur'ān can be divided into actions that pertain to rituals such as prayers, hajj, fasting, etc., which are termed *'ibāda* or worship, and nonritual actions (*mu'āmalāt*) including commerce, marriage, charitable deeds of various kinds, etc.
30. Abdul Aziz Sachedina, "Scriptural Reasoning in Islam," *Journal of Scriptural Reasoning*, 5 (2005): n.p.
31. William Graham, *Divine Word and Prophetic Word in Early Islam: A Reconsideration of the Sources, with Special References to the Divine Saying or Hadith Qudsi* (The Hague: Mouton, 1977), 15. See also Zafar Ansari, "The Contribution of the Qur'ān and the Prophet to the Development of the Islamic Fiqh," *Journal of Islamic Studies*, 3 (1992), 141–171.
32. Murteza Bedir, "An Early Response to Shafi'i: 'Īsā b. Abān on the Prophetic Report (Khabar)," *Islamic Law and Society*, 9 (2002): 303.
33. Graham, *Divine Word and Prophetic Word in Early Islam*, 12.

34. By conceptual relationship I mean to what extent were/are Sunna and the Qur'ān and Sunna and ḥadīth considered to constitute same bodies of knowledge.
35. By epistemological relationship I mean to what extent were/are Sunna and the Qur'ān and Sunna and ḥadīth considered to have been perpetuated by same mechanisms having the same epistemological value.
36. By hermeneutical I mean the function and role Sunna played in the overall theory of interpretation vis-à-vis the Qur'ān and ḥadīth.
37. In this context, Ansari's following remarks are quite pertinent: "Qur'ānic legislation differs from legal codes in form as well as in spirit and purpose. Its basic motivation is religious and moral rather than 'legal' in a narrow sense of the term. Its aim is to lay down certain standards of conduct that are intrinsically good and conducive to the good pleasure of God." Ansari, "The Contribution of the Qur'ān," 143.
38. Or more precisely legal norms were conceived more in ethico-religious terms.
39. Ansari, "The Contribution of the Qur'ān," 144–146.
40. Ibid., 103–104.
41. K. Reinhart, *Before Revelation—The Boundaries of Muslim Moral Thought* (Albany: State University of New York Press, 1995), 178.
42. Hourani, "Ethical Presuppositions of the Qur'ān," 25.
43. Ibid., 23.
44. M. A. Draz, *The Moral World of the Qur'ān* (London: I. B. Taurus, 2008).
45. Khaled Abou El-Fadl, "The Place of Ethical Obligations in Islamic Law," *UCLA Journal of Islamic and Near E.L.*, 4 (2005): 1–40.
46. Neuwirth, "Two Faces of the Qur'ān," 141–156.
47. Hamid Abu Zayd, *Reformation of Islamic Thought: A Critical Historical Analysis* (Amsterdam: Amsterdam University Press, 2006), 99.
48. Souaiaia, *The Function of Orality*. Also Auda, *Maqasid Al-Shariah*.
49. A. Souaiaia, "On the Sources of Islamic Law and Practices," *Journal of Law and Religion*, 20 (2005): 134–140.
50. This would exclude some of the Hanafī and Malikī jurists and legal theorists for whom the concept of Sunna remained epistemologically independent of the concept of sound hadith. On Malikī *madhhab*, see Umar F. Abd-Allah Wymann Landgraf, *Malik and Medina: Islamic Reasoning in the Formative Period* (Leiden: Brill, 2013). For Hanafīs, see Volkan I. Stodolsky, "A New Historical Model and Periodization for the Perception of the Sunna and His Companions" (PhD dissertation University of Chicago, 2012).
51. Such as the idea that Sunna represented and embodied certain abstract ethico-religious principles and norms.
52. See Zafar, Ansari, "Islamic Juristic Terminology before Shafi'i: A Semantical Analysis with Special Reference to Kufa," *Arabica*, 19 (1972): 255–300.
53. Ibid.
54. Duderija, "Evolution in the Concept of Sunna."
55. Ibid. For exceptions, see note 47.

56. Duderija, *Constructing a Religiously Ideal "Believer" and "Women" in Islam*. See Chapter 1 in particular.
57. Adis Duderija, "The Evolution in the Canonical Sunni Hadith Body of Literature, 1–27.
58. For example, Ibn Ashur, a contemporary proponent of such an approach, argues that premodern *uṣūl* legal theories disregard[ed] the purposes of the law, not including them in the fundamentals (of Islamic legal methodology) and merely studying them in a partial way within sections of analogical reasoning, under appropriateness and unrestricted interests, even though they were supposed to be the fundamental of the fundamentals. Tahir Al-Ashur, *Alaysa al-Subh bi Qarib? Al-Shakirah al-Tunisiyyah li-funun al-rasm* (Tunis: 1988), 237.
59. Hence the development of the *tafsīr al-ma'thūr* genre.
60. Several recent studies on the historical development of Islamic law have argued that the Qur'ān reflects the greater ethico-legal trends that were embedded in the late antiquity Near Eastern religions. See Wael Hallaq, *The Origins and Evolution of Islamic Law* (Cambridge: Cambridge University Press, 2005); Hina Azam, *Sexual Violence in Maliki Legal Ideology: From Discursive Foundations to Classical Articulation*, unpublished PhD dissertation (Duke University, 2007).
61. Generally on this, among many, see Asma Barlas, *Believing Women in Islam*. Also, Abou El-Fadl, *Speaking in God's Name*. Duderija, *Constructing a Religiously Ideal "Believer" and "Women" in Islam*.
62. See Barlas, *Believing Women in Islam,* Abou El-Fadl, *Speaking in God's Name,* and Duderija, *a Religiously Ideal "Believer" and "Women" in Islam*.
63. Not all aspects of stories in the Qur'ān were known to either the Prophet or his direct audience but their existence and general outlines were certainly known since a number of Jews and Christians lived in the area. For more on this, among many, see, for example, Keneth Cragg, *The Event of the Qur'ān: Islam in Its Scripture* (Oxford: Oneworld, 1971); Arthur Jeffery, *Qur'ān as Scripture* (New York: Russel Moore, 1952).
64. And only on rare occasions, the female gender equivalents are mentioned.
65. Halverson, *Theology and Creed in Sunni Islam*, 140.
66. There are many definitions of patriarchy but in our case we shall define it as control/rule of fathers/men over women at each or some levels of society (e.g., family, public life in terms socially acceptable norms and behaviors), law (e.g., family law), and politics (having a say in the way that a society is run).
67. Which does not imply that the Qur'ān is necessary or in essence a patriarchal text. In fact, the Qur'ān can sustain multiple interpretations, some of which can be seen as being anti-patriarchal. For example, Barlas, *Believing Women in Islam*. For a contrary view, see Souaiaia, *Contesting Justice*, 115 in particular.
68. J. Schacht and A. Layish, "Ṭalāḳ (a.)." *Encyclopaedia of Islam*, 2nd ed., ed. P. Bearman, Th. Bianquis, C. E. Bosworth, E. van Donzel, and W. P. Heinrichs, Brill Online, University of Melbourne, January 18, 2012.
69. Y. Ali's translation of the Qur'ān is used here.
70. O Prophet! When ye do divorce women, divorce them at their prescribed periods, and count (accurately) their prescribed periods: And fear Allah your Lord:

and turn them not out of their houses, nor shall they (themselves) leave (65:1). Thus when they fulfill their term appointed, either take them back on equitable terms or part with them on equitable terms (65:2).

71. They are available at http://mosshaf.com/web/.
72. So if a husband divorces his wife (irrevocably), he cannot, after that, remarry her until after she has married another man and he has divorced her.
73. O ye who believe! When ye marry believing women, and then divorce them before ye have touched them, no period of 'Iddat have ye to count in respect of them: so give them a present. Set them free in a handsome manner.
74. There is no blame on you if ye divorce women before consummation or the fixation of their dower, but bestow on them (a suitable gift), the wealthy according to his means, and the poor according to his means.
75. However, in cases dealing with spiritual or religious matters such as those pertaining to salvation and the Hereafter, the Qur'ān is gender egalitarian.
76. Men are the protectors and maintainers of women, because Allah has given the one more (strength) than the other, and because they support them from their means. It is interesting that some of the *mufassirun* (e.g., Al-Zamakhshārī) have given example of the husband's unilateral right to divorce his wife as one of the reasons why men are *qawwamuna* over women. Like in other verses discussed in the main text earlier, the vast majority of the *mufassrun* did not question the basic underlying premise of men's *qiwama* although some did link it to, among other religious or "naturally" inherent reasons, to the issue of *mahr*. For more on this see Karen Bauer, "Room for Interpretation: Qur'ānic Exegesis and Gender" (PhD dissertation, Princeton University, 2008).
77. And women shall have rights similar to the rights against them, according to what is equitable; but men have a degree (of advantage) over them.
78. On the significant prevalence of physical violence against women among the Muslim community during the life of Prophet Muhammad, see Manuela Marín, "Disciplining Wives: A Historical Reading of Qur'ān 4:34," *Studia Islamica*, 97 (2003): 5–40. Cf. Ayesha S. Chaudry, "Wife-Beating in the Pre-Modern Islamic Tradition: An Inter-Disciplinary Study of *Ḥadīth*, Qur'ānic Exegesis and Islamic Jurisprudence" (PhD dissertation, New York University, 2009). Chaudry states, for example, that both "Qur'ānic exegesis and Islamic jurisprudence *assume* a husband's right to discipline his wife and the ethical deliberations therein are concerned only with the procedure of hitting," viii.
79. On wife *nushuz*, see Chaudry, "Wife-Beating," 184–202.
80. See Qur'ān 4:11–12. For a detailed discussion of inheritance verses in relation to women from the Qur'ānic and classical Islamic law perspectives, see Souaiaia, *The Function of Orality*, and Souaiaia, *Contesting Justice*.
81. Khaled Abou El-Fadl, "The Pearls of Beauty," in *A Search for Beauty in Islam: The Conference of the Books* (Lanham, MD: University of America Press, 2001), 275.
82. Abu Zayd, "The Nexus of Theory and Practice," 164–165.
83. Let the women live (in *'iddat*) in the same style as ye live, according to your means: Annoy them not, so as to restrict them. And if they carry (life in

their wombs), then spend (your substance) on them until they deliver their burden: and if they suckle your (offspring), give them their recompense: and take mutual counsel together, according to what is just and reasonable. And if ye find yourselves in difficulties, let another woman suckle (the child) on the (father's) behalf.

84. A divorce is only permissible twice: after that, the parties should either hold together on equitable terms, or separate with kindness. It is not lawful for you (men), to take back any of your gifts (from your wives), except when both parties fear that they would be unable to keep the limits ordained by Allah. If ye (judges) do indeed fear that they would be unable to keep the limits ordained by Allah, there is no blame on either of them if she gives something for her freedom. These are the limits ordained by Allah; so do not transgress them if any do transgress the limits ordained by Allah, such persons wrong (themselves as well as others).
85. Verses such as 2:227; 2; 230 and 4:35 that address both parties in marriage suggest that there was "an incremental empowerment of women" scheme unfolding in the Qur'ān. El-Fadl, "The Pearls of Beauty," 275.
86. Madeleine Fletcher, "How Can We Understand Islamic Law Today?," *Journal of Islam and Christian–Muslim Relations*, 17 (2006): 159–172. In this context, she states: "Prophet's mission is not correctly indicated by reified content of Islamic Law but rather by the direction of his reforms," and more specifically to issues pertaining to women, "Prophet's message with respect to the Arab Sunna must be clearly understood. to benefit women and to reform the existing practices extremely prejudicial to women." Ibid., 163 and 165.
87. These legal injunctions mentioned in the Qur'ān, according to Abu Zayd, ought not to be considered to actually be Qur'ānic. The only purely or solely Qur'ānic values are those that have been *initiated* by the Qur'ān. He also adds that, based on this criterion, none of the Qur'ānic injunctions pertaining to punishments (*hudūd*), inheritance, or divorce laws (i.e., those that differentiate on the basis of gender or social status in general) are Qur'ānic or a divine imperative as they were not initially established by the Qur'ān. Rather they reflect the historical and cultural norms within which the Qur'ān was revealed and initially operated. The Qur'ān initially operated within this context, argues Abu Zayd further, in order that its immediate addressees would "get" or comprehend its ultimate message, which is theological and moral in nature. Elevating this historical aspect of the Qur'ān to a divine status or at the expense of the divine and perennial Qur'ānic values such as justice, argues Abu Zayd, would violate the actual Word of God. "The Nexus of Theory and Practice," 154–167.
88. Taha Al-Alwani, *Issues in Contemporary Islamic Thought* (London: International Institute of Islamic Thought, 2005).
89. Al Tahir Al Haddad, *Kalima Shukr*, reproduced in Al Tahir Al Haddad (Al Haj Yahya and Al Marzuqi editions, n.d.), 16.
90. Cf. Abu Zayd, "The Nexus of Theory and Practice." Souaiaia has also adduced evidence to argue that even the classical Islamic law and legal theory has

methodological and hermeneutical mechanisms in place that *theoretically* could be interpreted or construed to uphold the hermeneutical primacy of justice (*tahqīq al'adala'*) and social expediency (*maṣlaḥa*) as its purpose and core but that were never realized as the concepts of "justice" and "fairness" did not evolve past the formative period of Islamic thought. Souaiaia, *Contesting Justice*, 47.

91. See, for example, Ziba Mir-Hosseini, "Islam and Gender Justice," *Voices of Islam*, Vol. 5, *Voices of Change*, ed. V. Cornell, O. Safi, and V. Henry (Connecticut and London: Westport, 2007), 85–113.
92. Abu Zayd, "The Nexus of Theory and Practice," 154.
93. For example, 4:25. If any of you have not the means wherewith to wed free believing women, they may wed believing girls from among those whom your right hands possess: And Allah hath full knowledge about your faith. Ye are one from another: Wed them with the leave of their owners, and give them their dowers, according to what is reasonable: They should be chaste, not lustful, nor taking paramours: when they are taken in wedlock, if they fall into shame, their punishment is half that for free women. This (permission) is for those among you who fear sin; but it is better for you that ye practise self-restraint. And Allah is Oft-forgiving, Most Merciful.
94. The *fuqahā'* in the second and third centuries have made, for example, distinctions between the *'awra* (area of body to be covered during the prayer) of slave and free women. See Abou El-Fadl, *Speaking in God's Name*, 255–257, footnotes 106–107.
95. Azam, *Sexual Violence in Maliki Legal Ideology*, 17–20. Cf. Fatna Sabbah, *Woman in the Muslim Unconscious*, trans. Mary J. Lakeland (New York: Pergamon Press, 1984).
96. As based upon *corroborative* written evidence found in relevant *sīra*, *tarīh*, and ḥadīth sources.
97. Indeed, all books on explication of law (*usūl-ul-fiqh*) deal with subjects relating directly to slavery.
98. Azam, *Sexual Violence in Maliki Legal Ideology*, 17.
99. For other reasons in the context of status of women in Islam see Souaiaia, *Contesting Justice*.

Bibliography

al-ʿAbdallah, Yusuf Ibrahi. *Taʾrīkh al-Taʿlīm fi'l-Khalīj al-ʿArabī 1913–1971*. Doha: n.p., 2003.

Abdel-Fadil, Mona. "Islam Offline—Living 'The Message' behind the Screens," *Contemporary Islam*, 7:3 (2013): 283–309.

———. "The Islam-Online Crisis: A Battle of Wasatiyya vs. Salafi Ideologies?" *CyberOrient*, 5:1 (2011). http://www.cyberorient.net/article.do?articleId=6239.

ʿAbd al-Rahman, Taha. "Mashrūʿ Tajdīd ʿIlmī Li Mabḥath Maqāṣid al-Sharīʿa." al-Muslim al-muʿāṣir: special issue, maqāṣid al-sharīʿa 26:103 (1422/2002): 41–64.

———. *Suʾāl Al-Akhlāq: Musāhama Fī Al-Naqd Al-Akhlāqī Lil-Ḥadātha Al-Gharbīya. al-Ṭabʿah*, 1st ed. Casablanca: al-Markaz al-Thaqāfī al-ʿArabī, 2000.

———. *Tajdīd Al-Manhaj Fī Taqwīm Al-Turāth* [in Arabic], 3rd ed. Casablanca: al-Markaz al-Thaqāfī, 1994.

Abd Al Salam. Al-ʿIzz Ibn. *Qawaʿid al-Ahkam fi masaliḥ al-Anam*. Beirut: Dar al-nashr, n.d.

Abu-Lughod, Lila. *Dramas of Nationhood. The Politics of Television in Egypt*. Cairo: American University Press, 2005.

Abu-Rabiʿ M. Ibrahim. *Contemporary Arab Thought: Studies in Post-1967*. London: Pluto Press, 2004.

Abu Zayd, Nasr. *Mafhūm al-Naṣṣ: Dirāsa fi ʿUlūm al-Qurʾān*. Beirut: al-Markaz al-Thaqafi al-ʿArabi, 2000 [1999].

———. *Reformation of Islamic Thought—A Critical Historical Analysis*. Amsterdam: Amsterdam University Press, 2006.

———. *Re-Thinking the Qurʾān—Towards a Humanistic Hermeneutic*. Utrecht: Humanities University Press, 2004.

———. "The Nexus of Theory and Practice," in *The New Voices of Islam—Rethinking Politics and Modernity, A Reader*, edited by Mehran Kamvara. University of California Press: Berkley and Los Angeles, 2006, 153–176.

———. "The Qurʾān: God and Man in Communication," unpublished paper available at http://www.stichtingsocrates.nl/teksten/The%20Qu%27ran%20God%20and%20man%20in%20communication%20-%20Oratie%20Rijksuniversiteit%20Leiden.pdf.

Achrati, Ahmed. "Arabic, Qur'ānic Speech and Postmodern Language: What the Qur'ān Simply Says," *Arabica*, 54 (2008): 161–203.

Ahmad, Atif Ahmad. *Structural Interrelations of Theory and Practice in Islamic Law.* Leiden: Brill, 2006.

Aksoy, Sahin and Elmai, Abdurrahman. "The Core Concepts of the 'Four Principles' of Bioethics as Found in Islamic Tradition," *Medicine and Law*, 21 (2002): 211–224.

Ali, Kecia. *Marriage and Islam in Early Islam.* Cambridge, MA: Harvard University Press, 2010.

———. "Progressive Muslims and Muslim Jurisprudence: The Necessity for Critical Engagement with Marriage and Divorce Law." In *Progressive Muslims: On Justice, Gender and Pluralism*, edited by Omid Safi. Oxford: Oneworld, 2003, 163–189.

Alora, Angeles and Lumitao, Josephine (eds.). *Beyond a Western Bioethics* (Washington, DC: Georgetown University Press, 2001).

Al-Alwani, Taha. *Issues in Contemporary Islamic Thought.* Washington and London: IIIT, 2005.

———. *Maqāṣid al-Shari'ah*, 1st ed. Beirut: Dar al-Hadi, 2001.

Al-'Amiri, al-Faylasuf. *al-I'lam bi-Manaqib al-Islam*, edited by Ahmed Ghurab. Cairo: Dar al Kitab al-'Arabi, 1967.

Ansari, Zafar. "Islamic Juristic Terminology before Shafi'i: A Semantical Analysis with Special Reference to Kufa," *Arabica*, 19 (1972): 255–300.

———. "The Contribution of the Qur'ān and the Prophet to the Development of the Islamic Fiqh," *Journal of Islamic Studies*, 3 (1992): 141–171.

Arasta, Muhammad Jawad. *Tashkhīs Masleha Nizām: Azdidghahe fiqhi—Ḥuqūqi.* Tehran: Intisharat Kanun Andisheh Jawan, 2009.

Ardogan, Recep. "İslam'da İnsan Haklarının Teolojik Değeri." Paper presented at *İnsan Haklarında Yeni Arayışlar Sempozyumu*, Istanbul, May 27–29, 2006, 277–304.

Arjomand, Said Amir. "Authority in Shiism and Constitutional Developments in the Islamic Republic of Iran," in *The Twelver Shi'a in Modern Times*, edited by Rainer Brunner and Werner Ende. Leiden: Brill, 2001.

al-Atawneh, Muhammad. *Wahhābī Islam Facing the Challenges of Modernity: Dār al-Iftā' in the Modern Saudi State.* Brill: Leiden, 2010.

Attia, Gamal E. *Towards Realisation of the Higher Intents of Islamic Law—Maqāṣid Al Shari'ah—A Functional Approach*, translated by Nancy Robers. Kuala Lumpur: IIIT, 2010.

Auda, Jasser. "A Maqāṣidi Approach to Contemporary Application of the Shari'ah," *Intellectual Discourse*, 19 (2011): 193–217.

———. *Fiqh al-Maqāṣid: Ināṭah al-Aḥkām al-Šar'iyya bi-Maqāṣidihā.* Herndon, VA: International Institute of Islamic Thought, 2006.

———. *Maqāṣid al-Šarī'a ka-Falsafa li-l-Tašrī' al-Islāmī: Ru'ya Manẓūmiyya.* Herndon, VA: International Institute of Islamic Thought, 2012.

———. *Maqasid al-Shariah as Philosophy of Islamic Law: A Systems Approach.* Herndon, VA: International Institute of Islamic Thought, 2007.

Azam, Hina, "Sexual Violence in Maliki Legal Ideology—From Discursive Foundations to Classical Articulation," PhD thesis, Duke University, Durham, NC, 2007.

Bahry, Louay. 'The Arab Media Phenomenon: Qatar's Al-Jazeera," *Middle East Policy*, 8:2 (2001): 88–99.

Barlas, Asma. *Believing Women in Islam: Unreading Patriarchal Interpretations of the Qur'ān*. Austin, TX: University of Texas Press, 2002.

Baskan, Birol and Wright, Stephen. "Seeds of Change: Comparing State–Religion Relations in Qatar and Saudi Arabia," *Arab Studies Quarterly*, 33:2 (2011): 96–111.

Bauer, Karen. "Room for Interpretation: Qur'ānic Exegesis and Gender," PhD dissertation, Princeton University, Princeton, NJ, 2008.

Beauchamp, Tom L. "Comparative Studies: Japan and America," in *Japanese and Western Bioethics: Studies in Moral Diversity*, edited by K. Hoshino. Dordrecht: Kluwer Academic Publisher, 1997, 25–48.

———. "The 'Four Principles' Approach to Healthcare Ethics," in *Principles of Healthcare Ethics*, edited by R. E. Ashcroft, A. Dawson, H. Draper, and J. R. McMillan. Chichester: John Wiley & Sons, 2006 [1994], 3–10.

Beauchamp Tom L. and Childress, James F. *Principles of Biomedical Ethics* (Oxford: Oxford University Press, 2013 [1979]).

Bedir, Murteza. "An Early Response to Shafi'i: 'Īsā b. Abān on the Prophetic report (Khabar)," *Islamic Law and Society*, 9 (2002): 285–311.

Boozari, Amirhassan. *Shi'i Jurisprudence and Constitution*. New York: Palgrave Macmillan, 2011.

Brockopp, Jonathan E. (ed.). *Islamic Ethics of Life: Abortion, War and Euthanasia*. Colombia: University of South Carolina Press, 2002.

Al-Buti, Muhammad. *Dawabit al-maṣlaḥa fi al-sharī'a al-islamiyya*. Damascus: al-Maktaba al-Amawiyya, 1966.

Caeiro, Alexandre. "The Social Construction of Sharia: Bank Interest, Home Purchase and Islamic Norms in the West," *Die Welt des Islams*, 44:3 (2004): 351–375.

Caeiro, Alexandre and Mahmoud al-Saify. "Qaradawi in Europe, Europe in Qaradawi? The Global Mufti's European Politics," in *Global Mufti: The Phenomenon of Yusuf al-Qaradawi*, edited by Bettina Gräf and Jakob Skovgaard-Petersen. New York: Columbia University Press, 2009, 109–148.

Ceylan, Yasin. "Yaşar Nuri Öztürk'ün Misyonu." Accessed June 17, 2013. http://www.phil.metu.edu.tr/yceylan/works/ysr-nr-ztrk.html.

Chaudry, Ayesha S. "Wife-Beating in the Pre-Modern Islamic Tradition: An Inter-Disciplinary Study of Ḥadīth, Qur'anic Exegesis and Islamic Jurisprudence," PhD dissertation, New York University, New York, 2009.

Chipman, Leigh N. B. "The Professional Ethics of Medieval Pharmacists in the Islamic World," *Medicine and Law*, 21 (2002): 321–338.

Costet-Tardieu, Francine. *Un réformiste à l'université al-Azhar: Œuvre et pensée de Mustafâ al-Marâghî (1881–1945)*. Paris: Karthala, 2005.

Cragg, Keneth. *The Event of the Qur'ān—Islam in Its Scripture.* Oxford: Oneworld, 1971.

Daar, Abdallah. and al-Khitamy, Ahmed. "Health Care," in *A Companion to Muslim Ethics*, edited by Amyn B. Sajoo. London: I.B. Tauris, 2010, 119–130.

Dag, Mehmet. "İslam Dininde Reform, Ama Nasıl?," Cumhuriyet, October 4, 2004, 2.

———. "İslam'da Örtünme Üzerine," *İslam İlimleri Enstitüsü*, 5 (1982): 187–191.

Dalgın, Nihat. "İslam Hukuku Açısından Müslüman Bayanın Ehl-i Kitap Erkekle Evliliği," *İslam Hukuku Dergisi*, 2 (2003): 131–156.

———. "Özel Günlerdeki Kadınların İbadeti," *İslam Hukuku Araştırmaları Dergisi*, 9 (2007): 379–414.

Daly, Mary. *Beyond God the Father: Toward a Philosophy of Women's Liberation.* Boston, MA: Beacon Press, 1973.

Damad, Ayatullah Mohagheg. "The Role of Time and Social Welfare in the Modification of Legal Rulings," in *Shi'ite Heritage: Essays on Classical and Modern Traditions*, edited by Lynda Clarke. Binghamton: Global, 2001.

Doost, Abu'l QasimʿAli. *Fiqh va Maslahat.* Qum: Sazman-i Intisharat Pejushghah Farhang, 2000.

Denny, Frederick M. *Muslim Medical Ethics: From Theory to Practice.* Colombia: University of South Carolina Press, 2008.

Dien, Mawil Y. Izzi; Walker, P. E. "Wilāya (a.)." In *Encyclopaedia of Islam*, 2nd ed., edited by P. Bearman, Th. Bianquis, C. E. Bosworth, E. van Donzel, and W. P. Heinrichs. Brill, 2012. Brill Online. University of Melbourne, Australia, Novemebr 18, 2013.

Draz, M. *The Moral World of the Qur'ān.* London: I. B. Taurus, 2008.

Duderija, Adis. "A Paradigm Shift in Assessing/Evaluating the Value and Significance of Hadīth in Islamic Thought: From 'ulūmu-l-isnād/rijāl to *uṣūl al-fiqh*," *Arab Law Quarterly*, 23 (2009): 195–206.

———. *Constructing a Religiously Ideal 'Believer' and 'Woman' in Islam: Neo-Traditional Salafi and Progressive Muslim Methods of Interpretation* (manahij). New York: Palgrave, 2011.

———. "The Case study of Patriarchy and Slavery: The Hermeneutical Importance of Qur'ānic Assumptions in the Development of a Values-Based and Purposive Oriented Qurān-Sunna Hermeneutic," *Hawwa*, 11 (2013): 58–87.

———. "The Evolution in the Canonical Sunni Hadith Body of Literature and the Concept of an Sound Hadith During the Formative Period of Islamic Thought as Based on Recent Western Scholarship," *Arab Law Quarterly*, 23(2009): 1–27.

———. "The Evolution in the Concept of Sunna During the First Four Generations of Muslims in Relation to the Development of the Concept of an Sound Hadith as Based on Recent Western Scholarship," *Arab Law Quarterly*, 26 (2012): 393–437.

———. "Toward a Methodology of the Nature and the Scope of the Concept of Sunna," *Arab Law Quarterly*, 21 (2007): 269–280.

Eickelman, Dale F. and Armando Salvatore. "Muslim Publics," in *Public Islam and the Common Good*, edited by Eickelman and Salvatore. Leiden, The Netherlands: Brill, 2006, 1–27.

Eickelman, Dale F. and Jon W. Anderson. "Redefining Muslim Publics." In *New Media in the Muslim World. The Emerging Public Sphere*, edited by Eickelman and Anderson. Bloomington, IN: Indiana University Press, 1999, 1–18.

El Fadl, Khaled Abou. "Islamic Authority," in *New Directions in Islamic Thought*, edited by Karl Vogt et al. New York: I. B. Tauris, 2009, 129–144.

———. *Speaking in God's Name: Islamic Law, Authority and Women*. Oxford: Oneworld, 2001.

———. *The Great Theft: Wrestling Islam from the Extremists*. New York: Harper Collins, 2005.

———."The Pearls of Beauty," in *A Search for Beauty in Islam: The Conference of the Books*. Lanham, MD: University of America Press, 2001.

———."The Place of Ethical Obligations in Islamic Law," *UCLA Journal of Islamic and Near E.L.*, 4 (2005): 1–40.

Emon, Anver. "The Paradox of Equality and the Politics of Difference: Gender Equality, Islamic Law and the Modern Muslim State," in *Gender and Equality in Muslim Family Law: Justice and Ethics in the Islamic Legal Tradition*, edited by Z. Mir-Hosseini, Kari Vogts, Lena Larsen, and Christian Moe. New York: I.B. Tauris, 2013, 237–258.

Erdogan, Mehmet. *İslam Hukukunda Ahkamın Değişmesi.*Marmara: MÜİFV, 1990.

Esposito, J. and John, Voll. *Makers of Contemporary Islam*. Oxford: Oxford University Press, 2001.

Feldman, Noah. "Shari'a and Islamic Democracy in the Age of al-Jazeera," in *Shari'a: Islamic Law in the Contemporary Context*, edited by Abbas Madanat and Frank Griffel. Stanford, CA: Stanford University Press, 2007, 104–119.

Ferguson, D. *Biblical Hermeneutics: An Introduction*. Atlanta: John Knox Press, 1986.

Fletcher, Madeleine. "How Can We Understand Islamic Law Today?" *Journal of Islam and Christian–Muslim Relations*, 17 (2006): 159–172.

Fourest, Caroline. *Frère Tariq: Discours, stratégie et méthode de Tariq Ramadan*. Paris: B. Grasset, 2004.

Fromherz, Allen J. *Qatar: A Modern History*. Washington, DC: Georgetown University Press, 2012.

Gadamer, Hans-Georg. *Truth and Method*, 2nd revised ed., translated by rev. Joel Weinsheimer and Donald G. Marshall. London: Continuum, 2004.

Galal, Ehab. "Yusuf al-Qaradawi and the New Islamic TV," in *Global Mufti: The Phenomenon of Yusuf al-Qaradawi*, edited by Bettina Gräf and Jakob Skovgaard-Petersen. New York: Columbia University Press, 2009, 149–180.

Al-Ghannushi, Rachid. *al-ḥaraka al-islāmiyya wa mas'lat al-taghyyir. dar al-mujtahid lil-nashir wa al-tawzi'*, matba'at Tunis al-'ola, 2011.

———. *al-ḥurriyyāt al-'amma fi al-dawla al-islāmiyya*, 1st ed. Beirut: Markaz Dirasat al-Wihdah al-'Arabiyah, 1993.

———. "Freedom Comes First." Online article: http://www.onislam.net/english/shariah/contemporary-issues/human-conditions-and-social-context/420536-freedom-comes-first.html.

———. "Islamic Movements: Self-Criticism and Reconsideration," in *Palestine Times*, no. 94, April 1999. Or, *Middle East Affairs Journal*, Vol. 3 (1–2), Winter/Spring 1997. Or, online: http://www.islamonline.net/english/Contemporary/2002/05/Article16.shtml.

———. *ḥiwarat*. London: Khalil Media Service, 1992.

———. *ḥuqūq al-muwāṭana: waḍ'iyyat ghair al-muslim fi-l-mujtam' al-islāmi*. maṭba'at tūnis qarṭāj. November 1989.

———. *Muqārabāt fi al-'lmaniyya wa al-mujtama' al-madanī. Dar and Mujtahid lil-nashir wa al-tawzi'*. 2011.

———. "Participation in Non-Islamic Government," in *Liberal Islam: A Sourcebook*, edited by Charles Kruzman. New York, Oxford: Oxford University Press, 1998.

———. "Secularism In the Arab Maghreb," in *Islam and Secularism in the Middle East*, edited by John, Esposito and Azzam, Tamimi. New York: New York University Press, 2000.

Al-Ghazali, Abu Hamid. *Al-Mustasfa fi 'ilm ul usul*. Beirut: Dar al-Kutub al-Ilmiyyah, 1413.

———. *Marriage and Sexuality in Islam*, translated by Madelaine Farah. Kuala Lumpur: Islamic Book Trust, 2012.

Al Ghazali, Zainab. *Nazarāt fi kitāb Allah*. Cairo: Dar Ash Shuruq, 1994.

Gorgun, Tahsin. "Dünyevileşme ve Makasıd," *Din ve Hayat*, 3 (2011): 14–15.

Gorgun, Tahsin. "Siyasallaşan Dünyada Dini İlimlerin Değişen Statüleri," paper presented at *Türkiye'de İslamcılık Düşüncesi Sempozyumu*, Istanbul, May 17–19, 2013.

Gormez, Mehmet. "Sünnet ve Hadis'in Anlaşılması ve Yorumlanmasında Metodoloji Sorunu," *Journal of Islamic Research*, 10 (1997): 31–41.

Graf, Bettina. "IslamOnline.net: Independent, Interactive, Popular," *Arab Media & Society*, (2008).

Graf, Bettina and Jakob Skovgaard-Petersen. *Global Mufti: The Phenomenon of Yusuf al-Qaradawi*. New York: Columbia University Press, 2009.

———. "Introduction," in *Global Mufti: The Phenomenon of Yusuf al-Qaradawi*, edited by Bettina Gräf and Jakob Skovgaard-Petersen. New York: Columbia University Press, 2009, 251–254.

Graham, William. *Divine Word and Prophetic Word in Early Islam—A Reconsideration of the Sources with Special References to the Divine Saying or Hadith Qudsi*. Hague: Mouton, 1977.

Griffel, Frank. "Introduction," in *Sharī'a: Islamic Law in the Contemporary Context*, edited by Abbas Amanat and Frank Griffel. Stanford, CA: Stanford University Press, 2007.

Gulen, Fethullah. "Fethullah Gülen Bir Reformist Midir?" Last modified January 26, 2012. Accessed June 17, 2013. http://tr.fgulen.com/content/view/20201/5/.

Al Haddad, Al Tahir. *Kalima Shukr*, reproduced in Al Tahir Al Haddad, Al Haj Yahya, and Al Marzuqi editions, n.d.

al-Hakim, Muhammad Taqi. *al-Uṣūl al-'Āmma lil Fiqh al-Muqāran*. Beirut: al-Dār Andalus, 1983.

Hallaq, Wael B. *A History of Islamic Legal Theories: An Introduction to Sunni uæül al-fiqh*. Cambridge, UK: Cambridge University Press, 1997.
Halverson, J. *Theology and Creed in Sunni Islam: The Muslim Brotherhood, Asharism and Political Sunnism*. New York: Macmillan, 2010.
Hamed, Hamed A. "Islamic Religion in Qatar During the Twentieth Century: Personnel and Institutions," Unpublished Doctoral Dissertation. University of Manchester, England, 1993.
Hamel, Ian. *La vérité sur Tariq Ramadan: Sa famille, ses réseaux, sa stratégie*. Paris: Favre, 2007.
Hanafi, Hasan. *Islam in the Modern World*, Vol. II. Heliopolis: Dar Al Kebaa, 2000.
Haneef Sayed Sikandar. "Treatment of Recalcitrant Wife in Islamic Law: The Need for a Purposive Juridical Construct," *Global Jurist*, 12 (2012), n.p.
Harvey, Van A. "Hermeneutics," in *Encyclopedia of Religion*, edited by Lindsay Jones, Vol. 6, 2nd ed. Detroit: Macmillan Reference USA, 2005, 3930–3936.
Hashemi, *Ḥuqūq-i Asās-i Jumhūr-i Islām-i- Iran*. Qum: 1996.
al-Hilli, Ja'far ibn Yahya ibn al-Hasan. *Muhaqqiq*. Ma'ārij al-Uṣūl. Qum: Sayyid al-Shuhadā', 1983.
Hourani, G. "Ethical Presuppositions of the Qur'ān," *Muslim World*, 70 (1980): 1–28.
al-Husayni, Muhammad (ed.) *al-Ijtihād wa al-Ḥayāt*. Beirut: Markaz al-Ghadīr lil-Dirāsat al-Islāmiyya, 1998.
Khumayni, Ayatollah. *Saḥīfeh-i Nūr*. Tehran: Sazman-i madārik-i farhanghi-ye inqilab-i Islāmī, 1990.
Ibn Al-Athir, *Jamī' al Usul*. Cairo, 1969.
Ibn Ashur, Tahir. *Maqāṣid al-Shari'ah al-Islamiyyah*, edited by El-tahir el-Mesnawi. Kuala Lumpur: Al-fajr,1999.
Imam, Muhammad K. *Al-dalil al-irshadi Ila maqāṣid Al-Shari'ah al-islamiyyah*. London: Maqāṣid Research Centre, 2006.
Islamoglu, Mustafa. "Lafız, Mana, Maksat," *Yeni Şafak*, April 8, 2000.
al-Jabiri, Muḥammad 'Ābid. *Al-'aql Al-Akhlāqī Al-'arabī: Dirāsa Taḥlīlīya Naqdīya li Nazm Al-Qiyam Fīal-Thaqāfa Al-'arabīya*. Beirut: Markaz Dirāsāt al-Waḥda al-'Arabīya, 2001.
———. *Binyat Al-'aql Al-'arabī: Dirāsah Taḥlīlīyah Naqdīyah Li-Nuẓum Al-Ma'rifah Fī Al-Thaqāfah Al-'arabīyah. Naqd Al-'aql Al-'arabī* 2, 6th ed. Beirut: Markaz Dirāsāt al-Waḥdah al-'Arabiyah, 1986.
al-Jabiri, Muhammad 'Abid, and Mohammed 'Abed al-Jabri. Arab-Islamic Philosophy: A Contemporary Critique [published in French as: *Introduction à la critique de la raison arabe*. Originally written in Arabic], translated by Aziz Abbassi. Austin, TX: Center for Middle Eastern Studies, University of Texas at Austin, 1999.
Jackson, Sherman. "Literalism, Empiricism, and Induction," *Mich. St. L. Rev.*, (2006): 1469–1486.
al-Jawziyyah and Ibn Al-Qayyim. *I'lam al-Muwaqqi'in*, edited by Taha Abdul Rauf Saad. Beirut: Dar al Jil, 1973.

Jeffery, Arthur. *Qur'ān as Scripture*. New York: Russel Moore Company, 1952.
Johnston, David L. "A Turn in the Epistemology and Hermeneutics of Twentieth-Century Uæül al-Fiqh," *Islamic Law and Society*, 11 (2004): 233–282.
———. "Maqasid al-Shari'a: Epistemology and Hermeneutics of Muslim Theologies of Human Rights," *Die Welt des Islams*, 47 (2007): 149–187.
Al-Juwayni, Abu Al-Ma'ali. *Al-Burhan fi usul al-Fiqh*, edited by Abdul Al Azim al-deeb. Mansurah: Al-Wafa,1998.
———. *Al-Burhan fi usul al-fiqh*, annotated by Abdul-Azim al-Deeb. Qatar: Wazarat al-Shu'un al-Diniyyah, 1400 AH.
Kamali, Hashim. "Citizenship: An Islamic Perspective," *Journal of Islamic Law and Culture*, 11:2 (2009): 121–153.
———. *Civilisational Renewal : Revisiting the Islam Hadhari Approach : Definition, Significance, Criticism, Recognition, Support, Tajdid and Future Directions*. Kuala Lumpur: Arah Publication, 2008.
———. "Fiqh and Adaptation to Social Reality,"*The Muslim World*, 86 (1996): 62–76. Last accessed December 12, 2013. http://www.hashimkamali.com/index.php/about.
———. "Have We Neglected the Shari'ah-Law Doctrine of Maṣlaḥa?," *Islamic Studies*, 27 (1988): 287–303.
———. *IAIS Malaysia: Exploring the Intellectual Horizons of Civilisational Islam*. Kuala Lumpur: Arah Publications, 2008.
———. "Issues in the Legal Theory of Usul and Prospects for Reform," *Islamic Studies*, 40 (2001): 5–23.
———. "Istiḥsān and the Renewal of Islamic Law," Occasional Paper 58, 2004. Islamic Research Institute, Islamabad. Accessed November 26, 2013. http://www.hashimkamali.com/index.php/publications/item/119- istiḥsān-and-the-renewal-of-islamic-law.
———. "Law and Ethics in Islam: The Role of the Maqāṣid al-šarī'a," in *New Directions in Islamic Thought*, edited by Kari Vogt, Lena Larsen, and Christian Moe. New York: I.B. Tauris, 2009, 23–46.
———. "Legal Maxims and Other Genres of Literature in Islamic Jurisprudence," *Arab Law Quarterly*, 20 (2006): 77–101.
———. "Maqāṣid al-šarī'a: The Objectives of Islamic Law," *Islamic Studies*, 38 (1999): 193–208.
———. Maqāṣid al-šarī'a and Ijtihad as Instruments of Civilizational Renewal: A Methodological Perspective," *Islam and Civilisational Renewal*, 2 (2011): 245–271.
———. *Maqasid al-Shari'ah Made Simple*. Malaysia: IAIS, 2008.
———. "Methodological Issues in Islamic Jurisprudence," *Arab Law Quarterly*, 11 (1996): 3–33.
———. "Shari'ah and Civil Law: Towards a Methodology of Harmonization," *Islamic Law and Society*, 14 (2007): 391–420.
———. *Shari'ah Law: An Introduction*. Oxford: Oneworld, 2008.
———. *The Principles of Islamic Jurisprudence*. Cambridge: Islamic Texts Society, 1991.

Kamrava, Mehran. "Royal Factionalism and Political Liberalisation in Qatar," *The Middle East Journal*, 63 (2009): 401–420.

Karabasoglu, Metin. "Bediüzzaman'ı Anlamak Üzerine." Accessed June 17, 2013. http://www.cevaplar.org/index.php?content_view=3676&ctgr_id=138.

Karaman, Hayrettin. "Batı ve İslami Maksatlar," Yeni Şafak, October 6, 2011.

———. İslam'ın Işığında Günün Meseleleri, Vol. 2. İz Yayıncılık, 2003.

———. "Laikliğin Tarifi (3)," Yeni Şafak, October 27, 2006.

———. "Maksat İslam'ı Kuşa Çevirmek Değilse," *Altınoluk*, 114 (1995): 41–44.

———. *Yeni Gelişmeler Karşısında İslam Hukuku*. Istanbul: İklim Yayınları, 2nd ed., 1987.

Kerr, Malcolm, H. *Islamic Reform: The Political and Legal Theories of Muḥammad 'Abduh and Rashīd Riḍa*. London: Cambridge University Press, 1966.

Kerimoglu, Yusuf. *Fıkhi Meseleler*. Ölçü Yayınları, 1987.

Kirbasoglu, Hayri. *İslam Düşüncesinde Sünnet. Eleştirel Bir Yaklaşım*. Ankara Okulu, 2001.

Korner, Felix. *Revisionist Koran Hermeneutics in Contemporary Turkish University Theology*. Würzburg: Ergon Verlag, 2005.

Kugle, Scott and Stephen Hunt. "Masculinity, Homosexuality, and the Defense of Islam: A Case Study of Yusuf al-Qaradawi's Media Fatwa," *Religion and Gender*, 2 (2012): 254–279.

Landau, Paul. *Le sabre et le Coran: Tariq Ramadan et les Freres musulmans a la conquete de l'Europe*. Paris: Rocher, 2005.

Larsson, Goran. "Yusuf al-Qaradawi and Tariq Ramadan on Secularisation: Differences and Similarities," in *Muslim Societies and the Challenge of Secularization: An Interdisciplinary Approach*, edited by G. Marranci. Dordrecht: Springer, 2010, 47–63.

Mahallati, Amineh. "Women in traditional Sharīa: A List of Differences between Men and Women in Islamic Tradition," *Journal of Islamic Law and Culture*, 12 (2010): 1–9.

March, Andrew F. "Law as a Vanishing Mediator in the Theological Ethics of Tariq Ramadan," *European Journal of Political Theory*, 11 (2011): 177–201.

———. "Reading Tariq Ramadan: Political Liberalism, Islam and 'Overlapping Consensus,'" *Ethics & International Affairs*, 21 (2007): 399–413.

———. "The Post-Legal Ethics of Tariq Ramadan: Persuasion and Performance in Radical Reform: Islamic Ethics and Liberation," *Middle East Law & Governance*, 2 (2010): 253–273.

Marin, Manuela "Disciplining Wives: A Historical Reading of Qur'ân 4:34," *Studia Islamica*, 97 (2003): 5–40.

al-Marzuqi, Abu Ya'rub and Muhammad Sa'īd Ramadan al-Buti. *IshkālīYat Tajdīd Uṣūl Al-Fiqh* [in Arabic]. Damascus: Dār al-Fikr, 2006.

Masud, Muhammad Khalid. "Gender Equality and the Doctrine of Wilāya," in *Gender and Equality in Muslim Family Law: Justice and Ethics in the Islamic Legal Tradition*, edited by. Z. Mir-Hosseini, Kari Vogts, Lena Larsen, and Christian Moe. New York: I.B. Tauris, 2013, 127–152.

———. *Islamic Legal Philosophy: A Study of Abū Isḥāq al-Shatibi's Life and Thought.* Delhi: International Islamic Publishers, 1989.

Mir-Hosseini, Ziba. "Islam and Gender Justice," *Voices of Islam*, Vol. 5, Voices of Change, edited by V. Cornell, O. Safi, and V. Henry. Westport, CT and London: Praeger 2007, 85–113.

Moazam, Farhat. *Bioethics and Organ Transplantation in a Muslim Society: A Study in Culture, Ethnography, and Religion.* Bloomington, IN: University of Indiana Press, 2006.

Moosa, E. "The Debt and Burdens of Critical Islam," in *Progressive Muslims: On Social Justice, Gender and Pluralism*, edited by O.Safi. Oxford: Oneworld, 2003, 111–128.

Neuwirth, A. "Two Faces of the Qur'ān: Qur'ān and Mushaf," *Oral Tradition*, 25 (2010): 141–156.

Nie, Jing-Bao. *Behind the Silence: Chinese Voices on Abortion.* Boulder, CO: Rowman & Littlefield Publishers, 2005.

———. "Is Informed Consent Not Applicable to China? Intellectual Flaws of the Cultural Difference Argument," *Formosa Journal of Medical Humanities*, 2 (2001): 67–74.

———. "The Speciousness of an Asian Bioethics: Beyond Dichotomizing East and West," in *Principles of Healthcare Ethics*, edited by R. E. Ashcroft, A. Dawson, H. Draper, and J. R. McMillan. Chichester: John Wiley & Sons, 2006 [1994], 143–149.

Nursi, Bediuzzaman Said. *Risale-i Nur Külliyatı: Kaynaklı, İndeksli, Lügatli*, II Vols. Istanbul: YeniAsya, 1994.

Nyazee, Imran. *The Outlines of Islamic Jurisprudence.* Islamabad: Advanced Legal Studies Institute, 2000.

Opwis, Felicitas. *Maslaha and the Purpose of the Law.* Leiden: Brill, 2010.

———. "Maṣlaḥa in Contemporary Islamic Legal Theory," *Islamic Law and Society*, 12:2 (2005): 182–223.

Ozturk, Yasar Nuri. *Din ve Fıtrat* (Yaradılış), 2nd ed. Istanbul: Yeni Boyut, 1992.

———. *İslam Nasıl Yozlaştırıldı?* Yeni Boyut, 2000.

———. *İslam'ı Anlamaya Doğru*, 3rd ed. Yeni Boyut, 1997.

———. *Kur'an Uyarıyor* (Tevhid Mücadelesi), 4th ed. Yeni Boyut, 1999.

———. *Kur'an Verileri Açısından Laiklik.* Yeni Boyut, 2003.

———. *Kur'an'ı Anlamaya Doğru*, 10th ed. Yeni Boyut, 1999.

Pacacı, Mehmet. *Dirāsa fī Fiqh Maqāṣid al-Šarī'a: Bayna l-Maqāṣid al-Kulliyya wa-l-Nuṣūṣ al-Ğuz'iyya.* Cairo: Dar al-Shuruq, 2006.

———. *Dirāsa fī maqāṣid al-sharī'a: bayn al-maqāṣid al-kulliyya wa-l-nusus al-juz'iyya* ("A Study of the Shari'a's Purposes: Between the General Purposes and the Specific Texts"). Cairo: Dār al-Shurūq, 2006.

———. *Kayf Nata'aamal Ma'a al-Qur'ān al-'Azim*, 1st ed. Cairo: Dar al-Shoruq, 1999.

———. Kur'an ve Ben Ne Kadar Tarihseliz? Ankara Okulu, 2000.

———. *Madkhal li-Dirāsatal-sharī'a al-islamiyya* ("Introduction to the Study of the Islamic Shari'a," Beirut: MuŒassat al-Risāla), 2nd ed. Cairo: Maktabat al-Wahba, 2001.

———. *Siyāsa al-sharī'a fi daw' nusus al-sharī'a wa-maqāṣidiha* ("Political Governance in Light of the Shari'a's Texts and Objectives"). Cairo: Maktabat al-Wahba, 1999.

Pekcan, Ali. *İslam Hukukunda Gaye Problemi*, 2nd ed. Ankara: Ek Kitap, 2012.

PRA. "Diyanet Kurul Kararları, 2005." Accessed June 17, 2013. http://www.diyanet.gov.tr/turkish/dy/KurulDetay.aspx?ID=1134.

———. "Diyanet Kurul Kararları, 1980." Accessed June 17, 2013. http://www.diyanet.gov.tr/turkish/dy/KurulDetay.aspx?ID=3.

———. "Diyanet Kurul Kararları, 2000." Accessed June 17, 2013. http://www.diyanet.gov.tr/turkish/dy/KurulDetay.aspx?ID=8.

al-Qaradawi, Yusuf. *al-Ijtihād al-Mu'āṣir bayna l-Inḍibāt wa-l-Infirāṭ*. Cairo: n.p., 1998.

———. *Fī Fiqh al-Aqalliyyāt al-Muslima: Ḥayāt al-Muslimīn Wasaṭ al-Mujtama'āt al-Ukhrā*. Cairo: Dar al-Shuruq, 2001.

———. *Ibn al-Qarya wa-l-Kuttāb: Malāmiḥ Sīra wa-Masīra*, 4 Vols. Cairo: Dar al-Shuruq, 2002, 2004, 2006, 2011.

Al-Qarafi, Shihab al-Din. *al-Furuq*, edited by Khalil Mansour. Beirut: Dar al-kutub al-'ilmiyyah, 1998.

Al Qarni, Aid. *How to Become the Happiest Woman on Earth*. London: Al Firdous, 2006.

al-Qummi, Ibn Babawayh. 'Ilal al-Shara'i, edited by Mohammad Sadiq Bghar al-ulum. Najaf: Dar al Balaghah,1966.

Rahman, F. *Islam and Modernity: The Transformation of an Intellectual Tradition*. Chicago: Chicago University Press, 1982.

Ramadan, Tariq. *al-Iṣlāḥ al-Ġadrī: al-Aḫlāqāt al-Islāmiyya wa-l-Taḥarrur*, translated by A. Ayubi. Beirut: Arab Network for Research and Publishing, 2010.

———. *Islam, the West and the Challenges of Modernity*. Leicester: The Islamic Foundation, 2001.

———. Les Musulmans dans la Laïcité, responsabilités et droits des musulmans dans les sociétés occidentales. Lyons: Tawhid, 1994.

———. *Muslims in France: The Way Towards Coexistence*. Leicester: The Islamic Foundation, 1999.

———. "Préface" in *Conseil Européen des fatwas et de la recherché*, edited by Recueil de fatwas: Avis juridiques concernant les musulmans d'Europe. Lyons: Tawhid, 2001, 9–20.

———. *Radical Reform: Islamic Liberation & Ethics*. Oxford: Oxford University Press, 2009.

———. *To Be a European Muslim: A Study of Islamic Sources in the European Context*. Leicester: The Islamic Foundation, 2000.

———. *Western Muslims and the Future of Islam*. Oxford: Oxford University Press, 2004.

Ramadan, Tariq and Zemouri, Aziz. *Faut-il faire taire Tariq Ramadan?* Paris: L'Archipel, 2005.
Rawls, John. *Political Liberalism*. New York: Columbia University Press, 2005.
al-Raysuni, Ahmad. al-Kulliyyāt al-Asāsiyya li-l-Šarī'a al-Islāmiyya. Rabat: al-Tawhid wa-l-Islah, 2007.
———. *Imam al-Shatibi's Theory of the Higher Objectives and Intents of Islamic Law*, translated by N. Roberts. Herndon, VA: International Institute of Islamic Thought, 2005.
———. *Nazariyyat al-Maqāṣid 'ind al-imam al-Shatibi*, 1st ed. Herndon: IIIT, 1992.
Reinhart, Kevin. *Before Revelation—he Boundaries of Muslim Moral Thought*. Albany, NY: State University of New York Press, 1995.
Remien, Florian. *Muslime in Europa: Westlicher Staat und islamische Identität: Untersuchung zu Ansätzen von Yusuf al-Qaradawi, Tariq Ramadan und Charles Taylor*. Berlin: EB-Verlag, 2007.
Rida, Rashid. *Al-Wahi al Mohammadi: Thubut al-Nubuwwah bi al-Qur'ān*. Cairo: Mu'asasah 'izz al-din, n.d.
al-Rifa'i, Abd al-Jabbar (ed.) *Maqāṣid al-Sharī'a: Taḥrīr wa Ḥiwār*. Beirut: Dār al-Fikr al-Mu'āṣir, 2002.
Sabbah, Fatna. *Woman in the Muslim Unconscious*, translated by Mary J. Lakeland. New York: Pergamon Press, 1984.
Sachedina, Abdulaziz. *Islamic Biomedical Ethics: Principles and Applications*. Oxford: Oxford University Press, 2009.
———. "Scriptural Reasoning in Islam," *Journal of Scriptural Reasoning*, 5 (2005), n.p.
———. "The Search for Islamic Bioethics Principles," in *Principles of Healthcare Ethics*, edited by R. E. Ashcroft, A. Dawson, H. Draper, and J. R. McMillan. Chichester: John Wiley & Sons, 2006 [1994]), 117–125.
Saeed, A. "Rethinking Citizenship Rights of Non-Muslims in an Islamic State: Rachid Ghannūshī's Contribution to the Evolving Debat," *Islam and Christian-Muslim Relations*, 10:3 (1999).
Said, Edward W. *Representations of the Intellectual: The 1993 Reith Lectures*. London: Vintage Books, 1994.
———. "The Public Role of Writers and Intellectuals," in *The Public Intellectual*, edited by Helen Small. Oxford: Blackwell Publishing, 2002, 19–39.
Sajoo, Amyn B. *Muslim Ethics: Emerging Vistas*. London: I.B. Tauris, 2004.
Sakamoto, Hyaduki. "The foundation of a possible Asian bioethics," in *Bioethics: Asian Perspectives: A Quest for Moral Diversity*, edited by Ren-Zong Qiu. Dordrecht: Kluwer Academic Publishers, 2004.
Sanei, Ayatullah Yusuf. *Berabari-ye diyah*. Qum: Mu'assasah-ye Farhangi-ye fiqh-e Thaqalayn, 2005.
———. *Bulūgh al-Banāt*. Qum: Mua'ssasah Farhangi -ye fiqh-e Thaqalayn, 2003.
Schacht, J. and Layish, A. "Ṭalāḳ (a.)," in *Encyclopaedia of Islam*, 2nd ed., edited by P. Bearman, Th. Bianquis, C. E. Bosworth, E. van Donzel, and W. P. Heinrichs. Brill, 2012. Brill Online. University of Melbourne, Australia, January 18, 2012.

Shabistari, Ayatullah Muhammad Mujtahid. "Religion, Reason and the New Theology," in *Shi'ite Heritage: Essays on Classical and Modern Traditions*, edited by Lynda Clarke. Binghamton: Global, 2001.

Shahrudi, Mustafa Ashrafi. "Hamsuy-e fiqh ba tahavvulat va Niyazhay-e Jami-e," in *Ijtihād va Zamān va Makān*, 14 Vols. Qum: Mu'assi Chap v NashrUruj, 1995.

Shalabi, Muhammad. *Talıl al-ahkam*. Cairo: Matbaat al-Azhar, 1943.

al-Shatibi, Abu Ishaq. *Al-Muwāfaqāt Fī Uṣūl Al-Sharī'a*, edited by 'Allah Daraz, 4 Vols. Beirut: Dār al-Ma'rifa, n.d.

Skovgaard-Petersen, Jakob. "Yusuf al-Qaradawi and al-Azhar," in *Global Mufti: The Phenomenon of Yusuf al-Qaradawi*, edited by Bettina Gräf and Jakob Skovgaard-Petersen. New York: Columbia University Press, 2009, 27–54.

Soroush, Abdokarim. *Qabz wa bast-e ti'urik-e shari'at: Nazariyyah-ye takamul-e ma'rifat-e dini*. Tehran: Mu'assasah-ye farhangi-ye sirat, 1996.

———. *The Expansion of Prophetic Experience—Essays on Historicity, Contingency and Plurality in Religion*, translated by N. Mobasser, edited with an analytical introduction by F. Jahanbakhsh. Leiden: Brill, 2009.

Souaiaia, Ahmad. *Contesting Justice-Women, Islam, Law, and Society*. New York: SUNY, 2008.

———. "On the Sources of Islamic Law and Practices," *Journal of Law and Religion*, 20 (2005): 125–149.

———. *The Function of Orality in Islamic Law and Practices: Verbalizing Meaning*. Lewiston, NY: Edwin Mellen Press, 2006.

Steinberg, Guido. "Katar und der Arabische Frühling: Unterstützung für Islamisten und anti-syrische Neuausrichtunag," Stiftung Wissenschaft und Politik (February 2012), http://www.swp-berlin.org/fileadmin/contents/products/aktuell/2012A07_sbg.pdf.

Stodolsky, Volkan. "A New Historical Model and Periodization for the Perception of the Sunna and his Companions," PhD dissertation. University of Chicago, Chicago, IL, 2012.

al-Subhani, Ja'far. *Maṣādiq al-Fiqh al-Islāmī wa Manābi'uhu*. Qum: Mu'assasat al-Imām al-Ṣādiq, 2007.

al-Sughayyar, 'Abd al-Majid. *Al-Fikr Al-Uṣūlī Wa-Ishkālīyat Al-Sulṭa Al-'Ilmīya Fī Al-Islām:Qirā'at Fī Nash'at 'Ilm Al-Uṣūl Wa-Maqāṣid Al-Sharī'a*, 1st ed. Beirut: Dār al-Muntakhab al-'Arabī, 1994.

Tabatabai, Muhammad. *Tafsir Al Mizan*. http://www.shiasource.com/al-mizan/.

———. Tafsir Al Mizan, translated by Sayyid Saeed Akhtar Rizvi. Teheran: World Organisation for Islamic Services, 1990.

Tabrizi, Behrooz Ghamari. *Islam and Dissent in Post-Revolutionary Iran*. London: I.B. Tauris, 2008.

al-Tahanawi, Muhammad 'Ali (A'lā), and (ed) Rafiq al-'Ajam. *Mawsū'a Kashshāf Iṣṭilāḥāt Al-Funūn Wa Al-'ulūm*, 2 Vols. Beirut: Maktaba Lubnan, 1996.

Takim, Liyakat. "Revivalism or Reformation: The Reinterpretation of Islamic Law in Modern Times,"*American Journal of Islamic Social Sciences*, 25 (2008): 61–81.

———. *The Heirs of the Prophet: Charisma and Religious Authority in Shi'ite Islam.* Albany: State University of New York, 2006.

Tammam, Husam. "Yusuf al-Qaradawi and the Muslim Brothers: The Nature of a Special Relationship," in *Global Mufti: The Phenomenon of Yusuf al-Qaradawi,* edited by Bettina Gräf and Jakob Skovgaard-Petersen. New York: Columbia University Press, 2009, 55–84.

Tamimi, Azzam. *Rachid Ghannuchi: A Democrat Within Islamism.* New York: Oxford University Press, 2001.

Tarabishi, Jurj. Wahdat *Al-'aql Al-'arabī Al-IslāMī. Naqd Naqd Al-'aql Al-'arabī. al-Ṭab'ah,* 1st ed. Beirut: Dār al-Sāqī, 2002.

Telkenaroglu, Rahmi. "Makasıd İctihadına Dayanan Külli Kaideler," *Usul,* 10 (2008): 37–76.

Toprak, Binnaz and Ali Çarkoğlu. *Religion, Society and Politics in a Changing Turkey,* translated by Çiğdem Aksoy Fromm, edited by Jenny Sanders. Istanbul: Tesev, 2006.

Umar F. Abd-Allah Wymann Landgraf, *Malik and Medina-Islamic Reasoning in the Formative Period.* Leiden: Brill, 2013.

Virkler, Henry. *Hermeneutics: Principles and Processes of Biblical Interpretation.* Grand Rapids: Baker Book House, 1981.

Wadud, Amina. Foreword to Issue in *International Feminist Journal of Politics,* "Engaging Tawhid in Islam and Feminisms," 10 (2008): 435–438.

———. *Inside the Gender Jihad: Women's Reform in Islam.* Oxford: Oneworld, 2006.

———. "Islam Beyond Patriarchy Through Gender Inclusive Qur'anic Analysis," in *Wanted: Equality and Justice in Muslim Family,* edited by Zaina Anwar. Kuala Lumpur: Sisters in Islam, 2009.

———. *Qur'an and Woman: Rereading the Sacred Text from a Woman's Perspective,* 2nd ed. Oxford: Oxford University Press, 1999.

Warren, David H. "Whither the 'Global Mufti?' Shaykh Yusuf al-Qaradawi & the Arab Uprisings 2011–13: Between the Brotherhood, the Law, and Qatari Foreign Policy," *New Middle Eastern Studies* (forthcoming).

Weiss, Bernard. *The Spirit of Islamic Law.* Athens, GA: University of Georgia Press, 1998.

Wolterstorff, Nicolas. *Divine Discourse: Philosophical Reflections on the Claim that God Speaks.* Cambridge: Cambridge University Press, 1995.

Wright, Peter, M. "Modern Qur'ānic Hermeneutics," PhD dissertation. Chapell Hill, University of North Carolina, 2008.

Yaman, Ahmet. "Dinin Kaynağı Ben Miyim," Timetürk, August 17, 2011.

———. "İslam Hukuk Mirasını Algılama ve Uygulama Yöntemi Üzerine," *Divan,* 13 (2002/2): 307–313.

——— (ed.). *Makasıd ve İctihad.* Yediveren Yayınları, 2002.

———. "Nasdan Olguya Başörtüsü," *EskiYeni* 8 (2008): 103–108.

Yavuz, Hakan. "Islam without Shari'a?," in *Shari'a Politics,* edited by Robert Hefner. Indiana University Press, 2011, 146–178.

Yavuz, Yunus Vehbi. "Dindarlıkta Reform," Habervaktim, February 22, 2009.
———. "Kur'an Hükümlerinin Amaçları," *Bursa*, (1988): 1–33.
———. "Maksadi Yorum," *İHD*, 8 (2006): 41–78.
Al-Zamakhshari, Jar Allah Mahmud b. 'Umar, *Al-Kashshāf*, edited by Ahmad b. al-Munir al-Iskandari. Beirut: Dār al-Kitāb al-'Arabī, 1965, Vol. 1, 505.
Zaman, Muhammad Q. *Modern Islamic Thought in a Radical Age: Religious Authority and Internal Criticism*. Cambridge: Cambridge University Press, 2013.
———. *The 'Ulama' in Contemporary Islam: Custodians of Change*. Princeton, NJ: Princeton University Press, 2002.
———. "The "ulamā' of Contemporary Islam and their Conceptions of the Common Good," in *Public Islam and the Common Good*, edited by Armando Salvatore and Dale F. Eickelman. Leiden, The Netherlands: Brill, 2006, 129–155.
Zebiri, Kate. *Maḥmūd Shaltūt and Islamic Modernism*. Oxford: Clarendon Press, 1993.

Websites

http://www.systemoflife.com/articles/general/142-there-is-no-marriage-without-the-consent-of-guardian, accessed November 3, 2013.
http://one-islam.org/sahih_muhammad/sahih_Women.htm, accessed February 3, 2012.
http://mosshaf.com/web/.

Contributors

Adis Duderija is currently a visiting senior lecturer at the University Malaya, Gender Studies. He received his PhD in 2010 from the University of Western Australia. His research interests include contemporary Islamic hermeneutics, Islam and gender, contemporary Muslim reformist thought, and the role of religion in Western Muslims' identity construction. He is the author *of Constructing Religiously Ideal "Believer" and "Muslim Woman" Concepts: Neo-Traditional Salafi and Progressive Muslim Methods of Interpretation* (Manahij) (2011). His forthcoming volume includes: *The Evolution of the Concept of Sunna during the Formative and Classical Periods of Islamic Thought* (2014/2015). He has published extensively in his areas of research including articles such as: "Neo-Traditional Salafi Qur'an-Sunnah Hermeneutic and the Construction of a Normative Muslimah Image, *HAWWA-Journal of Women in the Middle East and the Muslim World* (2007); "The Hermeneutical Importance of Qur'anic Assumptions in the Development of a Values Based and Purposive Oriented Qur'an-Sunna Hermeneutic: Case Study of Patriarchy, Slavery, *HAWWA-Journal of Women in the Middle East and the Muslim World* (2013); "The Interpretational Implications of Progressive Muslims' Qur'an and Sunnah Manhaj in Relation to Their Construction of a Normative Muslim Construct, in Islam and Christian Muslim Relations (2010); "Critical-Progressive Muslim Thought: Reflections on Its Political Implications, Faith and International Affairs (2013), Islam and Gender in the thought of a Critical-progressive Muslim scholar activist Ziba Mir Hosseini, Islam and Christian Muslims Relations (2014, Forthcoming) and many others.

David L. Johnston is a visiting scholar at the University of Pennsylvania and teaches as an adjunct at St. Joseph's University. He served for 16 years as a pastor and teacher in Algeria, Egypt, and the West Bank. After completing his PhD in Islamic Studies at the Fuller Theological Seminary, he became a research affiliate and a part-time lecturer at Yale University. His research focuses on the intersection of Islamic law and theology and on Muslim-Christian dialogue. His articles and essays have appeared in *Islamochristiana*, *Islamic Law and Society*, *Die Welt des Islams*, *The Maghreb Review*, and *Comparative Islamic Studies*. He is the author of two books, *Evolving Muslim Theologies of Justice: Jamal al-Banna, Mohammad Hashim Kamali and Khaled Abou El Fadl* (2010), and *Earth, Empire and Sacred Text: Muslims and Christians as Trustees of Creation* (2010). He blogs on his own website www.humantrustees.org.

Aydogan Kars is a PhD candidate and teaching fellow at Vanderbilt University. He also works for the Divinity Library as a bibliographer in the field of "World Religions" and "Islamic Studies." He received his BS at Hacettepe University and his MA at the Middle East Technical University. He worked four years for the Scientific & Technological Research Council of Turkey, in the Social Sciences and Humanities Research Grant Committee. His MA thesis was a comparative study analyzing the ontology and hermeneutics of the Sufi Ibn al-ʿArabī (d.1240) by appealing to philosophical hermeneutics and occidental phenomenology. His readings in medieval philosophy and Sufism run parallel with those in modern continental philosophy. His doctoral dissertation focuses on negative theology and negative speech (*apophasis*) in thirteenth-century Sufism.

Ebrahim Moosa is professor of Islamic Studies in the Department of Religion at Duke University. His interests span both classical and modern Islamic thought with a special interest in Islamic law, ethics, and theology. In 2007 he delivered the prestigious Hassaniyyah lecture on the invitation of His Majesty King Mohammed VI in Fez. He was named Carnegie Scholar in 2005 to pursue research on the madrasas, the Islamic seminaries in South Asia.

Dr Moosa is the author of *Ghazali and the Poetics of Imagination,* winner of the American Academy of Religion's Best First Book in the history of religions (2006). His forthcoming book is titled: *What Is a Madrasa: Practices and Politics of Salvation in Contemporary Islam*. He has edited books on Modern Islam, Muslim family law, and Islamic revival with multiple publications on issues related to classical and modern Islamic thought. He is a senior fellow at the Kenan Institute for Ethics at Duke University.

Liyakat Takim is the Sharjah Chair in Global Islam at McMaster University in Hamilton, Canada. A native of Zanzibar, Tanzania, he has spoken at more than 80 academic conferences and authored a hundred scholarly works on diverse topics like reformation in the Islamic world, the treatment of women in Islamic law, Islam in America, the indigenization of the Muslim community in America, dialogue in post-9/11 America, war and peace in the Islamic tradition, Islamic law, Islamic biographical literature, the charisma of the holy man and shrine culture, and Islamic mystical traditions. He teaches a wide range of courses on Islam and offers a course on comparative religions. Professor Takim's second book titled *Shi'ism in America* was published by New York University Press in summer 2009. His first book, *The Heirs of the Prophet: Charisma and Religious Authority in Shi'ite Islam* (2006)and he is currently working on his third book, *Ijtihad and Reformation in Islam*. Professor Takim has taught at several American and Canadian universities and is actively engaged in dialogue with different faith communities.

David H. Warren is a doctoral candidate at the University of Manchester and his dissertation, due for submission in late 2014, sets out to examine the reformist efforts in the renewal of Islamic jurisprudence (*tajdīd al-fiqh*) in the context of Doha, with specific reference to Yusuf al-Qaradawi and his intellectual school. He has recently published articles based on his research in journals including *Contemporary Islam: Dynamics of Muslim Life* and *New Middle Eastern Studies* and he was previously a student, of primarily Maliki *fiqh*, at the madrasa of the late Muhammad Salim al-ʿAdud in Mauritania and has similarly studied at the University of Damascus, as well as in Yemen.

Index

Lightning Source UK Ltd.
Milton Keynes UK
UKOW01n1312070915

258209UK00004B/85/P

9 781137 323859